KU-161-510

THE ROUGH GUIDE to

Film Noir

by
Alexander Ballinger & Danny Graydon

Contents

THE ROUGH GUIDE to

Film Noir

ROUGH GUIDES

www.roughguides.com

30131 04217475 2
LONDON BOROUGH OF BARNET

Credits

The Rough Guide to Film Noir

Additional contributions: Barry Forshaw,
Andrew Lockett, Joe Staines
Editing: Sam Cook, Joe Staines, Ruth Tidball
Layout: Peter Buckley, Ankur Guha, Ruth Tidball
Picture research: Andrew Lockett
Proofreading: Jason Freeman
Indexing: Philippa Hopkins
Production: Aimee Hampson
& Katherine Owers

Rough Guides Reference

Series editor: Mark Ellingham
Editors: Peter Buckley,
Duncan Clark, Tracy Hopkins,
Sean Mahoney, Matthew Milton,
Joe Staines, Ruth Tidball
Director: Andrew Lockett

Publishing Information

This first edition published May 2007 by
Rough Guides Ltd, 80 Strand, London WC2R 0RL
345 Hudson St, 4th Floor, New York 10014, USA
Email: mail@roughguides.com

Distributed by the Penguin Group
Penguin Books Ltd, 80 Strand, London WC2R 0RL
Penguin Putnam, Inc., 375 Hudson Street, NY 10014, USA
Penguin Group (Australia), 250 Camberwell Road,
Camberwell, Victoria 3124, Australia
Penguin Books Canada Ltd, 90 Eglinton Avenue East, Toronto,
Ontario, Canada M4P 2YE
Penguin Group (New Zealand), 67 Apollo Drive, Mairongi Bay,
Auckland 1310, New Zealand

Printed in Italy by LegoPrint S.p.A

Typeset in Helvetica Neue and Bembo to an original design
by Henry Iles

The publishers and authors have done their best to ensure
the accuracy and currency of all information in *The Rough
Guide to Film Noir*; however, they can accept no responsibility
for any loss or inconvenience sustained by any reader as a
result of its information or advice.

No part of this book may be reproduced in any form without
permission from the publisher except for the quotation of
brief passages in reviews.

© Alexander Ballinger & Danny Graydon, 2007

312 pages; includes index

A catalogue record for this book is available from the British
Library

ISBN 13: 978-1-84353-474-7
ISBN 10: 1-84353-474-6

1 3 5 7 9 8 6 4 2

BARNET LIBRARIES	
Bertrams	03.07.07
791.43655	£9.99

Out Of The Shadows:

Casting Shadows:

Double-dealings:

Dark Side Of The Earth:

Private Investigations:

Introduction

Writing *The Rough Guide to Film Noir* has been an absorbing task for those involved and – aware that pleasing all of the people all of the time is a fool's mission – here are a few thoughts on what to look out for in this book's dark corners, and what blind alleys to expect.

Ever since French critics applied the term to a handful of Hollywood crime films that arrived in France just after World War II, film buffs have been arguing over precisely what is film noir, or – to put it another way – what makes a film *noir*. We have answered the question in a number of ways. In the opening chapter (**The Genre That Wasn't There: the origins**) we analyse the various ingredients – hard-boiled crime fiction, gangster movies and the arrival in 1930s Hollywood of (mostly German) *émigré* filmmakers – that helped create a new mood and style of crime movie. **Down These Mean Streets: the history** is a decade-by-decade overview, tracing noir's development, from the so-called classic era of the 1940s and 50s, through the lean years of the 1960s into its transformation and refashioning as neo-noir in more recent times. Then comes the core of the book: a detailed discussion of fifty great films (**The Canon: 50 essential film noirs**), of which the majority are selected from noir's great period but which also includes those truly groundbreaking neo-noirs (such as *Chinatown*,

Blade Runner and *L.A. Confidential*) that followed in their wake.

Of course, great films are the results of collaboration between great filmmakers, and in **The Out Of The Shadows: the icons** we profile some of the key actors, directors, cinematographers and others who have made a particularly striking contribution to noir. In **Double Dealings: noir crossovers** we tackle the issue of noir's interaction with other mainstream genres from sci-fi to comedy, and in **Casting Shadows: noir locations** we look at some of the places that have been favourite noir locations and inspired some of the most memorable scenes and moments. Los Angeles is the quintessential noir city but even from the early years the noir style could be discerned as far afield as Britain, France, Japan and Mexico – all of which (and more) are discussed in a brisk survey of world noir highlights, **Dark Side Of The Earth: international noir**. And there is always more to know. **Private Investigations: the information** suggests some of the best books and websites, which are highlighted along with other interesting alleyways of noir territory – from TV to graphic novels.

As well as the fifty long reviews that make up the Canon, there are over 130 short capsule **reviews** of the best of the rest, highlighting what makes them worth seeking out, along with several sidebars on other key topics – from *femmes fatales* to Existentialism. Divided in such a way, we hope that nearly all the important ground is covered. The continually shifting boundaries of noir as a concept inevitably mean that we will have left out titles regarded by some as noir and included others that are debatable. On the whole, we have avoided discussion of straightforward gangster films (except in the origins chapter), and although there are some titles that overlap with those in *The Rough Guide to Gangster Movies*, these are discussed from a different perspective.

On the whole we have emphasized noir as a filmmaking **style** rather than using some artificially watertight genre definition to guide us. We offer customary apologies if your favourite film has been omitted (though some omissions will have been intended) and welcome any suggestions and comments in the event of a second edition (sent to mail@roughguides.com). In the meantime, we hope you enjoy what is intended to lead you on to further exploration of a fascinating and dangerously beguiling territory.

More than one film noir

The French term "film noir" literally means black film but would be more accurately translated as "dark film". It is used to describe both the phenomenon in general (e.g. "Film noir emerged in Hollywood in the early 1940s") and individual examples (eg "Is *White Heat* a film noir or a gangster movie?"). The term became widely used in English from the 1970s onwards, to the extent that it is now treated by some writers as if it were English.

The problem is what to do when the need arises to pluralize the term. In French this would be "films noirs", which sounds odd in an English context but is usually employed by academics writing on the subject. Other writers favour "films noir", while a third alternative – and the one we have adopted – is "film noirs". This can, when necessary, be abbreviated simply to "noirs", and has the added advantage of being consistent with the less problematic pluralizing of "neo-noir".

Acknowledgements

Alexander Ballinger

For any writer on film noir, attendance at London's annual Crime Scene festival is essential so I would like to thank its inspired organisers Adrian Wootton and Maxim Jakubowski for programming films and events which have directly contributed to this book. Thanks should also be extended to Véronique Bahuet and Anne Marie Casalta from the Cannes Film Festival and to Giorgio Gosetti from the Noir In film festival. I attended the Noir In festival in 2002 with Andrew Spicer – whose intellectual support, friendship and provision of countless films and literature since – has enabled me to write this book's canon. Others who have generously provided key books, films and feedback include Geoff Andrew, Graham from Bookmark, Graeme Ginsberg, John Nichol, David Parkinson, Sebastian Thomas and Fred Zentner from the much-missed Cinema Bookshop. Librarians and libraries have played a key role in researching the canon and I would like to thank Noel Greenwood from the NFTS library and the excellent Sean Delaney and his superb staff at the BFI National Library. Closer to home thanks should go to Richard and Penelope Ballinger for looking after me while I carried out endless research and to Abigail and Plum for their continued support and love throughout this lengthy project. My thanks also goes to a duo of fine editors Sam Cook and more latterly Joe Staines – without his intelligent comments, courtesy and sheer hard work this book would not have seen the light of day. Lastly, a big thank you to Andrew Lockett of Rough Guides who commissioned this title and then went out of his way to accommodate its delays and difficulties: no writer could have hoped for a more understanding and honourable publisher.

Danny Graydon

At Rough Guides, I extend many thanks to Andrew Lockett for the opportunity and to Joe Staines for the subsequent editorial guidance and support – both appreciated. I am indebted to Andrew Spicer, whose highly accomplished academic studies of film noir, especially covering the British iteration of the form, were an essential and invaluable source of information. Endless thanks to my partner Manda, whose love and support (and supreme tolerance of this job's weird hours) serves to make everything worthwhile. Finally: to my late father, Tim Graydon (1944–2003), who was entirely responsible for igniting my passion for cinema, who adored a good crime movie and who would have undoubtedly been "as pleased as punch" by my contribution to this.

The Genre That Wasn't There:
the origins

Everyday settings and dark fatalism: noir anticipated in *Le jour se lève* (1939).

The Genre That Wasn't There:

the origins

Night-time city streets, an atmosphere of paranoia, a beautiful but treacherous woman, a gullible and morally weak man, a crime of passion, a crime for money: everyone knows the ingredients that make up the typical film noir, but why did such themes so fascinate Hollywood filmmakers in the period just after World War II? Along with the Western, film noir is often claimed as America's unique contribution to the movies but, as its French label suggests, its origins are a little more complex.

With literally hundreds of visually arresting and powerfully dramatic films made in the 1940s and 50s alone (the so-called classic era), film noir's indelible contribution to cinema history is indisputable. What is more, movies such as *The Maltese Falcon* (1941), *Double Indemnity* (1944), *The Big Heat* (1953) and *Touch Of Evil* (1958) have exerted a massive influence on subsequent generations of filmmakers worldwide, many of

whom have utilized noir's core thematic and stylistic elements to create a further movement, dubbed "neo-noir".

But what exactly *is* film noir? Is it a distinct genre or is it a style? Is the label only relevant to crime-related movies or can it be applied to other types of film? Does a film noir have to be in black and white? While these are questions that critics and theorists continue to argue about, some kind of consensus does exist. A typical film noir usually revolves around a doomed relationship set against the backdrop of a criminal and inveterately corrupt world. A male character (a cop, private eye, war veteran, hoodlum, government operative, down-at-heel lowlife) is caught between two women: one dutiful, responsible, devoted if unexciting, the other a *femme fatale* – sexually alluring, linked to the underworld, unreliable and duplicitous in the extreme. The male character makes a choice (or circumstances make the choice for him) and events spiral from there, inevitably to a tragic end. The protagonists occupy a world that is dark and malign: people are frequently trapped in a web of fear and paranoia, and are often overwhelmed by the power and consequences of uncontrollable sexual desire.

Visually, film noir is anchored in the imagery of a city environment at night. Dark streets soaked with rain reflect the harsh neon of signs and street lamps. The locales emit an atmosphere of claustrophobia (alleyways), sleaziness (nightclubs), paranoia (deserted docks) and temptation (opulent apartments). Film noir's foremost visual signature lies in the way the films are lit: high-contrast lighting accentuates deep, enveloping shadows, while a sense of a skewed reality and instability is created by the use of odd angles and wide shots.

In terms of narrative, the best noirs routinely display sophistication, experimentation and innovation, with the most common narrative modes being the first-person voice-over, the use of flashbacks and multiple viewpoints. All of which serve to provide the films with an unnerving ambiguity: noir narratives frequently possess a dream-like quality, in which objects and events are imbued with a supercharged and forbidding aura. Of course, not every film called "noir" possesses all of these characteristics.

There are plenty of blurry edges to the category, and the noir label has been applied to other genres (for instance Westerns) apart from crime dramas.

At the time they were produced, these films were for the most part derided by US movie critics, who wrote them off as possessing little artistic merit. The major Hollywood studios occasionally provided generous budgets, but more typically placed such films under the auspices of B-units, while the smaller studios regarded them with a production-line mentality, churning them out as filler material. And since the label was retrospective (and French in origin), few, if any, US filmmakers thought of themselves as making film noirs; what they were making were crime films, thrillers, mysteries and romantic melodramas. When released, such "crime films" were usually relegated to the first-half of a double bill, rarely as the main feature. While some, like *Double Indemnity* and *The Asphalt Jungle*, garnered critical attention, these were few and far between.

Critical reassessment

Noir's progress from widespread critical indifference at home to acclaim and influence at an international level was a slow and complicated one. As a label, the term "film noir" can be traced to the French film critic **Nino Frank**, who first employed it in August 1946 in his response to five US films, which were amongst the many released in France following the end of the Nazi occupation – *The Maltese Falcon* (1941), *Murder, My Sweet* (1944), *Double Indemnity* (1944), *Laura* (1944) and *The Lost Weekend* (1945). Frank identified these as a new darker style of crime film, replete with arresting visuals, complex narration and a focus on psychology.

The label was deliberately analogous to *roman noir* used first to describe the English gothic novel (see p.12), and then the American "hard-boiled" detective fiction that provided primary source material for these films. *Série noire* was the series title given to the French translations of such crime novels launched by the publisher **Gallimard** in 1945.

The subsequent popularity of the term amongst French intellectuals led to the first critical assessment of film noir in 1955. *Panorama du film noir américain* by **Raymond Borde** and **Etienne Chaumeton** characterized film noir as "nightmarish, weird, erotic, ambivalent and cruel" whose aim "was to create a specific alienation". But despite the intellectual enthusiasm towards film noir shown by the French, the lack of a similar approach to film criticism in the US meant that the term would not be much used outside of France until the late 1960s.

The first English-language assessment of film noir came in 1968 with the publication of *Hollywood In The Forties* by **Charles Higham** and **Joel Greenberg**. Two years later, **Raymond Durgnat** published his idiosyncratic essay *Paint It Black: The Family Tree Of Film Noir*, which sought to categorize film noir by themes and sub-genres while retaining its fluidity as a concept. Even more significant was an essay entitled "Notes On Film Noir" that appeared in *Film Comment* in 1972. Its author, **Paul Schrader** – who would go on to write the screenplay for the neo-noir classic *Taxi Driver* (1976) – placed film noir within a specific era as well as suggesting that its essential dark tone cut across different genres. Since then the field of criticism devoted to film noir has expanded rapidly, and there are now literally hundreds of books on the subject.

The sources of noir

Never an entirely American phenomenon, film noir's content and stylistic trademarks were derived from a fertile mixture of the following influences: US crime fiction of the "hard-boiled" variety, Hollywood gangster movies, German cinema of the Weimar years and French poetic realist films of the immediate prewar period. A less direct impact was made by the cycle of horror movies produced by Universal Studios in the 1930s, which in turn were influenced by gothic novels of the nineteenth century.

Hard-boiled crime writers

Of all noir's most immediate influences, the hard-boiled detective fiction of 1930s and 40s had the greatest impact. Much of noir's subject matter, characters and general milieu derived from it, in particular from the work of **Dashiell Hammett**, **Raymond Chandler**, **James M. Cain**, **David Goodis**, **W.R. Burnett** and **Cornell Woolrich**. Forming part of what became generally known as "pulp fiction" (so named because it was printed on cheap pulp paper), by the end of the 1930s hard-boiled crime fiction began appearing as paperbacks with lurid covers, securing a considerable audience among working-class men. It also provided Hollywood's native and European émigré directors with no shortage of material to adapt or imitate. It's been estimated that between 1941 and 1948 at least one fifth of all film noirs were derived from hard-boiled crime fiction.

Prior to the 1930s, crime fiction mostly appeared in cheap genre-specific magazines such as *Detective Story* and, most significantly, *Black Mask*. Launched in 1920 by **H.L. Mencken** and

George Jean Nathan, *Black Mask*'s most influential editor was **Joseph T. Shaw**. Under Shaw's editorship, the magazine became a platform for the swiftly growing genre of naturalistic crime thrillers, publishing the work of Hammett and later Chandler. Hammett is now regarded as the father of the hard-boiled crime style, and it was Shaw who first persuaded him to turn his hand to full-length fiction. For many, the golden age of film noir is initiated by **John Huston**'s powerful adaptation of Hammett's *The Maltese Falcon*, made in 1941 (see Canon).

Hammett developed a striking vernacular for his stories – a tough and terse idiom, closely following the cadences of ordinary speech. The fact that his stories were often narrated directly by the main character gave them an added element of urgency and speed. Chandler's contributions to the genre included his hugely atmospheric depictions of Los Angeles and his development of a key noir figure, the world-weary, wisecracking private eye. The third great literary influence was James M. Cain, whose stories usually revolve around the viewpoint of the criminal as opposed to the private eye. His protagonists are often forced into terrible deeds as the victims of circumstance, and many of his stories focus on the connection between money and sex. Cornell Woolrich was another significant writer; his elaborate prose, underlining the nightmarish element of city life, formed the basis of eleven films.

City Streets
dir Rouben Mamoulian, 1931, US, 75m, b/w

Adapted from a Hammett story, this gangster tale focuses on the love affair between The Kid (Gary Cooper), who runs a shooting gallery, and Nan (Sylvia Sidney), the daughter of a mobster. When Nan takes the rap for a crime her father committed, The Kid takes to crime in order to get her out of prison. Low on violence and high on romance, the noirish elements are visible in Mamoulian's stylish direction and Lee Garmes's atmospheric.

The Maltese Falcon
dir Roy Del Ruth, 1931, US, 80m, b/w

The first version of Hammett's *The Maltese Falcon* is a disappointment. Where Huston's later movie oozes sleaze and corruption, this one is just too breezy, despite the frank treatment of Sam Spade's womanizing. There's nothing remotely hard-bitten about Ricardo Cortez's unsubtle Spade, and while Bebe Daniels is rather better in the Mary Astor role, the whole thing fails to take off.

Gangster movies

While not as significant as the hard-boiled fiction of Hammett et al, the gangster movie, nevertheless, exerted a powerful influence on the general milieu of film noir. In Depression-era America, the gangster was a familiar figure; a routine presence on newspaper front pages and, for many, an attractive one, thanks to the combination of money, power and expensive clothes.

Gangster movies had been around since **D. W. Griffith**'s *The Musketeers Of Pig Alley* of 1912, but **Josef Von Sternberg**'s *Underworld* (1927) is the silent movie most often linked to noir. The first film to portray criminals with any degree of understanding, Ben Hecht's taut script (he had spent time as a Chicago crime reporter) was matched by Sternberg's atmospheric direction – although the two fell out during shooting. With its themes of alienation, paranoia, betrayal, revenge, and the omnipresence of death, *Underworld* stands as a potent sign of what was to come.

However, it was during the 1930s that the gangster film really established itself as one of

The Production Code

In 1930 the Motion Picture Producers and Distributors of America (**MPPDA**) established a set of guidelines about what should and shouldn't be shown in the movies. They did so in the face of a growing public perception that Hollywood was a stew of vice and immorality (both onscreen and off) and as a way of avoiding federal censorship. The guidelines were known collectively as the **Production Code**, or the Hays Code, and were drawn up by **Will H. Hays**, the former US Postmaster General who had been in charge of the MPPDA since 1922.

The Hays Code was extremely restrictive: its specific rules mainly concentrated on sex ("Excessive and lustful kissing, lustful embraces, suggestive postures and gestures, are not to be shown") and violence ("The technique of murder must be presented in a way that will not inspire imitation"), but also included social issues ("the existence of the [drug] trade should not be brought to the attention of audiences") and religion ("Ministers of religion in their character as ministers of religion should not be used as comic characters or as villains").

The rulings were not enforced, however, until July 1934 when **Joseph Breen** – a strict Catholic and secret anti-Semite – became head of the new Production Code Administration (**PCA**). From now on all scripts were strictly vetted for breaches of the guidelines and every film had to receive a certificate of approval before it could be released. Needless to say many producers, directors and scriptwriters were angered by the degree of interference they encountered, and there were regular standoffs with Breen's office.

With their heady combination of sex, duplicity and murder, films that we now think of as noir were par-

ticularly vulnerable to the heavy hand of the PCA and many were changed as a result of rulings from Breen's office. John Huston's 1941 remake of *The Maltese Falcon* (arguably the first great film noir) is an interesting case in point. Having refused the re-release of the 1931 version of Hammett's novel (on the grounds that Bebe Daniels was too skimpily dressed), Breen's report on the script of the 1941 version made a number of demands – mainly about the film's sexual content. These included removing any hint "of illicit sex between Spade and Brigid", and any suggestion that the character of Joel Cairo was a homosexual (or "pansy type" as the report put it).

Some critics have suggested that, far from limiting them, the restrictions actually stimulated filmmakers' imaginations, and it is certainly true that in many film noirs much is clearly implied through highly suggestive ambiguity and ellipsis. Thus – despite the request from Breen's office – it seems pretty obvious that Spade and Brigid do sleep together and that he has been sleeping with his partner's wife. Huston even managed to retain a reference to homosexuality with Spade's constant references to Wilmer Cook as a "gunsel". Though the word sounds as if it should mean gunman (which Wilmer is), it actually means a catamite or young homosexual companion to an older man.

Despite some successful challenges to its authority, the Production Code retained its power through most of the 1950s, but with the more permissive social climate of the 1960s its strictures seemed increasingly absurd and unenforceable. By 1968 the MPAA abandoned the Code altogether and replaced it with a rating system that has remained in place to this day.

the most daring and popular of all movie genres. Films like *Little Caesar* (1930), *The Public Enemy* (1931) and *Scarface* (1932) all contributed to the subversive notion that the gangster was a kind

of modern entrepreneur, as opposed to a mere criminal, embodying the dark underside of the American Dream. The popularity of such films also meant that the iconography and milieu of

Bull Weed (George Bancroft) considers his actions in *Underworld* (1927), Sternberg's early gangster film.

the criminal – crucial to film noir – was firmly fixed in the American consciousness.

Not all US crime movies were about mega-lomaniac mobsters, however. Petty hoodlums also got a look in and were often presented in a strikingly sympathetic way. In 1937 **Fritz Lang** pioneered the criminal-couple-on-the-run movie with *You Only Live Once* (1937), a darkly fatalistic tale (partly based on the real-life Bonnie and Clyde) that was to become the template for a whole spate of similar films, from Nicholas Ray's *They Live By Night* (1948) and Joseph Lewis's *Gun Crazy* (1950) to Terrence Malick's *Badlands* and Robert Altman's *Thieves Like Us* (both 1973).

Underworld
dir Josef Von Sternberg, 1927, US, 80m, b/w

Bank robber Bull Weed (George Bancroft) aids a down-and-out ex-lawyer (Clive Brook), who in return becomes his right-hand man but later falls for his moll girlfriend Feathers (Evelyn Brent). A violent showdown occurs when the volatile gangster discovers the truth. This is an influential milestone in the gangster genre, generating great mileage out of what became perennial noir themes: conflicts of love and loyalty.

Little Caesar
dir Mervyn LeRoy, 1930, US, 79m, b/w

Adapted from the novel by W.R. Burnett, *Little Caesar* is a cinematic landmark, a Depression-era parable of free enterprise pushed to murderous extremes. The film launched the career of Edward G. Robinson – who gives a mesmerizing performance as ruthless mobster Rico Bandello – and affirmed the dominance of the gangster film throughout the 1930s.

The Public Enemy
dir William Wellman, 1931, US, 83m, b/w

No less important than *Little Caesar*, *The Public Enemy* made James Cagney a star. Often acclaimed as the most realistic gangster film ever made, it is a thoroughly incendiary piece of work, with Wellman infusing character action and thought with waves of casual brutality. Firmly set in the criminal world – and rarely moving outside of it – Cagney presents one of the seminal portrayals of the gangster: volatile, hard and wholly without conscience.

You Only Live Once
dir Fritz Lang, 1937, US, 86m, b/w

Recently released convict Eddie Taylor (Henry Fonda) plans to go straight with the help of his girlfriend Joan (Sylvia Sidney), but things go badly wrong and they are forced on the run. This meticulously crafted tragedy has an often overwhelming grimness, with every shot adding to an atmosphere of unbearable futility. It was Lang's second US film and a prime example of what can be considered "pre-noir".

From Germany with angst

Aesthetically, the foremost influence on film noir came from Germany, and it is here that noir's shadow-laden visuals were born. After World War I and throughout the 1920s, German filmmakers made up for meagre budgets by using symbolism and *mise en scène* to insert mood and deeper layers of meaning into their films. Such films are often seen as examples of **Expressionism**, a movement across the arts that was profoundly anti-naturalistic and whose extreme subjectivity was conveyed by means of distortion and stylization.

The ultimate example of this type of cinema is **Robert Wiene**'s *Das Cabinet des Dr Caligari* (1920), a richly ambiguous horror story that uses bizarre painted décor and an exaggerated performance style to communicate the murderer/protagonist's demented inner world. Other expressionist films include **Paul Wegener**'s *Der Golem* (1920), about a monster created from clay, **F.W. Murnau**'s vampire film *Nosferatu* (1922) and **Paul Leni**'s *Waxworks* (1924). *Caligari*'s direct influence on film noir is debatable, but it was part of a cultural climate within German filmmaking that was innovative and experimental, visually, technically and in terms of story-telling.

Expressionist films typically dealt with madness, betrayal and the fantastic – classic subject matter that links them to German Romantic writers such as E.T.A. Hoffmann. But there was another stylistic strand of German filmmaking that emerged in the early 1920s called *Kammerspielfilm*. Derived from the theatre (the literal translation is "chamber play"), these were intimate dramas that usually homed in on the desperation of postwar urban life, the finest example of which is F.W. Murnau's tale of a demoted hotel doorman, *Der letzte Mann* (*The Last Laugh*, 1924).

Peter Lorre as murderer Hans Beckert amidst the expressive shadows and claustrophobic sets of *M* (1931).

The German influence on film noir manifested itself still further with the *Strassenfilm*, or "street film", which moved away from expressionism in favour of a more objective focus on the social realities of contemporary life. **Karl Grune's** *Die Strasse* (*The Street*, 1923) – the prototype for such films – dealt with an ordinary man's descent from respectability, seduced by the nocturnal lure of the city. Key elements of film noir are much in evidence: shadows, the rush of city life, forbidding underworld characters and, most pertinently, the attraction of illicit love in the beguiling form of a *femme fatale*. *Caligari*, *Der letzte Mann* and *Die Strasse* were all written by Carl Mayer, whose work emphasized the instinctive reactions of characters to their situations, in a way that meant that explanatory intertitles could be kept to a minimum.

The darkness and psychological depth of German filmmaking – which reflected the extreme economic privations suffered by ordinary Germans in the interwar years – began to impact on Hollywood after the Nazis came to power in 1933. Many German and Austrian film personnel – including directors Fritz Lang, Otto Preminger, Billy Wilder, Max Ophüls, Douglas Sirk, Robert Siodmak, William Dieterle and Fred Zinnemann – left their respective countries to seek work elsewhere. Several finished up in Hollywood where they were regarded as a highly desirable commodity given the prestigious reputation of German film. Their influence on the development of film noir, in combination with that of other European émigrés, was profound and far-reaching.

Das Cabinet des Dr Caligari
dir Robert Wiene, 1920, Ger, 71m, b/w

The most famous of German expressionist films tells the story of a sinister fairground magician, Dr Caligari (Werner Krauss), who hypnotizes his zomboid assistant Cesare (Conrad Veidt) into committing murder and abducting a young woman. The confusing plot is given a further twist by a framing device that suggests the whole thing may have been a lunatic's dream. Ultimately it is the disturbingly weird sets, designed by Hermann Warm, that linger longest in the memory.

Der letzte Mann (The Last Laugh)
dir F.W. Murnau, 1924, Ger, 100m, b/w

Emil Jannings plays a hotel doorman whose life falls apart when he is demoted to the job of lavatory attendant because of his age. His humiliation is complete when he is caught trying to steal back his uniform. If Jannings is the star, then so is Karl Freund's camera-work, which moves around the limited action with an amazingly graceful fluidity, acting as both eavesdropper and point of view.

Die Büsche der Pandora (Pandora's Box)
dir G.W. Pabst, 1928, Ger, 100m, b/w

As the seductive gamine Lulu – a showgirl who is both amoral yet a kind of innocent – American starlet Louise Brooks created one of the most enduring and archetypal of screen figures. The embodiment of pure sexuality, Lulu cuts a swathe through a series of weak-willed and emasculated men. A claustrophobic Berlin and the fog-filled streets of London provide the suitably oppressive backdrop.

Der blaue Engel (The Blue Angel)
dir Josef Von Sternberg, 1930, Ger, 99m, b/w

This co-production between UFA and Paramount (filmed in both German and English) launched the international career of Marlene Dietrich as the sexy cabaret singer Lola Lola. The actual star of the film was Emil Jannings, who plays a respectable school teacher whose career takes a nosedive after he ventures into *The Blue Angel* nightclub. Sternberg's *mise en scène* brilliantly conveys both the allure of the *demi-monde* and its essential shabbiness.

M
dir Fritz Lang, 1931, Ger, 105m, b/w

Centred around a mesmerizing performance from Peter Lorre as a serial child-killer, Lang's most chilling film – and his first in sound – concerns the attempts of Berlin's criminal underworld to apprehend the murderer. *M* possesses many innovative elements that would become staples of noir: expressive shadows, distorted angles, claustrophobic sets and the use of voice-over narration. It all adds up to a forensic view of the killer which is both creepy and moving.

Universal horror and the gothic novel

In 1931 Universal Studios – then suffering a downturn in its fortunes – released *Dracula* starring **Bela Lugosi**. An immediate hit, the film saved the studio and kickstarted a vogue for "horror" films that has lasted to this day. Universal had already achieved great success with films like *The Phantom Of The Opera* (1925) and *The Cat And The Canary* (1927), the latter directed by German Paul Leni, imported to Hollywood on the strength of his expressionist masterpiece *Waxworks* (1924).

Leni was just one part of a vital connection with Germany that helped inject a darker and more atmospheric feel to American films. An even more important figure was the great German cinematographer **Karl Freund**, who arrived in the US in 1929 with an impressive record, including the camera-work on *Der Golem*, *Der letzte Mann* and Fritz Lang's *Metropolis*. Freund was the key figure in defining Universal's visual style – as cinematographer on *Dracula* and *Murders In The Rue Morgue* (1932), and as the director of *The Mummy* (1932).

All Universal's horror films derived to some extent from the rich literary tradition of the **gothic**, which arose in the late eighteenth century and flourished in the first half of the nineteenth. Gothic novels were typically mysteries (often involving a

Mad love and gothic touches: Doctor Gogol (Peter Lorre) holds the hand of Yvonne Orlac (Frances Drake).

beautiful and vulnerable young woman) heavily tinged with horror and usually set against a background of medieval ruins and haunted castles. **Ann Radcliffe**, whose novels include *The Mysteries of Udolpho* (1794) and *The Italian* (1797), was the most influential of the early authors, while **Mary Shelley**'s *Frankenstein* (1818) is the most widely read. Gothic fiction can also be found in Germany, notably in the works of E.T.A. Hoffmann, and in the US where it was developed by such writers as Washington Irving, Nathaniel Hawthorne and **Edgar Allen Poe**.

Perhaps unsurprisingly, there are many overlaps between noir and horror: both focus on the darker side of human nature, where greed, desperation or unchecked desires can lead to acts of violence and betrayal. Both also employ many of the same aesthetic strategies, not least the often exaggerated and highly stylized use of darkness and light for symbolic purposes. This overlap is at its most marked in those films which derive from twentieth-century gothic (or neo-gothic) fiction, like **Daphne du Maurier**'s *Rebecca*, which was filmed by **Alfred Hitchcock** in 1940 (see p.26) – and is often cited as one of the first noirs – and **Ethel Lina White**'s *Some Must Watch*, filmed by **Robert Siodmak** as *The Spiral Staircase* in 1946 (see p.241).

Dracula
dir Tod Browning, 1931, US, 75m, b/w

The first authorized film of Bram Stoker's 1897 novel stars Bela Lugosi as the saturnine Count Dracula, a role he had played on Broadway. Browning's direction is largely uninspired and most of the atmosphere and eerie mood is generated by Freund's inventive cinematography, especially in the early Transylvanian scenes.

The Black Cat
dir Edgar G. Ulmer, 1934, US, 65m, b/w

The dream pairing of Bela Lugosi and Boris Karloff as arch-enemies delivers the creepy goods, even though the film's plot – supposedly based on a story by Poe – is utterly mystifying. Director Ulmer's background in German film is evident in the emphasis on the morbid psychology of Karloff's satanic architect and the designs of the modern gothic castle where he lives.

Mad Love (aka The Hands Of Orlac)
dir Karl Freund, 1935, US, 70m, b/w

Made for MGM, Freund's last film is his best. Peter Lorre plays Dr Gogol, who is obsessed with actress Yvonne Orlac (Frances Drake). When Yvonne's concert-pianist husband damages his hands, Dr Gogol surgically replaces them with the hands of an executed, knife-throwing murderer. Hokum, but of the highest order thanks to Lorre's brilliant performance and the murkily sepulchral settings.

The French connection

"Poetic realism" is the term often used to describe a group of French films of the 1930s that derived from realist literature. Set amongst the urban working class, such films have an over-riding mood of pessimism which is softened by a highly romanticized fatalism. As in Germany, the anxious brooding quality of these films reflects the bitter social and political reality of the times. Stories usually revolve around a criminal act or a hopeless love affair, and often feature a heroically doomed male protagonist – a role that the actor **Jean Gabin** came to epitomize. Poetic realist directors drew heavily on the work of French-language crime writers like **Georges Simenon**, **Pierre MacOrlan** and **Eugène Dabit**, but were also drawn to US writers; indeed, the first film adaptation of James M. Cain's novel, *The Postman Always Rings Twice,* was made in France by **Pierre Chenal** in 1939.

Other directors whose work encompasses poetic realism include **Jean Renoir**, whose *La* *chienne* (1931) owes a stylistic debt to German *Strassenfilm*; and **Julien Duvivier**, whose Algerian-based gangster film *Pépé le Moko* (1937) presents a quintessentially noir vision of the city as sinister labyrinth. But it's the three films made by director **Marcel Carné** in collaboration with scriptwriter **Jacques Prévert** that best encapsulate the poetic realist vision. *Le quai des brumes* (1938), *Hôtel Du Nord* (1938) and *Le jour se lève* (1939) all have a sense of lost innocence and hopelessness, a dark fatalism that is reinforced by the designs of **Alexandre**

Jean Gabin awaits the daybreak in *Le jour se lève*.

Trauner, which are rooted in realism but contain a subtle, painterly beauty.

Critically acclaimed in France (where they were sometimes referred to as film noir), poetic realist films were also admired in Britain and America for their sophisticated adult content and striking visual qualities. While not quite so misanthropic or cynical as American film noir, there is a clear kinship between the two movements. Consequently, many poetic realist films were remade in Hollywood, notably Jean Renoir's *La chienne* and *La bête humaine* (1938), remade by Fritz Lang as *Scarlet Street* (1945) and *Human Desire* (1954) respectively, and Carné's *Le jour se lève* which became *The Long Night* (1947), directed by Anatole Litvak.

French directors who went to Hollywood to escape World War II were relatively few: Jean Renoir was one of them, but the nearest he got to making a film noir was the mysterious melodrama *Woman On The Beach* (1947). It is worth noting that **Jules Dassin**, who is often thought to be French, was actually born in Connecticut to Russian parents, while **Jacques Tourneur**, who *was* French, largely learnt his craft in the Hollywood of the 1930s.

La chienne (The Bitch)
dir Jean Renoir, 1931, France, 91m, b/w

Renoir's first sound film tells the story of hen-pecked bank clerk and amateur painter Maurice Legrand (Michel Simon), and his obsession with a prostitute, Lulu (Janie Marèze), whom he eventually murders. Though her pimp is executed for the crime, Legrand is reduced to living as a tramp. Similar in theme to *Der blaue Engel*, Renoir's film – with its use of real locations – is grittier and less sentimental.

Pépé le Moko
dir Julien Duvivier, 1936, France, 93m, b/w

Pépé (Jean Gabin) is a gangster who rules the criminal roost in the Casbah – the Arab section of Algiers.

Homesick for France, he risks all by venturing outside his own turf when a beautiful young French woman (Mireille Balin) takes his fancy. Duvivier's direction makes great play with the shadowy world of the Casbah – all web-like alleyways and mysterious pools of light.

La bête humaine
dir Jean Renoir, 1938, France, 100m, b/w

Witnessing a murder leads train driver Jacques Lantier (Jean Gabin) into an affair with Séverine (Simone Simon), the stationmaster's wife. But Lantier has his own demon, a history of mental illness which unleashes murderous impulses. Renoir's quietly powerful film – based on Zola's novel – brilliantly utilizes the symbolism of the railway to suggest the destructive power of passion and the inexorability of fate.

Le jour se lève (Daybreak)
dir Marcel Carné, 1939, France, 87m, b/w

One of the finest examples of poetic realism opens with a murder committed by François (Jean Gabin), who then locks himself in his hotel room and waits for daybreak. The rest of the film, told in flashback, tells of the tragic love quartet between good girl Françoise (Jacqueline Laurent), the exploitative Valentin (Jules Berry) and classic *femme fatale* Clara (Arletty). Deeply despairing, the film is redeemed from melodrama by its makers' humanism.

Le dernier tournant (The Last Turn)
dir Pierre Chenal, 1939, France, 90m, b/w

The very first adaptation of Cain's *The Postman Always Rings Twice* succeeds because of the strength of its performances, in particular Michel Simon as the brutish garage mechanic Nick. Fernand Gravet as Frank and Corinne Luchaire as Cora generate the requisite steamy passion, and the whole thing makes the perfect link between prewar French and postwar American noir.

Fear and loathing in LA

All the different strands that make up film noir came together in **Los Angeles**, a town that had grown at a spectacular rate, thanks to petroleum, the aviation industry and, of course, the movies. In 1900 LA had a population of just over one hundred thousand, by 1940 it was one and a half million. The boom years of the early twentieth century were accompanied by a mythology of LA – and Southern California generally – as a healthy, sun-blessed land of opportunity. The reality was more a story of speculation, landgrabs and class war. Fuelled by the Depression, and LA's increasingly polarized politics, the novels of **Nathaniel West** and the hard-boiled fiction of Cain, Hammett and Chandler created the anti-myth of Southern California – a cynical, dystopian vision that would become central to noir. Whether writing about the disaffected middle class or a criminal underclass, these writers were presenting a picture of capitalism out of control.

This critique of Los Angeles as the symbol of a degenerate business culture was often sharpened when translated into film, by virtue of the fact that several key noir writers and directors were either left-leaning Americans or anti-fascist European émigrés. The latter brought an "old world" perspective to American life and were particularly scathing about LA's cultural shallowness, its suburban sprawl and its fake urbanity. Ironically, however critical these imported intellectuals were – whether from New York or Europe – they were there because Los Angeles institutions (the California Institute of Technology as well as Hollywood) were paying their wages.

There's a further paradox in the fact that studio bosses soon got wise to the commercial potential of noirish material (even if they didn't call it that), even permitting such self-lacerating movies as *Sunset Boulevard* (1950) and *The Bad And The Beautiful* (1952). Needless to say, not all noirs of the early years functioned as criticism.

Art of darkness

Whether directly or indirectly, the work of certain painters has had an influence on the visual style of film noir. As with the films themselves, these can be divided – broadly speaking – into two groups: one which favoured an objective, unflinching view of the world (realism), and one which attempted to convey, by distortion and stylization, a more subjective and disturbed vision of mankind (expressionism). Artists and movements with a relevance to noir include:

• **Caravaggio** (1571–1610) The most radical artist of his time, Caravaggio's mature religious paintings are striking for their extreme contrasts of light and shade (chiaroscuro), their implicit sense of violence, and the fact that ordinary working people were employed as models.

• **Realism** Though sometimes used in a general sense to mean the pictorial rendering of the visible world in a detailed and accurate manner, when spelled with a capital R it refers to a movement in mid-nineteenth-century France that rejected the idealization of academic art in favour of more down-to-earth subject matter, often peasant life. **Gustave Courbet** (1819–77) was Realism's most significant figure.

• **Expressionism** An artistic movement that expressed the unique, and often tormented, inner vison of the artist through exaggeration and distortion. The movement was particularly prevalent in Germany in the first quarter of the twentieth century.

• **Surrealism** An international movement, originating in France in the 1920s, that attempted to produce works of art that drew directly from the unconscious mind. Dreams, humour and sexual desire were especially valued as being untrammelled by the encumbrance of logic. Salvador Dali, the most famous Surrealist painter, designed the dream sequence in Hitchcock's *Spellbound* (1945).

• **Ashcan School** An informal group of American realist painters working at the beginning of the twentieth century, some of whose work focused on the everyday life of the urban poor. **George Bellows** (1882–1925), who was associated with the group, is best known for his noirish depictions of boxing matches, in which the straining bodies of the fighters are spot-lit by a harsh raking light.

• **Edward Hopper** (1882–1967) His cool and restrained urban scenes focus on solitary individuals within the city and are suffused with a sense of melancholy. His most famous painting, *Nighthawks* (1942), showing three customers in an illuminated night-time diner, is exactly contemporary with early film noir.

The studio system meant that a wide range of writers and directors of differing beliefs might be allocated a crime film. It's also true that many noirs were set in other cities, such as New York and San Francisco. But Los Angeles is the paradigm for the dream city that turned into a nightmare, and it has continued to fire the imaginations of filmmakers to this day.

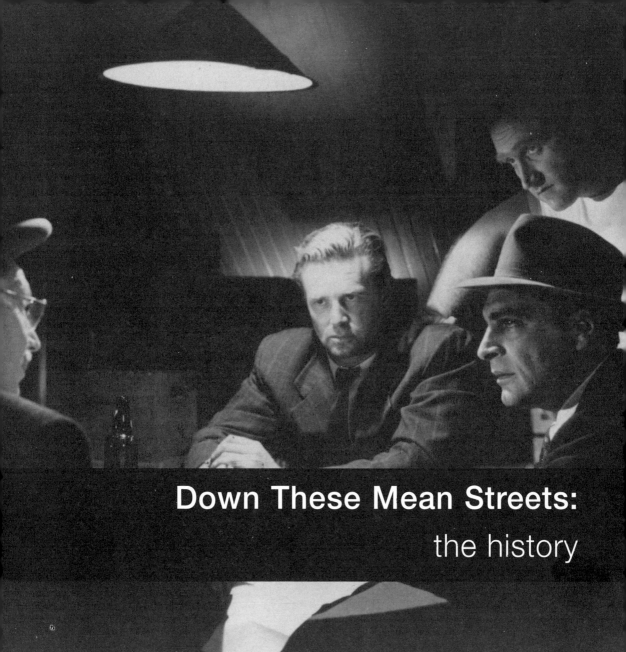

Down These Mean Streets:

the history

A scene from *The Asphalt Jungle* (1950)
– the first great heist movie, directed by
John Huston.

Down These Mean Streets:
the history

Debate still rages over which precise movie kick-started the film noir phenomenon: while many regard *The Maltese Falcon* (1941) as the most likely suspect, others look to pre-World War II films such as *Fury* (1936) and *You Only Live Once* (1937), both by Fritz Lang. Current critical consensus favours *Stranger On The Third Floor* (1940), an obscure RKO B-movie directed by the virtually unknown Latvian émigré Boris Ingster.

The 1940s

Stranger On The Third Floor may well be the prime candidate for "the first film noir", but its original critical reception was lukewarm at best. **Bosley Crowther** of the *New York Times* was particularly unimpressed: "The notion seems to have been that the way to put a psychological melodrama across is to pile on the sound effects and trick up the photography." In one sense this gets to the heart of film noir – a type of movie characterized by the extreme psychopathology of its protagonists, and the way in which stylized cinematography can express subjective experience. *Stranger* was also remarkable for assembling some influential noir figures, including actors Peter Lorre and Elisha Cook Jr, composer Roy Webb and cinematographer Nicholas Musuraca.

Citizen Kane and film noir

Citizen Kane, the first full-length feature film directed by the 25-year-old wunderkind **Orson Welles**, was released in May 1941. Expectation was huge, not least because newspaper tycoon **William Randolph Hearst** – on whom Kane was said to be based – tried to have the film banned. But despite the critical plaudits public reaction was unenthusiastic and the film lost money. It was only after *Kane* was screened in Paris in 1946 that it started to garner the kind of extreme praise that established its status as one of the greatest films ever made.

1946 was also the year that French critics applied the term film noir to certain American crime films, and *Kane* is sometimes viewed as a kind of honorary noir, largely on account of its flamboyant visual style. Welles was a questing and experimental artist, and *Kane* reveals his awareness of Surrealism and expressionism, Eisenstein's theories of montage as well as novelist William Faulkner's experiments with narrative structure and point of view.

The visual impact of *Kane* comes from the highly stylized and extravagant art direction of **Perry Ferguson** and the way the settings are lit and photographed by cinematographer **Gregg Toland**. In particular Toland employs the new technique of deep focus, whereby objects in both the foreground and background remain in focus. As well as providing greater fluidity by obviating the need for intercutting and reverse angles, it also creates a greater sense of space and allows figures to be placed in isolation from one another. Welles and Toland also utilized the whole repertoire of expressionist devices, including the use of wide-angle lenses, low-angled shots and high-contrast lighting.

Many noirs of the 1940s employ stylistic elements showcased in *Kane*: elaborate tracking shots, long takes, complex set design and shot composition as well as subjective perspectives generated through complex flashback narration. Welles's film – deemed by critics and film historians to be the pre-eminent example of "American Expressionism" – provides another major link between European modernist filmmaking and film noir.

 Citizen Kane
dir Orson Welles, 1947, US, 119m, b/w

Welles's masterpiece tells the fictional story of Charles Foster Kane, a powerful media magnate and a deeply flawed and complicated character. The film unravels his rise to power through interlocking flashbacks as a journalist tries to identify the meaning of "Rosebud" – the word on Kane's lips when he died. Its darkly cynical vision gives it a distinctly noir tinge although Kane is not a typical noir protagonist: he largely controls his own destiny and there is no destructive *femme fatale* in his life.

1940 also saw the release of **Alfred Hitchcock**'s first American feature, *Rebecca*, an adaptation of Daphne du Maurier's contemporary take on the gothic novel (see p.26). The film's English country house setting might not conform to the typical noir milieu, but the air of menace beneath the genteel surface and the moody camera-work of George Barnes give it the requisite paranoiac edge.

John Huston's directorial debut *The Maltese Falcon* (1941, see Canon) is unquestionably the first great noir. Hammett's novel had been filmed twice already, but Huston's is the definitive version, creating just the right hard-boiled tone and moral ambiguity through strong casting and dynamic camera-work. It also established a noir archetype in the tough-guy private investigator, and one of its greatest interpreters in **Humphrey Bogart**.

Hollywood had got wise to pulp novels in the 1930s, but it was only from the mid-1940s (the start of the classic noir era) that movies really began to do justice to the better-quality crime writers. *High Sierra* (1941) was based on the novel by **W.R. Burnett**; *This Gun For Hire* (1942), starring Alan Ladd and Veronica Lake, was taken from Graham Greene's *A Gun For Sale*; *The Glass Key* (1942) was another Hammett adaptation; while Orson Welles's *Journey Into Fear* (1943) – which Welles starred in and directed – drew broadly on the spy thriller by Eric Ambler.

The most inventive of these early crime novel adaptations was *Double Indemnity* (1944, see Canon), directed by Billy Wilder and co-written by him with crime novelist **Raymond Chandler**. It was Chandler who provided the quick-fire and witty dialogue – arguably an improvement on **James M. Cain**'s original novella. *Double Indemnity* also established something of a noir template, with its gullible and morally weak male protagonist manipulated and dragged down by an irresistible but ultimately heartless woman.

In the same year Chandler's own novel *Farewell My Lovely* was filmed by **Edward Dmytryk** as *Murder, My Sweet* (1944, see Canon), with Dick Powell as the legendary private detective Philip Marlowe. Cleverly exploiting the stylistic legacy of Welles's *Citizen Kane* – voice-over, expressionist lighting, distorting reflections – Dmytryk brought real depth to Marlowe's descent into an underworld hell. Two years later Humphrey Bogart added an extra layer of battered world-weariness to Marlowe in an equally fine Chandler adaptation, **Howard Hawks**'s *The Big Sleep* (1946, see Canon).

Noir on the couch

Many critics have observed that film noir's focus on individual paranoia and psychological disturbance is linked to the fact that by the 1940s there was a widespread awareness of psychoanalysis in the US. Freudian ideas and motifs crop up in many noirs. Characters are frequently propelled by sexual desire, often of a perverse nature and in a way that suggests deep psychological damage. Dream sequences are regularly used to shed light on some crucial aspect of the plot, and the common noir devices of voice-over and flashback have obvious parallels with the way psychoanalysis talks over the past in order to unravel the problems of the present. In 1940s noirs in particular, stylized camera-work and lighting suggest a highly subjective and disturbed point of view.

On a more superficial level, psychiatrists and psychoanalysts play key roles in a number of noirs, not always in a positive way. In Otto Preminger's *Whirlpool* (written by Ben Hecht), a sinister hypnotherapist achieves a hold over a kleptomaniac woman, whose psychoanalyst husband is too insensitive to be aware of her problems. But the most famous of all "Freudian" noirs is Hitchcock's *Spellbound*, once again written by Hecht, which takes place in a mental hospital where the director is about to retire and a new doctor take over. Unfortunately, as Hitchcock admitted, an uneasy tension exists in the film between the rather earnest outlining of psychoanalysis and the demands of a good thriller.

Spellbound
dir Alfred Hitchcock, 1945, US, 111m, b/w

Gregory Peck plays Dr Edwardes, a young psychiatrist who has just become director of a mental asylum. His behaviour, however, is erratic, prompting Ingrid Bergman's brilliant but emotionally cool doctor to suspect he is not who he claims. After falling in love with him, she helps him elude the police when he is accused of murder, and then attempts to cure him through dream analysis – a spectacular sequence designed by the Surrealist painter Salvador Dali. A film with noirish elements rather than a fully fledged noir, it is always gripping despite some ridiculous moments.

Meanwhile over in France, in an essay published at the end of 1946, critic **Nino Frank** identified a new darker strain in those US films – especially crime films – that had recently arrived in France with the end of World War II (see p.4). Surprisingly, Frank included *The Lost Weekend* (1945) and *Citizen Kane* (1941) as examples of the new noir sensibility, and it is true that – even in its early period – those films we think of as noir encompassed a strikingly wide range of subjects.

A publicity shot from *The Postman Always Rings Twice* (1946).

Comparing *Double Indemnity* with **Otto Preminger's** *Laura* (see Canon) – both made in 1944 and both cited by Nino Frank – reveals differences as marked as their similarities. In *Laura* the milieu is refined and glamorous, a crime is being investigated but we don't witness it, and the beguiling leading lady is no amoral *femme fatale*. The film is essentially a romantic melodrama, a "woman's film" given a noir dimension by a complex narrative framework and its stunning, dream-like *mise-en-scène*. Other "feminine" noirs include *Mildred Pierce* (1945, see Canon), *Leave Her To Heaven* (1945, see Canon), one of the first noirs filmed in colour, and *The Reckless Moment* (1949), in which the main character is an ordinary housewife faced with extraordinary circumstances.

The halfway mark of the decade saw some interesting developments in the way that noirs were produced, with some of the smaller, so-called **Poverty Row** studios starting to get in on the act. Producers Releasing Corporation was one such company. Largely specializing in B-movie Westerns, in 1945 it released two noirs directed by **Edgar G. Ulmer** – *Strange Illusion* and *Detour* (see Canon). The latter, which is Ulmer's masterpiece, is all the more remarkable for having been shot "on the fly" in just six days.

On a wider level, film noir was increasingly moving from the confines of the studio to the real-life city streets, a move prompted by the pioneering work of producer **Louis de Rochemont**, who from 1934 had

A, B and something in between

The economic Depression of the 1930s hit the movie industry, just as it did everyone else, not least in diminishing audience numbers. So, in order to make movie-going a more attractive proposition, cinemas introduced the "double feature", consisting of an A-grade film (featuring well-known stars) preceded by a shorter, and more cheaply produced, B-movie. While all the major studios had a B-movie unit, there were also smaller studios – so-called Poverty Row studios like **Republic** and **Monogram** – that made nothing but B-movies.

In the 1940s, budgets for an A-grade film were in the region of $1 million, while B-movies could be made for as little as $50,000. In between these two extremes were films, sometimes referred to as "intermediates", with budgets of around $350,000. Intermediates could appear either first or second on a double feature depending on how well they were initially received.

Though the majority of film noirs were B-movies, they were produced at every budgetary level and by all the major studios. Thus, *Double Indemnity* (1944) and *Laura* (1944) were both big-budget movies, *T-Men* (1948) and *Gun Crazy* (1950) are examples of inter-mediates, while down at the bottom of the scale were films like *Desperate* (1948) and *Detour* (1945), the latter with a budget of $117,000 (see p.83).

B-movie units and studios were good training grounds for fledgling directors and a way of getting yourself noticed. **Jacques Tourneur** worked for several years at the famous horror unit at RKO, directing the B-movie classics *Cat People* (1942) and *I Walked With A Zombie* (1943), before graduating to main features such as *Out Of The Past* (see Canon). A little later, **Anthony Mann** cut his teeth on a number of low-budget noirs for various companies (including RKO), winning slightly higher budgets at **Eagle Lion** where he made *T-Men* and *Raw Deal* (1948). By eking out quality with the meagrest of budgets, some directors became victims of their own success. The best of these was the Austrian-born **Edgar G. Ulmer** (the director of *Detour*) who despite his enormous talent never escaped the B-movie tag and never made a Hollywood A-movie.

masterminded the documentary newsreel series *The March Of Time*. In 1945 de Rochemont produced *The House On 92nd Street*, a noirish docu-drama, based on actual FBI cases, about an agent infiltrating a cell of Nazi spies. The film combined professional actors with real FBI operatives and much of it was shot in the locations where the incidents had taken place.

The House On 92nd Street was directed by **Henry Hathaway**, who went on to make other "docu-noirs" including *Kiss Of Death* (1947, see Canon) and *Call Northside 777* (1948). Aided by the newer, lightweight cameras developed by army documentary units during World War II, this type of film reached its apogee at the end of the decade with **Anthony Mann**'s *T-Men* (1948, see Canon) and **Jules Dassin**'s *The Naked City* (1948, see Canon). Docu-noir also provided an important link to later TV cop shows via the hard-hitting and detailed police procedural movie *He Walked By Night* (1949). Directed by Alfred L. Werker (with uncredited assistance from Mann), the film inspired one of its actors, Jack Webb, to create *Dragnet*, a radio show which was later developed into the long-running and extremely influential television series of the same name.

The birth of film noir coincided almost exactly with America's entry into World War II following the Japanese attack on Pearl Harbor in December 1941. While it would be simplistic to suggest that noir's prevailing mood of paranoia and alienation was a direct result of the war, wartime anxiety certainly helped to fuel it. The war also directly affected the studios, who lost their European markets and were further restricted by the rationing of raw materials and the loss of younger actors to the armed forces.

With the end of the war in 1945, other concerns began to surface, some of which – like the return home of large numbers of military personnel – were treated directly in several film noirs; relatively lightly in a film like *Dead Reckoning* (1947), more seriously in *The Blue Dahlia* (1946,

see Canon) and *Crossfire* (1947). The latter, directed by **Edward Dmytryk**, is an example of a film noir which tackles a serious social issue – racial prejudice – in an uncompromising manner that is implicitly critical of American society. Another film that held a mirror up to the shortcomings of US social institutions was **Jules Dassin**'s brooding *Brute Force* (1947), which is set in a nightmare prison where brutality is the norm.

Dmytryk and Dassin were both left-wing in their political sympathies, as were a number of figures associated with film noir. But with a virulently anti-Communist political agenda sweeping

Film noir and the HUAC

First formed in 1938, the House Committee on Un-American Activities (**HUAC**) was given a whole new lease of life at the end of World War II when the Soviet Union and the spread of global Communism were seen as the major threat to the American way of life. In 1947, a sub-committee of HUAC descended on Hollywood to investigate apparent Communist infiltration of the motion-picture industry.

The subsequent hearings, held in Washington in October of that year, saw testimony from an array of witnesses, some who cooperated with the committee, others who did not. The "**Hollywood Ten**" comprised a group who refused to testify on principle and were imprisoned for contempt as a result. The group – all of whom had at some time been members of the **American Communist Party** – included key noir figures such as director Edward Dmytryk, writer-producer Adrian Scott and screenwriters Dalton Trumbo and Albert Maltz. Dmytryck was later released when he agreed to give evidence against his colleagues, naming both Scott and Trumbo as Communists.

In a panic at the possible collapse of their industry, studio bosses agreed to deny employment to anyone

who had even the remotest connections to left-leaning causes. The Hollywood Ten were immediately fired and a blacklist established of undesirable employees. Many of those targeted were initially named in *Red Channels*, a pamphlet published by a right-wing magazine in June 1950. Further hearings in 1951 resulted in yet more artists being blacklisted, including the directors Abraham Polonsky, Robert Rossen and Joseph Losey.

The anti-Communist "witch-hunts" of the period led to an overwhelming climate of fear and persecution in postwar America and damaged or destroyed the careers of many important artists. A few directors – like Jules Dassin, Joseph Losey and Orson Welles – simply went and worked abroad, while several writers (including Dalton Trumbo) continued to provide screenplays either without credit or under a pseudonym. Others were less fortunate. The stress of appearing on the blacklist and of having to testify were undoubtedly contributing factors to the premature death, at 39, of actor **John Garfield**.

The unofficial end of the unofficial blacklist occurred in 1960 when Dalton Trumbo's own name appeared as a credited writer on the movie *Spartacus*.

The Committee for the First Amendment (CFA): Lauren Bacall and Humphrey Bogart in Washington lead a protest against the treatment of the "Hollywood Ten". Bogart later claimed he was "duped" into supporting them.

the US – following the Republican Party's capture of both houses of Congress in 1946 – everything was about to change. In 1947 an invigorated House Un-American Activities Committee turned the spotlight on Hollywood in its search for a Communist fifth column, and many careers were either destroyed or put on hold – often on the flimsiest of evidence (see opposite).

The "red scare", which was spearheaded by the rabble-rousing Senator **Joseph McCarthy**, prompted a number of anti-Communist films, of which *I Married A Communist* (1949) is the most memorable and the most noirish, thanks to the stylish camera-work of Nicholas Musuraca. The ideological stand-off between the US and the Soviet Union, which developed into the "Cold

War", nurtured a climate of suspicion and fear (not least of nuclear annihilation) which would be reflected in several film noirs over the following decade.

Amidst the wealth of fine films released in 1949, *White Heat* was another excellent and highly memorable amalgam of film noir and gangster movie directed by **Raoul Walsh**. With a combustible performance by **James Cagney** as the mentally unstable, mother-fixated Cody Jarrett, *White Heat* provides one of the most convincing portraits of the criminal psychopath as existential anti-hero.

Stranger On The Third Floor
dir Boris Ingster, 1940, US, 64m, b/w

A journalist is an important witness in a murder trial and his evidence is crucial in determining the guilty verdict. Afterwards, he becomes haunted by uncertainty, especially when his neighbour dies in exactly the same manner. Boris Ingster creates a nightmarish environment (including a brilliantly rendered dream sequence) that reveals the crucial stylistic influence of German expressionist films of the 1920s.

Rebecca
dir Alfred Hitchcock, 1940, US, 130m, b/w

A superb adaptation of Daphne du Maurier's gothic melodrama about a young woman who marries an urbane widower, Maxim De Winter (Laurence Olivier), and then gradually uncovers the terrible secret about his first wife's death. Hitchcock places the emphasis on the compelling struggle between the diffident new wife (Joan Fontaine) and the tyrannical housekeeper, Mrs Danvers (Joan Anderson).

High Sierra
dir Raoul Walsh, 1941, US, 100m, b/w

Outdoor noir meets gangster movie in this gripping tale of Roy "Mad Dog" Earle (Humphrey Bogart), recently sprung from jail and planning a raid on a swish hotel in the Sierra Mountains. Earle's attempts to do good by simple country girl Velma (Joan Leslie) only precipitate his existential despair when she rejects him. Though his final attempts at

freedom in the mountains are doomed, he achieves a kind of personal redemption.

This Gun For Hire
dir Frank Tuttle, 1942, US, 80m, b/w

An unsmiling Alan Ladd is Phillip Raven, a near-psychotic hitman who loves only his cat. Double-crossed by the man who hired him, he falls in with singer Ellen Graham (Veronica Lake), who helps him evade the police but is actually working as a federal agent. While the film never quite lives up to its electrifying opening, Ladd's "angel of death" was the prototype for a number of cool assassins, culminating in the open homage of Melville's *Le Samouraï* (see Canon).

Ministry Of Fear
dir Fritz Lang, 1945, US, 86m, b/w

Released from an asylum, Stephen Neale (Ray Milland) wanders into a village fête at night, where he wins a cake and is inadvertently caught up in a network of Nazi espionage. Based on a Graham Greene novel and set in England, Lang's film creates a brilliantly surreal world of darkness and deceit from which it seems impossible to escape. There are startlingly original images, not least the pinprick of light on a blackened screen as Neale's girlfriend Carla (Marjorie Reynolds) shoots her brother through a door.

The Postman Always Rings Twice
dir Tay Garnett, 1946, US, 113m, b/w

John Garfield plays drifter Frank Chambers, smitten by platinum blonde siren Cora Smith (Lana Turner), who is stranded in a loveless marriage to her café-owning husband Nick (Cecil Kellaway). The ensuing spiral of lust, murder and betrayal is recalled by Frank as he awaits execution. Production Code restrictions mean this version of Cain's novel never quite generates the requisite levels of heat from its two stars.

Brute Force
dir Jules Dassin, 1947, US, 98m, b/w

With a screenplay by Richard Brooks, this prison drama has a markedly anti-fascist agenda. Hume Cronyn plays Captain Munsey, the ruthless and sadistic chief guard of a prison that he runs with a fist of iron, while Burt Lancaster is the leader of a group of prisoners determined to make a break for it. With its suggestion that violence is self-perpetuating, this is a consistently dark movie which culminates in a classic, no-holds-barred riot.

Crossfire
dir Edward Dmytryk, 1947, US, 85m, b/w

A group of GIs on leave in Washington DC fetch up at the apartment of Joseph Samuels (Sam Levene) who is then murdered by the bigoted Montgomery (Robert Ryan). Told in flashback as Detective Finlay (Robert Young) and Sgt Keeley (Robert Mitchum) attempt to unravel what happened, this political noir confronts the issue of anti-Semitism head on.

Nightmare Alley
dir Edmund Goulding, 1947, US, 111m, b/w

Actor Tyrone Power broke with his usual swashbuckling image to play "The Great Stanton", a small-time huckster in a seedy travelling circus (marvellously recreated as a full-scale set). Aided by three women, he develops a money-spinning act as a fake spiritualist before exposure leads to a terrible descent. Goulding's direction, greatly assisted by Lee Garmes's hallucinatory camera-work, creates a nightmare vision of greed, gullibility and exploitation.

They Live By Night
dir Nicholas Ray, 1948, US, 95m, b/w

Bowie (Farley Granger) has joined forces with Chicamaw (Howard Da Silva) and T-Dub (Jay C. Flippen) in order to rob a bank. On the run, Bowie finds momentary peace when he elopes with a young woman (Cathy O'Donnell). But things get complicated when Chicamaw and T-Dub want to hook up with him for one more job. Nicholas Ray's first feature is one of the great "couple on the run" movies, given an added poignancy by the pair's genuine love for each other.

The Big Clock
dir John Farrow, 1948, US, 95m, b/w

George Stroud (Ray Milland) runs a true crime magazine owned by tyrannical press baron Earl Janoth (Charles Laughton). When Janoth sees a man leaving the apartment of his mistress Pauline (Rita Johnson), he murders her and then attempts to frame the mysterious visitor, enlisting Stroud to track him down. Unfortunately the fleeing man

was Stroud. The ensuing tension over who will take the rap is largely played out within Janoth's HQ, over which presides the relentless "big clock" of the title.

Key Largo
dir John Huston, 1948, US, 110m, b/w

As in *High Sierra*, Humphrey Bogart visits a hotel – this time in Florida – in another gangster-noir hybrid. Bogart is Frank McCloud, a disillusioned ex-soldier visiting the father (Lionel Barrymore) and young widow (Lauren Bacall) of a former buddy. When the hotel is taken over by gangster Johnny Rocco (Edward G. Robinson) and his gang, Frank doesn't want to get involved, but Rocco's treatment of his alcoholic mistress and the death of two Indians convinces him to take action.

Act Of Violence
dir Fred Zinnemann, 1948, US, 82m, b/w

World War II vet Frank Enley (Van Heflin) is back in the US having survived a POW camp in which all his comrades died – save the unbalanced Parkson (Robert Ryan). Aware of Enley's dark secret (he collaborated with the Nazis in exchange for food), Parkson wants his revenge on the so-called "war hero". Enley, now happily married to Edith (Janet Leigh), must confront his own cowardice, while evading his vengeance-driven ex-comrade.

White Heat
dir Raoul Walsh, 1949, US, 114m, b/w

Widely considered one of the great gangster films, *White Heat* is anchored in an incendiary performance by James Cagney as Cody Jarrett. A ruthless and psychopathic criminal responsible for two murder-filled robberies, he has an Oedipal attachment to his wily and determined old mother, "Ma" Jarrett (Margaret Wycherly). Walsh's direction is fast-paced and direct, but it is the script's emphasis on Jarrett's psychology and a kind of tragic grandeur (rather than any shadow-filled visuals) that give the film its noir credentials.

The Reckless Moment
dir Max Ophüls, 1949, US, 114m, b/w

This domestic melodrama focuses on Lucia Harper (Joan Bennett), a well-meaning but controlling housewife who tries to cover up her daughter's accidental killing of an unsuitable lover. When petty criminal Martin Donnelly (James Mason) is sent by his partner Nagel (Roy Roberts) to blackmail the family, he falls for Lucia instead. The noir elements may be light, but the strong script delivers a consistent darkness and Ophüls's direction has a hypnotic and lyrical beauty.

The 1950s

The second half of film noir's classic era began with the genre at its zenith, with over forty films released in 1950 alone. But whereas the noirs of the preceding decade were largely rooted in their expressionist stylings, with stories generally anchored around the plight of individuals, the 1950s saw a distinct shift towards tightly plotted, grittier fare, showcasing a greater degree of location work and with an increasing focus on organized criminals engaged in fierce battles with the authorities.

The decade began in some style with the release at the end of January 1950 of **Joseph** Lewis's *Gun Crazy* (see Canon), originally entitled *Deadly Is The Female*. It makes a revealing contrast to Nicholas Ray's *They Live By Night*, made just two years earlier, in that Lewis's young couple-on-the-run are markedly wilder, with a love of guns (he's a sharp-shooting army veteran, she a trick shooter in a Wild West show) and a flair for violence that anticipates *Bonnie And Clyde* (1967). The film was co-written by one Millard Kaufman, who, it was later revealed, was blacklisted screenwriter Dalton Trumbo.

In the same year **John Huston**'s archetypal heist movie, *The Asphalt Jungle* (1950), had an even more radical take on criminal psychology. If Lewis's couple were clearly amoral then Huston's were every shade of grey – from the fastidious mastermind Doc (a soon-to-be-blacklisted **Sam Jaffe**) to mixed-up former farm boy Dix (**Sterling Hayden**), each has his hopes and fears. Filmed in a crisp, semi-documentary style with virtually no music, the movie has a refreshingly taut and unsentimental feel to it. Particularly memorable is Huston's brilliant staging of the

Being and noirishness

Just as the Hollywood directors of the 1940s and early 50s weren't aware that they were making film noir, neither did they realize that such movies were "existential" – a term frequently applied by later critics to the films' (usually male) protagonists. As a philosophical outlook preoccupied with free will, **Existentialism** stresses the individual's responsibility for his or her own actions. For the existentialist, this responsibility for making choices within a meaningless universe engenders feelings of dread and the awareness of death.

Although Existentialism emerged as a school of thought in wartime France, it has been argued that it already existed as part of the zeitgeist, influencing film noir via its presence in hard-boiled fiction and through the general sense of unease that permeated the years before and during **World War II**.

In many noirs, the protagonist is an outsider trapped in an urban landscape, the frequent use of nocturnal settings simply adding to the mood of anxiety and alienation. He or she has no trust in traditional institutional supports – such as law and the police – which are often represented as hostile or corrupt. Instead, the individual must survive by his or her own wits, and plots often hinge on a crucial decision that determines the invariably tragic outcome of the film.

Every shade of criminality: Sam Jaffe as Doc Riedenschneider (left) outlines the plan for the jewellery robbery in *The Asphalt Jungle* (1950).

crime in a bravura, tension-filled eleven-minute sequence, in which the gang execute their plan in an unnervingly calm and precise manner, even in the face of a critical mishap.

Another classic noir director produced one of his best films in 1950. **Otto Preminger**'s *Where*

The Sidewalk Ends has at its centre a classic noir protagonist – the good cop who is, nevertheless, embittered with authority and out of control. It's a type that surfaces throughout the 1950s in such films as *The Big Combo* (see Canon) and *The Big Heat* (see Canon). Here, a Freudian dimension is added by screenwriter Ben Hecht in that the cop, Mark Dixon (**Dana Andrews**), is striving to rid himself of the taint of his dead father's career as a gangster.

Still in 1950, Hollywood cast a noirish eye over its own workings in two films – **Nicholas Ray**'s *In A Lonely Place* (see Canon) and **Billy Wilder**'s *Sunset Boulevard* (see p.33). The first has **Humphrey Bogart** as Dixon Steel, a scriptwriter whose violent temper is destroying his career. Some commentators have seen Steel's condition as a metaphor for life on the blacklist – marginalized, embittered, unable to recover. If anything, *Sunset Boulevard* is even more cynical. Again the protagonist is a writer (played by **William Holden**) who – having fallen on hard times – prostitutes himself in a last-ditch attempt to make it in the "dream factory". Working on a fantasy comeback for faded silent star Norma Desmond (**Gloria Swanson**), the ill-matched couple's desperation reveals both the allure of Hollywood and its capacity to swallow up talent and spit it out.

Wilder had already extended the range of acceptable subject matter with his noirish exploration of alcoholism in *The Lost Weekend*, and in 1951 he turned his sardonic gaze on unscrupulous, or "yellow", journalism. *Ace In The Hole* (aka *The Big Carnival*) tells of how a washed-up reporter exploits a caving accident to resurrect his career by prolonging the rescue operation and turning the media spotlight onto the incident. Not since **Fritz Lang**'s *Fury* (1936) had there been such a withering account of human nature and the film duly offended many – especially journalists.

Given that film noir habitually dealt with hard-edged themes involving crime, psychosis and dark sexuality, battles with censorship had been routine during the 1940s. However, in the 50s they became increasingly sporadic, thanks to a Supreme Court ruling in 1952 that films were "a significant medium for the communication of ideas", meaning that filmmakers could invoke the First Amendment of the US Constitution that guaranteed certain personal freedoms, in this case the freedom of speech. Consequently, the Production Code was swiftly recognized as outmoded and unrepresentative of wider public tastes and attitudes.

Though there were still restrictions, filmmakers rapidly responded to the weakening of the Production Code's hold with an increasing number of noirs in which the sex and violence quotient increased and became much more graphic. Few pushed the boundaries of violence further than **Phil Karlson**, a jobbing director who made four classic noir B-movies in the 1950s beginning with *Kansas City Confidential* (1952). Once again the police are treated with a marked lack of sympathy in this tale of a bank heist, masterminded by an embittered ex-cop, in which an ex-con (played by Karlson regular **John Payne**) gets framed. After a shockingly brutal beating from the police, his alibi holds and he sets off to track down the real culprits.

There's a sense in which the raw, on-the-hoof quality of B-movies was better equipped to convey the sheer sordidness of criminal violence. Like Karlson, **Sam Fuller** was a director who excelled with this kind of fare. Shot in just twenty days, Fuller's *Pickup On South Street* (1953, see Canon) starred **Richard Widmark** as Skip McCoy, a pickpocket who steals a wallet that contains a microfilm of top-secret government information. Though one of the people after the microfilm is a Communist agent, Fuller is more interested in the film's lowlife characters and milieu than in ideology.

Despite the election of Eisenhower in 1952 – the first Republican president in twenty

Noir in colour?

Dramatic contrasts of light and shade are such a defining feature of film noir, especially of those films made in the 1940s and 50s, that the idea of a noir filmed in colour can cause a momentary cognitive hiccup. Colour noir sounds like an oxymoron, but there are at least five films from the classic era that fit such a description.

In the first of these, *Leave Her To Heaven* (1945), the colour is employed in a frequently non-naturalistic and symbolic manner in order to underscore the charged emotional content on display (see p.128). Eight years later **Henry Hathaway**'s *Niagara* achieves a more mixed mood; its combination of Technicolor, Cinemascope and outdoor locations feels, at times, like watching a kind of epic holiday home movie, but its interior scenes achieve just the requisite noir claustrophobia.

Slightly Scarlet (1956) and *Party Girl* (1958) are disappointing films but both have wonderfully dramatic moments. The former is enhanced by some virtuoso camera-work from **John Alton**, who lights the film as if it were in black and white. The latter, set in the gangster world of the 1930s, stars **Cyd Charisse** and looks and feels as if the team for a bold and brash MGM musical had been handed the wrong script.

The best of the early colour noirs is Hitchcock's tale of doomed love, *Vertigo* (1958). Shot by **Robert Burks** in and around San Francisco, the hallucinatory, suspended look of the movie was achieved, as Hitchcock disclosed to François Truffaut, "by shooting through a fog filter. That gave us a green effect, like fog over the bright sunshine." The resulting dream-like quality finds its perfect aural complement in **Bernard Herrmann**'s unnervingly hypnotic music.

Niagara
dir Henry Hathaway, 1953, US, 90m

A tale of two contrasting married couples staying at a holiday motel at Niagara Falls. Ray Cutler (Casey Adams) and his wife Polly (Jean Peters) are young, sweet and conventional, whereas George Loomis (Joseph Cotton) is an unstable World War II veteran married to the much younger and gorgeous Rose (Marilyn Monroe). Sexual jealousy and murderous intent occur against the backdrop of the thunderous falls, as Ray and Polly become reluctant witnesses to the unfolding psychodrama of the other couple.

Vertigo
dir Alfred Hitchcock, 1958, US, 128m

One of Hitchcock's most mesmerizing and disturbing films has ex-San Francisco cop Scottie Ferguson (James Stewart) recovering from a breakdown brought on by his fear of heights. Hired by a former friend to trail his disturbed wife Madeleine (Kim Novak), he gradually falls in love with her but is unable to prevent her apparently suicidal fall from a church tower. Recovering once again, he spots Madeleine's lookalike on the street and obsessively pursues her in an attempt to recreate the woman he has lost – with ultimately disastrous results.

years – the paranoia over the internal threat of Communist subversion began to decrease in the mid-1950s, partly as a result of the declining influence and popularity of the rabble-rousing **Senator McCarthy**. However, anxiety over the external threat posed by the Soviet Union and nuclear weapons was ever-increasing. **Robert Aldrich**'s *Kiss Me Deadly* (1955, see Canon) is arguably the high-water mark of both Cold War cinema and of film noir. In adapting **Mickey Spillane**'s crude pulp novel, Aldrich and scriptwriter A.I. Bezzerides tapped into popular fears and created a genuinely disconcerting movie in which that noir staple – the tough-guy private investigator – is portrayed as a posturing anachronism.

Mike Hammer (Ralph Meeker) puts the squeeze on
Friday (Marian Carr) in *Kiss Me Deadly* (1955).

The first serious study of the noir phenomenon, *Panorama du film noir américain*, appeared in 1955. Written by **Raymond Borde** and Etienne Chaumeton, it identified the years 1946–48 as the crucial period, and stressed the films' importance in terms of the way they challenged and disorientated their audience. Interestingly, a photograph exists of Robert Aldrich clutching a copy of the book on the set of his war movie *Attack* (1956), but what impact it had on him, or whether he ever read it, is not known.

At this point, film noir was clearly on the decline, its essential qualities of anxiety and despair at odds with the more upbeat mood brought about by greater economic prosperity. The movies in general were suffering from TV's rapid rise in popularity, while a police series like *Dragnet* (1953–59) was both inspired by and a direct competitor with film noirs. Needless to say, noir did not end abruptly: the young director **Stanley Kubrick** breathed new life into it with his innovative heist movie *The Killing* (1956, see Canon), which was released in the same week as old-timer **Fritz Lang**'s penultimate noir outing, *While The City Sleeps*.

Despite the stylistic shifts that film noir adopted in this decade, it is notable that the film now seen as signalling the end of the classic era – **Orson Welles**'s *Touch Of Evil* (1958, see Canon) – was a highly expression-istic work that harked back to his incredibly influential *Citizen Kane* made seventeen years earlier. Ironically, the film fared very poorly on its release, thanks mainly to Universal, who deemed it too confusing (after editing it themselves) and gave it little or no publicity. Like film noir as a whole, *Touch Of Evil* gained its first serious following in France where it ran for two years in Parisian cinemas.

The Asphalt Jungle
dir John Huston, 1950, US, 112m, b/w

Based on the novel by W.R. Burnett, John Huston's second noir masterpiece shows the planning and execution of an audacious jewel theft by a disparate group of criminals. The tense all-male meetings of the gang members are cleverly contrasted with their domestic lives and the women that wait for them – a sympathetic approach that was strongly at odds with the strict guidelines of the Production Code.

Where The Sidewalk Ends
dir Otto Preminger, 1950, US, 95m, b/w

Dana Andrews plays Mark Dixon, a New York cop who is a little over-enthusiastic about roughing up hoodlums. After accidentally killing a suspect, he attempts to cover it up by framing a local gangster. Things get complicated when he falls for the victim's wife (Gene Tierney) and even more so when her taxi-driving father becomes the chief suspect. Ben Hecht's powerful script focuses on Dixon's redemptive quest to free himself from his own rage.

Sunset Boulevard
dir Billy Wilder, 1950, US, 110m, b/w

Narrated as a flashback by a drowned man, this supremely opulent-looking noir mixes gothic melodrama, romance, black comedy and horror to dizzying effect. William Holden plays a down-on-his-luck screenwriter drawn into the fractured fantasy world of Gloria Swanson's faded, comeback-seeking actress. Hollywood legends Cecil B. DeMille, Buster Keaton and Erich von Stroheim all collude in Wilder's merciless dissection of the ephemerality of fame.

Ace In The Hole (aka The Big Carnival)
dir Billy Wilder, 1951, US, 111m, b/w

No one gets out of this film with any dignity, least of all the ruthless journalist Charles Tatum (a brilliantly manic Kirk Douglas), who manipulates the attempted rescue of a man trapped underground to further his flagging career. His venality is matched by the victim's insensitive wife (Jan Sterling) and a sheriff seeking to get himself re-elected. Largely filmed in the New Mexico desert, this is the last of Wilder's four noirs and one of the most cynical visions of human greed on film.

Kansas City Confidential
dir Phil Karlson, 1952, US, 98m, b/w

Joe Rolfe (John Payne), an ex-con and now a florist's van driver, gets set up to take the rap for a bank heist. When the gang re-convenes in Mexico to pick up their takings, Rolfe plans to get even, pursuing them with a ruthless single-mindedness. The twist is that he then falls in love with the lawyer daughter (Coleen Gray) of the gang's mysterious boss. This hard-hitting noir has few stylistic frills, but boasts a particularly malevolent trio of heavies (Jack Elam, Lee Van Cleef and Neville Brand).

The Night Of The Hunter
dir Charles Laughton, 1955, US, 104m, b/w

In Charles Laughton's only film as a director, Robert Mitchum gives a chilling performance as a preacher (with "Love" and "Hate" tattooed on his knuckles) who befriends a widow and her two children in order to get his hands on some hidden money. Laughton drew heavily from expressionist films, and with his cinematographer, Stanley Cortez, created some beautiful and dream-like sequences – several from the viewpoint of the pursued children – perfectly complemented by Walter Schumann's haunting score.

While The City Sleeps
dir Fritz Lang, 1956, US, 100m, b/w

Set in the offices of a newspaper, where the proprietor has offered the editorship to whoever discovers the identity of a serial sex murderer, this is a movie with as cynical a view of the press as *Ace In The Hole*. Dana Andrews plays Ed Mobley, a reporter who reluctantly joins the game, eventually becoming as sleazy and self-seeking as everyone else – even using his girlfriend (Sally Forrest) as bait for the killer (John Barrymore Jr). A tight script and some fine ensemble acting help deliver one of Lang's finest American films.

The Wrong Man
dir Alfred Hitchcock, 1956, US, 105m, b/w

A New York musician (Henry Fonda) finds himself arrested and accused of a hold-up that he never committed. Unfortunately, all the circumstantial evidence points to his guilt and he is brought to trial. This nightmare premise – based on a real case – was filmed by Hitchcock from the wronged man's point of view. It shows how his world falls apart, culminating in the breakdown and eventual madness of his wife (Vera Miles). It's an extremely bleak film made all the more affecting by the relatively restrained way in which it is filmed.

Sweet Smell Of Success
dir Alexander MacKendrick, 1957, US, 96m, b/w

This caustic look at the abuse of power homes in on J.J. Hunsecker, an arrogant and unscrupulous society columnist (played with menacing aplomb by a bespectacled Burt Lancaster), and ambitious hustler Sidney Falco (Tony Curtis). Falco will do anything to get on, so Hunsecker sets him the task of sabotaging the relationship between a young musician and Hunsecker's young sister Susan. It's unusual noir territory (no deaths occur), but Hunsecker is the equal in evil to many a crime boss and the New York depicted is brittle and soulless.

Odds Against Tomorrow
dir Robert Wise, 1959, US, 98m, b/w

One of the last gasps of noir's classic era is notable for being the first to feature a black protagonist, played by Harry Belafonte (who also produced). Dave Burke (Ed Begley) is a burnt-out cop who asks ex-con Earl Slater (Robert Ryan) to rob an upstate bank with him. He also recruits debt-ridden nightclub entertainer Johnny Ingram (Belafonte), who has serious gambling debts. But when they embark on the robbery, tension mounts between Johnny and the racist Earl with cataclysmic consequences. Also features a great jazz score by John Lewis.

The 1960s

The 1960s was the leanest of all decades for film noir. While there were a few stragglers – like *Cape Fear* (1962) and the films of **Sam Fuller** – that fit fairly neatly into the noir rubric, the rest are a heterogeneous bunch, stretching noir's stylistic parameters and crossing over into a range of genres. And while there was plenty to be scared about in the 1960s (the Cold War was still raging, with Vietnam its bloodiest manifestation), life was more affluent, there was a greater emphasis on youth culture, and the counter-cultural ideas of the 1950s were developing into a diverse chorus of dissenting voices – from Hippies and Yippies to feminists.

Meanwhile Hollywood had to adapt to the fierce onslaught of TV, which was competing for largely the same audience. To lure people back into the cinema, the studio bosses decided to show people things they couldn't see at home. This meant large-scale spectacle in all its Technicolor, widescreen glory – the very antithesis of film noir.

Consequently, many of the talents who worked on noir during the classic era found a new home in TV, where they began generating a wide array of noir-inflected fare. The first broadly popular crime series of an unmistakably noir nature was *Peter Gunn* (1958–61), created by **Blake Edwards** with Craig Stevens as the eponymous private investigator. But by far the most prominent example of 1960s noir TV was *The Fugitive*, which ran from 1963 to 1967 and starred **David Janssen** as a doctor falsely accused of murder. (For a more detailed look at noir TV see p.277.)

If film noir was struggling in America, it was exploding into life in France, where noir thrillers had long been incredibly popular. US directors were extravagantly celebrated in the pages of *Cahiers du cinéma* by young critics like **François Truffaut, Jean-Luc Godard** and **Claude Chabrol**, who went on to become key directors of the *nouvelle vague* (New Wave, see p.257). Classic noir director **Jules Dassin** made his brilliant French heist movie *Rififi* in 1955, the same year that **Jean-Pierre Melville** (who would become the most consistent French noir director of the 1960s) produced his *hommage* to US crime movies *Bob le flambeur*. Meanwhile Godard's innovative modern noir *A bout de souffle* (*Breathless*, 1959) was followed by Truffaut's *Tirez sur le pianiste* (1960, see Canon). (For more on French film noir see p.255.)

The first distinguished US movie of the 1960s with a strong noir component was Hitchcock's *Psycho*, a film still shocking for its violence and for the artful way that the audience is made to identify with both the victim and the killer. It's shot in black and white, which still seemed to be the norm for this kind of material, and begins in classic urban noir vein before moving, seamlessly, into the darkest horror territory.

Two slightly more conventional noirs (both in black and white) appeared in 1962. Blake Edwards's *Experiment In Terror* begins with the terrorizing of a young woman (**Lee Remick**) in the darkness of her suburban garage by a psychopath trying to extort money from her. In *Cape Fear*, Robert Mitchum (in one of his best roles) plays a recently released convict, hell-bent on avenging himself on the lawyer (**Gregory Peck**) who had him put away.

Also released in 1962 was *The Manchurian Candidate*, an ambitious noir variant, based on a novel by Richard Condon. Its complex Cold War plot hinges on a couple of veterans from the 1950s Korean War, and a plan to kill the US president concocted by a bizarre alliance of home-grown neo-fascists and foreign Communists. There was an unnerving resonance in the fact that the assassination of President Kennedy occurred almost exactly a year after the film was released.

Of those noir directors flourishing in the 1950s, the one who maintained the highest noir profile in the 1960s was Sam Fuller, with a trio of startlingly brash movies – *Underworld USA* (1961), *Shock Corridor* (1963) and *The Naked Kiss* (1964). All three were forthright attacks on bourgeois hypocrisy and suburban values and the closest in feel to the noirs of the classic era. In Fuller's uncompromising vision, the cynicism, pessimism and dark existentialism of film noir were far from dead.

While insanity and mental illness were recurring themes in early 1960s noirs – **William Conrad**'s *Brainstorm* (1965) is another example – by the middle of the decade that old noir stalwart, the private investigator, was making a comeback. Beginning with **Paul Newman** as slobbish Lew Harper in *Harper* (1966), the new-style PI was a rather more easy-going figure than his predecessors. Although Frank Sinatra would up the traditional macho stakes as Miami private eye Tony Rome, first in *Tony Rome* (1967), then in *The Lady In Cement* (1968), the decade would end with an interesting contemporary version of **Raymond Chandler**'s *The Little Sister*. Set in a bright and brittle LA, *Marlowe* (1969) anticipates Altman's more radical critique of the private eye myth, *The Long Goodbye* (1973, see Canon).

The police procedural also got something of a makeover in an attempt to bring it into line with more permissive attitudes following the demise of the Production Code. In *The Detective* (1968) **Frank Sinatra** plays Joe Leland, a hard-nosed cop with a conscience who questions authority and himself. Don Siegel's *Madigan* (1968), with Richard Widmark in the title role, is less "liberal" in its concerns. Both films highlight the troubled domestic lives of their protagonists (in the shape of "difficult" wives), but their attempts to be modern are undermined by characters (and stars) who seem to belong to an earlier era.

In the same year, that other noir standard, the heist movie, got a lively outing in *The Split*. Unusual at the time for having two black actors (Jim Brown and Diahann Carroll) in lead roles, the story of a daring raid on the LA Coliseum during a football game only takes off when the money disappears and **Gene Hackman**'s bent cop stumbles on it. The film's noir credentials come courtesy of an amazing cast and the striking camera-work of veteran noir cinematographer Burnett Guffey.

The year before, Guffey had contributed to the look of one the decade's most significant films, **Arthur Penn**'s *Bonnie And Clyde* (1967). Loosely based on the true tale of two young Depression-era bank robbers, Bonnie Parker and Clyde Barrow, the film refashions the classic crime spree movie into a parable of youthful rebellion that tapped into the spirit of the times. Stylistically, it brought a radical and experimental quality to mainstream American film (that was partly indebted to *nouvelle vague* directors like Godard) and introduced a particularly graphic level of violence in its blood-spattered denouement.

Of equal, if not greater, significance in the story of noir's development was **John Boorman**'s *Point Blank* (1967). Based (like *The Split*) on a Donald Westlake novel, its ultra-cool look and fractured narrative make it much closer to European art-house movies (Resnais and Antonioni in particular) than to Hollywood. Set mostly in the brightly lit and oppressive terrain of corporate LA, the film has a near-abstract quality in the way colour and space are employed within the widescreen frame.

Though *Point Blank* was not as successful as *Bonnie And Clyde* on its first release, both films helped to rejuvenate American cinema and provided an example for later "neo-noir" directors to follow.

Psycho
dir Alfred Hitchcock, 1960, US, 109m, b/w

In a rash moment, Marion Crane (Janet Leigh) steals a large sum from her employer and hits the road. Driving through the night, she decides to stop off at a motel run by the shy and awkward Norman Bates (Anthony Perkins), a young man seemingly dominated by his mother. What happens next includes one of the most brilliantly constructed and horrific scenes in all cinema. Aside from being one of the greatest horror films of all time, *Psycho* can also be seen as the hugely shocking, unexpected sting in the tail-end of noir's classic era.

Underworld USA
dir Samuel Fuller, 1961, US, 99m, b/w

One of Fuller's most uncompromising and intense works, this revenge thriller takes no prisoners in a scenario that's cut to the bone. Cliff Robertson is Tolly Devlin, an ex-convict determined to extract vengeance for the murder of his father – a devastating experience he witnessed as a child. Robertson is used as a blunt instrument for the director's unvarnished narrative; his opponents are granted

no measure of sympathy whatever, and the result is a grim predecessor of John Boorman's *Point Blank*.

The Manchurian Candidate
dir John Frankenheimer, 1962, US, 126m, b/w

This masterpiece of Cold War paranoia has Major Marco (Frank Sinatra) battling with nightmares and wondering why one of his men (Laurence Harvey) returned from the Korean War highly decorated, and what he intends to do

The ultra-cool and fractured *Point Blank* (1967), with Lee Marvin (right) as the relentless Walker.

now. Treading a fine line between satire and suspense, the film utilized the prevailing fears of both the right and the left. The film's crowning glory, though, is Angela Lansbury's scene-stealing turn as the repellently manipulative mother of Harvey's brainwashed soldier – a *femme fatale* of an extremely menacing kind.

Cape Fear
dir J. Lee Thompson, 1962, US, 105m, b/w

Robert Mitchum gives one of his most chilling performances as Max Cady, a psychopathic ex-con hell-bent on revenge. The target of his wrath is respectable lawyer Sam Bowden (Gregory Peck), whose testimony helped put Cady in prison, and the best way to get at him is via his lovely wife and daughter. The success of the film lies in how much of the violence is implied, as Cady – exuding sexual menace – tries to goad Bowden into action. As with *Psycho*, Bernard Herrmann's insinuating score helps to ratchet up the tension.

Bonnie And Clyde
dir Arthur Penn, 1967, US, 111m

With half a nod to 1950s classic *Gun Crazy* and another to 1960s radicalism, Arthur Penn tells the tale of how two young hoodlums, Clyde Barrow (Warren Beatty) and Bonnie Parker (Faye Dunaway), form a gang of incompetent bank robbers and become folk heroes. An astute meditation on America's obsession with gun culture and fame, the film's mixture of period detail, impoverished rural landscapes and unflinching violence shocked and exhilarated its original audience in equal measure.

Point Blank
dir John Boorman, 1967, US, 92m

An elliptical and violent thriller which begins with the apparent death of Walker (Lee Marvin) at Alcatraz, following a heist. The culprits are his accomplices – wife Lynne (Sharon Acker) and best friend Mal Reece (John Vernon) – who turn out to be lovers. The remainder of the film follows Walker's single-minded and relentless quest to retrieve his share of the money. Despite undercutting noir conventions, Boorman's cool avant-garde style succeeds in creating the authentic noir mood of unease and disorientation.

The 1970s

After the fallow years of the 1960s, the 1970s was a period of reinvigoration and renewal for film noir. This was partly due to the revival of the industry as whole, which had been in serious decline in the mid-1960s but had been rescued by the huge success of films such as *The Graduate* (1967), *Bonnie And Clyde* and *Easy Rider* (1969). As a result of this, the director had become a more powerful player within the industry, and there was a greater openness to new ideas and new talent.

US society of the early 1970s was certainly one in which there was an audience for a darker and more socially critical type of film. The Vietnam War was still raging and was seen to be unwinnable, while Richard Nixon's presidency was progressively mired in scandal and would end with his resignation. Cynicism and pessimism were in the air, qualities that several directors were quick to tap into.

The first great noir of the 1970s was *Klute* (1971, see Canon), directed by **Alan J. Pakula**, which takes a noirish scenario – honest cop investigating a series of murders befriends vulnerable prostitute Bree – and filters it through a liberal sensibility, so that Bree's inner life (brilliantly conveyed by **Jane Fonda**) becomes as important as the thriller element of the plot. *Klute* was one of a series of cop movies made that year, which gave the genre a new edge and a greater realism.

William Friedkin's *The French Connection* (1971), and its John Frankenheimer-directed sequel, *The French Connection II*, both starred **Gene Hackman** as "Popeye" Doyle, a cop utterly unconcerned with judicial bureaucracy. On one level he's a classic noir type – the rogue cop out of control as he works to his own agenda, but unlike his

"Notes On Film Noir"

The spring of 1972 saw a significant moment in the critical study of film noir with the publication of an essay, "Notes On Film Noir", in the US film magazine *Film Comment*. Written by critic **Paul Schrader** to accompany an LA retrospective of seven film noirs, it proved to be a hugely influential contribution to the ongoing critical exploration of noir, most notably by defining its stylistic qualities and by placing it within "a specific period of film history". Furthermore, Schrader divided the period of film noir – a type of film he saw as developing out of the gangster movie – into three phases: 1941–46 was the era of the private eye; 1945–49 saw a focus on criminality, corruption and the police; while 1949–53 ("the cream of the film noir period") produced films of "psychotic action and suicidal impulse".

Like **Raymond Borde** and **Etienne Chaumeton** in their seminal *Panorama du film noir américain*, Schrader displayed huge enthusiasm for noir, calling it "probably the most creative [period] in Hollywood's history". He also observed that film noir seemed particularly relevant during periods of political turmoil, and suggested that his own time was ripe for "taking a look at the underside of the American character". Like the critics of *Cahiers du cinéma*, Schrader was able to put his ideas about noir into practice – first as a screenwriter on a trio of noir-inflected 1970s movies – *The Yakuza*, *Taxi Driver* and *Obsession* – then as a director of his own scripts beginning with *Blue Collar* (1978) and following this with the intensely noirish *Hardcore* (1979). Schrader's "Notes On Film Noir" was recently reprinted in *Schrader On Schrader* by UK publisher Faber & Faber.

counterparts in 1950s noirs (eg Bannion in *The Big Heat*) his motivation always remains an enigma.

Both *Klute* and *The French Connection* depict the city as an unfathomable urban jungle, a theme also explored in **Don Siegel**'s seminal *Dirty Harry* (1971), a film in which the maverick cop (played by Clint Eastwood) is another outsider, whose constant frustration with the system manifests itself with sudden and shocking outbursts of violence. Harry justifies his methods as necessary given how sick – in his mind – society has become. Siegel's film recognizes the seductiveness of Harry's vigilantism, while never actually condoning it.

The theme of vigilantism was rather more crudely handled in **Phil Karlson**'s *Walking Tall* (1973) and Michael Winner's *Death Wish* (1974), while Robert Aldrich's *Hustle* (1975) offered a more quizzical and philosophical response to the ineffectiveness of the modern cop.

When it came to the private eye movie, a degree of directorial cynicism enters the frame. In the ground-breaking "Blaxploitation" movie *Shaft* (1971), there's a strong element of parody in the name character's super-cool, wisecracking approach. But it's with **Robert Altman**'s *The Long Goodbye* (1973, see Canon) that we get a wholesale dismantling of the private eye persona, with Elliott Gould turning Chandler's downtown knight errant into a shambling, ineffectual oddball. Gene Hackman's Harry Moseby functions only slightly better in *Night Moves* (1975, see Canon), while in **Robert Benton**'s affectionate *The Late Show* (1977, see Canon) Art Carney plays a geriatric PI whose outmoded values are at odds with the modern world.

Chinatown (1974, see Canon) marks an even more significant moment in noir revisionism. Set in the period of classic noirs and dominated by **Jack Nicholson**'s iconoclastic private detective, the film functions as both a celebration and a critique of noir conventions, thanks, in no small part, to **Robert Towne**'s intelligent and multi-layered script. *Chinatown*'s attention to period detail would instigate a taste for "retro" noir, as in the following year's *Farewell My Lovely* (1975), a Chandler remake which – despite employing *Chinatown*'s cinematographer and starring Robert Mitchum – does little more than go through the motions.

Another noir standard to get a fresh approach was the crime spree movie. In particular **Terrence Malick**'s *Badlands* (1973) made

his maladjusted, fame-seeking couple highly image-conscious, with **Martin Sheen**'s Kit priding himself on his likeness to **James Dean**. *Badlands* was set in the 1950s, whereas Robert Altman's low-key *Thieves Like Us* (1974) takes place in Depression-era Mississippi. Based on the same novel as Nicholas Ray's 1940s classic *They Live By Night*, the Altman film de-romanticizes the story, presenting his criminals as ordinary and unheroic.

From the summer of 1972, when the Watergate Hotel burglars were first arrested, until President Nixon's resignation in the autumn of 1974, the

Noir for the 1970s: Robert De Niro as Travis Bickle attempts to redeem child prostitute Iris (Jodie Foster) in Scorsese and Schrader's nightmare vision of New York, *Taxi Driver*.

public became more and more fascinated as the "dirty tricks" and cover-ups of Nixon's inner circle were slowly revealed. Disenchantment and paranoia about the political process became widespread, a fact reflected in the number of noirish political thrillers that started to appear. Conceived before the Watergate scandal, **Francis Ford Coppola**'s *The Conversation* (1974) had disturbingly prescient parallels with it. It was not an overtly political film, being more an elliptical examination of surveillance and voyeurism, but it hit a public nerve about the misuses of technology. Next came **Alan J. Pakula**'s *The Parallax View* (1974) and **Sidney Pollack**'s *Three Days*

Of The Condor (1975), two films that presented the view that ideological conspiracy could (and did) extend right to the heart of the state. They were followed, logically enough, by *All The President's Men* (1976), Pakula's thrilling dramatization of how journalists Carl Bernstein and Bob Woodward broke the Watergate scandal.

The 1970s was also a significant decade for unleashing a new generation of US filmmakers that included Francis Ford Coppola, **Walter Hill**, **Martin Scorsese** and **Paul Schrader**. All were cinéastes – as well-versed in the classics of European cinema as they were in film noir – and their work would reflect this. The increasingly

What is neo-noir?

Film historians may argue about precise dates, but there's a general consensus that the classic era of film noir occurred in the 1940s and 50s. But if noir never quite disappeared in the 1960s, at what point did its reinvention and reinvigoration become neo-noir? And how does a film style so strongly defined by high-contrast black-and-white photography succeed in colour?

Most critics would agree that an element of self-conscious revivalism was apparent as early as the late 1950s. In *A bout de souffle* (1959), **Jean-Luc Godard** took some of the stylistic hallmarks of classic-era noir and reconfigured them to reflect a contemporary, partly ironic, viewpoint. Something similar occurred in Melville's *Le Samouraï* (1967) and Boorman's *Point Blank* (1968). Both were filmed in colour but whereas the cool colours of Melville's film were an attempt to find a correlative to the harsh shadows of classic noir, *Point Blank* had a consistently bright and distinctly modern look.

The 1970s was the crucial decade: assisted by a richly stylized cinematography, both *Klute* (1971) and *Taxi Driver* (1976) created a very noirish vision of the modern city as a labyrinth of sleaze and decay. Similarly

their protagonists – prostitute-victim in *Klute*, alienated Vietnam veteran in *Taxi Driver* – were drawn from noir archetypes but inhabited a world of completely different values. And in an era of less strict censorship, this meant making what was once implicit highly explicit – in terms of both what could be seen and what could be said. *Chinatown* (1974) helped establish another trend – started by *Bonnie And Clyde* (1968) – that of noirs set in the past, in which there is an almost fetishistic attention to period detail. But *Chinatown* is also much more than just "retro-noir": it works both as a homage to and a critique of classic noirs.

But the movie which really established neo-noir in its own right was *Body Heat* (1981), a film for which its director **Lawrence Kasdan** plundered the noir back catalogue in his steamy tale of *amour fou* and deception. There's a different kind of knowingness on offer here, a mixture of postmodern parody and nostalgia, with the audience simultaneously enjoying a hot, steamy thriller and being in on the joke. Although set in Florida, the film really takes place in a "noir land", a lustful place of dark shadows and Venetian blinds, where people speak largely in wisecracks.

influential notion of the auteur–director as the key creative force in filmmaking gave them the confidence to experiment and to see their films as vehicles for creative self-expression.

Scorsese's *Mean Streets* (1973), in which he explores the Little Italy of his youth via a couple of minor hoodlums, established him as a director of great visual flair and one preoccupied by a male world of crime, guilt and redemption. Three years later he teamed up with Paul Schrader to make *Taxi Driver*, in which Robert De Niro plays Travis Bickle, a maladjusted Vietnam veteran so disaffected and disturbed by the sleaze of New York that he takes it upon himself to purge the city of its ills. Of all the noirs released in the 1970s, *Taxi Driver* was the one that most effectively gave film noir a vivid contemporary edge.

 ### The French Connection
dir William Friedkin, 1971, US, 104m

Friedkin's taut, thrilling tale of a maverick New York cop's obsessive pursuit of a French drug smuggler (the urbane Fernando Rey) was responsible for presenting the cop archetype in a strikingly cynical and anti-authoritarian manner. Gene Hackman is outstanding as the combustible, porkpie-hat-wearing "Popeye" Doyle, battling his way through a series of contrasting cityscapes in New York and Marseilles, while the film's legendary breakneck car chase remains a thrilling and much-imitated model.

 ### Dirty Harry
dir Don Siegel, 1971, US, 104m

Clint Eastwood – at his chilliest – plays the cynical and brutal San Francisco cop Harry Callaghan, who's armed with "the world's most powerful handgun" and has no hesitation in using it. In his pursuit, through a lawless city, of an equally single-minded criminal (Andy Robinson), Harry adheres to his own street justice rather than the law. Derided by liberals for the extremity of his vision, Siegel captured the growing cynicism of American society while never extolling Harry's fascistic values.

 ### Mean Streets
dir Martin Scorsese, 1973, US, 110m

Robert De Niro plays Johnny Boy, a daredevil, small-time hoodlum who is the cousin of the more circumspect Charlie (Harvey Keitel). Both exist on the edges of violent crime and respectability, in Charlie's case unsure of how best to improve his criminal prospects while paying lip service to God. Scorsese's homage to New York's Little Italy is refreshingly exuberant, not least in the wild improvisatory nature of Keitel and De Niro's scenes together. The exemplary rock soundtrack stokes up the film's wild energy.

 ### The Conversation
dir Francis Ford Coppola, 1974, US, 113m

On one level a Hitchcockian thriller, this subtle and complex film focuses on Harry Caul (Gene Hackman), a consummate professional so dedicated to his job – he's a surveillance expert – that he has next to no life outside of it. Listening to a fragment of conversation, he becomes obsessed with the idea that some terrible event is about to occur, and as he tries to uncover what it is – endlessly playing and manipulating taped recordings – he descends into an ever more self-destructive paranoia.

 ### Taxi Driver
dir Martin Scorsese, 1976, US, 112m

Travis Bickle (Robert De Niro) is a New York cab driver, lonely, isolated and full of disgust with the city and with himself. His attempt to reconnect with society and his own feelings focuses on Betsy (Cybill Shepherd), a political campaign worker. When this fails he refashions himself as the avenging saviour of a child prostitute (Jodie Foster) and all hell breaks loose. One of the bleakest and most lurid accounts of individual urban alienation, in which the logic of paranoid psychosis is meticulously unravelled.

 ### The Driver
dir Walter Hill, 1978, US, 91m

With the same cinematographer, Philip Lathrop, who filmed *Point Blank*, this film has a similarly austere aesthetic. The title character, played by Ryan O'Neal, is the perfect getaway driver – laconic and unflappable. Bruce Dern plays the detective determined, to the point of obsession, to nail him by any means possible. None of the characters has a name nor any backstory, which gives the film a quality that is both mythic and like a graphic novel. It also contains some of the most vital and exhilarating car chases on film.

The 1980s

The 1980s was the decade when Hollywood really emerged from the commercial doldrums, but arguably did so by demanding rather less of its audience's intelligence. It was an era defined by the proliferation of blockbusters, such as *E.T.* (1982) and the continuing *Star Wars* cycle. Nevertheless neo-noir was firmly established as an important contemporary trend in filmmaking. Indeed, this was the period when noir mutated, spreading itself into a variety of different genres – from cartoon to documentary – with varying degrees of success.

The decade started strongly with Scorsese, Schrader and De Niro following up their *Taxi Driver* success with the brutal, and brutally honest, *Raging Bull* (1980). Based on the autobiography of middleweight boxing champion Jake LaMotta, this was a noir biopic, filmed mostly in black and white, which self-consciously referenced the look of classic boxing movies, such as *Body And Soul* (1947) and *Somebody Up There Likes Me* (1956).

The same year saw the release of *American Gigolo*, another exploration of individual spiritual decay by writer-director **Paul Schrader.** Set in a sleek but soulless LA, **Richard Gere** plays a narcissistic prostitute (costumed by Armani) dedicated to his work but emotionally hollow. When he is framed for murder, the sham that is his life is finally exposed. A rather more satisfying, character-focused noir arrived with the outstanding *Cutter's Way* (1981). This unpredictable thriller boasted a wonderfully overwrought performance from John

Heard as a damaged but endearing Vietnam veteran who discovers a new purpose to his life when his friend Bone stumbles on a murder.

Cutter's Way did rather less well at the box office than two other neo-noirs out in 1981, both of which pay more obvious tribute to movies of the past. **Bob Rafelson's** *The Postman Always Rings Twice* (with a script by David Mamet) was the fourth screen adaptation of James M. Cain's novel of the same name, and while the sexual charge was very much stronger than in the 1946 version (see p.26), there were longueurs and **Jack Nicholson** seemed just too intelligent as the drifter Frank. A much more convincing take on the same theme can be found in **Lawrence Kasdan's** *Body Heat* (1981, see Canon), an updated, and startlingly effective, combination of *The Postman* and *Double Indemnity* set in the steamy heat of Florida.

Ridley Scott's *Blade Runner* (1982, see Canon) was a hybrid of an even more radical nature. Presenting a dystopian vision of Los Angeles circa 2019, the protagonist was a private eye figure, replete with raincoat and a world-weary voice-over drawn straight from classic noir. So successful was this film in combining noir with science fiction that it created the new genre of "tech" or "future" noir, which spawned such films as *The Terminator* (1984) and *Robocop* (1987). If *Blade Runner* was a big-budget extravaganza, then the Coen brothers kept the spirit of B-movie noirs alive with their first feature *Blood Simple* (1983, see Canon). This seminal neo-noir was shot for a mere $1.5 million and established its reputation largely by word of mouth.

Having been somewhat sidelined in the 1970s, the key noir figure of the *femme fatale* made a big comeback in the 1980s. One of the archetypes of classic noir, the *femme fatale* was – like the tough-guy private dick – something of an anachronism in a post-feminist era, and neo-noir directors treated her with varying degrees of irony. Bob Rafelson's rather lame *Black Widow* (1987) starred Theresa Russell as a psychotic woman who marries rich men in order to kill them and inherit their wealth.

Upping the psycho stakes was **Adrian Lyne**'s *Fatal Attraction* (1987), in which Dan (Michael Douglas), a complacent married man, is relentlessly pursued by Alex (Glenn Close), a woman with whom he has enjoyed an illicit weekend of very raunchy sex. Essentially a Hitchcockian thriller, but without the subtlety, the film's climax has the now utterly demented Alex terrorizing Dan's wife and daughter (she even boils the pet rabbit) before getting her comeuppance. Roundly attacked by feminists as misogynistic, the film is redeemed by Close's full-throttle performance.

Along with the Coen brothers, **Michael Mann** was one of the finest directorial talents to emerge in the 1980s and, like them, he was fascinated by the possibilities of neo-noir. Graduating from TV, Mann's first feature, *Thief* (1981), was the tale of a safe-breaker, Frank (James Caan), who dreams of a better life but gets embroiled with a crime boss (Robert Prosky) who takes over his business and his life. Mann's achievement was to integrate some powerful and often violent action scenes with detailed character development. He was greatly helped by a high-voltage performance from Caan as a man desperate to control his own destiny.

Five years later – and by now the executive producer of the hugely successful TV series *Miami Vice* – Mann released his third feature, *Manhunter* (1986), the first film adaptation of Thomas Harris's Hannibal Lecter novel *Red Dragon*. The film concentrates on the FBI agent, played by William Petersen, who has been persuaded out of retirement to track down a serial killer. Both *Thief* and *Manhunter* have a highly distinct visual style, with something of the cool abstraction of *Point Blank* in their use of strong colours and starkly composed settings. No less disturbing was **David Lynch**'s *Blue Velvet* (1986), a stylish unpeeling of the bland surface of middle America to reveal the violence and warped desires beneath.

Throughout the decade, neo-noir's strategies and stylistic traits were infiltrating a number of different genres. Thus in 1981 there was *Pennies From Heaven*, a musical neo-noir about a lonely sheet music salesman in the Depression era (Steve Martin), who fantasizes about living out the sentiments of the songs he peddles. Next year, the brilliantly constructed comedy *Dead Men Don't Wear Plaid* wove together actual scenes from classic noirs, linking them with newly shot material starring Steve Martin as an incompetent private detective. **Alan Parker**'s *Angel Heart* (1987) was a gothic horror-noir set in New Orleans, with Robert De Niro as a mysterious Satanic figure who hires private eye Harry Angel (Mickey Rourke) to track down a singer.

In the closing years of the decade, crossover noirs even produced a noirish documentary, *The Thin Blue Line* (1988), about a man on death row wrongly accused of murder; and a feature-length cartoon, *Who Framed Roger Rabbit* (1988), that was informed by noir, not least in the presence of the *femme fatale* Jessica Rabbit. Finally **Tim Burton**'s *Batman* (1989), with its noirish Art Deco look, sharply dressed gangsters, corrupt cops and glamorous molls, managed to inject a true sense of darkness into the Dark Knight's character.

Raging Bull
dir Martin Scorsese, 1980, US, 129m, b/w

The tragedy of a man, Jake LaMotta (Robert De Niro), whose profession is violence, but whose rage and brutality outside of the ring leads to the estrangement of his wife (Cathy Moriarty) and brother (Joe Pesci). De Niro brilliantly inhabits the role, famously feeding himself up so that he was convincingly transformed from the lean fighting machine of LaMotta's brief glory years to a shambling, self-pitying slob. The stylized and hallucinatory fight scenes are mesmerizing and revolting by turns.

Cutter's Way
dir Ivan Passer, 1981, US, 109m

One night, the laid-back Richard Bone (Jeff Bridges) spots a man loading something into a garbage can which later turns out to be a murdered woman. When Bone alerts his buddy Alex Cutter (John Heard), an embittered, disabled Vietnam vet, they start to sniff a conspiracy emanating from local businessman J.J. Court (Stephen Elliot). Sensitively performed, with Lisa Eichhorn outstanding as Cutter's vulnerable wife Mo, this is a murder mystery shot through with the poignancy of lost dreams and wasted lives.

Manhunter
dir Michael Mann, 1986, US, 122m

A very frightening film which follows the attempt by FBI "profiler" Will Graham (William Petersen) to track down a serial killer, "The Tooth Fairy" (Tom Noonan). To do so he must first reconnect with the psychotic mind by interviewing the imprisoned Hannibal Lecter, played by Brian Cox (less histrionic but no less scary than Anthony Hopkins). With little horror actually shown, the film works through watching Petersen convey Graham's thought processes as he struggles to do his job without going insane.

Blue Velvet
dir David Lynch, 1986, US, 122m

From the start the film propels you into abnormal normality, small-town America as viewed by a Surrealist: red roses, white picket fences, blue sky, all in rich saturated colours. From here naive Jeffrey Beaumont (Kyle MacLachlan) – investigating the mystery of a severed ear – stumbles into another, nightmarish world, that of the psychotic Frank Booth (Dennis Hopper at his evil best) and his mysterious and violent relationship with chanteuse Dorothy Vallens (Isabella Rossellini). Like the viewer, Jeffrey is a willing voyeur – at once both fascinated and disturbed.

House Of Games
dir David Mamet, 1987, US, 102m

This, the first feature from leading US playwright David Mamet, is very much a writer's film – eschewing fancy camera-work and strong visuals in favour of a tightly structured script. Margaret Ford (Lindsay Crouse) is a successful psychiatrist who decides to investigate the gambling debt of one of her patients by visiting the seedy gambling den "The House of Games". Befriended by con-man Mike (Joe Mantegna), Margaret becomes initiated into the art of the sting, gradually getting lured deeper and deeper into the world of bluff and double bluff.

The 1990s

If the 1980s was the decade when neo-noir really took flight – with a profusion of crossover material – then the 1990s was the time when it became ever more elastic as a concept. Indeed so widely stretched are the parameters for what constitutes neo-noir that several critics have questioned the usefulness of the term at all (see p.41 for further discussion). Hence the reluctance of many to refer to it as a genre, preferring to think of it as a style, a mood, a set of character types, that colours all or part of a film. Certainly, some of the most creative filmmakers of the 1990s – like the **Coen brothers** or **Quentin Tarantino** – have used it as an idea to be subverted and played around with. Their background in independent cinema gave them an ability to think outside the box and the confidence to produce idiosyncratic and highly original films.

The Coens got the decade off to a blazing start with *Miller's Crossing* (1990), their homage to the gangster films of the 1930s and Dashiel Hammett's crime fiction in particular. But the first great out-and-out neo-noir of the 1990s is surely *The Grifters* (1990, see Canon). This story

Quentin Tarantino – postmodern noir auteur

Despite his fervent insistence that "I don't do neo-noir", the sensational trio of films that opened Quentin Tarantino's directing career – the heist noir *Reservoir Dogs* (1991), the postmodern, brilliant *Pulp Fiction* (1994) and the pulp noir classic *Jackie Brown* (1997) – certainly suggest otherwise.

Something of a cult figure, Tarantino's career is defined by an unabashed passion for trash culture, allusions to which fill his movies, both verbally and visually. His work's core reference point, however, is clearly crime films and film noir – albeit viewed through a postmodern lens that transforms such material for an audience well-versed in pop-culture sensibilities. But while Tarantino subverts the staples of film noir, he does not mock them. His vigorous debut, *Reservoir Dogs*, was a superb update of the heist noir, exemplified by classic films such as *The Asphalt Jungle* (1950) and Kubrick's *The Killing* (1955). In *Reservoir Dogs*, the plot trails the tortuous and bloody aftermath of a failed heist, allowing for an incisive deconstruction of noir character types.

Tarantino's next film, *Pulp Fiction*, is rightfully regarded as a modern classic, as well as a high point of postmodern noir. The film is anchored in a complex, time-shifting narrative filled with pulp culture references. It showed Tarantino's adeptness at infusing particularly grim situations (male rape, heroin overdose) with a strain of humour that plays with the audience's expec-

tations and on several occasions masks the repeated themes of morality and honour.

In contrast, *Jackie Brown* saw Tarantino go for a (relatively) straight adaptation of Elmore Leonard's novel *Rum Punch*, the result being a more concerted effort at rounded characterization.

While *Kill Bill Vols 1 & 2* (2003 and 2004) strayed even further from the neo-noir path, Tarantino has managed to retain his noir credentials through his "guesting" directorial role on *Sin City* (see p.52), and both screenwriting and directorial credits for episodes of the distinctly noirish TV series *CSI: Crime Scene Investigation*.

Pulp Fiction
dir Quentin Tarantino, 1994, US, 154m

With its tagliatelle of storylines and complicated characters, *Pulp Fiction* offers a knowingly comic-book glimpse of life in LA's seedy underbelly. Samuel L. Jackson's elegizing hitman spins his tale around a discovery of personal belief, while Bruce Willis puts in a stunning performance as the downtrodden Butch the boxer. Everything about this film is tight and exquisitely considered, with the immensely colourful script – which rollercoasts from the apocalyptic to the hilarious to the heart-stopping – being the strongest tool in Tarantino's box.

of the bizarre relationship between three low-level con artists – a young man (**John Cusack**), his consuming mother (**Angelica Huston**) and new girlfriend (**Annette Bening**) – was directed by Stephen Frears from a Jim Thompson novel. Part of its noirishness is achieved by a somewhat unspecific period setting – a kind of approximation to the 1950s. It was produced by **Martin Scorsese**, who the following year directed an entirely unnecessary remake of *Cape Fear*, with

a demonic, tattooed **Robert De Niro** going way over the top as the vengeful ex-con. Rather more effective was *Reservoir Dogs* (1991), the astonishing feature debut of **Quentin Tarantino**. Filmed mainly in a warehouse, where the robbers meet after a diamond heist has gone badly wrong, it's a brilliant ensemble piece, packed full of pop culture and movie references.

In 1991 the Coen brothers had another noirish outing with *Barton Fink*, their whimsical take on the Hollywood of the 1940s. Like *Sunset Boulevard* (1953, see p.33), this is a highly cynical tale of a writer – in this case a budding Broadway playwright – who sells his soul when he agrees to take the Hollywood dollar. No less original was **Carl Franklin**'s brilliant directorial debut, *One Last Move* (1992), written by and starring **Billy Bob Thornton**. It's another film about the aftermath of a brutal crime, with an oddball gang of three holed up in a small Arkansas town, attempting to evade both the smart LA cops and the hick local police chief.

In a decade of pretty extreme crime movies, one of the most hard-hitting was **Abel Ferrara**'s *Bad Lieutenant* (1992). Focusing on the activities of an utterly corrupted New York policeman – played with a body-and-soul-baring honesty by **Harvey Keitel** – it has all the urban sleaze of *Taxi Driver* but with the protagonist colluding in the corruption, until the rape of a nun gives him the opportunity to redeem his sanity and his soul.

With **Paul Verhoeven**'s *Basic Instinct* (1992) we are back in *femme fatale* territory, with a memorable, star-making turn from **Sharon Stone** as Catherine Trammell, the sexually voracious novelist, and possible murderer, who ensnares **Michael Douglas**'s cop. Its soft-core sex scenes – which formed a large part of its appeal – aroused controversy, as did its equation of bisexual women with twisted psychopaths. A much more intelligent take on the *femme fatale* came from **John Dahl**, a director whose first two films, *Kill Me Again* (1989) and *Red Rock West* (1992), both explored noir territory. In *The Last Seduction* (1995, see Canon), Linda Fiorentino plays Bridget Gregory, a completely amoral and self-serving woman who destroys all the men who cross her path. As with *Thelma And Louise* (1991), her single-minded agenda to beat men at

their own game was seen as a fantasy of female empowerment rather than misogynistic.

Controversy surfaced again with **Oliver Stone**'s *Natural Born Killers* (1994), in which a trailer-trash couple (played by **Woody Harrelson** and **Juliette Lewis**) go on a mad killing spree, then get taken up by a disreputable talk show host. An extreme variant on the couple-on-the-run theme, some critics saw it as a biting satire on the symbiotic relationship between the media and violence, others as merely opportunist and unnecessarily gruesome.

In a bumper year for neo-noir, 1995 saw the release of three outstandingly good films. *The Usual Suspects* was a *tour de force* of intriguingly complex storytelling, centred around the identification of Keyser Soze, a criminal "Mr Big" who may or not exist. Next up was *Se7en* (1995, see Canon), which played out a classic theme of a serial killer playing mind games with the cops who are trying to outwit him. Filmed at audaciously low lighting levels, the resulting dark shadows and sense of claustrophobia constantly threatened to overwhelm the characters. There was much excited anticipation for the arrival of **Michael Mann**'s *Heat* (1995), not least because it paired up **Robert De Niro** (as gang boss Neil McCauley) and **Al Pacino** (as LA cop Vincent Hanna) for the first time. Ostensibly a heist movie, it's the relationship between two single-minded professionals – albeit on different sides of the law – that makes the film so compelling.

A few months later came what is, arguably, the Coens' best and most original spin on noir. *Fargo* (1996), which takes place in the snowy landscape of Minnesota, mixes the humorous with the harrowing, and has, in the charming Frances MacDormand, one of the most un-noir-ish police chiefs on film. But for many, the finest neo-noir of the 1990s was **Curtis Hanson**'s

L.A. Confidential (1997, see Canon). A retro-noir based on a James Ellroy novel, this movie does for LA in the 1950s what *Chinatown* (1974) did for it in the late 1930s – turns the spotlight on the seething corruption and power struggles beneath the brash, glittering surface.

The decade ended with two very quirky homages to Raymond Chandler. In *Twilight* (1998), **Robert Benton** reprised the theme of his *The Late Show* (1977) with the story of a washed-up, elderly private eye (Paul Newman) who does odd jobs for an actor with cancer (Gene Hackman) and his wife (Susan Sarandon). It fizzles towards its end but is saved by its veteran stars turning on the style. The Coens' *The Big Lebowski* (1998) is a much more ambitious and artful look at the LA myth, while also presaging the comedy and parody noir of the 2000s. Jeff Bridges plays Jeffrey Lebowski (aka "the Dude"), a laid-back wastrel who gets roughed-up by a couple of debt-collecting thugs who mistake him for a multi-millionaire of the same name. The Dude decides to seek compensation from the "other" Lebowski and a typically convoluted and very funny series of mishaps then occurs (see p.237).

One False Move
dir Carl Franklin, 1991, US, 105m

Three misfit criminals, coke addicts Ray (Billy Bob Thornton), his girlfriend Fantasia (Cynda Williams) and stab-happy hardman Pluto (Michael Beach), go on a killing spree in suburban LA before hot-footing it to Arkansas with the drugs and money they were after. An exceedingly raw and brutal movie, it also taps a vein of humour when gauche local sheriff "Hurricane" Dixon (Bill Paxton) has to work alongside two big-time LA cops (Jim Metzler and Earl Billings).

Reservoir Dogs
dir Quentin Tarantino, 1991, US, 118m

A group of men assemble to discuss a raid on a diamond warehouse, identified only by the names of colours. When the raid goes wrong, it becomes clear that one of them is a police plant, but which one? Tarantino's film has achieved cult status for a number of reasons: the unusual dialogue (a Madonna song is analyzed), the realistically prolonged agony of the wounded Mr Orange (Tim Roth), the sadistic violence of Mr Blonde (Michael Madsen) – all put together with the precision of a well-oiled machine.

The Usual Suspects
dir Bryan Singer, 1995, US, 106m

This clever heist noir marked the arrival of Bryan Singer and elevated Kevin Spacey from character actor to genuine star. Spacey is astounding as the crippled con-artist who "tells" cops investigating a dockside bloodbath the story of the group of criminals whose activities led to it, and the possibility of it all being orchestrated by the mysterious Keyser Soze. There are many smart moments but the finale is a masterpiece of editing, with fact and fiction colliding to bewildering, captivating effect.

Heat
dir Michael Mann, 1995, US, 171m

A routine robbery, organized by master criminal Neil McCauley (Robert De Niro), goes wrong when one of the gang gets trigger-happy. Enter Lt Vincent Hanna (Al Pacino), an obsessively dedicated police officer determined to bring McCauley to justice. At nearly three hours, this is a pretty epic battle of wits as the two men try to get the better of each other – irrespective of anything else in their lives, including those closest to them. A big, bruising movie with a full-scale, street shoot-out at its climax.

Fargo
dir Joel Coen, 1996, US, 98m

To solve his financial problems, Jerry Lundegaard (William H. Macy) hires two weirdo thugs (Steve Buscemi and Peter Stormare) to abduct his wife, hoping that her father will pay the ransom which he will then split with the abductors. When one of the thugs kills three people, folksy Police

Chief Marge Gunderson arrives to investigate – despite being pregnant. A wonderful Coenesque mix of unexpected elements, rural noir has never been more eccentric nor – despite some nasty moments – more charming.

The 2000s

Neo-noir's worst slump since the mid-1970s continued well into 2000, with the exception of **John Frankenheimer**'s *Reindeer Games* (aka *Deception*) and **James Gray**'s *The Yards*. In both films an ex-con (Ben Affleck and Mark Wahlberg respectively) tries to go straight but is driven to crime by his attraction to a complex woman – in each case played by Charlize Theron. But in September of that year came **Christopher Nolan**'s über neo-noir *Memento* (see p.51), which bewildered audiences with its fractured narrative encircling amnesiac protagonist Guy Pearce and his stop-start investigation into the rape and murder of his wife. Not since *Point Blank* (1967) had neo-noir undergone such a radical shake-up. Nolan followed this postmodern puzzler with *Insomnia* (2002), a deft Hollywood remake of Erik Skjoldbjaerg's 1997 Norwegian film of the same title (see p.274). Here, short-term memory loss is replaced by sleep deprivation as addled police investigator Al Pacino solves a murder in a wintry Alaskan town.

Yet as the new millennium dawned noir was casting more than one uneasy look over its shoulder. Kicking off retro-noir in the new decade was the Coens' *The Man Who Wasn't There* (2001), a near-perfect black-and-white reconstruction of classic film noir. Cult director **David Lynch**'s systematically weird *Mulholland Dr.* (2001) was seen as a return to form, although its overall feel harked back to the Lynch of *Blue Velvet* (1986) rather

than to the 1940s classics of the Coens' meticulous pastiche. Both films found huge favour with the critics, sharing the Best Director prize at Cannes. Far more central to noir's own dark history but also with foregrounded LA settings was **Brian DePalma**'s disappointing *The Black Dahlia* (2006), which reverted to one of the most notorious unsolved murders of the 1940s via pulp author James Ellroy's novel. *Hollywoodland* (2006) went one better, delving into the mysterious suicide of 1950s *Superman* actor George Reeves, with Ben Affleck in the lead.

The events of 9/11 and the ongoing Gulf War inspired a spate of politically oriented films. In *The Assassination Of Richard Nixon* (2004), director **Niels Mueller** follows the relentless decline of Sean Penn's downtrodden Sam Bicke, who just wants "a little piece of the American dream". Fat chance, as he loses his job and family and sees his prized entrepreneurial idea quashed. Like its 1970s predecessor *Taxi Driver*, *Assassination* is dominated by its protagonist's coiled, pent-up performance. **John Sayles**'s talky *Silver City* (2004) was the indie director's most noirish outing since *Lone Star* (1996), with a disarmingly self-effacing Danny Huston as a private investigator uncovering corruption behind the election campaign of a would-be governor with a strong resemblance to George W. Bush. Also in 2004 came **Jonathan Demme**'s remake of the Cold War classic *The Manchurian Candidate* (1962), with Denzel Washington's disturbed Gulf War survivor replacing Frank Sinatra's brainwashed Korean War vet. Washington and his decorated ex-platoon sergeant Liev Schreiber become unwitting pawns in a political assassination attempt intended to ensure a fraudulent and dangerous president comes to power.

Washington has chalked up a number of standout neo-noir performances in the 2000s. In

Troubled Man: Billy Bob Thornton as luckless barber Ed in *The Man Who Wasn't There* (2001).

Carl Franklin's sweaty, Florida-bound *Out Of Time* (2003), his easy-going police chief is lured into embezzlement by a duplicitous *femme fatale*. His heinous narcotics cop in *Training Day* (2001) represents one of the few occasions in neo-noir in which a black officer is not incorruptible.

Rogue cops have been patrolling the streets of noir throughout the 2000s. First off was **Jack Nicholson**'s Jerry Blick in *The Pledge* (2001). A homicide detective on the cusp of retirement, Blick becomes so obsessed with his promise to find a child killer that he abandons retirement, happiness and finally his own sanity in his doomed quest. No such motivation was need-

ed for **Brendan Gleeson**'s monumentally evil LAPD officer Jack Van Meter in Ron Shelton's underrated *Dark Blue* (2002), based on a James Ellroy story. Set in an atmospheric New York, *In The Cut* (2003) was one of the few neo-noirs of the 2000s directed by a woman (Jane Campion). Repressed academic Frannie (an unrecognizable Meg Ryan) tries to determine whether or not her intense lover, homicide detective Mark Ruffalo, is a serial killer.

Retro-noir got another boost in 2003 with a remake of Dennis Potter's *The Singing Detective* (see p.279), featuring an extraordinary performance from **Robert Downey Jr** as the slick detective. Downey reappeared two years later as Harry Lockhart – burglar, would-be Hollywood actor and inept private investigator – in Shane Black's rollicking *Kiss Kiss Bang Bang* (see Canon). Although high-school loner Brendan Frye (Joseph Gordon-Levitt), the chief protagonist in Rian Johnson's 2005 *Brick* (see p.53), is too young to hold a detective's license, his dogged investigation into the murder of his ex-girlfriend qualifies him as an honorary private investigator. Kevin Kline's Guy Noir – Garrison Keillor's fictional detective refashioned in Robert Altman's swan song *A Prairie Home Companion* (2006) – was a sleuth in a more whimsical vein.

The mid-2000s saw a welcome return to neo-noir from directors **Martin Scorsese** and **Michael Mann**. Scorsese's *The Departed* (2006) was the director's finest neo-noir since *Casino* (1995) and, like Mann's *Miami Vice* (2006), dealt with the tribulations of undercover police work. Although *Miami Vice* added new layers of grit to the slick television series, it is Mann's *Collateral* (2004, see p.53) which stands out as one of the decade's key neo-noirs. A masterclass in Los Angeles topography, it should be watched with honorary neo-noir *Los Angeles Plays Itself* (Thom Anderson, 2004), a riveting documentary that charts the relationship between Los Angeles and the movies.

If anything, the proliferation of noir sensibility and style across an even wider spectrum of film genres was the keynote of the 2000s. Josh Hartnett (a disappointment in *Black Dahlia*) was impressive as an ingénu mistaken for his debt-ridden friend in *Lucky Number Slevin* (Paul McGuigan, 2006). *Slevin* was the last in a quartet of fantasy neo-noirs which included *Batman Begins* (Christopher Nolan again), *A History Of Violence* (David Cronenberg) and *Sin City* (Robert Rodriguez and Frank Miller), all released in 2005. Based on comic-book stories or graphic novels, they were all in various ways immersed in an exaggerated noir style. *A History Of Violence* was also a modern example of rural noir. Superhero noir *Batman Begins* (2005) employed noir styling to bring the winged one back to his dark roots, while the hilarious, hugely underrated *Kiss Kiss Bang Bang* flawlessly melded noir and comedy. *Derailed* (2005), starring Clive Owen and Jennifer Aniston, was an effective "menaced-couple" noir, a sub-genre also drawn upon in art-house favourite Michael Haneke's *Caché* (*Hidden*, 2005). Some thirteen years after *Unforgiven*, Tommy Lee Jones revived the Western noir with *The Three Burials Of Melquiades Estrada* (2005) while, most bizarrely of all, *The Lady From Stockholm* (2005) united film noir with sock puppets! It's a dark, dark movie world and seemingly getting darker all the time.

Memento
dir Christopher Nolan, 2000, US, 113m

Nolan's amnesia storyline and back-to-front narrative were two of several dazzling twists on stock noir formulae. Detective Leonard Shelby (Guy Pearce) seeks to track down his own wife's murderer. His problem: since the event he has been unable to remember anything much beyond a few minutes. A confused chronology and a myriad of details which don't add up until the very end leave the spectator (like the investigation) in a miasma of uncertainty. This was the film which upped neo-noir's game and anointed Nolan as a new master.

The Man Who Wasn't There
dir Joel Coen, 2001, US, 115m, b/w

Nothing much seems to trouble Billy Bob Thornton's near-silent barber Ed Crane – not even his mind-numbing job, or his loveless marriage to a vulgar cheating wife. That is, until he decides to invest $10,000 in the hare-brained dry-cleaning enterprise of a sleazy entrepreneur. Blackmailing his wife's lover (James Gandolfini) leads Crane inexorably to the chair – and not of the barbershop variety.

Sin City – ultra noir?

With the release of *Sin City* in 2005, audiences saw perhaps the most stylized expression of film noir ever produced. Based on the highly acclaimed comic-book series, written and drawn by **Frank Miller** (who also co-directed the film with **Robert Rodriguez** along with "Special Guest Director" **Quentin Tarantino**), the film is an anthology-style collection of three of Miller's full-length Sin City stories – "The Hard Goodbye", "The Big Fat Kill" and "That Yellow Bastard" – with the addition of a short story, "The Customer Is Always Right", that acts as the film's introduction.

Rodriguez was adamant that the film should be "a translation, not an adaptation". The resulting movie is breathtaking, and has been hugely praised for being the most faithful rendition of a comic ever committed to screen. All the film's character action was shot against green-screen and then the various comic-strip back-drops and environments were added using CGI (computer-generated imagery) technology. Miller's distinctive

black-and-white artwork was thus faithfully translated to the big screen, with many shots in the film being almost exact replications of panels from the graphic novels. The process also allowed the filmmakers to achieve a style of chiaroscuro (an Italian word meaning the pictorial representation of strongly contrasting light and dark) that would have been impossible to emulate in "real" conditions.

Yet, can *Sin City* be considered noir? Is it even neo-noir? The answer is both yes and no: the film undoubtedly showcases many elements of film noir – first-person voice-overs, a retro-1940s setting, *femmes fatales*, clipped dialogue, an oppressive and labyrinthine urban environment … the list goes on. Yet, despite these signi-fiers, *Sin City* is first and foremost a tremendously faith-ful translation of a comic book, which in turn presents an incredibly stylized idea of what noir is, primarily influenced by the work of Mickey Spillane and at times indulging in a ridiculous level of ultra-violence.

Sin City (2005): comic book *and* noir to the nth degree.

Mulholland Dr.
dir David Lynch, 2001, US, 145m

Laura Elena Harring plays the enigmatic Rita – in voluptuous Hayworth mould – who takes refuge in the LA apartment of Hollywood hopeful Betty Elms (Naomi Watts). Their personalities split, merge and eventually destruct in a sublime haze of broken Hollywood dreams. Lynch fans applauded the trademark eerie suspense ratcheted to ever-higher levels, but detractors noted that even dreams in movies could benefit from a convincing plot.

Insomnia
dir Christopher Nolan, 2002, US, 188m

Robin Williams was a natural choice for creepy crime novelist and prime suspect Walter Finch in Nolan's remake of Erik Skjoldbjaerg's Norwegian midnight-sun noir. Detective Will Dormer (Al Pacino) investigates the murder of a teenage girl in a quiet Alaskan town. Neither lead disappoints, as suspect and insomniac policeman (whose judgement becomes progressively impaired) are entwined in a cat-and-mouse game laced with irony and moral ambiguity. Hollywood gloss meets European complexity with impressive results.

Collateral
dir Michael Mann, 2004, US, 120m

Getting $600 for a night ferrying a realtor round a nocturnal LA to close a series of deals seems like a good proposition to Max (Jamie Foxx). But once his first stopover is interrupted by a corpse ricocheting off his roof, a complex relationship develops as Max tries to outwit his captor Vincent (Tom Cruise). *Collateral* may be a technical *tour de force* but its real revelation is Cruise, a worthy successor to Alain Delon's assassin in *Le Samouraï*.

Brick
dir Rian Johnson, 2006, US, 110m

The crowning – and wholly compelling – achievement of this low-budget indie is to take the core components of film noir and apply them to the environment of an American high school. Surprisingly, the results are staggeringly good, utilizing dialogue, cinematography and even renditions of specific scenes from classic noirs. Even the characters' language drew heavily on Hammett-style detective-fiction slang, and the actors were dressed in an intriguing blend of teenage wear and classic noir-style costumes. Tremendously assured and finely observed.

The Departed
dir Martin Scorsese, 2006, US, 151m

It sounds like an odd fit – Andrew Lau's Hong Kong cult actioner *Infernal Affairs* (2002) remade by an Italian-American director and transferred to Boston's largely Irish police force. But this noir-heavy fable references Scorsese's *Mean Streets* (1973) and *Taxi Driver* (1976). Informers Leonardo di Caprio and Matt Damon are both surrogate sons to Irish mobster Costello (Jack Nicholson). Once he discovers something isn't quite right with either of them, Costello's depraved antics and violent outbursts easily exceed noir's legions of corrupt fathers.

From darkness into light? The final ambiguous moment from
The Big Combo superbly lit by camera wizard John Alton

The Canon: 50 essential film noirs

The Top Ten

1 Chinatown
1974; see p.74

It might be a Technicolor neo-noir and have arrived a few decades late, but Robert Towne's magnificent screenplay and Roman Polanski's tight direction propel noir to the top of its game.

2 Criss Cross
1948; see p.77

Siodmak's finest film stars Burt Lancaster as a weak-willed protagonist in thrall to his past, Yvonne De Carlo as a money-grubbing *femme fatale* and Dan Duryea as the reptilian hoodlum caught in between them.

3 Double Indemnity
1944; see p.86

Thanks to the combined talents of Raymond Chandler and Billy Wilder, James M. Cain's tale of a diligent insurance salesman derailed by Barbara Stanwyck's seductive *femme fatale* reaches the level of classical tragedy.

4 Touch of Evil
1958; see p.170

Orson Welles both stars in and directs the tragic tale of lawless policeman Hank Quinlan as he manipulates Charlton Heston's Hispanic official in a shady border town. A *tour de force* that belies its B-movie status.

5 Out Of The Past
1947; see p.151

Robert Mitchum's world-weary gumshoe Jeff Bailey lacks the cultural resonance of a Sam Spade or a Philip Marlowe, but he gives both a run for their money when he's rehired to track down doe-eyed Jane Greer.

6 L.A. Confidential
1997; see p.116

Three mismatched LAPD officers join forces to investigate a spate of gruesome massacres. Based on James Ellroy's seemingly unadaptable novel, Curtis Hanson's masterpiece is the standout neo-noir of the 1990s.

7 The Big Combo
1955; see p.57

A police lieutenant's obsessive pursuit of a charismatic crime lord clouds his judgement in this darkest of noirs, courtesy of cinematographer John Alton and king of the Bs, Joseph H. Lewis.

8 Kiss Me Deadly
1955; see p.109

Marvel at how Aldrich turns Mickey Spillane's fascistic pulp into Cold War allegory, or simply revel as private eye Mike Hammer slugs his way round a gleaming Los Angeles in a naive search for the "great whatsit".

9 The Maltese Falcon
1941; see p.133

In Huston's dazzling adaptation of Dashiell Hammett's novel, Bogart's unrivalled Sam Spade is up against noir's first great *femme fatale* and a gallery of grotesques – all desperately questing for a priceless antique statuette.

10 The Big Sleep
1946; see p.62

Howard Hawks's dazzling riff on Chandler's novel is anything but soporific as Bogie and Bacall blister the screen in a convoluted plot that even its sozzled originator couldn't fathom.

The Canon:
50 essential
film noirs

The Big Combo

dir **Joseph H. Lewis, 1955, US, 89m, b/w**
cast **Cornel Wilde, Richard Conte, Jean Wallace, Helen Stanton, Brian Donlevy** *cin* **John Alton** *m* **David Raksin**

All Lt Leonard Diamond (**Cornel Wilde**) has achieved after a dogged six-month investigation into the criminal activities of ruthless Combination chief Mr Brown (**Richard Conte**) is an $18,600 departmental deficit, the ire of his superior and an unhealthy obsession with Brown's icy society mistress, Susan Lowell (**Jean Wallace**). So when Susan is hospitalized after a botched suicide attempt – precipitated by her sado-masochistic relationship with the magnetic Mr Brown – Diamond is on hand to question her under a preposterous homicide charge.

His bedside interrogation fleshes out one tiny lead, Susan's drug-addled murmur of "Alicia", a name she witnessed Brown tracing and guiltily wiping from a misted windowpane. Further liberal use of departmental resources follows as Diamond corrals the Combination's 96 hoods for questioning, even submitting Brown to a lie detector test, but still Alicia's identity remains unknown. Having pushed Brown too far, Diamond is kidnapped and undergoes wincing torture-by-hearing-aid at the hands of Brown, aging Irish hood Joe McClure (**Brian Donlevy**) and a duo of hip, homosexual hoodlums – Fante (**Lee Van Cleef**) and Mingo (**Earl Holliman**).

Shadows and silhouettes in a movie "bereft of greys".

Released, but still determined to establish Alicia's identity, Diamond starts to unravel Brown's ruthless rise to power, despite the latter's murderous attempts to thwart him. Diamond's quest leads him initially to ex-Combination book-keeper Bettini (**Ted de Corsia**), suave antiques dealer and former ship's captain Nils Dreyer (**John Hoyt**), and finally to the mysterious Alicia herself.

To 1950s American audiences used to headline-grabbing stories of Senate hearings into organized crime, *The Big Combo* (despite its suggestive title) must have disappointed. Although Brown is described as running the "largest pool of illegal money in the world", the Combination's workings remain mostly mysterious. Instead the film concentrates on the psychopathological relationship between Diamond and Brown, and their obsessive attitudes towards power and sex. Frustrated by his low salary and dysfunctional relationship with Rita (**Helen Stanton**), Diamond craves both. Brown, on the other hand, regards them not just as his right but in some way intricately connected: "Women know the difference, they got instinct, first is first and second is nobody." He seduces a convalescent Susan with what an irate Production Code committee assumed was cunnilingus. Lewis recalled their questions in a 1975 interview:

> Committee: Well, where did Dick Conte go?
> Lewis: How the hell do I know? What does an actor do when you move in on a close-up of someone else? Go sit down somewhere, I guess.

Wherever it was Brown went, the committee's suspicions were shared by Jean Wallace's shocked off-screen husband Cornel Wilde, who refused to talk to Lewis for the rest of the filming.

Relations were better between Lewis and cinematographer **John Alton**. In a film that has been described as "bereft of greys", Alton and his gifted gaffer Harry Sundby achieved the apogee of noir high-contrast, shadow-filled cinematography, often with audaciously simple single-source lighting. Lewis recalled Alton's lighting technique: "It was magic. He'd put a light there, a backlight there, and a front light kicker here, and say, 'Ready.'" A blacker than black example is the composition of Diamond's torture scene, where the eyes of Fante and Mingo appear like white specks on an inky background.

Alton saved his greatest light effects for the final mist-filled hangar sequence, in which a desperate Brown tries to escape with the kidnapped Susan. Sporadically illuminated by a stark revolving flashlight, Brown is cornered by Diamond only to be blinded by a car searchlight directed by Susan. Out of ammunition and pleading to be shot, he is dragged out of the hangar followed by the silhouetted figures of Diamond and Susan, soon to be ominously enveloped by the mist. Some have claimed that their departure together is a positive ending; if so, it is about as close as noir gets to a traditional Hollywood walk-into-the-sunset finish.

The Big Heat

dir Fritz Lang, 1953, US, 89m, b/w
cast Glenn Ford, Gloria Grahame, Alexander Scourby, Jocelyn Brando, Lee Marvin *cin* Charles B. Lang Jr *m* Daniele Amfitheatrof

"Ah yes, we should love **Fritz Lang**. Toast the premiere of each new film, rush to see it, return again and again…" wrote François Truffaut in his 1954 *The Big Heat* review, heralding the beginning of Lang's canonization as an auteur. Lang later explained to Peter Bogdanovich how hate, murder and revenge and "the fight against fate" unconsciously ran through his pictures, making them the most consistently noir in any director's career. *The Big Heat* is the jewel in their thorny crown.

In 1953 the situation was quite different for the jobbing 62-year-old émigré director. Hired for the first time by second-tier studio Columbia, he was allotted 28 days to shoot William McGivern's newspaper serial about an explosive Philly cop and his vengeful crusade against organized crime. Ex-crime reporter and noir specialist **Sydney Boehm** came on board to tighten up McGivern's cod philosophizing, his crackling screenplay aided by **Charles B. Lang**'s unnerving mobile camera-work and William Kiernan's meticulous set decoration.

Detective Sgt Dave Bannion (**Glenn Ford**) has had ten years too many with Menport's corrupt police force, but with a family to support he has stomached a queasy status quo enforced by hoodlum Mike Lagana (the mellifluous **Alexander Scourby**). That is, until he and his wife (**Jocelyn Brando**) receive an abusive telephone call from one of Lagana's thugs warning him off the unravelling suicide case of police bureau chief Tom Duncan. A headstrong, fist-flying visit to Lagana's baroque mansion ensues, followed by accusations of Lagana's involvement in the brutal torture and murder of Duncan's mistress Lucy Chapman (**Dorothy Green**).

Lagana's brutal retaliation (and the Police Commissioner's feeble response to it) drives the embittered, and now badge-less, Bannion into the kind of hate binge that is usually the reserve of noir's most extreme psychotics. He still has some way to go before descending to the depths of Lagana's chief fixer Vince Stone (Lee Marvin), whose terrifying rages tend towards "working women over" by burning, scalding or strangulation. Bannion's humiliation of Stone in a nightclub confrontation wins him the respect of Stone's flirtatious girlfriend Debby Marsh (**Gloria Grahame**). Challenged by Bannion, the free-spirited Debby justifies her hedonistic lifestyle by telling him: "I've been rich and I've been poor – believe me rich is better."

Debby's enjoyment of the good life comes to an abrupt end when Stone discovers she's been talking to Bannion. Enraged, he pitches a pot of boiling coffee into her off-screen face, her agonized screams and hysterical confusion bolstering the impression that the entire act has been filmed. It is one of the most notorious sequences in noir and reflects Lang's belief that as long as his audience no longer feared "punishment after death" they were afraid of "only one thing – pain".

A bandaged Debby seeks shelter in Bannion's hotel and proceeds to single-handedly bring down Lagana's organization. After she has ambushed Stone with a pot of boiling water (the act this time shown in its wincing entirety), Bannion has little problem overcoming his handicapped adversary – remarkably, he is one of noir's few detectives who survives a case without receiving a punch. Meanwhile Debby has been fatally shot by Stone; even in her dying throes she frets about her appearance and buries her half-scarred face in her mink coat.

The last scene places Bannion not with what remains of his family but back at work. As he heads out on a job, his final words to "keep the coffee hot" carry an ominous weight. Perhaps it is not too far-fetched to think that if Debby can describe herself and Duncan's avaricious wife Bertha (**Jeanette Nolan**) as "sisters under the mink", then perhaps Bannion and Stone are akin to brothers under their respective gaberdine and camel hair.

The Big Sleep

dir Howard Hawks, 1946, US, 114m, b/w

cast Humphrey Bogart, Lauren Bacall, Martha Vickers, Elisha Cook Jr, Bob Steele *cin* Sid Hickox *m* Max Steiner

Humphrey Bogart (Philip Marlowe) came onto *The Big Sleep*'s set and asked director **Howard Hawks**: "Who pushed Taylor off the pier?" It was an innocuous question about the second of five corpses that cross Marlowe's path during his investigation into

On-screen and off-screen chemistry: Humphrey Bogart and Lauren Bacall with a sleeping Martha Vickers.

The Luzon versus the New York release

It was the American servicemen stationed in Luzon in the Philippines who were first in line to see *The Big Sleep* in August 1945. Released to the American public a year later, it was shorn of eighteen minutes to incorporate an additional twenty minutes of mostly Bogie-Bacall sparring and innuendo, in order to cash in on their off-screen romance. More significantly for generations of bewildered viewers, it also drastically cut Marlowe's face-off with the DA (in which the killer of chauffeur Owen Taylor was named) and a lengthy plot recap. Until its restoration in 1996 by the UCLA archive, the Luzon release was only available in a rare 16mm print, its scarcity only enhancing *The Big Sleep*'s cult status.

the blackmailing of Carmen Sternwood (**Martha Vickers**), but suddenly "everything stopped" on the Warner Bros soundstage. Nobody knew! Screenwriters **William Faulkner** and **Leigh Brackett** drew a blank, and even Marlowe's creator, Raymond Chandler, had no idea. The perpetrator of Taylor's fate was to remain unknown to the public for the next forty years, and even by noir's standards *The Big Sleep*'s narrative is still maddeningly difficult to follow.

This was the least of Hawks's worries, however, as he struggled with a schedule rapidly spiralling out of control (the production overran by 34 days) and Bogart's increasingly erratic on-set behaviour (prompted by the actor's imploding marriage to the alcoholic and paranoid Mayo Methot). In a triangular relationship the equal of any in noir, Hawks looked on sullenly as his favoured protégée, **Lauren Bacall** (who was playing Vivian Sternwood), became a smitten victim of the vicissitudes of Bogart's emotional see-sawing. Hawks had also – in the absence of screenwriter Faulkner – started shooting with a temporary screenplay, with "Butch" Brackett on hand to provide harder-boiled lines for Bogart. These concerns would have unseated a lesser director; Hawks, however, relished the impromptu approach, prompting Jack Warner to send the memo: "Word has reached me that you are having fun on the set. This must stop."

In this picaresque story of Marlowe's obstinate quest for the missing Sean Regan, via assorted hoods, extortionists and members of the decadent Sternwood family, it is the individual scenes that stay fixed in the mind after the film's bizarre storyline has faded. Marlowe's hothouse encounter with the dying patriarch General Sternwood (**Charles Waldron**) which starts the film, and the killing of the tough little grifter Harry Jones (**Elisha Cook Jr**) by Canino (played by B-movie Western star "Battlin' **Bob Steele**) are two of many played out with skilful leisure. His literary counterpart's knightly good looks replaced by an endearing streetwise grubbiness, Bogart appears in almost every scene. His trademark tics – finger quizzically tugging at his ear lobe, or thumbs emphatically tucked behind his waistband as he detonates Chandler's hard-boiled dialogue – led the author to write: "Bogart is the genuine article. Like Edward G. Robinson, all he has to do to dominate a scene is to enter it." Certainly no actor before or since has nailed the cadence of Chandler's dialogue with such snappy rigour. Even with a gun trained on him, Marlowe has time to sit down on a chinoiserie throne to exchange barbed quips with blackmailer Eddie Mars (**John Ridgeley**).

Despite its iconic status, *The Big Sleep* sits uneasily in noir's top fifty. It has little in the way of pronounced noir style, its stand-out sequences being the gritty low lighting in the death scene of Geiger (**Theodore von Eltz**) and the final confrontation between Marlowe, Vivian and Mars. The screenwriters (who latterly included Jules Furthman and Philip Epstein of *Casablanca* fame) had to take great liberties with Chandler's novel to appease the production code and to indulge a Bogart-Bacall mad public. The result is a far cry from Chandler's vision, but one which provides some of the most electrifying sparring sessions between private detective and faux *femme fatale* in noir's history:

> Marlowe: I can't tell till I've seen you over a distance of ground, but you've got a touch of class – but I dunno how far you can go…
> Vivian: A lot depends on who's in the saddle. Go ahead Marlowe, I like the way you work. In case you don't know, you're doing alright.

It has been a sentiment shared by generations of "Bogey Cult" fans, for whom St Bogart remains the quintessential Philip Marlowe.

Blade Runner

dir **Ridley Scott, 1982, US, 112m**

cast **Harrison Ford, Rutger Hauer, Sean Young, M. Emmet Walsh, Daryl Hannah** *cin* **Jordan Cronenweth** *m* **Vangelis**

Twenty-five years after its first release *Blade Runner* is still the benchmark film in tech noir or future noir – a bleak fusion of sci-fi and noir. **Ridley Scott** had wanted to make "a film set forty years hence, presented in the style of forty years ago". He even went so far as retrofitting Warners' Burbank backlot – famed for its use in noir classics such as *The Maltese Falcon* (1941) and *The Big Sleep* (1946) – to realize

Harrison Ford clings on to the Bradbury Building in *Blade Runner*'s rain-soaked tech-noir landscape.

Most overrated noir: *Blade Runner*

A Google search on *Blade Runner* throws up a staggering 5 million-plus hits. Its legions of fans continue to dissect the film's innumerable versions, including original studio prints, home releases and the director's cut. Does *Blade Runner* really merit such attention? Critic Pauline Kael thought not, writing: "some of the scenes seem to have six subtexts but no text, and no context either". While Harrison Ford, whose performance was trashed as "more cardboard than hard-boiled", remembers standing around "in some vain kind of attempt to give some focus to Ridley's sets".

Ironically, much of the film's fascination has to do with its unfinished qualities. Multiple screenwriters pulled Philip K. Dick's seemingly unfilmable novel in various directions. Production exigencies piled on further continuity errors and plot problems. However, these narrative glitches are overwhelmed by the film's bravura visuals and Vangelis soundtrack. But, after repeated viewings a nagging doubt remains as to whether the film is nothing more than a sophisticated riff on noir style, with a hazy nod to Dick's disquieting novel on the responsibilities of being human in a catastrophic near future.

his vision of trash-chic, retro-deco downtown Los Angeles. Other noir locations include LA's Union Station (used for the police HQ) and the fin-de-siècle Bradbury building as the crumbling home of genetic engineer J.F. Sebastian (**William J. Sanderson**).

Blade Runner's challenge to noir conventions begins with the opening title, which identifies the film's setting as LOS ANGELES, NOVEMBER 2019, before a mesmeric aerial sequence reveals a landscape of belching refineries and monumental skyscrapers. But this is like no other LA noir landscape; rather it is a nightmarish hybrid of Los Angeles, New York, Hong Kong and Beijing. Trying to navigate this neon-lit, acid-rain-swept cityscape is ex-blade runner (or replicant killer) Rick Deckard (**Harrison Ford**) and the AWOL replicants he has been co-opted to "retire". These "skin jobs" are *übermensch* androids desperate to extend their limited life spans – as featured in the film's cult sci-fi source novel, **Philip K. Dick**'s *Do Androids Dream Of Electric Sheep?* (1968).

At first sight Deckard seems every inch the neo-noir detective, with his battered trenchcoat and his battle with alcohol and authority. However, his monotone, emotionless voice-over (excised in the 1992 Director's Cut – now the film's official version) and his cowardly, ham-fisted attempts to destroy the all-too-human replicants make him less and less convincing as he becomes consumed by doubt, self-loathing and empathy for the very things he's employed to destroy.

Deckard's love interest Rachael (**Sean Young**) seems the quintessential *femme fatale*, with her Joan Crawford look and Rita Hayworth sashay. But when Deckard uncovers her as a replicant during his investigations into the Tyrell Corporation – the organization responsible for creating replicants – she still "loves" him enough to save him from vengeful, renegade replicant Leon (**Brion James**). Rachael's life-saving act initiates a violent, questionable relationship between them as they desperately attempt to function in a dysfunctional society, in which androids seem more humane than humans and the majority of the population have emigrated to off-world colonies.

Once the anti-hero and head replicant Roy (**Rutger Hauer** in scenery-chewing form) starts to dominate the storyline, Deckard's noir protagonist status is rapidly sidelined. Not only does Roy get the choicest lines, but he also runs away with the most gutsy, guignol role in all neo-noir as he fights for his remaining life and toys with Deckard. Roy is often filmed from exhilaratingly extreme low angles in a way which explodes the boundaries of noir cinematography. So much so that the first two weeks had to be re-filmed when the footage turned out to be pitch-black because of cinematographer **Jordan Cronenweth**'s risk-taking exposure levels.

After repeated viewings, *Blade Runner* remains an unsettling visual experience: it is impossible to digest its wealth of set details and light effects, such as the probing crime control searchlights that slice into scenes already shrouded by an ubiquitous squint-inducing fug. Objects or moving figures constantly interrupt viewpoints and characters are positioned off-centre, reinforcing the nagging feeling that something crucial is happening just out of eyeshot.

For 25 years there has been festering speculation as to what actually did go on off screen in *Blade Runner*'s troubled, gruelling production, during which Scott and Ford barely spoke and the crew nearly mutinied. Perhaps the real story will emerge in the forthcoming anniversary DVD, which promises a re-mastered director's cut (long only available in a shoddily produced DVD), its myriad edits, as well as a mass of commentaries and extras.

Blood Simple

dir **Joel Coen, 1984, US, 99m**
cast **M. Emmet Walsh, Frances McDormand, Dan Hedaya, John Getz** *cin* **Barry Sonnenfeld** *m* **Carter Burwell**

It is not only indigestion troubling dyspeptic roadhouse owner Julian Marty (**Dan Hedaya**). His errant wife Abby (**Frances McDormand**) has just slept with one of his barkeeps, Ray (**John Getz**), and the scumbag private investigator he has arranged to tail her is relishing a blow-by-blow account of the couple's motel assignation. This is Loren Visser (**M. Emmet Walsh**), whose otherworldly drawl accompanies *Blood Simple*'s blighted Texan-tableaux opener, warning noirishly: "The world is full of complainers. But th' fact is, nothing comes with a guarantee … somethin' can always go wrong."

Rest assured it will, in ways the protagonists least expect, once an apoplectic Marty – humiliated in his crotch-crunching efforts to

Blood money: paying for *Blood Simple*

Blood Simple's pre-production history began in wintry Minneapolis in early 1982. Here, ex-NYU film student **Joel Coen**, with only three assistant film editor credits to his name, including low-budget nasty *The Evil Dead* (1981), set about raising the film's $775,000 budget. Schlepping a 16mm projector and a bloody two-minute trailer – depicting a man being buried alive and a detective's colourful attempt to shoot his way out of a corner – he visited local businesses, from auto junkyards, bowling alleys to banks, projecting and pitching *Blood Simple* to his incredulous fellow Minnesotans.

His brother **Ethan** – a Princeton philosophy dropout with a penchant for Wittgenstein – partnered him when his Macy's job permitted, and remarkably, by October, the film's budget had been independently raised by Minnesotan, New York and Texan investors. So, with a rookie crew, whose most experienced member was key grip Tom Prophet Jr, and a cinematographer who later recalled not knowing where the on/off switch was on the film's camera, Joel Coen entered a feature film set for the first time, partnered by his co-screenwriter/producer brother.

Due to the Coens' meticulous storyboarding and rigorous pre-planning, *Blood Simple*'s eight-week Austin/Hutton-based shoot ran smoothly, only to be followed by two frustrating years of post-production and thwarted attempts cajoling distributors to buy a film "which was too bloody to be an art movie and too arty to be an exploitation film". That is, until it began generating interest on the festival circuit and audiences like those at the 1984 New York Film Festival started "cheering themselves hoarse". It was not the usual reaction to neo-noir, but with its sledgehammer horror effects, overcooked Texan ambience and irreverent attitude towards its noirish antecedents like Hammett and Cain, it stretched the category's woolly parameters almost to breaking point.

strong-arm his wife back into his life – contracts Visser to murder Abby and Ray. The odious investigator has other plans, however, such as doctoring the couple's death-scene photographs, pocketing a $10,000 fee from his duped client and framing Abby for her husband's murder. What he doesn't foresee is Marty's stubborn refusal to die, Ray happening upon his erstwhile employer's apparent corpse, and his bloody, muddy efforts to cover up what he perceives to be Abby's crime of passion.

Blood Simple borrows its title from Hammett's pulp novel *Red Harvest* (1929), in which the term describes a tough investigator's dissolving psyche and fears over his appetite for killing as he reforms a corrupt mining town. Visser, hulking around in a misshapen pastel-yellow leisure suit and fly-blown Stetson, has no such qualms or reforming qualities. Wearing a frightful grimace and often emitting a curdling laugh, he is prepared to play assassin or turn murderer for money, making his forebears like Sam Spade and Mike Hammer seem positively saintly in comparison.

Almost his equal in sleaziness is hirsute Greco-American Marty – all medallions, tight-fitting epauletted shirts and sneer. His three scenes with Visser singe a screen already burnished by cinematographer **Barry Sonnenfeld**. So much so, that it is their intense pairing, rather than that of Abby and Ray, which becomes the film's perverse equivalent to James M. Cain's passion-filled, murderous couples, so often cited as a key influence on the movie.

Mischance, miscommunication and misunderstanding reach an uncontrollable pitch in *Blood Simple*'s final, escalating thirty minutes. As an unhinged Ray starts to believe that he is a hapless pawn in Abby's duplicitous attempts to extricate herself from Marty, Abby herself becomes increasingly anxious about Ray's sanity, assuming that Marty is still alive and responsible for her lover's irrational behaviour. Meanwhile Visser is convinced Abby and Ray are onto him and is forced to take radical measures. As the plot bloodily unravels around the doomed characters, prepare yourself for a denouement guaranteed to leave you aghast, horrified and helpless.

The Blue Dahlia

dir George Marshall, 1946, US, 98m, b/w

cast Alan Ladd, Veronica Lake, William Bendix, Howard Da Silva, Doris Dowling *cin* Lionel Lindon *m* Victor Young

Raymond Chandler explained to producer **John Houseman** that he could only finish *The Blue Dahlia* screenplay "at home – drunk". Other requirements were two cadillacs on standby to deliver fresh pages to Paramount; six secretaries working round the clock; and

Dreamy encounters: Alan Ladd and Veronica Lake in a publicity still for *The Blue Dahlia*.

a medical team to administer vitamin shots during his eight-day Bourbon-fuelled writing marathon. A few months before, Chandler had wowed Paramount by hammering out a ninety-page story from his unfinished novel, *The Blue Dahlia*. It had a familiar noir plotline of veterans returning to civilian life, in this case Johnny, George and Buzz, "the last survivors of a bomber crew that made too many missions".

It was the perfect fit for a studio desperate to eke out a vehicle for one of their top stars, **Alan Ladd**, prior to his imminent army recall. However, Chandler had not counted on the US Navy censor banning the murder of Johnny's wife, Helen, by the war-damaged Buzz who has a plate in his head "as big as your brains". The writer had to find a less politically sensitive murderer as the film's ultra-dependable director **George Marshall** raced through the unfinished screenplay.

Johnny (Ladd), Buzz (**William Bendix**) and George (**Hugh Beaumont**) return to Los Angeles from their South Pacific tour to find the city in flux and seething with corrupt undercurrents. Johnny's troubles begin on interrupting the party of his wife Helen (**Doris Dowling**) as he right hooks her paramour and owner of *The Blue Dahlia* club, Eddie Harwood (**Howard da Silva**) with the line "You've got the wrong lipstick on, Mister!" After learning from his unapologetic wife (clad in a voluptuous Edith Head lamé trouser suit) that their son was killed in a car crash due to one of her alcohol-fuelled spins, Johnny hits the rainswept road and wanders listlessly through one of the greatest downpours in noir's history.

Johnny is picked up that same night by Eddie's ex-wife Joyce (**Veronica Lake**) – and the two of them embark upon a trance-like ride down the Pacific Coastal Highway. His halting farewell words, "Every guy has seen you before, somewhere – the trick is to find you", sets the mood for their dreamy encounters throughout the film. Hardly has Joyce had time to don a hair band over her luxurious fringe than Helen's corpse is discovered. Johnny becomes the prime suspect and archetypal noir fugitive in a bid to prove his innocence. In the background, George and Buzz blunder around trying to help Johnny, who (worryingly) they believe to be guilty.

Buzz is a classic example of noir's many damaged veterans. With the exception of Johnny, he threatens all those unfortunate to cross his path and rants against bebop or "monkey music", which triggers an uncontrollable cacophony in his head. When this is accompanied by **Lionel Lindon**'s camera tracking into an extreme close-up of his pained, angry face, the effect is unnerving – a technique later used to great effect by the cinematographer on the damaged Korean veterans in *The Manchurian Candidate* (1962).

Buzz is not the only one of the veterans to return from combat damaged. Helen's words to Johnny – "Maybe you've learnt to like hurting people?" – are prescient. It is difficult to guess what is going on under his icily controlled exterior, but shocking glimpses appear as he descends into a world of shifty wartime extortionists and a Los Angeles gone to seed. Here low-angled lighting predominates, and the final fight between Johnny and *The Blue Dahlia*'s manager, Leo (**Don Costello**), has a jarring, realistic quality.

His name cleared, Johnny is free to be reunited with Joyce in an unconvincing ending demanded by the studio and a public hungry for more Ladd-Lake chemistry. They would be teamed up again sooner than they thought in *Variety Girl* (1947), as Ladd did not eventually re-induct into the US army – an irony no doubt not wasted on the exhausted and hungover Chandler.

Body Heat

dir Lawrence Kasdan, 1981, US, 109m

cast William Hurt, Kathleen Turner, Ted Danson, Richard Crenna, J.A. Preston *cin* Richard H. Kline *m* John Barry

It is not just the heat wave stifling indolent lawyer cum listless Lothario Ned Racine (played by a moustachioed and permanently perspiring **William Hurt**). His criminal practice is going nowhere and his personal life is little more than a series of unfulfilling one-night stands, glibly recounted to his bored colleagues – Assistant DA Peter Lowenstein (**Ted Danson**) and police detective Oscar Grace (**J.A. Preston**). When a chance encounter – or so he imagines – with rich and unhappily married out-of-towner Matty Walker (**Kathleen Turner**) segues into a torrid, no-holds-barred affair, his dream ticket out of small-town Miranda Beach seems assured. However, the insatiable Matty has other plans for the duped attorney, including the brutal murder of her crooked businessman-husband Edmund (**Richard Crenna**), as well as arson, perjury and much, much more.

Having spent the 1960s and 70s smouldering on the sidelines of neo-noir, the *femme fatale* was back – bad and supercharged. Combining Jane Greer's guile with Barbara Stanwyck's sexiness, Kathleen Turner makes her noir sisters seem nun-like in comparison. As she throatily tells Ned, her body temperature "runs a couple of degrees high, around the hundred … the engine or something. Runs a little fast." In a response uttered in the time it takes him to put down his ubiquitous cigarette, he replies: "Maybe you need a tune up?" To which she fires back: "Don't tell me; you've just

Femme fatale Kathleen Turner and her besotted victim William Hurt cooling off from their exertions.

the right tool?" Not since Stanwyck and MacMurray in *Double Indemnity* and Bacall and Bogart in *The Big Sleep* have a noir couple had so much verbal fun. Not that it lasts long, once Ned realizes that the get-rich plan he has been lulled into thinking was his own idea is merely part of Matty's bigger scheme.

Convinced that *Body Heat* might be his first and last shot at directing, Kasdan determined to do "everything with the camera that [he] could think of" in the hope of producing "something very extravagant". The result initiated neo-noir's exciting 1980s/90s resurgence and introduced a new type of baroque noir style realized by veteran cinematographer **Richard H. Kline**, whose career had included camera-assisting on the noir classic *The Lady From Shanghai*. Among the visual high points are the Venetian blind shadows enfolding Ned's salt-caked torso as he is slavered over by Matty during a clandestine tryst, and the impenetrable ocean mist which threatens to subsume the couple after they dispose of Edmund's corpse. Throughout the film, Kline's restless camera constantly tracks or moves around Ned, its movement becoming a more complex, sinister dance as Matty gradually ensnares him.

Ned Racine ranks as one of noir's most doomed and infatuated protagonists, and by the film's end he is in the state penitentiary on charges of murder, criminal malpractice and manslaughter. Matty has nullified his fake alibi, doctored Edmund's will in Ned's name to ensure she gets the maximum payout, and been (apparently) killed by an incendiary device while being threatened by Ned. It being Florida, Ned presumably faces the death sentence, and yet all he can discuss with Oscar is how Matty engineered his downfall and how she could have feigned her own death. Take one look in his crazed eyes and all you can see is admiration for the woman who set him up – just how noir is that?

As for Matty's future, you will have to watch the film to find out…

Chinatown

dir **Roman Polanski, 1974, US, 131m**
cast **Jack Nicholson, Faye Dunaway, John Huston, Roman Polanski** *cin* **John Alonzo** *m* **Jerry Goldsmith**

Chinatown's pre-production was hardly auspicious. Nobody at Paramount could understand **Robert Towne**'s convoluted 180-page screenplay with its Hammett-inspired plot and Chandleresque imagery – all loosely based on the ruthless expansion of Los Angeles and the rape of the water-rich Owens Valley. It would be up to **Roman Polanski** to bully and cajole a structured narrative from Towne during a two-month rewrite. But by the first day of shooting the two men still disagreed on the film's ending and relations got so bad between them that Towne was banned from the set for the rest of the shoot.

The sequel: *The Two Jakes*

Chinatown's long-awaited sequel, *Two Jakes*, was first slated for production in 1986 with **Jack Nicholson** returning as Jake Gittes and *Chinatown*'s maverick producer **Robert Evans** as the second Jake. However, with its screenwriter/director **Robert Towne** worried about Evans's rusty acting ability and his screenplay only 80 percent finished, the project imploded. The trio's professional and – in Evans and Towne's case – personal partnership was left in tatters.

Thanks to Nicholson's resilience and his considerable Hollywood clout, a new deal was eventually struck and production of *The Two Jakes* (as it was now called) restarted in 1989. Nicholson was to combine acting and directing duties, while **Harvey Keitel** would play Gittes' troublesome client Jake Berman. Nicholson would also be desperately rewriting throughout the production, since the screenplay remained unfinished and Towne's revisions soon dried up.

All these problems meant that *The Two Jakes* evolved into a fascinating two-hour plus oddity that is six parts Nicholson to four parts Towne. Nicholson's contribution is a nostalgic, discursive companion piece to *Chinatown* and paean to a lost Los Angeles; Towne's is a sprawling detective story, peopled by a swathe of is unscrupulous characters all linked circuitously to Gittes' traumatic past.

The Two Jakes is peppered with stand-out moments – such as the sporadic quakes which emphasize both Los Angeles' and the investigation's unstable fault lines. Even so, there's a gnawing suspicion that a remarkable sequel was only a rewrite away. Just how different the outcome might have been had an exiled Roman Polanski directed and cajoled a final draft from Towne

is an enticing thought. Perhaps Nicholson's cumbersome voice-over could then have been avoided, and Frederic Forrest's and Eli Wallach's woefully underdeveloped roles excised.

However, don't let the "might haves" stop you savouring a rich retro noir – from **Vilmos Zsigmond**'s "hard and perfect" 1940s look to Gittes' extravagantly lapelled jackets and streamlined deco offices. *Chinatown* aficionados should not be disappointed either. Gittes' careworn associate Lawrence Walsh (Joe Mantell) is still on hand assiduously warning the detective not to return to the Mulwray case. A promoted Capt. Lou Escobar (Perry Lopez), having lost a leg at Guadalcanal, remains a thorn in Gittes' side and Allan Warnick's pesky public records clerk reappears as an obnoxious public notary.

A word of warning – a *Chinatown*/*Two Jakes* double bill is not recommended. Better to see *Chinatown* first: digesting its background material will save a lot of head scratching when it comes to enjoying *The Two Jakes* a bit later.

The Two Jakes
dir Jack Nicholson, 1990, USA, 138 mins

1948 and it's boom-time in Los Angeles. Eleven years on and Jake Gittes (Jack Nicholson) – with a distinguished war record and a successful detective agency – divides his leisure time between his fiancée and the Wilshire Country Club. But when a client, Jake Berman (Harvey Keitel), shoots his wife's lover (who just happens to be his business partner), Gittes is forced to clear himself as a possible accessory to murder. His efforts take him into a murky Los Angeles of rapacious land and oil developers, and right back into the heart of the tortured Mulwray family.

Two weeks into filming, Polanski felt he was making just another "imitation of classic movies shot in black and white". One problem was veteran cinematographer **Stanley Cortez**, who was "out of touch with mainstream developments", required a vast amount of lights and insisted on using diffusion for filming Faye Dunaway's close-ups. Replacing Cortez at a day's notice was the speedier **John A. Alonzo**, whose preferred "camera eye" was the 40mm Anamorphic widescreen lens, ideal for capturing claustrophobic medium close-ups of the actors which dominate a film almost bereft of reassuring establishing shots.

With Alonzo completing the film's gifted team of key technicians (including Dick and Anthea Sylbert on production design and costume respectively), Polanski started making "a film about the thirties seen through the camera eye of the seventies". By doing so, he facilitated a vision of Los Angeles more resonant and evocative of the city than many classic noirs encumbered by technical and Production Code restrictions. Walking these burnished streets was a new type of private detective embodied by languid counter-culture actor Jack Nicholson. His brash Hollywood detective, specializing in "discreet investigations", combined effortless glamour and self-confidence as he becomes mired in a case of environmental and domestic corruption that is wholly beyond him.

When Gittes is duped into investigating Hollis Mulwray (**Darrell Zwerling**), the chief engineer of the Los Angeles Water & Power department, by a woman claiming to be his wife (**Diane Ladd**), the result is a headline-grabbing exposé of his apparent liaison with a much younger woman. Unfortunately for the detective, the real Evelyn Mulwray (**Faye Dunaway**) then appears with a lawsuit, only to mysteriously drop it "quicker than the wind from a duck's ass".

When soon after this, Mulwray is discovered suspiciously drowned, Gittes decides to follow up the commissioner's solitary investigations into the mysterious draining of LA's reservoirs. Lowering the water levels, as Gittes discovers, is the clandestine part of a campaign to persuade drought-ridden Angelinos to back a controversial dam construction. Mulwray has vetoed the scheme, which is being masterminded by his depraved ex-partner and father-in-law Noah Cross (played with chilling relish by iconic noir director **John Huston**). Ex-water baron Cross wants to use the dam to irrigate vast tracks of land that he is ruthlessly and cheaply acquiring in the North West Valley.

Undaunted by a horrific reservoir-side encounter in which he receives a wincing knife thrust to his nostril from a diminutive hoodlum played by Polanski, Gittes determines "to find the boys making the pay-offs" and "sue the shit out of them". This is the first of a number of violent encounters that he will experience, with the result that he spends the next third of the film sporting a monstrous bandage spread-eagled across his nose.

However not before – in a bizarre volte-face – he is commissioned by an agitated Evelyn to investigate Hollis's death and then hired by Cross to find Hollis's young companion. From here on in Gittes' naive and blundering quest into civil corruption will become hopelessly intertwined with a family that is outwardly respectable but deeply and perversely dysfunctional.

Chinatown, and Gittes traumatic past links to it, barely feature in the film; instead it seems to function as a metaphor for the real workings of the city as something impenetrable, nefarious – a law unto itself. It is, however, the setting for the film's tragic and disturbing denouement, in which Noah Cross and his daughter are brought together for the only time. It's the bleakest of endings, which the well-intentioned but arrogant Gittes has inadvertently engineered but is now completely powerless to prevent.

Criss Cross

dir Robert Siodmak, 1949, US, 98m, b/w
cast Burt Lancaster, Yvonne de Carlo, Dan Duryea,
Stephen McNally *cin* Franz Planer *m* Miklós Rózsa

Brace yourself for one of noir's most urgent *in media res* openers as **Franz Planer**'s aerial camera descends over a nocturnal Los Angeles and taxies towards Steve Thompson (**Burt Lancaster**) and his ex-wife Anna (**Yvonne De Carlo**) embracing in a nightclub car lot. It's the night before a payroll heist in which Steve (a security van driver) is the inside man and the couple are furtively finalizing their scheme to elope with fifty percent of the takings. In transit to Long Beach, Steve recalls the tumultuous events leading up to the job, which starts a forty-minute series of dreamy flashbacks as complex as any in noir.

After two years away from a disastrous seven-month marriage to Anna, Steve returns to his family in Los Angeles, his voice-over claiming ominously: "I didn't come back on account of her, it had

Most underrated noir: *Criss Cross*

Although highly regarded by those in the know, *Criss Cross* (1949) is rarely screened and remains almost unknown to the public. Its director Robert Siodmak is more celebrated for his noirish Hemingway adaptation *The Killers* (1946), its star Burt Lancaster better known for his late career flourishes in *Atlantic City* (1980) and *Field Of Dreams* (1989), and its *femme fatale* Yvonne De Carlo more likely to be remembered as Lily from the 1960s TV show *The Munsters*.

This is a puzzling oversight as *Criss Cross* is arguably the most complete noir of the classic era. It combines archetypal characters – a doomed protagonist, a calculating *femme fatale*, a reptilian hoodlum – with the tale of a meticulously planned then botched heist, all seasoned by a complex flashback and Lancaster's self-deluding voice-over. For the perfect introduction to classic Los Angeles noir there can be no better place to start than here, in the rundown streets of the Bunker Hill district – noir's most quintessential locale.

nothing to do with that … But then from the start, it all went one way, it was in the cards or it was fate or a jinx or whatever you want to call it." Once Steve sees Anna sashaying with **Tony Curtis** (in his screen debut) in the Round-Up club, he is transfixed. No sooner have the couple met for an early morning Zuma beach dip than their earthy relationship is on again.

Warned away from Steve by his family and threatened by his vindictive friend Lt Pete Ramirez (**Stephen McNally**), Anna marries her gangster boyfriend Slim Dundee (**Dan Duryea**). However, a chance encounter between Steve and Anna in Union Station re-ignites their affair. That is, until Slim and his henchman pay them a visit during one of their afternoon assignations. Thinking on his feet, Steve claims that he was proposing a plan for a payroll heist and the wary Slim takes the bait. Whether or not Anna has tricked the infatuated, gullible Steve into this corner is a moot point.

Although planned with military precision, the heist turns into a smoke-filled, brawling, surreal gun battle as Steve retaliates against the double-crossing Slim. Having taken a terrible beating and now hospitalized, Steve comes out of the ordeal a hero, although the suspicious Ramirez tries to eke out a confession from him. Unperturbed, Steve is more concerned about the no-show of Anna and whether Slim has further plans for him. Kidnapped by one of Slim's men, he is being driven to the gang's hideout, but can he bribe the man to take him to Anna and his Palos Verdes rendezvous instead?

Following the premature death of producer Mark Hellinger in 1946, **Robert Siodmak** capitalized on his greater autonomy and re-wrote **Anthony Veiller**'s screenplay with **Daniel Fuchs**. Whereas Hellinger had wanted to provide a panoramic role to Los Angeles (akin to that given New York in *The Naked City*), Siodmak chose to confine the bulk of the action to the city's Bunker Hill district, a working-class neighbourhood, filled with crowded lodging houses reached by precipitous ascents and descents. Here the cluttered Thompson family home and the labyrinthine rooming house where the heist is planned provide a nightmare reflection of Steve's confused, besieged mind.

As the love interest, Yvonne de Carlo's Anna is one of the most vulnerable, working-class and pragmatic of noir *femmes fatales*. Stuck in a dire triangular relationship between an infatuated ex-husband, who holds little interest for her other than the physical, and the wife-beating Slim, she decides to make off independently with her fifty percent of the takings. Her decision is vindicated by the return of an impotent, bewildered Steve (virtually mummified in a mass of bandages and casts). But with a vengeful, limping Slim emerging out of the inky blackness, it looks as if she may be stuck with Steve for good.

Cry Of The City

dir Robert Siodmak, 1948, US, 96m, b/w
cast Victor Mature, Richard Conte, Berry Kroeger, Shelley Winters, Debra Paget *cin* Lloyd Ahern *m* Alfred Newman

"Go fry!" murmurs a bullet-ridden Martin Rome (**Richard Conte**) to shyster attorney Niles (**Berry Kroeger**) before being wheeled into emergency surgery and an uncertain future. It is an apt line from a cop-killer bound for the electric chair which repels the attorney's cynical efforts to eke out a false confession for the notorious De Grazia jewellery job. Overseeing this sordid exchange is Lt Vittorio Candella (**Victor Mature**) who, like Rome, has grafted his way up from Little Italy's tenements, but to a life of police enforcement rather than crime.

Spurred on by the visitation of his angelic girlfriend Teena Riconti (**Debra Paget**), Rome makes a miraculous recovery and escapes. Having ensured Teena's safety, lodged with his sympathetic nurse Pruett (**Betty Garde**), Rome attempts to extort money from the meddling Niles. When their ensuing skirmish reveals the attorney to have masterminded the De Grazia job, he draws a gun on Rome and receives a knife in the back for his trouble. This leaves Rome with the hot jewellery, a cash flow problem and the need for a new ID and a passage south. With only floozy Brenda Martingale (**Shelley Winters**) and his impressionable kid brother Tony (**Tommy Cook**) to rely on, Rome is now wanted for two murders. He is also the prime suspect for the De Grazia job and, to add to his troubles, his beloved Teena is suspected of being his accomplice.

Hunted obsessively by Candella through an unforgiving nocturnal New York, Rome encounters a nightmare assortment of personalities who are the equal of any in noir's roster of misfits. These include furtive émigré Dr Veroff (**Konstantin Shayne**) and the gargantuan Rose Given (**Hope Emerson**), the real De Grazia accomplice with a nasty predilection for torturing and then strangling her victims. The feverish Rome (an effect helped by the fact that Conte suffered a virus during filming) survives her over-enthusiastic neck rub to see his attempted jewellery pick-up from a subway locker go spectacularly awry. In the ensuing chaos, Candella takes a bullet meant for Rome as he leaps over the subway turnstiles. The two men now have more in common than ever.

Candella's obsessive quest to bring Rome to justice is at the heart of this intense movie. The cop is a lone figure, single-minded and ruthless. When Rome asks, "You ever bet a hundred bucks on a horse or maybe give a girl a big bunch of orchids just 'cause you like her smile?", Candella's answer, through gritted teeth, "No, but I sleep good at nights" does not quite ring true. His home life is non-existent, lived vicariously through repeated visits to Rome's close-knit family.

Cry Of The City is a celebrated example of semi-realist noir and helped pioneer the use of gritty, authentic location shooting favoured by Twentieth Century-Fox. Although the use of actual Manhattan locations (such as the 18th St Subway entrance) is unquestionable, spotting where location work stops and studio set starts is a challenge. This is not surprising for a director who professed to "hate locations – there's so much you can't control". The hospital locations are a case in point. They were filmed at LA County Hospital, but the labyrinthine corridors and echoing monastic interiors suggest some inspired manipulation by art directors Albert Hogsett and Lyle Wheeler.

Cry Of The City is also steeped in religious imagery, especially in Rome's final night-time meeting with the saintly Teena in the neighbourhood church where he and Candella fight for her soul. Still severely wounded, Candella is beaten to the ground by Rome before collapsing in a Christ-like pose that echoes a painting in the church. Raising himself up, he then shoots Rome, who falls to the pavement silhouetted in deep focus, his arms spread out as if in crucifixion. Rome's young brother Tony arrives to find him dead, and then helps Candella to the waiting car. Framed within the confining car's rear window and its ominous POLICE lettering, the two of them make a grotesque and disturbing image.

D.O.A.

dir Rudolph Maté, 1950, US, 83m, b/w
cast Edmond O'Brien, Pamela Britton, Luther Adler,
Neville Brand *cin* Ernest Laszlo *m* Dimitri Tiomkin

Spare a thought for Frank Bigelow (**Edmond O'Brien**), striding determinedly through the endless corridors of downtown LAPD. Barely 36 hours into a bachelor break and this small-town accountant has been poisoned, kidnapped, shot at and driven to manslaughter. On top of which, he has some explaining to do:

Edmond O'Brien (Frank Bigelow) retaliates against an unknown assailant in *D.O.A.*

Bigelow: I want to report a murder.
Captain: Where was this murder committed?
Bigelow: San Francisco, last night.
Captain: Who was murdered?
Bigelow: I was.

Following this exchange, Bigelow's flashback begins the day before on a stiflingly hot morning in his hometown of Banning. Frustrated by one tax return too many and constrained by a predictable future with his devoted fiancée, Laura (**Pamela Britton**), he embarks on a week of pleasure in San Francisco. No sooner has he leered his libidinous way through the St Francis Hotel – accompanied by **Dimitri Tiomkin**'s incongruous wolf-whistle composition – than he is ensconced in a bar grooving to the manic sax notes of Illinois Jacquet. Sidestepping one potential pick-up, he arranges an (unfulfilled) assignation with another "jive-crazy chick", while he is slipped a toxic Mickey Finn.

Waking next morning with stomach pains, Bigelow is horrified to learn – two hospitals and a glowing phial sample later – that he has been poisoned by a luminous toxin and has only a week to live. Adrift in San Francisco, his only lead in his own murder case is Eugene Phillips, a Los Angeles-based client apparently driven to suicide after being tricked into buying stolen iridium, notarized by Bigelow. After some against-the-clock detective work, Bigelow concludes that his client's murder and his poisoner are one and the same man. This is Raymond Rakubian who, in partnership with his wife Marla (**Laurette Luez**), tricked Phillips into buying the iridium and who has his reasons to suppress the notarization.

It's a neat theory – until Bigelow is kidnapped by Rakubian Snr, aka Majak (**Luther Adler**), and shown Raymond's ornate funerary urn. Off beam about his murderer, he is right on the nail about Rakubian's nefarious involvement in the iridium transactions and now poses a major threat to Majak's security. So with just hours to live, Bigelow has to evade Majak's goons and confront a murderer, who has a more personal motive for wanting to keep the notarization under wraps.

It's best not to try to disentangle *D.O.A.*'s increasingly absurd plotline, and instead revel in one of noir's most animated performances as Edmond O'Brien careers, chases and skids his way across Los Angeles and San Francisco, all under the lens of noir specialist cinematographer **Ernest Lazslo**. The film's velocity has led one expert to describe it as "the closest any film noir got to being a Warner Bros cartoon".

That's not to say it's comic. Look for instance at the exhilarating sequence when Bigelow runs blindly through streets crowded with people, after discovering that he has been poisoned. In a spectacular crane shot he crosses a main road, dodges a taxi and comes to an exhausted halt outside a newsstand. In three succinct shots he looks at the sunset (possibly for the last time), picks up a ball for a child that rolls his way (his chances of fatherhood are finished), and sees a couple embracing (his loving relationship with Paula will never blossom).

Probably more than any other noir protagonist, Bigelow runs the gamut of noir archetypes – from bewildered outsider adrift in an alien city and beset by arbitrary fate, to ruthless investigator bereft of fear as he psychotically empties his chamber into the cowering figure of his murderer. As if his dying words – "All I did was notarize a bill of sale" – were not enough to prove his status as noir's unluckiest protagonist, the film has one more cruel trick in store – the Captain's choice to nullify Bigelow's story with instructions to make the report D.O.A.

Detour

dir Edgar G. Ulmer 1945, US, 68m, b/w
cast Tom Neal, Ann Savage, Claudia Drake, Edmund MacDonald *cin* Benjamin H. Kline *m* Leo Erdody

Few Hollywood filmmakers have had to contend with the kind of draconian constraints imposed on **Edgar G. Ulmer** during *Detour*'s production. In a burst of unparalleled creativity, Ulmer completed the film in six days (shooting eighty set-ups a day), stretching every cent of his $117,000 budget. As if this was not enough, the director was rationed to 15,000ft of film and the picture's locations were limited to a fifteen-mile radius from the studio's headquarters in West Hollywood. After a three-and-a-half-day edit, Ulmer had produced a 67-minute masterpiece, whose heady concoction of fatalistic doom, poetic gutter dialogue and expressionist wizardry would

A deceptively benign publicity shot of *Detour*'s hellish couple (Ann Savage and Tom Neal).

showcase the prodigious technical skills that he had picked up on the UFA sets of Fritz Lang and F.W. Murnau.

Detour is dominated by a voice-over from noir's most pessimistic and untrustworthy narrator. This is disillusioned pianist Al Roberts (**Tom Neal**), slumming it in a crummy Reno diner and recalling his ill-fated hitch-hike from New York to Los Angeles to join his singer girlfriend Sue (**Claudia Drake**). Despite his permanently pained expression, Al gets picked up by ex-bookie turned hymnal salesman, Charles Haskell Jr (**Edmund MacDonald**), who is going "all the way" to Los Angeles. Figuring he will be nailed for Haskell's suspicious heart attack in transit, Al assumes the dead man's identity.

Before Haskell's untimely death, Al questions him about the deep scratches on his right hand. Haskell's reply heralds the arrival of one of the most aggressive, tragic and needy women in postwar American cinema – more *femme febrile* than *femme fatale*. Al picks up the consumptive Vera (**Ann Savage**) at a petrol station, his demented voice-over going into overdrive as he tries to justify his actions: "Man, she looked as if she had just been thrown off the crummiest freight train in the world, yet in spite of this, I got the impression of beauty … a beauty that's almost homely because it's so real." Perhaps Al sees something in the cold cream that Ulmer had smeared all over Savage's hair, but what Al's voice-over claims and what Ulmer reveals are alarmingly different. The director repeatedly prompted Ann Savage to quicken her dialogue delivery, wanting her – as he later recalled – to have "a voice like a buzz-saw and the eyes of a gorgon".

After Vera accuses him of murdering Haskell and stealing his identity, Al has no other choice but to become embroiled in her outlandish plan to hock the car and to claim a substantial inheritance from Haskell's dying father. Holed up in an airless apartment, masquerading as Mr and Mrs Haskell in a sickening parody of marriage, their drunken arguments become increasingly sado-masochistic as Vera attempts to engage Al in some kind of psycho-sexual relationship. Her advances rebuffed, and chafing with pain and anger, she grabs the phone, threatening to hand Al over to the police. When Al tugs frantically at the phone trying to disconnect it, he is unaware of what the outcome will be – a macabre scene which, according to Savage, was unscripted and improvised by Ulmer on the day. Al is now destined to wander the highways like an eternal hobo, until, that is, he is picked up by a cruising squad car. In the end, his nihilistic voice-over gets the last word: "Some day a car will pick me up … that I never thumbed. Yes, fate or some mysterious force can put the finger on you or me for no good reason at all."

Double Indemnity

dir Billy Wilder 1944, US, 106m, b/w

cast Barbara Stanwyck, Fred MacMurray, Edward G. Robinson, Tom Powers *cin* John Seitz *m* Miklós Rózsa

With its hard-boiled **James M. Cain/Raymond Chandler** provenance, low-key **John F. Seitz** cinematography, stylish **Edith Head** costumes and anxiety-filled soundtrack by **Miklós Rósza**, *Double Indemnity* is noir's defining movie. Its plot, of insurance salesman Walter Neff (**Fred MacMurray**) willingly pushed by intoxicating *femme fatale* Phyllis Dietrichson (**Barbara Stanwyck**) to "crook the house" and murder her husband, thunders along, like its protagonists, "stuck with each other … to the end of the line". Interspersed with an embittered, confessional voice-over by the dying Neff, its acrid dialogue ricochets around a nightmarish Los Angeles.

Based on the notorious 1927 Snyder Grey case, Cain's novel of unpunished adultery, greed and murder had languished for over a decade in censorial limbo until Paramount let director **Billy Wilder** loose on the material. In the absence of Cain, producer Joe Sistrom suggested that Wilder team up with newcomer to the screen, novelist Raymond Chandler. This was to be the start of a combative but productive relationship which led Chandler to write: "Working with Billy Wilder on *Double Indemnity* was an agonizing experience and has probably shortened my life, but I learned from it about as much about screenwriting as I am capable of learning, which is not very much."

While keeping to the spirit of Cain's writing, Wilder and Chandler improved on the book's narrative excesses, while dexterously navigating their way around the Hays Code. They added Neff's voice-over, which provides a wry commentary on his downfall, and replaced Cain's operatic ending with a sequence that Wilder described as one "of the best scenes I've ever shot in my whole life". (The scene, in which Walter is executed in the San Quentin gas chamber, was eventually removed during the editing process after previewing badly.) Greater emphasis is placed on the love/hate relationship between Walter and claims manager Keyes (**Edward G. Robinson**), whose obsessive work has led him to trust nobody. The screenwriter's suggestive dialogue between Phyllis and Neff was

Double Indemnity at the Oscars

It was not **Billy Wilder**'s night at the 1944 Oscar ceremony. The Bing Crosby vehicle, *Going My Way* swept the board, while *Double Indemnity*'s seven Oscar nominations – best picture, script, cinematography, music, leading actress – came to nothing. Hollywood myth has it that Wilder, disgruntled and tiring of *Going My Way*'s endless awards, stretched out his foot at an opportune moment and sent the jubilant Best Director, **Leo McCarey**, flying as he went to collect his statuette. History proves that in fact his frustration was very appropriate – he could see it was a great movie, but others couldn't.

accepted by the Hays Office, but left the audience in no doubt as to their immediate sexual attraction. So impressed was Cain by the adaptation that he conceded: "It's the only picture I ever saw made from my books that had things in it I wish I had thought of."

Although set in the summer of 1938, *Double Indemnity*'s 1943 A-status production was affected by wartime constraints. Film stock rationing limited the budget to under $1 million. Seitz's gritty night-for-night cinematography was aided by wartime dim-out regulations, and the film's urgent newsreel-style lighting was suited to his "no filler lighting". Having already proved his noir credentials on the bleak *This Gun For Hire* (1942), Seitz showcased his technical skills in the opening sequence, where the wounded Walter drives recklessly through a night-time Los Angeles to make his confession, and in the night location shoots where Walter and Phyllis abandon Dietrichson's corpse to stage his accidental death and ensure the double indemnity payout.

Seitz took especial care in lighting the Dietrichson house where Walter has his first fateful meeting with Phyllis, and to which he returns for three increasingly chilly encounters. For the initial lascivious encounter, Wilder wanted an effect of the sun slanting "through the windows of those old crappy Spanish houses … (and) you see dust in the air". To achieve this, Seitz "invented a sort of aluminium powder which we blew into the air just before we started shooting". For Walter's final deathly encounter with Phyllis, the living room has become a monstrous shadowy lair, with Walter's figure adding shadows upon shadows. The extraordinary lighting and sets prompted Stanwyck to say: "The way those sets were lit, the house. Walter's apartment, those dark shadows, those slices of harsh light at strange angles – all that helped my performance. The way Billy staged it, it was all one sensational mood." Combine this with Chandler's dialogue, Cain's diabolical plot and a trio of actors all igniting sparks off each other and the result is quite possibly the darkest, most entertaining and influential film in Hollywood's history.

The Element Of Crime

dir Lars von Trier, 1984, Denmark, 103m
cast Michael Elphick, Esmond Knight, Me Me Lai, Jerold Wells *cin* Tom Elling *m* Bo Holten

In **Lars von Trier**'s hilarious commentary on *The Element Of Crime* DVD he tells his jocular editor **Tómas Gislason** and wheezy cinematographer **Tom Elling**: "I'm not sure what it's all about." It is a sentiment shared by most of *Element*'s viewers. So here goes with a rough summary.

In a sweltering sanatorium some time in the future, an obese Levantine doctor intones to camera: "I want you to leave Cairo, the sun, the desert … You're going to see Europe again, for the first time in thirteen years." His off-screen patient is ex-police detective Fisher (**Michael Elphick**), a headache-riven amnesiac undergoing hypnosis to exorcize a recent horrific murder investigation. It could be an opener from any number of amnesiac-themed 1940s noirs – well, leaving aside the monkey feverishly preening itself on the psychiatrist's shoulder.

Fisher's extended flashback – peppered intermittently by Elphick's droning voice-over and the shrink's increasingly bewildered interruptions – returns him to a semi-submerged, totalitarian Northern Europe. Torn between his old criminology professor Osborne (played by blind actor **Esmond Knight** in his last great role) and police chief Kramer (**Jerold Wells**), he is assigned to investigate a grisly series of killings in which child lotto sellers are being brutally eviscerated throughout a post-apocalyptic police state.

While Osborne is reduced to an incoherent wreck by his failure to satisfactorily solve the murders, Fisher re-enacts the movements of missing chief suspect Harry Grey. His nightmare journey sees him

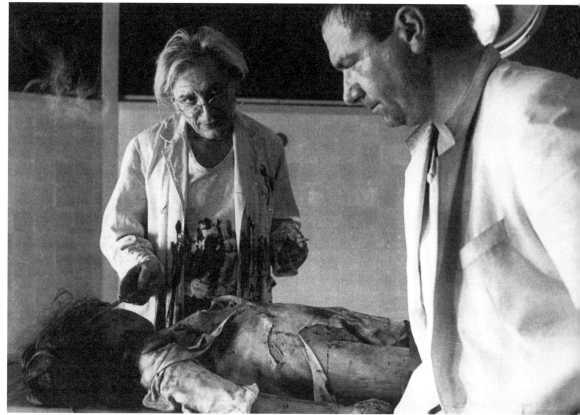

Forensic attention: Dt. Fisher (Michael Elphick) investigates the latest child murder in *The Element Of Crime.*

gradually take on Grey's character: popping Thorazin pills to experience his doppelgänger's racking headaches and reliving a sadistic relationship with Grey's mistress Kim (**Me Me Lai**). Wilfully ignoring Osborne's maxim that the criminologist "must remain untouched, detached, clinical, objective" as outlined in his mentor's celebrated police primer – *The Element of Crime* – Fisher determines to solve the case at all costs, irrespective of the appalling consequences.

Von Trier's eccentric aim of making "the first film noir shot in colour" and his controversial use of sodium lighting – more commonly used on European autoroutes – ensured *Element* has a sickening black and yellow patina, unique in neo-noir. **Peter Høimark**'s extraordinary production design, seen for example in Fisher's abseil into the bowels of the submerged police archives or his disastrous attempt to lure Grey with a decoy lotto seller in a disused bottle factory, also contributes to the "special kind of evil" – as Osborne puts it – that overwhelms the film's obtuse narrative.

In the centre of this season-less, nocturnal world wanders a catatonic and bewildered Elphick, his soused performance apparently aided by copious amounts of Gammeldansk, a heady Danish brew. It is a remarkable interpretation that evokes noir icons Humphrey Bogart in its general world-weariness and Dana Andrews in its hungover taciturnity.

Over-stylized it might be, but *Element* overflows with noir and neo-noir references, from *Touch Of Evil* and *The Third Man* to *The Conversation* and *Taxi Driver*, while paying homage to German Expressionism and Tarkovsky's *Stalker*. The last word however goes to von Trier who, when referring to one of *Element*'s trance-like sequences on the DVD commentary, says excitedly to his colleagues: "Nobody will ever surpass that…" And he's probably right, unless another director decides to shoot a scene in which a drug-addled police detective is orally relieved while boating through the sewers, with both cast and crew working alongside to noisy extracts from Wagner's *Götterdämmerung*!

Force Of Evil

dir Abraham Polonsky, 1948, US, 78m, b/w
cast John Garfield, Thomas Gomez, Marie Windsor, Beatrice Pearson, Roy Roberts *cin* George Barnes *m* David Raksin

Joe Morse (**John Garfield**) has escaped the Lower East Side slums thanks to the self-sacrifice of his brother Leo (**Thomas Gomez**) and rides high as a successful lawyer in his swanky Wall Street office. He is a day away from his first million, courtesy of nefarious dealings with his top client and numbers racketeer Ben Tucker (**Roy Roberts**).

The numbers "game" is an illegal lottery in which bets are placed on an unpredictable three-digit number that is, in Joe's words, "selected from the totals bet at some race track that day". On the fourth of July many bet on the number 776 (1776 being the year of the Declaration of Independence), which, of course, never comes up. Tucker has fixed it so that this year it will. The result will break all the betting shops (known as "banks"), at which point Tucker will bail out the largest so that they keep running, in exchange for two-thirds of the profits.

Leo, an honest man in a dishonest business, has stayed in the Lower East Side and heads up a local numbers bank with a small, devoted workforce. Refusing to compromise his battered integrity, he ignores Joe's entreaties to join Tucker, with tragic results. When the mob moves in, Leo's terrified book-keeper, Bauer (**Howland Chamberlain**), starts tipping off the authorities before falling prey to Bill Ficco (**Paul Fix**), a rival gangster who wants part of the action. Joe, meanwhile, faced with the direct consequences of his greed and corruption, descends inexorably into a noirish world of fear, duplicity and violence.

Polonsky wanted the film's dialogue to "play an equal role with the actor and visual image and not run along as illustration". The result is a lilting voice-over from Garfield and speech that is a mixture of authentic city slang and lyricism. The scene in which Leo is set up by Bauer in an all-night restaurant is particularly brilliantly realized: dialogue, visuals and music (from Beethoven's *String Quartet 14*) are all perfectly matched, while Leo's exhausted, poignant speech to Bauer is almost unbearable to listen to: "I'm a man with heart trouble, I die almost every day myself, that's the way I live, it's a silly habit. You know sometimes you feel as though you're dying … you're dying while you're breathing."

Polonsky asked future director **Robert Aldrich** to organize the movie's crucial New York exteriors – on Wall Street, Trinity Church and under the Manhattan Bridge – so he could concentrate on working his magic with the actors. The director had a difficult time with newcomer **Beatrice Pearson** as Doris Lowry, Leo's seemingly incorruptible secretary who is seduced and corrupted by Joe but tries to redeem him. Relations became so poor between her and Gomez that Polonsky was reduced to shooting some of their scenes separately. In contrast, the scenes between Joe and Tucker's *femme fatale* wife Edna (**Marie Windsor**) were filmed effortlessly and fairly sizzle with sexual tension.

Unhappy with the polished Hollywood look provided by veteran cinematographer **George Barnes**, Polonsky showed him an Edward Hopper monograph and as a result Barnes started using simple single-source lighting. Although the film is largely studio set, the exterior New York scenes have an almost surreal quality, especially where an overhead camera captures Joe running down a deserted Wall Street – a tiny figure in a De Chirico-esque cityscape. As if to accentuate Joe's gradual descent, he is sometimes shot with the camera looking down on him and is often overshadowed by others in the frame.

The ravaged Joe eventually finds his brother's corpse among the flotsam and jetsam under the towering Manhattan Bridge, and the film finishes with one of the bleakest and most regretful voice-overs in noir: "It was like going to the bottom of the world to find my brother. I turned back to give myself up to Hall because if a man's life can be lived so long and come out this way, like rubbish, then something was horrible and had to be ended one way or the other and I decided to help."

The "I decided to help" was a necessary coda for the film to get past the strictures of the Production Code. It was a compromise that Polonsky was willing to make, unlike his testimony to the HUAC (see p.24), which prevented the director from making another film for 21 years – one of the great losses to American and world cinema.

Gilda

dir Charles Vidor, 1946, US, 110m, b/w
cast Rita Hayworth, Glenn Ford, George Macready, Steven Geray *cin* Rudolph Maté

Gilda's opening credits fade to black, and from below floor level **Rudolph Maté**'s camera cranes up to reveal a pair of gigantic dice tumbling towards the lens. Throwing the dice in a crooked crapshoot is Johnny Farrell (**Glenn Ford**), adrift in Buenos Aires at the close of World War II. It's a masterfully concise introduction to a noir world of gambling, shifting uncertainties and a grifter whose self-made luck is about to change.

Leaving with his winnings, Johnny is rescued mid-beating by enigmatic dockside cruiser Ballin Mundson (**George Macready**) and his handy retractable dagger-stick. Hardly has Ballin re-sheathed the dagger – which will be symbolically erected at key points during the two men's homo-erotic relationship – than Johnny is managing Ballin's casino and has his own set of keys to his boss's luxurious home.

Johnny is obsessively faithful to his mentor Ballin, who entrusts him with "all the things that belong to me". Unfortunately this includes his beautiful new wife Gilda (**Rita Hayworth**), who happens to be Johnny's ill-treated ex-girlfriend. Thus begins one of the most tortuous and wayward of noir's many troubled triangular relationships. In one of several voice-overs, which usually express either jealousy, obsessive love or regret at his treatment of her, Johnny says of Gilda: "I hated her, so I couldn't get her out of my mind for a moment. She was in the air I breathed and the food I ate."

The role of the mesmerizing Gilda established Rita Hayworth's status as Hollywood's "love goddess", and was also to haunt her disastrous personal life, prompting her infamous words: "Every man I knew had fallen in love with Gilda and wakened with me." Gilda is still in love with Johnny and will do anything to excite feelings of jealousy in her ex-lover and disrupt his relationship with Ballin. "If I had been a ranch, they would have named me the bar nothing!" she exclaims to Johnny before roaring off in the sports car of playboy Gabe Evans (**Robert Scott**). Perversely, this does not have the required effect on Johnny, who obsessively protects Ballin from Gilda's increasingly lascivious behaviour.

Johnny is caught between his love/hate for Gilda and his attachment to Ballin, who offers him an escape from his past (always an attractive proposition for a noir protagonist). Ballin is a charismatic, vampire-dandy figure, immaculately coiffured and with a curiously clipped German accent. Often filmed in shadow, he has a tendency to disorient compositions either in profile or in the foreground. He controls his casino from a central panopticon-like office and has Nazi-esque plans for world domination through his ruthless tungsten cartel.

After the apparent suicide of his boss (as a result of his collapsing cartel plans), Johnny inherits Ballin's casino and business interests, before pushing his relationship with Gilda into ever more sado-masochistic depths. Literally transforming himself into Ballin, Johnny controls her every movement until she starts to behave more and more irresponsibly and wantonly in order to excite his jealousy and anger.

Rita Hayworth as Gilda sings
"Put The Blame On Mame".

That dress

Outside of the fashion business, few dresses can be said to have achieved iconic status: one that has is the strapless evening gown worn by **Rita Hayworth** in *Gilda*'s most famous scene, in which she sings "Put The Blame On Mame" while performing a very public "clothed striptease". Both the dress and the woman inside it have become the abiding image of the movie, her bold sexuality perfectly complemented by the slit-to-the-thigh, black satin dress and long black gloves.

The dress was the creation of Jean Louis Berthault (known simply as **Jean Louis**) who was then head costume designer at Columbia Studios (see p.192). The inspiration for the dress came from John Singer Sargent's no less infamous *Portrait of Madame X*, which caused a scandal when it was exhibited at the Paris Salon in 1884. The two dresses are similar but not identical: in Sargent's portrait the sitter – one Madame Gautreau – has thin chain-like straps supporting her dress. No such support was necessary for Hayworth who, when asked by a journalist what held up her dress, replied "two things".

After the emotional vicissitudes and the mental torture meted out to each other, Johnny and Gilda's sudden reconciliation at the film's end comes like a bolt from the blue – no doubt required by the Hays Office or Columbia's commercial imperatives. So it comes as something of a dramatic relief when Ballin suddenly reappears with his swordstick to make a claim for his wife. Who gets speared next should be left to the viewer to find out. However ludicrous the ending, it did not hurt the film's fortunes, as it took a whopping $3.75 million at the box office.

The Grifters

dir **Stephen Frears, 1990, US, 110m**

cast **Anjelica Huston, John Cusack, Annette Bening, Pat Hingle** *cin* **Oliver Stapleton** *m* **Elmer Bernstein**

The grifters – introduced in a slick 1970s-style triptych at the film's start – are Lilly Dillon (a gorgon-like **Anjelica Huston** in a blonde wig), her estranged son Roy (**John Cusack**) and his licentious girlfriend Myra Langtry (**Annette Bening**). Lilly handles playback money for ruthless Baltimore bookmaker Bobo Justus (Pat Hingle) while skimming her own take, Roy is a short-con artist working the twenties, the smack and the tat while fronting as a tool salesman, and Myra is an ex-long-con roper on her uppers. Understand any of this? If not, then check out the sidebar below.

After a foiled grift sees Roy floored by an irate barman, the last person he wants to see is his youthful mother, dropping by Los Angeles en route to a La Jolla race meet. Not that he has much say about it after she rushes him to hospital with an internal haemorrhage. Begrudging her life-saving intervention and her perverse efforts to control him, Roy is soon back on the grift and on his way to La Jolla for a weekend break with Myra.

Wise to Roy's alter ego – having spotted him working the tat on some gullible sailors – Myra does her lascivious best to rope him into the life of the long con. But any spark of interest in partnering her is rapidly dampened after visiting Lilly the following morning to settle his hospital bill. Shaken up, and with her hand still smarting from a cigar-inflicted wound courtesy of a punishing encounter with Bobo, Lilly warns her unsympathetic son: "Grift's like anything else Roy, you don't stand still, either go up or down. Usually down sooner or later."

Little wonder Roy gives the scheming Myra – whose bloodred wardrobe has begun alarmingly to resemble his mother's – the brush-off. Myra blames the rejection on Lilly, even accusing Roy of incest. His response is to beat her to the ground and then, in a moment of contrition and loathing, tell her: "That's not like me, I don't do this … You're disgusting, your mind is so filthy it's hard to look at you." No need, as all hell breaks loose after Myra proceeds to shop Lilly and her grifting skim to Bobo.

Stephen Frears's first US-based film was essentially neo-noir in its witty revivalism and knowing revisionism, and holds its own against classic noirs of the 1940s and 50s. This was achieved in part by the film's unspecific period setting and the verbatim use of the hard-boiled dialogue from Jim Thompson's original novel. Further layers of ambiguity were added by costume designer Richard Hornung's fusion of 1940s and 80s fashion in Lilly's and Myra's tailored outfits and the seamless integration of iconic Los Angeles noir locations into the film (like Roy's anodyne apartment in the Bryson Tower building, which is cited by Chandler in his 1943 novel *The Lady in the Lake*). But above all, it is in Frears's unshowy direction that *The Grifters* vies with the best of classic noir.

Unbelievably, Anjelica Huston only got the role of Lilly after Melanie Griffith turned it down and Cher became unaffordable.

Grifters slang

grifter a short-con operator

mark subject to be conned

playback money controlled betting to protect bookies from excessive long-shot pay-outs

long-end big con/long-con a complex well-planned scam involving multiple grifters

tat dice fixing

roper a grifter (usually an attractive woman) who inveigles a mark into a loss-making scam

smack crooked coin tossing

working the twenties flipping/palming $20 for $10 bills to ensure maximum payback when buying drinks etc in bars

However, Frears was swept away by the intensity of her acting, with the cumulative force of her performance reaching giddy guignol heights in her final confrontation with Roy. On the run from Bobo, and having ruthlessly swapped identities with an avaricious Myra after a bloody motel encounter, she will do anything to prize her son's grifting stash: "What if I told you I wasn't really your mother? ... You'd like that wouldn't you? Sure you would ... And why would you like that, Roy?" Likened by screenwriter Donald Westlake to rounds in a boxing match, these exchanges mix menace, unspoken lust and a shockingly bloody outcome with a numbingly cold-hearted aftermath. Westlake would later recall Huston's bone-chilling wails echoing throughout the studio building and Cusack remembered her being carried off the set at the end of the encounter: "We didn't call cut and she didn't say 'I think that was good' ... they carted her off weeping."

Gun Crazy

dir **Joseph H. Lewis 1949, US, 87m, b/w**
cast **Peggy Cummins, John Dall, Berry Kroeger, Morris Carnovsky, Anabel Shaw** *cin* **Russell Harlan** *m* **Victor Young**

Obsessive noir protagonists do not come much stranger than *Gun Crazy*'s Bart Tare (**Rusty Tamblyn**) who always carries a gun, saying to his friends: "Nobody can tell what might happen." And nothing

The Hampton Bank hold up

Take one stretch Cadillac, strap two soundmen to its luggage carrier, then squeeze in a script girl, head grip, cameraman and director. Ensure this leaves enough room for two actors, the camera with its 1000ft film magazine and a hefty length of two 2x12ft ply board greased together, on which the whole unwieldy rig sits and slides. It might sound like the antics of the *Wacky Races*' Anthill mob, but this is how **Joseph H. Lewis** prepared for streamlining a complex 17-page bank heist into one three-minutes-twenty-seconds continuous shot.

Without the help of back projection, the back-seat camera records Bart and Annie's nervy drive from city outskirts to Hampton's downtown bank, the concealed button mikes eavesdropping on their nervy, impro-vised exchanges. Bart enters the bank leaving Annie primed for the getaway. Then suddenly the camera nudges forward and pans to witness Annie's flirtatious exchange with a passing policeman turn ugly as Bart flees the bank and the two make their urgent escape. It's only now that the camera moves in on Annie's thrilled expression as she looks behind for pursuers, enticing the audience into what Myron Meisel in his book on Lewis calls "a dizziness of irresponsibility".

The hold-up – filmed in two takes with no rehearsal – was so realistic that off-screen bystanders hollered: "They held up the bank! They held up the bank!" The response of the studio was similarly hysterical as Lewis was inundated with calls enquiring how this incredible sequence had been achieved. His audacious docu-mentary technique would be rapidly subsumed into Hollywood film grammar and the scene would continue to influence and impact down the years on films from *Bonnie And Clyde* (1967) to *Reservoir Dogs* (1992).

much does in the sleepy railroad town of Cashville while Bart attends the eighth grade and is brought up by his sister (**Anabel Shaw**) – that is, until his beloved handgun is confiscated. Still gun-fixated, Bart bungles an attempt to steal a replacement and is soon on his way to reform school, followed by army service "teaching guys to shoot".

An adult Bart (**John Dall**) returns home to a sister transformed into a domestic drudge and an awkward reunion with childhood chums Dave (**Nedrick Young**) and Clyde (**Harry Lewis**), now stultified into the town's local hack and sheriff. So, offered the chance to join a visit-ing carnival after a sexually charged, victorious shootout with main attraction Annie Laurie Starr (**Peggy Cummins**), he is soon assisting the shapely sharpshooter in his own Wild West buckskin costume.

When Bart is sacked by Packett (**Berry Kroeger**), Laurie's jilted partner, the couple marry, but within a brisk ten-shot riches-to-rags montage are soon penniless in a flea-ridden hotel. Bart suggests getting employment with gun-manufacturers Remington, however Laurie, fresh from her bath, wants "to do a bit of living" with "a guy with spirit" and threatens to walk out unless he joins her in a life of crime. Unable to resist combining his two competing obsessions – handling guns and Laurie's quivering bathrobed body – Bart and his trigger-happy wife are soon staging elaborate hold-ups, rapidly becoming noir's most intoxicated lovers on the run.

Granted unprecedented freedom by his producers, a generous thirty-day shooting schedule and a $500,000 budget, **Joseph H. Lewis** treated the film like an über B-movie, applying all he had learned from a decade grafting on Poverty Row. He was, however, astute enough to ensure that key crew members were all A-list technicians: writer – the blacklisted **Dalton Trumbo** (fronted by Millard Kaufman), responsible for carving some sense into Mackinlay Kantor's screenplay, which ran to over 180 pages; composer – **Victor Young**; production designer – **Gordon Wiles**, and cinematographer – **Russell Harlan**. The main actors were less experienced, with Dall having just four films behind him and 24-year-old British actress Cummins in her Hollywood debut. The casting gamble paid off, as their combination of awkwardness and carnal chemistry – in their carnival encounter, Lewis instructed them to pretend to be a female and male dog on heat – would be an essential factor in the film's status as one of the cult B-movie classics of all time.

Lewis took a hands-on approach to filming, and, for the uninterrupted shot of Bart's impetuous and fateful return to Laurie after their final heist "lay right across the hood of that car, holding on for dear life, operating a mounted camera by means of a hand switch". Fleet Southcott's superb camera operation was no less inventive, as in the film's opening in which the camera moves towards a young Bart sprawled on a noirish nocturnal wet city street. Bart's helter-skelter emotions were also reflected in unorthodox editing, for example as he exits the bottom of the frame when being warned out of Cashville by Dave and Clyde, after which the camera dollies into his anguished medium close-up.

Having returned to his sister's house, Bart and Laurie flee to the San Lorenzo mountains and their final swamp-filled refuge. Eschewing a real location, Lewis staged it on a fogbound soundstage and used a shadowy reed effect (inspired by various duck shooting trips) to cast eerie bar-like shadows over the fugitives. As the couple wake up to the sounds of the approaching Dave and Clyde, and a dizzying array of dolly shots swoop ever closer to their desperate close-ups, Bart shoots Laurie before she can open fire. Traditional readings posit that he dies protecting his friends, but noir historian Jim Kitses is more convincing when he writes: "Bart despatches his love to protect her from herself, and the shedding of more blood."

In A Lonely Place

dir **Nicholas Ray 1950, US, 93m, b/w**

cast **Humphrey Bogart, Gloria Grahame, Frank Lovejoy, Art Smith** *cin* **Burnett Guffey** *m* **George Antheil**

"There goes Dix again" remarks Fran Randolph (**Alix Talton**) archly as her mercurial ex sends a precocious young film executive flying into a banquette. It might be just another evening at

Laurel Gray (Gloria Grahame) has second thoughts about her volatile lover Dix (Humphrey Bogart).

Paul's Restaurant for washed-up, embittered screenwriter Dixon Steele (**Humphrey Bogart**), but after picking up hat-check girl, Mildred Atkinson (**Martha Stewart**) – so that she can explain to him the plot of a bestseller he has no intention of adapting – the temperament of this most paranoid of noir protagonists will be tested beyond breaking point.

When Mildred is discovered strangled, Dix is questioned by his wartime buddy Det. Sgt Nicolai (**Frank Lovejoy**) and Capt. Lochner (**Carl Benton Reid**). His cynical posturing – "you plan to arrest me for lack of emotion?" – is cut short by an ambiguous alibi from his new neighbour, Laurel Gray (**Gloria Grahame**), who claims to have "noticed him because he looked interesting. I like his face". Sparks soon fly between the couple as Laurel parries Dix's impulsive advances with responses like "I said I liked it. I didn't say I wanted to kiss it." Barely 48 hours into their relationship, however, and Laurel has reciprocated Dix's impassioned avowals of love and put her fledgling Hollywood acting career on hold, becoming muse, cook and typist to the reinvigorated screenwriter, now hard at work adapting the bestseller.

With the hat-check murder still unsolved and Dix regarded as prime suspect, Lochner treats an indignant Laurel to a potted history of the celebrity screenwriter's well-publicized violent outbursts. No need, it turns out, as Dix's discovery of her clandestine visit to the police drives him into a psychotic rage. Careering recklessly down Mulholland Drive, he sideswipes a college boy's car, with only Laurel's terrified entreaties preventing him burying a rock into the hapless driver's face. Her faith in Dix's innocence shattered, Laurel is gradually left with no choice but to leave a disintegrating relationship with potentially fatal results.

Take a good look at Bogart's eyes in his rear-view mirror behind the credits, or his hooded features as he realizes that Laurel intends to leave him, and director **Nicholas Ray**'s words, "he was an image of our condition. His face was a living reproach", do not sound so grandiloquent. Bogart's intense performance was also influenced by years of bitter contractual squabbles with Jack Warner and constant fights with producers and agents.

Ray's involvement in the film was no less personal, but certainly more bizarre. He slept on set rather than invite speculation about the end of his marriage to Grahame, and ensured that her RKO loan-out contract granted him "full professional control over everything she did, from 9 to 6, six days a week" – the kind of control that Dix would like to have exerted over Laurel. He also based the Beverly Patio complex (home to Dix and Laurel) on his first Hollywood home – his complex and symbolic use of interconnecting courtyard, staircase and increasingly claustrophobic apartments reflecting an internalized noir vision. When the film does embrace noir stylistics, it is in explosive jolts – unnerving visual equivalents to Dix's psychotic outbursts, such as the sudden, paranoid close-up of Dix and Laurel as their romantic reverie is interrupted by an off-duty policeman.

Ray and Bogart were unhappy with the film's first ending, which stuck closely to Holt's screenplay. In this scenario, Dix, his innocence proved, becomes enraged by Laurel's suspicions and efforts to escape. He strangles her, before completing his screenplay and getting picked up by the police. Instead the re-shot, and largely improvised, scene sees Dix's uncontrollable throttling of Laurel interrupted by Lochner's urgent and revelatory call. Even with this last-minute reprieve, it is now too late for the couple to salvage their battered relationship, as Dix leaves the apartment under Laurel's gaze in an ending as deflated and sombre as any in noir.

The Killers

dir **Robert Siodmak, 1946, US, 105m, b/w**
cast **Edmond O'Brien, Burt Lancaster, Ava Gardner, Albert Dekker, Charles McGraw, William Conrad** *cin* **Woody Bredell** *m* **Miklós Rósza**

At night two men drive through New Jersey, the silhouettes of their backs contrasting starkly with the front-projected road ahead. It's an urgent and frightening image, made more so by **Miklós Rózsa's** thunderous and ominously repetitious refrain. The men enter downtown Brentwood casting giant shadows under the streetlights. As they turn to walk towards Henry's Diner their stern faces momentarily catch the ambient light to reveal Max (**William Conrad**) and Al (**Charles McGraw**). They have come to kill ex-boxer "The Swede" (**Burt Lancaster**, in his debut role).

As Max and Al prepare themselves for the hit in the Swede's favoured diner, Woody Bredell's unnerving wide-angle and deep-focus cinematography creates a confined and claustrophobic atmosphere, accentuating their faces by top- and low-angled lighting. It comes as a relief when the Swede doesn't appear, instead stoically awaiting his fate in his spartan lodgings. One of noir's great existentialist heroes, he says to his informant Nick: "There's nothing I can do about it … I'm through with all that running around … I did something wrong, once."

This is where Hemingway's story ends, but in John Huston's and Anthony Veiller's adaptation the killers track down the Swede and empty their revolvers into his supine body, the explosive discharges casting ghastly flashes on their emotionless faces. From this narrative springboard, the writers adopted a *Citizen Kane*-like structure, introducing Jim Reardon (played by noir everyman **Edmond O'Brien**), whose investigation into the Swede's life insurance policy leads him through a rogue's gallery of the dead man's friends and criminal colleagues. It's through their eleven interconnecting and non-chronological flashbacks that the Swede's doomed trajectory emerges.

There is a heartbreaking nobility to the Swede – few other noir protagonists suffer so much and with such resignation. His boxing career cruelly foreshortened by a pummelling that leaves his right hand crushed, he gets involved with criminal Jake the Rake (**John Miljan**) and his underworld cronies. Transfixed by Kitty Collins (**Ava Gardner**) singing "The More I Know Of Love" at one of Jake's parties, he ditches good girl Lilly (**Virginia Christine**) and is soon taking the rap for a hawked diamond-encrusted spider brooch Kitty

The Prentiss hat factory payroll heist

Director **Robert Siodmak** once claimed that he would be happy "if, out of an entire feature, I can place on film 500ft of pure cinema". In *The Killers* he achieved this in the heist sequence, which was filmed "entirely in one take, utilizing 18 camera stops and upwards of 60 changes of focus". Here a raised camera on a crane follows the criminals entering through the factory gates, tracking with them as it cranes up to show the payroll robbery and moves to cover their getaway. It is an exhilarating shot, leading Siodmak to say: "Everything was very confused, with people not knowing where they ought to be, a car backed up wrong and left in the middle of the road … but curiously enough the result turned out to give just the right effect." Its criminal authenticity received the stamp of approval from underworld figures at a clandestine preview of the film arranged by its well-connected producer Mark Hellinger.

is spotted wearing. By the time he gets out of jail, Kitty is back as the mistress of crime boss Big Jim Colfax (**Albert Dekker**), but all it takes is one lazy stretch of her leg for the Swede to be joining the gang's payroll heist. Duped by Kitty into believing he is being set up, he holds up the gang, only to find himself on the receiving end of "the double cross of all double crosses".

Producer **Mark Hellinger** wanted the film to have a newsreel quality, which in Siodmak and Bredell's hands became a kind of heightened realism. As Swede is "murdered" by his opponent in the boxing ring, Bredell replaces the usual bright white lighting with distanced overhead lights which create unsettling deep shadows. Lighting Gardner in her iconic introductory scene, Bredell only used the lamps on the tables to give "a soft glow, making her appear even more sensuous", and even talked her into wearing no make-up: "All we did was rub a little Vaseline into her skin for a sheen effect."

The real noir protagonist in *The Killers* is Reardon. His obsessive quest to discover the reasons behind the Swede's murder has disastrous consequences, and all that his work achieves – as his long-suffering boss points out – is to lower his company's basic insurance rate by one-tenth of a cent. His behaviour implies that he would have done better in the world of Colfax than of the Swede, especially as he flirts with Kitty: "I would have liked to have known the old Kitty Collins." His expression as Kitty implores the dying Colfax to plead her innocence is a far cry from the Swede's doomed nobility.

The Killing

dir **Stanley Kubrick, 1956, US, 84m**
cast Sterling Hayden, Coleen Gray, Elisha Cook Jr, Marie Windsor, Jay C. Flippen *cin* Lucien Ballard *m* Gerald Fried

Fresh from a five-year stretch in Alcatraz, Johnny Clay (**Sterling Hayden**) describes his current associates to his anxious fiancée, Fay (**Coleen Gray**): "None of these men are criminals in the usual sense, they've all got jobs, they all live seemingly normal, decent lives, but they got their problems and they've all got a little larceny in 'em" Cast from a cohort of noir's finest character actors,

Johnny Clay (Sterling Hayden) drops off a concealed gun in *The Killing*'s meticulously planned heist.

this disparate group will help coordinate Johnny's latest caper – a doomed $2 million racetrack heist, set to unravel in a tense series of interweaving and overlapping flashbacks.

The heist's inside men are weaselly window teller George Peatty (**Elisha Cook Jr**), desperate to impress his tramp-ish, two-timing wife Sherry (**Marie Windsor**), and world-weary barman Mike O'Reilly (**Joe Sawyer**), driven to crime by the medical needs of his invalid partner Ruthie (**Dorothy Adams**). On the outside, it is up to bent book-keeper Marvin Unger (**Jay C. Flippen**), who holds more than just a paternal torch for Johnny, to float the operation, while corrupt patrolman Randy Kennan (**Ted De Corsia**) plays inconspicuous bagman. This just leaves philosophizing wrestler Maurice (played by Kubrick's chess chum **Kola Kwariani**) and squinting, mumbling marksman Nikki Arcane (**Timothy Carey**) to provide essential diversions: creating a fracas in the cavernous betting hall and picking off Lansdowne Stakes favourite Red Lightning mid-race respectively.

In the event all goes according to plan, and during the ensuing commotion it's Johnny who sidles into the darkened bowels of the betting hall and, locating a concealed automatic rifle and donning a surreal clown mask, successfully holds up the cashiers' office. But despite the gang's methodical efficiency and rigorous time-keeping – increasingly at odds with a chronologically muddled and self-important voice-over – the heist will prove fatally flawed due to the avaricious schemes of Sherry and her slick hoodlum boyfriend Val Cannon (Vince Edwards).

A pivotal work in **Stanley Kubrick**'s fledgling movie career, *The Killing*'s $320,000 budget, provided by United Artists and his partner and producer James B. Harris, meant that the film was a quantum leap from his previous home-made independents. But it's the radically splintered flashback structure (taken verbatim from **Lionel White**'s novel *Clean Break*) and the numbingly nihilistic closing scenes that give *The Killing* the edge over other heist movies, such as *The Asphalt Jungle* (1950) or *Plunder Road* (1957).

Blurring the lines between guerrilla filmmaking and traditional Hollywood methods (something he was to pursue throughout his maverick career), Kubrick took a hands-on approach to filming, even going as far as using a hand-held camera to suggest George's point-of-view as he staggers through the shocking after-effects of his revenge on Val. Kubrick's eye for high-contrast black-and-white cinematography (honed by his lengthy apprenticeship as a *Look* magazine photographer) is also much in evidence, notably in the scenes when the gang move in and out of darkness, lit by a sole over-head light, as they finalize the heist. Or in the low-angled shots of Sherry and Val discussing their plans, a standard lamp eerily casting shadows onto the faces. Whether by Ballard or Kubrick, the film's striking cinematography would prompt *Time* magazine to write of how "the camera watches the whole shoddy show with the keen eye of a terrier stalking a pack of rats".

The film's final unravelling sees the fatally wounded George stagger back to his apartment to avenge the faithless Sherry as Johnny puts plan B into action, heading straight to the airport with the money for a later split. It is now that his calm starts to implode as he buys "the biggest suitcase he can find" and proceeds to decant the money. Unable to take the suitcase as hand luggage, he watches helplessly as it falls off a swerving luggage carrier only to spew its bank notes into swirling eddies scattered by the plane's propellers. As Fay tries to rush him to the nearest taxi, George can barely summon the energy to escape, merely murmuring "What's the difference?" as two feds walk menacingly towards him.

Kiss Kiss Bang Bang

dir Shane Black, 2005, US 99m
cast Robert Downey Jr, Val Kilmer, Michelle Monaghan, Corbin Bernsen, Larry Miller, Rockmond Dunbar *cin* Michael Barrett *m* John Ottman

Take a script rejected by every Hollywood studio, an elusive director emerging from a decade-long struggle with writer's block and two notoriously difficult lead actors. It hardly sounds the ideal springboard for the first significant neo-noir of the twenty-first century. And yet with a meagre $15 million budget and a lean 35-day schedule, **Shane Black**, the wünderkind screenwriter who had revitalized the action genre with *Lethal Weapon* only to see his savvy screenplays *The Last Boy Scout* and *The Long Kiss Goodbye* mauled by the studios, was back. This time, however, he was behind the camera armed with a script so tight "you could bounce a dime" off it.

Taking the 1940s pulp novel *Bodies Are Where You Find Them* by **Brett Halliday** (aka David Dresser) as a loose starting point, *Kiss Kiss Bang Bang* mixes romance, thriller and mystery elements with dazzling brio. It abounds in noir pastiche, plundering Chandler's impenetrable plotlines – with telling section titles such as *Trouble Is My Business* and *The Simple Art Of Murder* – and with a private eye, Harry Lockhart (**Robert Downey Jr**), who interrupts his flashback narration with challenging and cajoling voice-over asides. At one

Noir moving in a comic and violent direction.

point he brings the film to a frame-stopping halt to comment on his poor narrating skills. Chandler's Philip Marlowe never had it so tough…

Harry is not even a bona-fide private investigator. Rather he is a bungling ex-burglar who, via a series of outlandish mishaps, fetches up in Los Angeles being groomed for the role of a movie detective. Fiction becomes reality while on work experience with slick Hollywood private eye Perry Van Shrike, aka Gay Perry (a coiffed, butch **Val Kilmer** with a hint of real-life LA dick Anthony Pellicano), when a routine stakeout culminates in the unlikely duo fishing their strangled subject out of a nearby lake. When the corpse reappears in Harry's hotel room, the bickering couple are thrown into a gaudy LA world of apparent kidnapping, murder and extortion.

Toss into the mix Harry's unrequited childhood love for Harmony Faith Lane (**Michelle Monaghan**), now a disillusioned Hollywood hopeful, and the case of her shot-up little sister, and a lovelorn Lockhart is soon masquerading as a private eye for real. His ham-fisted investigation leads him and a reluctant Perry to businessman Harlan Dexter (**Corbin Bernsen**) and his noirish psychiatric clinic. An ex-actor, Dexter's CV includes the role of TV detective Johnny Gossamer, whose colourful exploits in tales such as *Straighten Up And Die Right* prepare the couple for the outlandish plot twists ahead.

Despite receiving universally glowing reviews and euphoric festival screenings at Cannes and London, *Kiss Kiss Bang Bang* suffered a lacklustre, limited release. It is too early to say whether it will become a post-release cult classic in the style of *Blade Runner* or *Shawshank Redemption*, but its DVD format is ideal for scrutinizing Black's efforts to realize "all these ideas I had and how I felt about private eye novels. I wanted to cram it all into one picture."

And crammed it is, with the dizzying effect that *Kiss Kiss Bang Bang* appears more meta-noir than neo-noir. It captures the self-reflexive, mocking tone of Chandler and classic film noir and then takes it in wildly unexpected directions – usually blackly and comically violent. One critic described *Kiss Kiss* as a cross between *Chinatown* and *As Good As It Gets* and it is not too far off the mark. That is, leaving aside the most imaginative, climactic car chase and epilogue of the last decade, all of which begins with wincing torture by electrodes, a coffin with a life of its own and concludes with a would-be detective turned bloodied, redemptive knight.

Kiss Me Deadly

dir Robert Aldrich, 1955, US, 105m, b/w
cast Ralph Meeker, Albert Dekker, Paul Stewart, Maxine Cooper, Gaby Rodgers *cin* Ernest Laszlo *m* Frank De Vol

By the mid-1950s the private detective in noir had all but hung up his trenchcoat and fedora; stragglers included veteran English director/producer Victor Saville's maverick productions of **Mickey Spillane**'s best-selling Mike Hammer private eye novels, the best of which was **Robert Aldrich**'s *Kiss Me Deadly*.

As the film's guerrilla crew tore into its meagre 22-day schedule, neither Aldrich nor Saville could have guessed they were embarking on a film so radical in technique and apocalyptic in vision that it would, in Paul Schrader's words, render "for all practical purposes the forties private-eye … defunct". With its heady atmosphere of noir, horror, Cold War nuclear paranoia and veiled anti-McCarthyism, *Kiss Me Deadly* would atomize the parameters of classical private eye noir forever. Reviewers were not so appreciative: the *Hollywood Reporter* was perplexed by the plot, the Legion of Decency black-balled it and the British banned it outright.

Aldrich and screenwriter **A.I. Bezzerides** shared a healthy scepticism for Spillane's original ultra-right-wing story about a private detective's vengeful exploits in Albany, New York state's unforgiving capital. Instead Aldrich wanted to depict his "utter contempt and loathing for the cynical, fascistic private eye", while Bezzerides transformed Hammer into a slick, amoral bedroom dick, hopelessly out of his depth in a self-serving quest for the mysterious "great whatsit" throughout a hellish Los Angeles.

The film screeches into life on a pitch-black Calabras freeway, its soundtrack dominated by the rasping sobs of hysterical asylum escapee Christina (**Cloris Leachman**), clad only in a trenchcoat as she attempts to flag down passing cars. In a frenzy of jumpcuts she manages to stop Hammer (**Ralph Meeker**), almost totalling his pristine Jaguar. His unsympathetic, gnomic response, "You almost wrecked my car! Well? Get in!", is almost as disconcerting as the subsequent reverse rolling credits, which segue into the middle distance. Three days later, Hammer regains consciousness in a Los Angeles hospital, having miraculously survived incarceration, a rigged car crash by Christina's pursuers and witnessed her horrific, ear-splitting torture-to-death by pliers. This is just the first ten minutes.

Convinced that the Rossetti-poetry-spouting Christina – really a scientist held in involuntary custody by government agents – must be "connected with something big", Hammer reins in his divorce work for more profitable freelance footslogging. His expression fixed in an increasing rictus of incomprehension, unfazed by bomb-rigged cars or switchblade-wielding assailants, Hammer pummels his way to Christina's pursuers, Carl Evello (the effortlessly sinister **Paul Stewart**) and his sidekicks Sugar Smallhouse (**Jack Lambert**) and Charlie Max (**Jack Elam**), via a grotesque gallery of terrified Angelenos, all unfortunate enough to be linked to Christina and her coveted device. Meanwhile it is up to Hammer's exploited, curvaceous secretary Velda (**Maxine Cooper**) – taking a break from woo-baiting prospective clients' husbands – to provide essential detective know-how.

The production's breathtaking B-movie schedule would result in glaring technical errors, such as mikes, lights and actors' floor marks coming into view in key scenes. However, this barely matters in a film whose "inventiveness" François Truffaut described as so rich "that we don't know what to look at". Look out for impossible camera positions (behind Gabrielle's bedhead or placed at the rear of the device deposited in its locker) or the surreal overhead shots of Gabrielle's Bunker Hill Jalisco Hotel rooms, with their obtuse banister shadows.

Pumped full of the truth drug Sodium Pentathol, corpses rapidly piling up around him and the excoriating words of Lt Pat Chambers

(**Wesley Addy**) ringing in his ears – "You penny ante gumshoe. You thought you saw something big. Let him go to hell. Let the big slob sit there and think about his girl, what's likely to happen to her" – Hammer lurches towards his climactic encounter with the mysterious Dr Soberin (**Albert Dekker**), his wayward accomplice Gabrielle (**Gaby Rodgers**) and the kidnapped Velda. It is only now that he gets to see, in Aldrich's words, "what havoc he has caused". Although what inflammatory climax and contaminated nourish future awaits this ground-zero foursome can barely be envisaged.

Kiss Of Death

dir Henry Hathaway, 1947, US, 98m, b/w
cast Victor Mature, Richard Widmark, Brian Donlevy,
Coleen Gray, *cin* Norbert Brodine *m* David Buttolph

When **Victor Mature** was told that actors were not accepted in the exclusive Los Angeles Country Club, he wisecracked: "Hell, I'm no actor, and I've got 28 pictures and a scrapbook of reviews to prove it!" However, take one look at his subtle performance as ex-con and stool pigeon Nick Bianco in *Kiss Of Death* and his two-dimensional image as "Hollywood's beautiful hunk" takes on a noirish shade.

A year on the outside, and rehabilitation still eludes Nick. Jobless and with no Christmas presents for his wife and two daughters, he opts for a disastrous Christmas Eve jewellery heist which ends with a twenty-year stretch. Despite pressure to squeal from Assistant DA DeAngelo (**Brian Donlevy**), Nick – hoping to protect his family – keeps schtum. Three years into his prison sentence, however, he learns of his wife's suicide and makes a deal with DeAngelo: he will give information about his accomplices in return for a visit to his girls, parole and a new identity.

With a job in a bricklayer's yard, a faithful new wife, Nettie (**Coleen Gray**), and his kids back, Nick's worries are over. But not for long. Recalled by DeAngelo to gather evidence on his fellow Sing Sing con, the psychotic Tommy Udo (**Richard Widmark**, remarkable in his debut role), Nick is subsequently requested to

Ex-con (Victor Mature) and his wife (Coleen Grey) look suitably alarmed in a *Kiss Of Death* publicity shot.

give evidence in Udo's murder trial. Catastrophically, Udo, who has a liking for shooting squealers in the belly "so they can roll around for a long time, thinking it over", is found not guilty.

Kiss Of Death was one of a handful of so-called "semi-realist" noirs made in the 1940s, which pioneered the use of real locations. Wherever possible actual locales were used, including the Chrysler Building (where the heist takes place), the Criminal Courts Building (where Nick is sentenced) and Sing Sing (its factory workshop is where Nick hears about his wife's suicide). Director Hathaway even ensured cast and crew were "transported to" and "processed through" the Tombs prison and Sing Sing "as if they were convicts".

This rehearsal procedure clearly worked on Oscar-nominated Widmark, whose Tommy Udo rates as one of noir's greatest psychopaths. With a wig that lowered his hairline and beset by terrible stage fright, Widmark peppers his delivery with unhinged giggles and toothy leers, interspersed with throwaway lines such as "Picked up for shoving a man's ears off his head – driving ticket stuff!" He is the nightmare antithesis of Nick: driven ("can't stand sleeping, that's for squits"), drug-addled and amoral. In one chilling scene, he terrorizes, binds and then despatches a fellow hood's wheelchair-bound mother down a tenement staircase with one brief hideous smile. No wonder Nick is prepared to do anything to rid himself of this maniac.

Kiss Of Death is a profoundly uneasy and ambiguous film. Sentimental or quasi-religious scenes of Nick and family continually jar against the film's gritty location work and harsh story. Never more so than in Nick's first visit to his eerily well-adjusted girls in the orphanage, or his cloying farewell to his family while being menaced by one of Udo's men (or so he thinks) at a desolate, wind-swept railway station. Throughout, there is an angelic voice-over by one of noir's few female narrators, the optimistic Nettie. Even when Nick is finally stretchered off with five bullets in the stomach, courtesy of a cackling Udo, her voice intones: "Sometimes out of the worst comes the best. Mr DeAngelo got what he wanted, Nick got what he wanted and I got all I ever wanted, I got Nick." The kind of future in store for a man who has taken this kind of punishment as well as being a well-publicized stool pigeon hardly bears thinking about. Will Nick have the stomach for it?

Klute

dir Alan J. Pakula, 1971, US, 114m

cast Jane Fonda, Donald Sutherland, Charles Cioffi, Roy Scheider, Vivian Nathan *cin* Gordon Willis *m* Michael Small

Nothing much happens in small-town Tuscarora, that is until respected family man Tom Gruneman (**Robert Milli**) goes missing, leaving a trail of obscene letters to New York call girl Bree Daniel (**Jane Fonda**). Time for his best friend John Klute (**Donald Sutherland**) to ditch his Penn State police badge, turn private investigator and head to New York under the employ of Gruneman's boss, Peter Cable (**Charles Cioffi**). After six months of FBI surveillance, Bree is still getting heavy-breathing calls and has started being stalked.

When Klute's attempts to interview the call girl are rebuffed, he stakes out in her tenement basement, recording her explicit telephone conversations and tailing her with an obsessiveness that is worryingly similar to that of her stalker. Threatening to hand over the incriminating tapes to the authorities, and resisting her attempted seduction, Klute questions Bree about Gruneman and whether he could be an ex-client. When their conversation is interrupted by the sound of the stalker hovering on her roof – shortly to evade Klute through a terrifying maze of descending torch-lit, dilapidated rooms – Bree warily agrees to help the detective.

So begins their journey into New York's underbelly, where they come up against Bree's former pimp Frank Ligourin (**Roy Scheider**), brothel madams and two fellow prostitutes. The problem is that nobody recognizes Gruneman's photo. Eventually a horrified Klute realizes that his investigation has led the sex-offender-turned-murderer to the third victim able to identify him – a fact of which the audience has been frustratingly aware from the first menacing shots of Cable stalking Bree or repeatedly playing recordings of her call girl routine.

Meanwhile an uneasy love affair has developed between Klute and an increasingly disturbed Bree, as she is torn between returning to Ligourin's world or an uncertain future with the investigator. But, with her apartment trashed and her clothes shredded by a maniacal Cable, she opts for Ligourin. Klute responds by attacking the pimp, only to receive a retaliatory scissor swipe from a hysterical Bree. On her own and friendless in New York, the call girl is now an easy target.

Throughout the film Bree's anxieties are voiced in intense sessions with her psychotherapist (**Vivian Nathan**). These mostly straight-to-camera monologues have a disturbing tendency to overlap into a voice-over undermining Bree's more intimate scenes with Klute. They also showcase Fonda's powerful performance in a role for which she had prepared meticulously and which was to win her a well-deserved Oscar. Here was a new gender-busting noir heroine, combining a mass of contradictory qualities – the complex traits of a controlling whore, a compulsive *femme fatale*, an angst-ridden victim to a would-be good woman.

To accentuate Bree's nocturnal, claustrophobic existence Pakula and cinematographer **Gordon Willis** framed many shots "with the back of another character in front to mask a part of the screen". A further sense of alienation was achieved by filming her apartment as if it was "at the end of a long tunnel". Tense verticals constantly contrast with the film's horizontal Panavision format in shots of lift shafts, staircases and in a vertiginous plunge pan from Cable's glacier-like office building. Willis's highly expressive manipulation of light and shade reaches its apogee in Bree's final confrontation with an incensed Cable. Forced to listen to the graphic recording of a fellow-prostitute's murder, Bree's terrified face is almost completely silhouetted before emerging out of the shadows.

Surviving Cable's assault after Klute's last-minute arrival, Bree is all set to leave her deserted apartment to go to Tuscaroro with Klute. Ominously, she is wearing the outfit she wore when turning her first trick in the film and her voice-over, taken from a session with her shrink, undercuts the intimate departure: "I know enough about myself to know that whatever lies in store for me is not going to be … housekeeping for somebody in Tuscarora and darning socks." She adds: "I've no idea what's going to happen … Maybe I'll come back. You'll probably see me next week." However long it takes, the implication is that Ligourin and his world will be waiting.

L.A. Confidential

dir Curtis Hanson, 1997, US, 132m
cast Kevin Spacey, Russell Crowe, Kim Basinger,
Guy Pearce, Danny DeVito *cin* Dante Spinotti *m* Jerry
Goldsmith

Working on *L.A. Confidential* (1990) – the third novel in his celebrated LA quartet – **James Ellroy** wanted "to write the biggest, baddest, ugliest, deepest, darkest crime novel of all time set in LA, my fatherland throughout the 1950s". Sounds outlandish? Then try staggering through Ellroy's ferocious quasi-cinematic onslaught on the senses, with its characters mired in civil, media and police corruption, mixed with plotlines unplumbed since Chandler's heyday. Film rights were soon snapped up but who could wrestle this four-hundred-page beast into a manageable film?

Chief volunteer was long-term Angelino **Curtis Hanson**, a former film journalist turned maverick screenwriter/director. His co-screenwriter **Brian Helgeland** remembers *L.A. Confidential* as "a project where I got taken right to the brink of what I had to give". Excising great swathes of head-spinning backstories and extraneous characters, Hanson and Helgeland concentrated the action around three interlinked events: the Hollywood precinct riot at the film's start, aka "Bloody Christmas", in which six Chicano inmates are set upon by a drunken, racist LAPD mob; the Nite Owl Massacre, where a number of late-night diners are butchered, and the subsequent capture, escape and brutal shooting of the apparent "Negro" suspects; and thereafter the startling investigations into the real perpetrators of the massacre and why.

Central to the investigations, and attempting to save their police careers, are ruthless careerist Det. Lt Edmund "Shotgun Ed" Exley (**Guy Pearce**); Det. Sgt Jack Vincennes (**Kevin Spacey**), aka "Hollywood Jack", the sartorially slick advisor to hit television cop show *Badge Of Honour* (read *Dragnet*); and Officer Wendell "Bud" White (**Russell Crowe**), the greatest maladjusted cop this side of 1950s psychotic noir. As events unfold, the detectives are drawn ever deeper into a world of high-class hookers and eventually to world-weary Veronica Lake look-alike Lynn Bracken (an awkward **Kim Basinger**), who becomes

Officers Smith (James Cromwell), Exley (Guy Pearce), White (Russell Crowe) and Vicennes (Kevin Spacey).

buffeted between her lover White and his nemesis Exley. Overseeing events are slippery pimp cum powerful business magnate Pierce Morehouse Patchett (**David Straithairn**), cadaverous police captain Dudley Smith (**James Cromwell**) and sleaze-monger Sid Hudgens (**Danny DeVito**), who is on hand to provide a helpful amount of exposition and who, like Bracken, exposes the rift between image and reality in a "city of manufactured dreams".

Steeped as he was in Los Angeles movie history and noir, Hanson "wanted to avoid telling the story through the lens of nostalgia" and hoped that "the audience … at a certain point would be allowed to forget they were watching a period movie at all". Even the inclusion of historical figures – the clunky bane of many a period movie – such as LA mobster Mickey Cohen, his sidekick Johnny Stompanato and Lana Turner are introduced seamlessly. Crucially, Hanson cast virtual unknowns – Australians Pearce and Crowe – in two lead parts. Six weeks of intensive rehearsal (including secondment with LAPD patrols and a rigorous study of old training films) helped create performances with a genuinely authentic ring.

L.A.Confidential wears its neo-noir style lightly, with cinematographer Dante Spinotti creating "a kind of naturalistic look where the audience would understand where the light was coming from in every scene." Noir staples such as skewed camera angles and chiaroscuro lighting hardly feature, except in the visceral Victory Motel shoot-out finale, in which White and Exley come head-to-head with the corrupt forces attempting to take over LA law enforcement.

However, in the coda Hanson does return to core neo-noir territory: as a bandaged, wired White and his fiancée Lynn Bracken bid farewell to the now decorated Captain Exley, she murmurs ruefully: "Some men get the world, others get ex-hookers and a trip to Arizona." Although, one look at Exley's stern world-weary expression at the film's close shows it is obvious that his world will still be mired in corruption and compromise.

The Lady From Shanghai

dir Orson Welles, 1948, US, 87m, b/w

cast Orson Welles, Rita Hayworth, Everett Sloane, Ted De Corsia, Glenn Anders *cin* Charles Lawton Jr *m* Heinz Roemheld

The last thing that Columbia chief Harry Cohn wanted was box-office sensation Rita Hayworth having her lustrous red locks removed. And yet, with much fanfare, her soon-to-be-ex husband Orson Welles oversaw the remodelling of her hair into a cropped peroxide curl for the role of iconic *femme fatale* Elsa in *The Lady From Shanghai*.

This would be the least of Cohn's worries as Welles and his team set off for seven weeks filming in the Pacific aboard Errol Flynn's yacht. The Conradesque expedition was plagued by fatalities, accidents and delays, which increased its schedule to fifteen weeks and the budget to $2 million. Welles's first cut of the film ran to two and a half hours and even when butchered down to eighty-odd minutes by editor Viola Lawrence, Cohn was offering $1000 to anyone who could explain the plot to him.

As waterfront agitator Michael O'Hara (Welles) rescues mysterious white Russian Elsa from a hold-up in Central Park, his blarney voice-over intones in flashback mode: "Once I had seen her I was not in my right mind" – a condition worth aspiring to when watching this most dream-like of noirs. Seduced by the charms of the supposedly vulnerable Elsa and persuaded by her crippled husband Arthur (**Everett Sloane**), "the world's greatest criminal lawyer", Michael agrees to captain their East–West Coast cruise via Panama. Hopelessly adrift, Michael falls prey to the machinations of his shark-like hosts as they holiday restively on the Mexican coastline, and has to contend with a couple of noir's true grotesques – Arthur's unctuous, scheming partner Grisby (**Glenn Anders**) and his snarling private detective Broome (**Ted De Corsia**), who travels incognito as the yacht's steward.

Docking in San Francisco and desperately needing cash to fund his planned elopement with the bewitching Elsa, Michael is duped into accepting Grisby's offer of $5000 in return for signing a phoney murder confession. The ruse is that the victim will be Grisby who, excessively paranoid, wants to disappear. The plan is apparently foolproof – with no corpse discovered, Michael's confession will be null and void. Before disappearing off to the South Seas, Grisby (with Elsa) intends to exploit his cast-iron alibi, but a blackmailing Broome and fatal rendezvous with a panicked Elsa puts paid to his scheme. When Michael ends up in the dock on a murder rap for Grisby, with a vengeful Arthur as his defence lawyer, his nightmare has barely begun.

Even in its bastardized form – with an inappropriate score (vetoed by Welles), contributions from three cinematographers, and jarring studio inserts – *The Lady From Shanghai* still rates as one of the greatest noirs. Stand-out episodes include Michael's vertiginous

Orson Welles's infatuated protagonist confronts the split personalities of Elsa Bannister (Rita Hayworth).

cliff-top conversation with the leering Grisby, full of low-angled shots, sweaty choker close-ups and suffused with a free-wheeling flavour more 1968 than 1948, and Michael's meeting with Elsa at the San Francisco aquarium, their breathless, erotic conversation subsumed by the ominous background images of octopus, sharks and conger eels.

The magic mirror maze

Mirrors play a significant role in film noir and often signal the duplicity or destructive vanity of those who gaze at them. They appear in compacts, wall hangings, vanity tables or – in *The Lady From Shanghai*'s spectacular example – a magic mirror maze. Here, in the culmination of Michael's Crazy House tour, he witnesses the shattering exchanges – both verbal and explosive – between unwelcome fellow participants Elsa and Arthur.

The maze was planned by Welles, cinematographer Charles Lawton Jr, and special effects wizard Lawrence W. Butler and was part of the Crazy House set which filled two conjoining Columbia soundstages. Its staggering 2912 square feet of "reflecting surface" comprised a series of twenty-four distortion and eighty 7x4ft plate glass mirrors – some of the latter two-way so that cameramen could film through their non-reflecting sides. Despite having been cut down from the scripted version, compromised by a ruthless studio re-edit and with a soundtrack which Welles disowned, the resulting 2-minute-15-second sequence is still a technical and symbolic *tour de force*.

The sequence starts with Elsa admitting her murderous guilt to Michael as their multiple images fragment and stretch away to infinity. Then, when Arthur appears all visual hell breaks loose. Triple split screens in which projected footage of Arthur vies with stills and fragments of Elsa crosscut with superimpositions of an enraged Arthur over close-ups of Elsa's eyes. As the couple repeatedly fire at each other, their multiple images/personalities fracture and explode until the scene's bloody finale.

Just how this spellbinding sequence was achieved still remains unknown. However, Welles did tell Peter Bogdanovich that had the studios approved his initial two-and-a-half-hour edit, the mirror maze sequence would have seemed a mere appendage to the rest of the Crazy House footage. Anybody looked in Columbia's vaults lately?

The film's surreal ending sees Michael's disoriented state of mind literally realized as he wakes up in the Crazy House, having escaped the confines of the courtroom to be catapulted into the clutches of Elsa and her sinister Chinese gangster accomplices. The sequence is now a pale shadow of what Welles intended, as Michael wanders like a somnambulist through a series of fantastical chambers before somersaulting down a 125ft elevated chute for his final confrontation with Elsa and Arthur.

Despite the loss of its original cut, Welles's abridged film certainly feels like a noir, with its themes of eroticism and greed, its flashback structure, inconclusive voice-over, camera technique, and its *femme fatale*. However, Welles also constantly undermines the narrator's character, pushes performances to extremes and produces a multiplicity of camera angles and extended tracking shots that often border on parody. Perhaps film historian Mark Graham is right to suggest that "the viewer, like Michael, is the butt of a prolonged practical joke. Yet, unlike Michael, we don't mind at all."

No wonder Cohn lost the plot.

The Last Seduction

dir John Dahl, 1994, US, 105m

cast Linda Fiorentino, Peter Berg, Bill Pullman, Bill Nunn

cin Jeffrey Jur *m* Joseph Vitarelli

The last place New Yorker Bridget (**Linda Fiorentino**) wants to wind up is upstate Beston or "cow country" as Harlan (**Bill Nunn**), the hapless private eye who is tailing her, dismisses it. Having absconded with the proceeds of a pharmaceutical drug deal – filched from her abusive medic husband Clay (**Bill Pullman**) – she wanders into a neighbourhood bar and the life of embittered claims adjuster Mike (**Peter Berg**).

In the next hundred or so minutes detective, doctor and local dupe will suffer spectacularly at the hands of the avaricious and predatory Bridget, twentieth-century cinema's last great *femme fatale*. So, hold onto your seats or – in the case of this trio of unfortunate male saps – your trousers.

The third and most accomplished of Dahl's neo-noir trilogy, after *Kill Me Again* (1989) and *Red Rock West* (1992), *Last Seduction* is a giddy mixture of preposterous B-movie plot and low-budget art film. It is also a variant on a strand of neo-noir, coined "rural" or "cowboy" noir, initiated by *Blood Simple* a decade earlier. Set in a landscape of motorcourt motels, faceless institutions and close-knit neighbour-hoods, it's the kind of society that Montana-raised Dahl: and the film's Arizona-based screenwriter Steve Barancik knew first-hand.

Across this colourless canvas swaggers a fearless Fiorentino – all monochrome power dressing, high heels and fiery lipstick. Not the first choice to play Bridget, Fiorentino advised Dahl: "There are only two women who can play this role, me and Barbara Stanwyck – and as she's dead you'll have to take me." Fortunately he did, letting her run riot with a blackly comic creation, whose actions so stretched credulity on the page that Dahl comments on the special edition DVD: "I kept on thinking, well she's going to be redeemable at some point, she just can't be all that bad ... then she never does a good thing in the movie." Not that it matters much to Mike, who at one point says to Bridget with not much conviction: "I thought we were going to be more than sex partners."

Linda Fiorentino as Bridget – the twentieth century's last great *femme fatale*.

Some hope ... until the ball-breaking Bridget breezes into a top executive position in Mike's insurance company, where she plans the grotesque downfall of her blinkered boyfriend, the "rural Neanderthal" or "designated fuck" as she witheringly calls him. By "bending the rules, playing with peoples' brains" and judiciously cross-referencing the company's database, she hatches a plan to market a bespoke killing service for the vengeful wives of cheating clients.

With the kind of scheming that would impress a Lucrezia Borgia or Lady Macbeth, Bridget cajoles Mike into joining her and playing would-be assassin. Without giving too much away, she does this by playing on Mike's shady past in Buffalo, his fear of his own repressed homosexuality and his desperate desire to leave Beston for the Big Apple – even if it is to "off" a client. However, it turns out that his unfortunate victim is more intimately linked to Bridget than he dares believe.

The Last Seduction's pragmatic visual style – sequences are often covered in one efficient camera move – takes its cue from time and budgetary constraints. Added to which, Joseph Vitarelli's jazzy clarinet-dominated soundtrack provides an incongruously upbeat counterbalance to the action on screen. So what makes it rise above being just a ferocious black comedy-thriller into one of the best neo-noirs of the last 25 years? The answer is Bridget Gregory, who not only reveals depths of seduction, guile and ruthless violence hitherto unseen in noir women, but who also balances her heinous exploits with a vulnerable streak that floors all her male antagonists.

Perhaps the last word should go to the cult 1990s website *The Last Seduction Club*, "dedicated in honor of Linda Fiorentino", which counselled: "We believe that women should be more like Bridget and less like helpless little fools." Fortunately for male saps everywhere, the website no longer seems to be online.

The Late Show

dir Robert Benton, 1976, US, 93m
cast Art Carney, Lily Tomlin, Bill Macy, Ruth Nelson, Howard Duff, Joanna Cassidy *cin* Charles Rosher Jr *m* Kenneth Wannberg

After thirty years working the mean streets of Los Angeles, private eye Ira Wells (**Art Carney**) has nothing to show for it except a perforated ulcer, a bust leg and a hearing aid. As he says ruefully to fellow old-timer Charlie Hatter (**Bill Macy**), "There aren't many guys left from the old days." And there are even less when his dying ex-partner Harry Regan (played by radio's Sam Spade and *Naked City* actor **Howard Duff**) turns up on his doorstep full of bullet holes.

Ditching any plans of retirement, Ira teams up with Harry's most recent client, kooky Margo Sperling (**Lily Tomlin**), and Charlie, who is still "the best information man in town". Margo desperately wants to find her beloved cat Winston, brutally kidnapped and threatened with strangulation by her ex, Brian Hemphill, who is demanding the $500 that Margo owes him. Despite the fact Ira doesn't talk much and Margo seldom draws breath, a see-sawing mutual attraction builds up between them.

Ira's journey through a Los Angeles of cheap apartments and Spanish colonial-style and neo-baronial piles (by public transport or Margo's beige Dodge van) embroils him in a plot as befuddling as any of the great private eye noirs of the 1940s. Though Margo is eventually reunited with Winston, after Hemphill is gunned down in front of Ira's rundown lodgings and his accomplice Ray Escobar winds up in his own refrigerator, the old detective is still no nearer finding the louse that nailed his partner.

He does, however, come across a terrified Laura Birdwell (**Joanna Cassidy**) in Escobar's apartment, and it's her mysterious disappearance from the crime scene that prompts Ira to re-investigate her estranged husband and Hemphill's ex-boss, Ron Birdwell (**Eugene Roche**). A smirking fence in monogrammed flannel jumpsuit, Birdwell fatally underestimates the detective, commenting sarcastically: "You're a little late Pop, about forty years." But along with his vengeful, adulterous wife and flash flunky Jeff Lamar (**John Considine**), Birdwell is inextricably linked to an escalating pile-up of corpses, as Ira is soon to discover.

Noir aficionados might wonder why an offbeat private eye comedy tagged "The nicest, warmest, funniest and most touching movie you'll ever see about blackmail, mystery and murder" is included in the Canon. However, look beyond Margo's dippy perspective on Ira's old-school professionalism and an incredibly bleak picture of 1970s Los Angeles begins to emerge. In part this is achieved by the cinematography of Charles Rosher Jr, who wanted to create "a colour equivalent of those old black-and-white Warner Bros films" and achieved his aim by mixing colours in such a way that "there was never a pure red or a pure blue or a pure yellow in this picture". The result brings an appropriately grubby, muted look to a Los Angeles bereft of sun and bright colours.

Grubbiness also defines most of the characters in the film. Everyone except Ira is on the make: from Margo, whose original theft of $500 while schlepping hot goods to Bakersfield results in Harry's murder, to Harry himself, who attempts to blackmail Birdwell after discovering incriminating evidence against Laura. Even Charlie turns two-bit chiseller as he attempts to extort money from the trigger-happy Birdwell just as the resourceful Ira is turning in the criminal trio to the police in a bloody finale that rivals *The Maltese Falcon* in intensity.

Waiting for a bus after Charlie's funeral, Ira and Margo's friendly bickering suggests that the soon-to-be-homeless detective might just move into Margo's next-door apartment and the couple team up professionally. There's even a hint at a more intimate relationship, but given that Ira had earlier justified his frugal existence with the words, "I'm by myself now because I like it that way. Nothing personal but I don't like to talk a lot, there's too much talk in the world as it is", the signs don't look that promising.

Laura

dir Otto Preminger 1944, US, 88m, b/w
cast Gene Tierney, Dana Andrews, Clifton Webb, Vincent Price, Judith Anderson *cin* Joseph LaShelle *m* David Raksin

Laura's tumultuous production history started poolside at **Darryl F. Zanuck**'s home in 1943. Here, in a classic Hollywood encounter, **Otto Preminger**, having clashed one too many times with the boss of Twentieth Century-Fox, was told that he would never direct again as long as Zanuck was studio head.

Undeterred, Preminger turned to developing **Vera Caspary**'s multi-narrated novel *Laura*, with some of Hollywood's finest writers. He then successfully lobbied to upgrade *Laura* to A-picture status, only to suffer the ignominy of seeing his work turned down by Hollywood's frontline directors – until the cash-strapped **Rouben Mamoulian** took on the job. Eighteen days into shooting, Mamoulian had still failed to put his stamp on the film, and Zanuck – appalled by the rushes – handed the directorial responsibilities over to Preminger.

Having mollified the suspicious actors, the new director quickly brought in cinematographer **Joseph LaShelle**, changed the sets, costumes, and replaced Azadia Newman's portrait of Laura with Frank Polony's painted-over photograph. With the film's technical

Laura's theme

Preminger wanted a specific musical theme to be linked to the sophisticated, and apparently dead, Laura. But Ira Gershwin refused permission for his first choice, "Summertime", and the film's composer **David Raksin** dissuaded him from using Duke Ellington's "Sophisticated Lady". That left Raksin just 48 hours to come up with an alternative. Working under intolerable pressure, further intensified by the news that his wife intended to leave him, he felt the last of his strength go, "and then – without willing it – I was playing the first phrase … and stumbled through it again and again in a sweat of catharsis and self-indulgence". The result was a haunting and song-like melody that recurs obsessively throughout the film, as if in acknowledgement that Laura dominates the thoughts of all the main characters – even when she's not there.

Such was the popularity of the music that fairly soon after the film's release **Johnny Mercer** was asked to add lyrics to the melody. The resulting song was first performed by Johnny Johnston on his radio show and became a hit for no less than four other performers in 1945 alone, including Dick Haymes and Woody Herman. Part of its success can be put down to the way Mercer's poignant, dreamy lyrics tapped in to the mood of the film without ever being too specific:

Laura is the face in the misty light,

Footsteps that you hear down the hall,

The laugh that floats on a summer night

That you can never quite recall…

team in place, Preminger now started undermining that Hollywood staple, the traditional murder mystery. First off, he took it from the drawing room into the hothouse atmosphere of Manhattan's acerbic *haut monde*, where a gruesome murder has just been committed. And then, in what has been justifiably described as "one of the great moments of postwar cinema", he introduced the eponymous victim/heroine (**Gene Tierney**) more than halfway into the film.

Laura starts with streetwise, taciturn cop Lt Mark McPherson (**Dana Andrews**) waiting to interview the journalist, social commentator and connoisseur Waldo Lydecker (**Clifton Webb**) in his sweltering objet-filled apartment. Lydecker, it transpires – via a dreamily subjective flashback recounted mellifluously to the detective – was Laura's mentor and confidant, who had moulded her from an ambitious designer into a beautiful, cultured and successful advertising executive. Completing Laura's inner circle are her spinster aunt, the pragmatic, cynical Ann Treadwell (**Judith Anderson**), and her fiancé, slippery Southern playboy Shelby Carpenter (**Vincent Price**). The fact that Shelby and Ann seem to be lovers adds just one more undercurrent of seething sexuality to this story of obsessive love and mistaken identity.

With few colleagues in evidence, McPherson appears to have carte blanche to wander around wherever he likes, and for much of the first half of the film plays a reserved bystander to the machinations of the waspish Lydecker and his cronies. Indeed, so convincing is Andrews at playing the emotionless professional that his burgeoning obsession with the apparently dead Laura is bizarre, even unsettling. Rather more credible are his sudden bursts of violence after Laura returns and becomes a suspect herself – the vicious punch to Carpenter or his harsh interrogation of Laura. The incongruous casting of Andrews merely adds another deliberate layer of obfuscation to a bewitching, dream-like film.

However, Preminger's odd casting did not stop with Andrews. Tierney spectacularly fails to live up to the fascinating image conjured up by Lydecker, the effete Price makes an unconvincing playboy, while Anderson struggles to convince as the sexually predatory aunt. So, what makes Laura such a mesmeric film, even after countless viewings? The answer lies in Webb's extraordinary Lydecker, an asexual, fastidious aesthete whose Svengali-like obsession with Laura skews his rationality and colours the thoughts of all those around him – including the audience.

After catastrophic previews, Preminger was forced by Zanuck to film an alternative ending, with a voice-over from Gene Tierney explaining that the story had all been in Lydecker's imagination. But once again Zanuck had to change his mind when the influential journalist Walter Winchell was mystified by the voice-over after attending one of the film's final previews. It was just as well that Zanuck listened to him as *Laura*, despite receiving mixed reviews, rapidly became one of Fox's most critically acclaimed films of the 1940s and still remains the cult noir *par excellence*.

Leave Her To Heaven

dir **John M. Stahl 1945, US, 107m**
cast **Gene Tierney, Cornel Wilde, Jeanne Crain, Darryl Hickman** *cin* **Leon Shamroy** *m* **Alfred Newman**

Once novelist Richard Harland (**Cornel Wilde**) notices the piercing stare of Ellen Berent (**Gene Tierney**) on the Jacinto Express, he doesn't stand a chance. Barely introduced to the dysfunctional Berent family, Richard accepts Ellen's marriage proposal – an offer primarily motivated by his striking resemblance to her father. Thereafter he is pitched helplessly into the psychotic hands of an icily deranged *femme fatale*, a woman in the grip of a Freudian nightmare, who, in her mother's words, "loves too much", and, when she tells the captivated, helpless novelist, "I'll never let you go, never, never", means it.

Leave Her To Heaven is not a conventional noir. It is a woman's picture and was director John Stahl's first foray into Technicolor: altogether a bold choice for 1945 when colour was typically used for costume dramas and musicals, not for contemporary subjects. And cinematographer Leon Shamroy's work on the film was anything but Technicolor's usual studied pastel colours. Instead he saturates the frame with a sickly, amber patina which lends it the same degree of foreboding that is found in the black-and-white noirs of the period.

Although Shamroy's cinematography earned him an Oscar, the film's subtleties failed to connect with its audience. Critics were unconvinced by its preposterous storyline but impressed by the film's technical virtuosity. There can now, however, be no doubt that the intensity of the film's Technicolor hues accentuate the seething emotional undercurrents of the film. As Martin Scorsese says: "Shamroy's cinematography conjured up an unsettling superrealist vision. This was a lost paradise, its beauty ravished by the heroine's perverse nature." A careful eye should also be cast over the film's symbolic mixing of cold and hot colours, illuminating examples being Ellen's manic costume changes – from cool domestic green or blue pastels to a clinging, blood-red swimsuit.

Gene Tierney's performance as the possessive, controlling Ellen Berent is delivered as if it was to be her last. (It did earn her an Oscar nomination, but she lost out to Joan Crawford's Mildred Pierce.) The bravura sequence when Ellen scatters her father's ashes on the blood-red New Mexican landscape before impulsively flinging the casket away leaves an indelible impression on the mesmerized Richard. Ellen's pained words, "I love you so, I can't bear to share you with anybody", lead to a lurid carnage that is more than a match for noir's monochrome urban crimes.

The first unlucky victim of Ellen's insane jealousy is Richard's paraplegic brother Danny (**Darryl Hickman**), unwise enough to entrust her with his swimming training. Sitting on a boat on a placid lake and encouraging him to swim beyond his limits, she intones, "You're not making very much progress, Danny", as she calmly watches him slip beneath the surface. Desperate to patch up their crumbling relationship, Ellen imagines that having a child will secure her place in Richard's strained affections, but not before paranoid jealousies of her cousin Ruth (**Jeanne Crain**) possess her. No sooner has she told her startled doctor that "This baby's making a prisoner out of me", and Ruth "Look at me, I hate the little beast, I wish it would die", than she is pitching headlong down the stairs, putting an end to Richard and Ruth's bootie-buying sprees. After admitting her heinous crimes to a bolting Richard, Ellen implicates Ruth from beyond the grave after her cyanide-induced suicide. Though the jury finds Ruth innocent, Richard gets two years for withholding evidence.

Upon his release, Richard has Ruth waiting for him at the quayside. A happy ending then, or so it would seem – Ruth's resemblance to Ellen, combined with the foreboding lighting of their twilight reunion, suggests this psychologically maladjusted family has more horrors yet in store.

The Long Goodbye

dir Robert Altman, 1973, US, 112m

cast Elliott Gould, Nina Van Pallandt, Sterling Hayden, Mark Rydell, Henry Gibson *cin* Vilmos Zsigmond *m* John Williams

By the time Hollywood got round to adapting Raymond Chandler's novel *The Long Goodbye* (1953), the Los Angeles it describes had become a city of hippies, health food and yoga. Private eye Philip Marlowe – to borrow Chandler's simile – belonged in this city of cool like "a pearl onion on a banana split". While making the film, screenwriter **Leigh Brackett** (who had worked on the 1946 film of *The Big Sleep*), director **Robert Altman** and **Elliott Gould** (who played Marlowe) would refer to Chandler's sardonic detective as Rip Van Marlowe as they transformed him into a befuddled, helpless onlooker who had awakened into a morally bankrupt Los Angeles of the future.

The labyrinthine plot begins with Marlowe's return to LA after dropping off his friend Terry Lennox (**Jim Bouton**) in Tijuana.

Manhandled by two burly police detectives, what really gets to him, as he shrugs off his arrest with a characteristic "it's okay with me", is that he cannot find his cat. Held as an accessory to murder – Terry's wife Sylvia having been brutally killed the night of his visit – he is released after his friend's dubious suicide and murder confession. Back to gumshoe work, Marlowe is employed by bruised blonde Eileen Wade (**Nina Van Pallandt**) to extricate her alcoholic author-husband Roger (**Sterling Hayden** in best Hemingway mode) from the

Elliott Gould (left) as a befuddled Marlowe interviews Dr Verringer (Henry Gibson) in *The Long Goodbye*.

clutches of sinister Dr Verringer (**Henry Gibson**) and his Burbank sanatorium. As Malibu socialites and neighbours of the Lennoxes, the Wades are inextricably involved with the deceased couple.

With barely time to holler for his cat, Marlowe is rounded up by theatrical gangster Marty Augustine (played by actor/director **Mark Rydell**), who demands the $355,000 Terry owes him. Pressing his point home, Augustine smashes a bottle across the face of his subservient mistress (**Jo Ann Brody**) with the chilling words: "That's someone I love, and you I don't even like."

A quick trip to Mexico to check on Terry's suicide and Marlowe visits the Wades' beach party, where he fails to prevent Roger's drunken, stumbling ocean suicide. With the actors convincingly thrashing about in the surf as a storm breaks, the camera remains with Roger's Doberman barking forlornly at his master's washed-up stick. Discovering from Eileen that Roger had murdered Sylvia after the end of their affair and her return to Terry, a drunken Marlowe rails at Det. Farmer (**Stephen Coit**) with the news, but the police already know.

Taken to Augustine, Marlowe is only saved from getting "cut" by Eileen's return of the $355,000. Chasing after her car in nocturnal LA, Marlowe is run over, only to miraculously wake up next to a bandaged patient who randomly hands him a baby harmonica – Altman would later cite this enigmatic moment as the film's key scene! Returning to Mexico, Marlowe discovers that Terry did murder his wife and fake his suicide, and is now living with Eileen in Mexico. This time it will not be "okay with me", and he sets out to confront the friend who has betrayed him.

Stylistically, *The Long Goodbye* is radically anti-noir. Marlowe's typical first-person, voice-over narration – as heard in *Murder My Sweet* (1944) – is replaced by Gould's constant mumblings and musings, and the usual noir camera techniques are instead replaced by a constantly roving camera, zooming in and out of subjects, brilliantly encapsulating the characters' mutual mistrust.

The film opened disastrously in Los Angeles in March 1973 to almost uniformly bad reviews from critics such as *Time*'s Jay Cocks, who wrote: "Any resemblance between Chandler's book and this movie is not only coincidental but probably libellous." Pulled from distribution, *The Long Goodbye* would be re-released as an art film in New York to greater acclaim, but its reputation was irretrievably damaged.

Over thirty years on, Altman's remarkable version of the novel more than holds its own alongside classic Hollywood Chandler adaptations, while also providing an unnerving exploration of friendship, betrayal, suicide and righteous anger. However, according to Altman, the film's real mystery is "where Marlowe's cat had gotten to".

The Maltese Falcon

dir John Huston 1941, US, 100m, b/w

cast Humphrey Bogart, Mary Astor, Sydney Greenstreet, Peter Lorre, Elisha Cook Jr *cin* Arthur Edeson *m* Adolph Deutsch

"You go and make *The Maltese Falcon* exactly the way Hammett wrote it, use the dialogue, don't change a goddam thing and you'll have a hell of a picture." So recommended **Howard Hawks** to first-time director **John Huston**. Taking Hawks's advice, the 34-year-old director instructed his secretary to break up Hammett's 1930 book into basic shots, using "the novel as a word-for-word guide".

In the summer of 1941, studio executives regarded *The Maltese Falcon* as yet another standard Warner Bros detective melodrama with an $81,000 B-movie budget and a six-week shooting schedule. Their contract star, **George Raft**, had refused the role of Sam Spade and was replaced by character actor Humphrey Bogart, better known for his many secondary roles in 1930s gangster films. It was the novel's third outing, already filmed as *The Maltese Falcon* (1931) by **Roy Del Ruth** (see p.6) and *Satan Met A Lady* (1935) by **William Dieterle**. From these inauspicious beginnings, *The Maltese Falcon* gave birth to the great director-actor partnership of Huston and Bogart, set the standard for all subsequent private eye films, and virtually launched the film noir style.

Action and events in *The Maltese Falcon* unfold tumultuously. Before we know it, Spade's partner, Miles Archer (**Jerome Cowan**), ends up on the wrong end of a Webley .45 after taking on a mundane job for the beautiful Mrs Wonderly (**Mary Astor**). Investigating Archer's death, Spade balances his desire for and mistrust of Wonderly

Humphrey Bogart as private detective Sam Spade handling the "stuff that dreams are made of".

(aka Brigid O'Shaughnessy) and encounters a grotesque gallery of characters – **Sydney Greenstreet** as the fat man Kasper Gutman, **Elisha Cook Jr** as his "gunsel" Wilmer Cook (see p.7) and **Peter Lorre** as the effeminate Levantine Joel Cairo – and their ruthless quest to find the elusive Maltese falcon. The film is dominated by the unshaven, world-weary Bogart as Spade – streets away from Hammett's hawkish "blond satan". His morally ambiguous detective, menacing and jaunty, is as at ease in the company of district attorneys as he is with perverse criminals.

The actors and director were a tight bunch, breakfasting together and often socializing at the Lakeside Country Club after filming. Huston's approach on set was no less refreshing, making Astor run round the studio before takes to induce her breathless and deceptively vulnerable delivery. Huston even cast his father, **Walter Huston**, in the non-speaking role of Hammett's 7ft Captain Jacoby, who delivers the falcon to Spade in his death throes.

Leaving nothing to chance, Huston sketched each of the film's main set-ups and bucked the Hollywood norm by shooting most of the film sequentially. With imperious cinematographer Art Edeson – aka "Little Napoleon" – they continually filmed over Bogart's shoulder, dolly tracked behind him or showed his point of view to get into the detective's mindset. Characters are composed in medium shots in unnerving tableaux, for instance Spade flanked by police investigators Dundy (**Barton MacLane**) and Polhaus (**Ward Bond**) in his shadowy apartment. In the film's final tense sequences, as the protagonists await the falcon's arrival, the frame can hardly contain Gutman's bulk, the electric presence of Spade and the seething Cairo in the background. Unnerving low angles, such as those of Gutman or the shock cuts of Wilmer's alarmed point of view as he looks at Gutman, Cairo, Spade and Brigid, led critic Manny Farber to describe Huston as having an "Eisenstein-lubricated brain".

Visual excess takes a secondary role in Spade's memorable confrontation with Brigid at the movie's close. Here, Hawks's advice would be proved right, as Hammett's dialogue crackles on screen. With the couple covering an extraordinary amount of detailed plot exposition, Brigid insists on the sincerity of her love for Spade while simultaneously revealing the depths of her deceit. Whatever the tragic outcome, Spade's self-justifying words to her, "When a man's partner is killed, he's supposed to do something about it", have a particularly hollow ring to them.

The *Maltese Falcon* prop

The *Maltese Falcon* prop has had as chequered a history as its fictional sixteenth-century counterpart. After completion of filming, the falcon was passed between members of the cast, including Humphrey Bogart, and reappeared as a prop in Curtis Bernhardt's *Conflict* (1945). It then resurfaced at a Christie's 1994 auction, where it was bought by jeweller to the stars Harry Winston Jr, for the world auction record for a movie prop of $398,500. Although the fictional falcon was supposed to be made of solid gold, the prop was enamel-plated with a lead base and core. Taking two years, the Winston workshop replicated the prop in gold, malachite, cabochon rubies and a 42-carat diamond. So at last the "stuff that dreams are made of" became a reality – at an $8 million price tag.

Mildred Pierce

dir Michael Curtiz 1945, US, 113m, b/w
cast Joan Crawford, Ann Blyth, Jack Carson, Bruce
Bennett, Jo Ann Marlowe *cin* Ernest Haller *m* Max Steiner

Joan Crawford bestrides James M. Cain's noirish southern California
like a shoulder-padded colossus, yet the ageing ex-MGM glamour

Veda (Ann Blyth) and Mildred Pierce (Joan Crawford) try to keep Monte Beragon (Zachary Scott) in the family.

star was an unlikely and unpopular choice for the role of Mildred Pierce. With a tenacity not unlike Mildred's, the diminutive, fading star badgered Warner Bros producer Jerry Wald for the role and insisted on testing "with each potential member of the cast". This was certainly not the expected behaviour of a star whose previous power of contract had extended to approval over her own close-ups. When hard-hearted director **Michael Curtiz** broke down during her test scene, competitors Bette Davis, Rosalind Russell and Barbara Stanwyck were out and Crawford was in, later describing her Oscar-winning role as "the easiest thing I've ever done".

The Ranald MacDougall screenplay was a radical departure from Cain's novel. Gone was daughter Veda Pierce's immense musical talent and the suppressed incestuous longings which Mildred has for her. Instead it was replaced by a more streamlined story of adultery, greed and ambition, culminating in murder, thwarted suicide and the death penalty. It borrowed the flashback structure (fast becoming a noir staple) from *Double Indemnity* (see Canon), with events proceeding from its explosive opening scene of Monte Beragon (**Zachary Scott**) being peppered by bullets in his beach house. From here on in, the film goes into noir stylistic overdrive as a staggering, hunched Crawford contemplates suicide from the glistening, rain-swept shadows of Santa Monica's pier. The disorienting compositions, low lighting and menacing shadows conjured up by cinematographer Ernest Haller and art director Anton Grot never let up as Mildred, now transformed into a *femme fatale*, lures Wally Fay (**Jack Carson**) to the crime scene to frame him for murder.

With the main protagonists gathered in the menacing, nocturnal shadows of the office of Inspector Peterson (**Moroni Olsen**), the film flashbacks into daytime melodrama. Crawford, now attired in floral pinafore, bakes away interminably in her drab Glendale tract home as one of noir's rare female voice-overs plaintively intones: "I was always in the kitchen – I felt as though I had been born in a kitchen and lived there all my life, except for the few hours it took to get married." Fed up with her out-of-work, philandering husband Bert (played by ex-Olympic shot putter Bruce Bennett), she goes it solo, waitressing and baking herself into the ground to provide for her daughters, Kay (**Jo Ann Marlowe**) and Veda (**Ann Blyth**). Mildred's meteoric rise in the restaurant business is assured when Crawford dons her iconic mannish pinstriped skirt suit – Milo Anderson's creation being one of the great contributions to Crawford's enduring camp/cult status. Commentators have expounded on how Mildred's success reflects the changing roles of women in postwar society, but few of these businesswomen would have had to contend with the kind of heinous punishment meted out to Mildred by Veda.

The spoilt, sluttish Veda represents a nightmarish flipside to her mother, and one that is only ever hinted at by the streetwise Mildred. Their mother-daughter relationship, combined with their increasingly similar hairstyles, is as warped as any in the canon. On the receiving end of Veda's venomous diatribe, "with this money I can get away from you and your chickens and your pies and your kitchens and everything that smells of grease", Mildred, unable to contain her rising fury, slaps her daughter, shouting, "Get out, before I kill you!", after which the camera dollies into devastating close-up. Through extortion of the wealthy Forrester family, her job as a nightclub singer and dancer, and increasingly desperate acts, Veda continues to drag Mildred down. Her parting words – "Don't worry about me mother, I'll get by" – are, in the light of her dire predicament, as chilling as those uttered by any *femme fatale* in the history of film noir.

Murder My Sweet

dir **Edward Dmytryk, 1944, US, 95m, b/w**
cast **Dick Powell, Claire Trevor, Anne Shirley, Otto Kruger, Mike Mazurki** *cin* **Harry J. Wild** *m* **Roy Webb**

Fans hoping for another routine song and dance number from one of Hollywood's favourite crooners, Dick Powell, were to have their expectations cruelly shattered in this film version of Raymond Chandler's *Farewell My Lovely*. In his dogged, haphazard search for a jade necklace, a missing showgirl and a brutal killer, Powell's Philip Marlowe gets bludgeoned by blackjacks, pistol-whipped and beaten senseless, showing, as one contemporary reviewer noted, "a capacity for taking a beating that is downright admirable". So worried was RKO about confounding expectations that it replaced the original title with the more explanatory *Murder My Sweet*. Even the cantankerous Chandler praised the adaptation of his work.

Taking advantage of the studio's under-exploited property (previously filmed in 1942 as the six-reeler, *The Falcon Takes Over*), producer Adrian Scott employed **John Paxton** to adapt and simplify the novel's labyrinthine plot. Despite adjustments, *Murder My Sweet*'s storyline defies any kind of pithy description. Marlowe himself has great difficulty in following the unfolding events as they lurch to their bloody conclusion. Powell's voice-over helps, combining as it does just the right amount of street savvy, honour and uncomprehending persistence to make his omniscient narrator believable. Here was a detective who was as bewildered as the audience and who suffered like the common man.

Although *The Big Sleep* is claimed as the greatest Chandler adaptation and Humphrey Bogart as the definitive Marlowe, *Murder My Sweet*, with its B-status and less starry cast, gives it a run for its money. Dmytryk and cinematographer **Harry J. Wild** drew inspiration from the work of nineteenth-century satirical artist Honoré Daumier, and there is more than a hint of his caricatures in the bizarre physiognomies of Moose Malloy (**Mike Mazurki**), Jules Amthor (**Otto Kruger**), Dr Sonderberg (**Ralf Harolde**) and Mr Grayle (**Miles Mander**). Menacing encounters generally take place at night, with Wild placing his camera at low angles and testing the limits of the film stock. Examples include the neon-reflected figure of Moose looming over the startled detective in his office window as he is first introduced. In another instance, lighting levels are virtually non-existent as *femme fatale* Helen Grayle (**Claire Trevor**) lies like a coiled dragon on a chaise longue, the slight plumes of cigarette smoke the only evidence of her vampish presence.

Having reinvented herself as a society woman, Helen cannot escape her tawdry "showgirl" past and is prepared to murder, seduce and exploit all men who cross her. From her first encounter with Marlowe (who can barely keep his eyes off her unravelling legs), she exudes sexuality – were it not for Claire Trevor's assured performance, her revealing playsuit with exposed midriff would seem ludicrously out of place in the refined Grayle mansion.

After Marlowe fails to bluff blackmailing psychiatrist Amthor and Moose, he is half-strangled and bludgeoned to the ground. There then follows an expressionistic dream sequence of *Alice*-like tumbles, leering close-ups and Magritte-like perspectives which would influence many subsequent noirs. The nightmare continues as Marlowe's voice-over intones: "The window was open, but the smoke didn't move. It was a grey web woven by a thousand spiders. I wondered how they got them to work together." In a debilitating wide-angled overhead, Marlowe lashes out at the cobwebs and screams for help in a terrifying close-up. It is now up to the detective to drag himself out of the nightmare. "Okay Marlowe, I said to myself, you're the tough guy, you've been sapped twice, choked, beaten silly with a gun, shot in the arm until you're as crazy as a couple of waltzing mice. Now let's see you do something really tough, like putting your pants on…" With this bewildered, disoriented, sweaty performance, Powell set new standards for the interpretation of private investigators on the screen. One thing was for sure, he didn't work for Busby Berkeley again.

The Naked City

dir Jules Dassin, 1948, US, 96m, b/w
cast Barry Fitzgerald, Howard Duff, Dorothy Hart, Ted De Corsia, Don Taylor, Frank Conroy *cin* William H. Daniels *m* Miklós Rósza, Frank Skinner

A magnificent aerial shot of Manhattan's skyline is accompanied by a confiding, cajoling and cosmopolitan voice-over: "Ladies and gentlemen, the motion picture you are about to see is called *The Naked City*. My name is Mark Hellinger; I was in charge of its production. And I may as well tell you frankly, that it's a bit different from most films you've ever seen…" Based on a screenplay culled from a range of NYPD's unsolved cases, and with a cast of largely unknown screen actors criss-crossing 107 New York locations, *The Naked City* is as close to documentary as noir gets.

Ten weeks of location shooting in the gruelling heat of New York's hottest summer on record, a spiralling budget and the efforts of marshalling an estimated 200,000 inquisitive onlookers put intolerable pressure on the hard-living Hellinger. Three months after the end of principal photography, he suffered a fatal heart attack, shortly after recording his complex voice-over narration.

The film's story was devised by screenwriter **Malvin Wald** after months of research in New York talking to police and leafing through

Rooftop shooting: a *Naked City* moment filmed precariously outside Universal's New York offices.

the files. Based on a true story, the "Bathtub Murder" involves ex-fashion model Jean Dexter as the victim, who in partnership with the mendacious Frank Niles (Howard Duff) fixes a series of jewellery thefts using the society connections of her duped lover, the elusive

Weegee's *Naked City*

The title of *The Naked City* was taken from the pioneering 1945 book of photographs, *Naked City*, by New York photographer Arthur Fellig (1899–1968), aka **"Weegee"**, whose nickname (a variant on "Ouija") was apparently given him because of his unerring ability to arrive at the crime scene before the police.

An immigrant from Zloczów in Austria (now part of Poland), Fellig grew up in Manhattan's Lower East Side. After working as a darkroom technician for Acme Newspictures he became a freelance press photographer in the mid-1930s, specializing in scene-of-the-crime pictures in Lower Manhattan. These black-and-white photos – of murder victims, arrested gangsters, prostitutes and down-and-outs – have a brutal directness and uncensored quality which was unprecedented

in newspaper pictures. His rapid results were partly due to the fact that his car was equipped with both a police radio and a small darkroom.

The connection between *Naked City* and Dassin's movie was due to the film's screenwriter Malvin Wald, who had been shown a copy of the book by a friend. Wald persuaded Mark Hellinger to buy the rights, in part because he thought the title was so poetic. Hellinger in turn showed the book to the film's eventual director Jules Dassin who, with cinematographer William Daniels, attempted to recreate the raw immediacy of Weegee's photographs. There is no evidence that the photographer had any consultative role in the film (as has been suggested) and he does not appear in the credits.

Mr Henderson. That is, until their handymen – dipso Pete Backalis (Walter Burke) and psychotic ex-wrestler Willie "the harmonica" Garzah (Ted De Corsia) – decide to go freelance.

Picking up the pieces (stolen jewellery and otherwise) along the way are wily, old-timer Lt Dan Muldoon (Barry Fitzgerald) and his enthusiastic assistant Jimmy Halloran (Don Taylor). Their methodical police work takes them from swanky Park Avenue apartments to grimy Lower East Side tenements. Once Henderson's identity and confession ("I had to wallow in my own filth") are established and Niles's squalid scam unravels, Halloran's legwork leads him to the grinning, zealous Garzah and a relentless nine-minute chase scene, culminating in a vertiginous finale on the Williamsburg Bridge.

Ultimately, *The Naked City*'s noirish heart lies embedded in New York itself, with its ferocious summer heat and pulsating street life providing a disorienting daytime or inky night-time backdrop to murder investigation and manhunt. This urban angst is best summed up in the embittered words of Jean's careworn father (Grover Burgess): "We'll go home, we don't like this place, this *fine city*." Catch sight of cinematographer William Daniels's peripheral images, such as kids cooling off around a burst hydrant, and it's as if Weegee's iconic New York photographs come alive before your eyes (see box).

For reasons of practicality and speed, director Jules Dassin and Daniels used new fast film and portable lighting units to augment exterior sunlight and create a raw look for locations. In order to make the street scenes more lifelike, the film was shot secretly from trucks panelled with opaque two-way mirrors and the actors were filmed without make-up. Almost a third of the schedule was devoted to the final sequence, in which Garzah is hunted on the Lower East Side. Eventually hemmed in and wounded by the police, he drags himself up a Williamsburg Bridge tower. Once he has lurched to the top, he looks over an unreachable panorama of New York before being shot and plunging into a dizzying maze of beams and girders.

Having worked on the editing for ten weeks, Dassin was bitterly disappointed by the final cut, which seems to have been supervised by Hellinger and tailored to his extensive voice-over. Just how much more noir Dassin intended the film to be will never be known. Despite its director's reservations, the film was a huge commercial and critical success, and earned Oscars for Daniels and editor Paul Weatherwax. It would become even more famous for spawning the television series of the same name from 1958–63, which took as its celebrated opening lines the closing narration of its original: "There are eight million stories in the naked city…"

Night And The City

dir **Jules Dassin, 1950, UK/US, 100m, b/w**
cast **Richard Widmark, Gene Tierney, Googie Withers, Francis L. Sullivan, Herbert Lom** *cin* **Max Greene** *m* **Benjamin Frankel (UK), Franz Waxman (US)**

Reviled by the English, feted by the French, *Night And The City* is now justly celebrated for its treatment of the opportunistic rise and unlucky fall of neurotic noir trickster Harry Fabian (**Richard Widmark**). On the receipt of the screenplay, it prompted its source novelist, **Gerald Kersh**, to advise Twentieth Century-Fox to have the script "suitably perforated" and hung "in a tramp's lavatory", *Times* critic Dilys Powell to describe it as "squalid and brutal", and French publisher Editions de Minuit to immortalize it on the cover of *Panorama du film noir américain* (1955), the first book devoted to film noir.

Its frenetic production began with an unannounced late-night visit by Twentieth Century-Fox head **Darryl F. Zanuck** to Dassin's Beverly Hills house in late 1949. Realizing that the black-listed Dassin's Hollywood career was over, the gap-toothed mogul instructed the director to leave immediately for London. As Dassin recalled in 1957, Zanuck urged him to finalize the script and start "with the most expensive sequences first – that way no one would force him to fire me".

Harry is a frustrated tout for the *Silver Fox* clip joint, bustling about London's West End in a blur of clashing pinstripe and corresponding Oxfords, his eyes forever glinting with ambitious plans and scams. Until now his failed business ventures have been subsidized by his long-suffering girlfriend Mary (**Gene Tierney**), a singer at the *Silver Fox*, run by the sinister Phil Nosseross (**Francis L. Sullivan**) and his disillusioned, cattish wife Helen (**Googie Withers**).

Busted for touting at a wrestling match, Harry witnesses an impassioned argument between London wrestling magnate Kristo (**Herbert Lom**) and his ageing father Gregorius, "the greatest wrestler the world has ever known" (played by ex-world heavyweight champion, **Stanislaus Zbyszko**). Immediately inveigling his way into Gregorius's company, he passes himself off as a Greco-Roman promoter and signs up Gregorius's protégé Nikolas (**Kenneth Richmond**). Arrogantly, Harry believes that, with his well-connected new partner in tow, he "has the means to control wrestling in all London", and instigates a dangerous game, playing off father against son.

Unfortunately his desperate business dealings with the predatory Helen and duplicitous Nosseross fail to conjure "the biggest wrestling match London will ever see" between Nikolas and the Strangler (**Mike Mazurki**). Instead he sees the Strangler's drunken insults incite Gregorius to enter the ring for one last bone-crushing encounter. With Kristo on hand to witness the calamitous result, Harry becomes a fugitive, embarking on a staggering 25-minute descent into a treacherous London of bomb sites, beggars' dens and barges. The cumulative horror and desperation gathers pace as Kristo's words spread through London: "I want Fabian, get the word around, the East End, Soho, the Embankment – £1000 for the man who hits Fabian, I want him."

Nightmare merges with real life as Harry's exhausted legs give way while he lurches across Hammersmith Bridge to collapse at his final refuge, the black marketing outfit of riverside woman Anna O'Leary (**Maureen Delaney**). Although overwhelmed with exhaustion and remorse – "All my life, I've been running from welfare offices, things, my father" – his eye is still on the main chance. He desperately tries to persuade a distraught Mary to hand him over to Kristo for the £1000 reward, not realizing the irony of his final words to her: "For the first time in my life it's a foolproof idea." With only thirty minutes of dawn light to film Harry's sacrificial final run, Dassin and cinematographer Max Greene set up six cameras and completed a staggering twenty-two shots in eighteen minutes. Hardly surprising, then, that Widmark's overriding memory of the film fifty years later was that he "was always running, the whole sixty days of the shoot; I musta lost twenty pounds".

Night Moves

dir Arthur Penn, 1975, US, 99m,
cast Gene Hackman, Jennifer Warren, John Crawford,
Melanie Griffith, James Wood *cin* Bruce Surtees *m*
Michael Small

Ex-football pro turned private eye Harry Moseby (**Gene Hackman**) is reduced to solving crummy divorce cases, and to make matters worse his own wife Ellen (**Susan Clark**) is cheating on him. But by treating her affair just like another case – making her incriminate herself and tailing her lover, Marty Heller (**Harris Yulin**) – Moseby pushes the marriage into freefall. Time to escape Los Angeles and throw himself into a new job – to find and return missing nymphet Delly Grastner (a debuting Melanie Griffith) to her ex-starlet lush of a mother, Arlene Iverson (**Janet Ward**).

Straightforward legwork via Delly's most recent bedfellows – studio mechanic Quentin (**James Woods**) and stuntman Marv Ellman (**Anthony Costello**) – leads Moseby to a New Mexico film location overseen by stunt coordinator Joey Ziegler (**Edward Binns**) and then to the Florida Keys. Here he finds Delly settled into a curious *ménage à trois* with her fly-by-night stepfather Tom Iverson (**John Crawford**) and his enigmatic partner Paula (**Jennifer Warren**).

Case solved it seems, but Moseby is in no hurry to return home and cut short his flirtatious exchanges with Paula. However his Florida idyll soon becomes nightmare as a nocturnal boat outing with Paula and Delly leads to the discovery of a ditched airplane

Gene Hackman as Harry Moseby, a neo-noir private eye.

with decomposing pilot – which, unbeknownst to Moseby, is all part of the Iversons' illicit Yucatan statuary smuggling racket. With the plane accident now apparently in the hands of the Coast Guard, the detective and his charge make their departure.

Back in LA, Moseby deposits a traumatized Delly with the sluttish Arlene while ignoring the sounds of drunken mother and daughter exchanging blows on his departure. Realizing his success in returning Delly has merely exacerbated her troubled life, he determines to change career and rebuild his relationship with Ellen. And it looks as if this might happen until Delly's suspicious death on Ziegler's film precipitates Moseby's return to Florida in a finale so desolate, maddening and labyrinthine that even he is reduced to asking imploringly, "What the hell is going on?"

If Moseby was puzzled, then so were the film's director, Arthur Penn, and Hollywood-based Scottish screenwriter Alan Sharp. Even after six months of intensive and unsatisfactory script rewrites, shooting began with an unfinished script, merely accentuating the film's mass of already unresolved issues and red herrings. Just who, for instance, planned Delly's death and why? Was it Quentin, Arlene or Ziegler? Having recognized Marv Ellman in the submerged cockpit, did she know too much about the smuggling operation?

Penn would later explain that the film's mystery was never delineated properly, saying "we're part of a generation which knows there are no solutions", thus underlining *Night Moves'* key place in America's post-Watergate cinema of paranoia, alongside such films as *The Conversation* (1974), in which Hackman plays another puzzled Harry. Despite the unresolved narrative and Penn's skittery eleventh hour re-edit in order to simplify Paula's character and make Moseby more sympathetic, *Night Moves* still rips along thanks to editor Dede Allen's dexterous cutting of the miles of footage demanded by coverage-obsessed Penn.

The film's extraordinary ending secures its place as one of the greatest neo-noirs of the 1970s. Here Moseby, after admitting to Paula that he "didn't solve anything, just fell in on top of it", finally has the chance to achieve something and retrieve the submerged contraband, perhaps even sail off into the sunset with his glamorous companion. Isolated on a silvered ocean waiting for Paula to locate the priceless antique objects, an aircraft descends and strafes Moseby's vessel, ripping his leg open. As he looks on helplessly, he attempts to warn Paula of the now water-bound plane tearing mercilessly towards them. Bloodied and cursing, Moseby attempts to set his vessel on course as Bruce Surtees' aerial camera shows the detective endlessly circling the ocean under a pallid morning sun, like his investigation going nowhere.

On Dangerous Ground

dir Nicholas Ray, 1951, US, 80m, b/w
cast Robert Ryan, Ida Lupino, Ward Bond, Sumner Williams, Charles Kemper *cin* George E. Diskant *m* Bernard Herrmann

"He's getting tougher to work with all the time" wearily comments Pete Santos (**Anthony Ross**) to fellow San Francisco detective Pop Daly (**Charles Kemper**) after preventing their out-of-control colleague Jim Wilson (**Robert Ryan**) from publicly pummelling an innocent suspect.

This is a jaw-dropping understatement as their night shift unravels and Jim proceeds to squeeze out information sadistically from prostitute Myrna Bowers (**Cleo Moore**) and savagely beats up cop-killer accomplice Bernie Tucker (**Richard Irving**), screaming: "I'm going to make you talk, I always make you punks talk, why do you do it? WHY? WHY?"

With a citizen's committee concerned about police brutality, Jim is shunted upstate to the snowy wilderness of Westham to investigate a child murder. Immediately he is plunged into the world of Walter Brent (Ward Bond), who craves vengeance for his daughter's shocking death: "It was my kid and it's going to be my gun that takes care of him." A suspicious, combative partnership ensues between the two men as they hunt down chief suspect Danny Malden (**Sumner Williams**) through a wintry landscape.

Led to the house of Danny's blind sister Mary (**Ida Lupino**), Jim is forced to confront his own violence as he stops Brent strong-arming Danny's whereabouts from Mary. And in a remarkable turnaround, he starts to open up to the self-assured and intuitive blind woman as he leaves behind the city's "crooks, murderers, winos, stoolies, dames, all with an angle". Though unable to see his shame-

Jim Wilson (Robert Ryan and Mary Malden (Ida Lupino) snowbound *On Dangerous Ground*.

filled face, Mary senses his alienation: "The city can be lonely too. Sometimes people who are never alone are the loneliest, don't you think so?" Hardly has the snow melted from his encrusted city shoes than Jim is agreeing to protect the deranged Danny (sheltered by Mary), leading to a snowbound, melodramatic finale.

Nicholas Ray worked closely with key noir screenwriter **A.I. Bezzerides** (who cameos as the grinning, unctuous bar owner Gato at the film's start), adapting British crime writer Gerald Butler's *Mad With Much Heart* (1947). Producer John Houseman described the partnership as "a combination of an almost feminine sensitivity [Ray] with a strong macho streak [Bezzerides]". Throwing himself into the film's pre-production, Ray spent weeks being driven out with police squad cars in the toughest district of Boston in order to study police psychopathology.

For cinematographer **George Diskant** there were virtually two separate films to be lit. The night-time exteriors of the opening city sequences were mostly shot in San Francisco's Tenderloin district at daringly low lighting levels. In one extraordinary sequence, Jim chases a mobster down a pitch-black alleyway, his pursuit peppered with two bursts of disorienting subjective hand-held camera-work. Both men's faces are so enshrouded that they become indistinguishable from each other, before Jim is wrenched away from repeatedly pistol-whipping his victim under a lone door light. Switching to a higher contrast film for the Westham exterior sequences (actually shot in the Colorado Rockies), Diskant had to contend with delays caused by blizzards and juggle with an ever-changing snowscape.

The film suffered two years in limbo before a lacklustre release and a $425,000 loss for RKO. Contemporary reviewers were puzzled and unready for such a raw and bizarrely structured film. Fifty years on, and the film is still an extraordinarily unsettling experience with its jarring two-part structure and enforced saccharine ending (Houseman and Ray going against Bezzerides' more realistic ending). Its final sequence shows a numb-faced Jim driving back to the city and then unexpectedly dissolves to his return, reconciliation and subsequent embrace with Mary. Hollywood legend has it that Lupino and Ryan self-directed this scene rather than an uninterested Ray. It would be nice to imagine that he had a darker conclusion in mind and could have avoided one of the canon's most compromised endings.

Out Of The Past

dir Jacques Tourneur, 1947, US, 96m, b/w
cast Robert Mitchum, Jane Greer, Kirk Douglas, Virginia
Huston, Steve Brodie *cin* Nicholas Musuraca *m* Roy Webb

With its sun-dazzled opening scenes set in High Sierra country, *Out Of The Past* is a world away from noir's dark rain-slicked streets, but do not be fooled – all is not quite right in bucolic Bridgeport. This small town is home to ex-private detective Jeff Bailey (**Robert Mitchum**), now seeking a life of anonymity minding his remote service station with his young deaf-mute assistant the Kid (**Dickie Moore**).

Jeff's attempt at a quiet life – fishing and courting local girl Ann Miller (**Virginia Huston**) – are cut short when he is spotted pumping gas by a heavy from his gumshoe days, Joe Stephanos (**Paul Valentine**). Hardly has Jeff had time to swap his natty fishing attire for one of noir's most crumpled and stained trenchcoats than he is visiting Joe's boss – big-time gambling operator Whit Sterling (**Kirk Douglas**) – and making a return to a past that he would rather forget.

As Jeff starts to tell Ann about his former life – while driving to Whit's Lake Tahoe house – his account segues into a virtuoso flashback punctuated by his resigned voice-over. Originally employed by a wounded Whit to locate his trigger-happy mistress Kathie Moffat (**Jane Greer**) before she hightails with $40,000, Jeff tracks her down to Acapulco. But after a series of highly charged encounters, the last thing Jeff intends to do with Kathie is return her to Whit. Their subsequent life together (back in California) comes to an explosive end, however, as Jeff's old partner Jack Fisher (**Steve Brodie**) comes calling and is ruthlessly dispatched by Kathie, who deserts Jeff and leaves him with just a corpse for company.

Cut to the present and Jeff's meeting with Whit where he discovers, to his disgust, that Kathie is "back in the fold". With no alternative but to become an unwilling player in Whit's plans to retrieve his financial records from blackmailing attorney Leonard Eels (**Ken Niles**), Jeff heads to San Francisco only to discover he's the intended victim of an incriminating double-cross.

For a film so celebrated for its noir style, *Out Of The Past* has a surprising lack of the usual stylized noir camera-work. Instead, cinematographer Nicholas Musuraca concentrated on creating a "modulated atmosphere lighting", often using a single source with a tiny amount of light to accentuate faces or details. When sequences called for more dramatic lighting, such as Jeff's catastrophic fight with Fisher or his confrontation with Kathie, he used realistic low-level lighting sources like a fire or table light to create an unnerving, shadow-filled effect reminiscent of his earlier work with Tourneur.

Humphrey Bogart and Dick Powell were both considered for the role of Jeff Bailey. But it was RKO's top star, **Robert Mitchum**, who was to plumb hitherto undiscovered depths of world-weariness, fatalism and resigned cynicism as the former private detective. Look at him kissing Greer during the Acapulco beach scene – he is barely able to keep his eyes open as he responds to her lies with an exhausted "Baby, I don't care" before resuming their embrace.

As Kathie, the 22-year-old Jane Greer produced a performance of great depth by doing very little. In one of the most sexually assured entrances of any noir *femme fatale*, she appears like an apparition "out of the sun" into the La Mar Azul bar and Jeff's half-waking life. Whether he awakes from this dream state during their affair is a moot point. Certainly his heightened memories of her are a world away from the woman who shoots three men who get in her way. But as she says to Jeff, "I never told you I was anything but what I am. You just wanted to imagine I was, that's why I left you."

Jeff does finally escape his past – though not in the way he had hoped to – when he tips off the police about his attempted getaway with Kathie. Whether the film's good girl Ann will escape hers is a question that only gets answered in the film's poignant coda.

Pickup On South Street

dir Samuel Fuller, 1953, US, 80m, b/w

cast Richard Widmark, Jean Peters, Thelma Ritter, Richard Kiley, Murvyn Vye *cin* Joseph MacDonald *m* Leigh Harline

Brash and ballsy openers are a prerequisite of any Fuller film, and none more so than in this, the first of his celebrated noir sextet. In the muggy bustle of New York's subway rush hour, recent ex-con

Skip McCoy (**Richard Widmark**) moves in on streetwise Candy (**Jean Peters**) in what looks like a pick-up. That is, until he dexterously picks her purse – the contents of which include sensitive government film she is unknowingly couriering to a top Communist agent – as they exchange charged stares under the gaze of two horrified FBI agents. It is a masterful introduction to a relationship which will vacillate between mistrust, violence and sexual attraction, and a chance pick that will propel Skip into a world of industrial espionage, Feds, reds and the lovable tie-peddling stoolie Moe Williams (Oscar-nominated **Thelma Ritter**).

With the FBI and Candy desperate to locate Skip and his now secreted celluloid, Moe is soon doing a brisk trade in overpriced "persoinality neckwear". Meanwhile, Skip is hauled in front of his growling nemesis Capt. Dan Tiger (**Murvyn Vye**) and his new Fed friends. Suspicious of their efforts to retrieve the film in return for waiving charges against him, Skip proves impervious to their patriotic appeals – "If you refuse to cooperate, you'll be as guilty as the traitors that gave Stalin the A-bomb" – and promptly embarks on noir's most treasonable shakedown. When Candy's lascivious visits to his extraordinarily rickety waterfront hideout (built to Fuller's precise specification by noir specialist **Lyle Wheeler**) are met with punches, kicks and cynical kisses, it seems that nothing will prevent him from "playing both ends against the middle" and demanding $25,000 from a calculating, apolitical syndicate, which includes Candy's exploitative ex Joey (**Richard Kiley**).

Without a detective hero, *femme fatale* or psychotic in sight, *Pickup* is hardly conventional noir, but what it has in abundance is small-time crooks. As an experienced ex-crime reporter for *The New York Graphic*, Fuller had first-hand experience of grifters, muffins, stoolies, big thumbs and cannons such as these. In this world, a stoolie, ex-hooker and pickpocket can become heroes, whether through uncompromising loyalty and an adherence to the code of the street, unreciprocated love or righteous indignation.

Complementing this "skid row hysteria", cinematographer Joe MacDonald's technical realism was later praised by Fuller: "To make other scenes look real, MacDonald took a helluva lot of risks for me. He shot sequences in one single camera movement, not knowing what the hell we had in the can until we looked at the dailies." Examples include Moe's heart-rending monologue to Joey in her pitiful Bowery tenement, covered largely in one

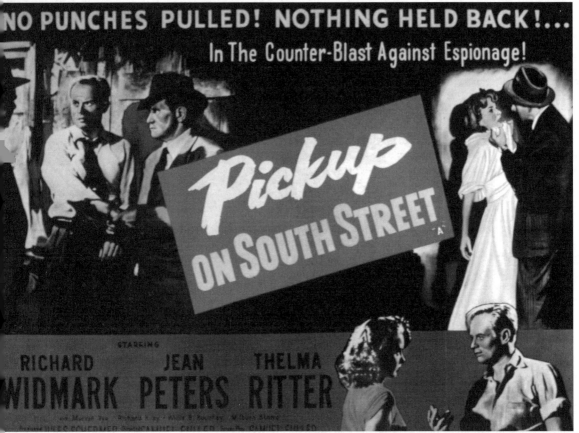

A classic example of Twentieth Century-Fox's vigorous, lithographic poster art.

dirge-like track towards her. Fuller then recuts to her close-up at the scene's end as she says, "Look Mister, I'm so tired, you'd be doing me a big favour if you blew my head off", while the camera pans respectfully to a revolving record on her Victrola. The penultimate subway scene, where Skip finally confronts Joey, is similarly brutal, dominated by a giddy panoply of shots ranging from overheads, brutal medium shots and a reverse track barely able to contain the scrapping duo. Fuller was particularly pleased with the effect of Skip dragging Joey down the subway stairs by the ankles mid-fight, later drawing attention to the musicality of the heavy's chin hitting every step.

Pickup's pervasive strain of cynicism continues to its unresolved close when a sneering Skip is told by Tiger: "You'll always be a two bit person … I give you thirty days before I pick ya up with your hand in somebody else's pocket." Tiger's forecast is probably right. Can the couple's borderline sado-masochistic relationship possibly outlast the temptation of further seductive subway grifts?

Pitfall

dir André de Toth, 1948, US, 86m, b/w
cast Dick Powell, Lizabeth Scott, Jane Wyatt, Raymond Burr, Byron Barr *cin* Harry Wild *m* Louis Forbes

Johnny Forbes (**Dick Powell**) is stuck in a rut "six feet deep" at Olympic Mutual Insurance and feels "like a wheel within a wheel, within a wheel." His ossifying suburban existence is not much better, with a predictable routine, an unsympathetic wife and a young son racking up the bills. So when an insurance case takes him to glamorous fashion model Mona Stevens (**Lizabeth Scott**) and she castigates him with "You're a little man with a briefcase; you go to work every morning and do what you're told", he decides to disobey company orders.

Ditching his inventory – he is in the middle of reclaiming gifts given to Mona by her embezzler-jailbird fiancé Bill Smiley (**Byron Barr**) – Johnny spends a dreamy session roaring around in her speedboat (aptly called the *Tempest*), topping it off with intimate afternoon cocktails and dinner. Meanwhile, Olympic's odious private investigator MacDonald (**Raymond Burr**) has developed an unhealthy obsession with Mona and is maddened by Johnny's extracurricular activity. So much so, that he warns his erstwhile employer off Mona with a savage beating.

With Mona crushed by the discovery of Johnny's family and off the scene with barely a whimper, a battered Johnny resumes his life with his guilty secret intact – but not for long. In his absence MacDonald continues to menace Mona and, with his advances unreciprocated, threatens to disclose the couple's clandestine affair. Left with no choice but to re-enter the fray and dust down his intercollegiate boxing skills, Johnny warns off MacDonald with disastrous results. Determined to eviscerate his competitor, Mac visits Smiley in prison with news of his fiancée's affair and stokes up the paroled ex-con to a frenzied, fatal visit to Johnny's home.

Pitfall's story of a protagonist's "temporary insanity" and descent into a bog of accumulated lies, deceit and homicide is a favourite plotline of noir and neo-noir. But what sets it apart is its lean direction by de Toth, which is as taut as Johnny's immaculately tailored suits. Take a look at how the camera pans with Johnny and his wife Sue (**Jane Wyatt**) before and after the shooting of Smiley in the dark confines of their living room and a flavour of de Toth's deceptively simple style emerges.

Every character in *Pitfall* gets a rum deal. The Assistant District Attorney sets the tone when he tells Johnny: "You killed a man, and that's not a pleasant thing to live with for the rest of your life." As for the others: Smiley is horribly manipulated by MacDonald and gets gunned down as a common prowler; MacDonald is shot by Mona as he goads her into teaming up with him after (what he sees as) the fortuitous death of Smiley; and Mona faces a possible murder rap as MacDonald's life hangs in the balance. She is the film's single most fascinating character, changing chameleon-like from *femme fatale* (look at the way she spars and flirts with Johnny in the opening scenes) to stoically accepting Johnny's duplicitous behaviour and then becoming vulnerable victim to both Smiley and MacDonald.

The final word goes to Sue, who not only is devastated by the outcome of Johnny's "filthy conscience", but also singularly fails to convince her husband to protect the family from scandal. After Johnny has made a full confession to the Assistant DA, she collects him from the Courts of Justice and tells him that she is prepared to try to save their marriage. However, take one look at her pained, drawn expression, fixed on the road ahead, and critic Philippe Garnier's description of the film's finish – "One of the most chilling endings in the history of cinema" – might just be an understatement.

Raw Deal

dir **Anthony Mann, 1948, US, 82m, b/w**
cast Dennis O'Keefe, Claire Trevor, Marsha Hunt,
Raymond Burr, John Ireland *cin* John Alton *m* Paul Sawtell

Faced with a three-year rap for mobster Rick Coyle (**Raymond Burr**), Joe Morse (**Dennis O'Keefe**) tells his faithful girlfriend Pat (**Claire Trevor**): "I want to breathe, that's why I want out of this place, so I can take a deep breath again." Concerned that Joe might "scream loud enough for the DA to hear", Rick fixes Joe's prison break-out, knowing there is only an infinitesimal chance that he'll ever reach Crescent City for his $50,000 pay-off and passage to Panama.

With a bullet-ridden gas tank and a dragnet closing in, Joe and Pat kidnap Ann Martin (**Marsha Hunt**) – an assistant lawyer who now has good reason to regret her sympathetic visits to Joe in prison – and commandeer her car. An unlikely trio, their triangular relationship becomes increasingly fraught as they sidestep an ineffectual police force in noir's bleakest road movie. Pat's problem is that Joe is falling in love with Ann, and Joe's problem is that Ann regards him as "something from under a rock".

In his baroque apartment, Rick is rattled that Joe has made it safely over Idaho's Blue Mountain Range and sends his leering sidekick Fantail (played by noir stalwart **John Ireland**) to the planned rendezvous with the admonition "I don't want him to meet me – EVER!" The ensuing confrontation is fought out against a bizarre location – Grimshaw's Taxidermy – and sees Ann's hesitant gunplay winging Fantail and saving Joe from being impaled on a taxidermist's probe. Following a clinch on the beach and Ann's avowal of love, Joe selflessly decides to leave her with an unconvincing "We go together like a bird and a cat." Arriving in San Francisco, Pat talks Joe out of visiting Rick and the couple prepare for their passage south. The trouble is, Pat knows that Ann is being held by the misogynistic Rick, who has a worrying habit of throwing flaming punch cups at women who irritate him. Minutes away from departure, will she reveal the situation to Joe and forestall their chances of a new life together?

Raw Deal is infused by a disquieting female voice-over as Pat comments on her disintegrating relationship with Joe to the ethereal strands of Paul Sawtell's theremin. More worrying still is her inability to control her thoughts, which tumble into her speech during especially tense moments. So, when racked by indecision about whether to tell Joe about Ann, she shouts out her rival's name, leaving no choice but to tell the truth. Her outburst is prefigured by an audacious close-up of her in dark profile flanked by a wall clock in deep focus, followed by a reflection of her anguished face on the clockface, and culminating in a slow track towards a devastating close-up.

Mann was teamed up for the second time with cinematographer **John Alton** and they worked at breakneck speed, often completing seventy set-ups a day during the film's three-week schedule. To embody the shadowy world the fugitives inhabit, Alton daringly left large areas of the frame in total darkness or placed the actors in inky silhouette as he worked from the floor with minimum lights. Illuminating fog and mist was one of Alton's specialities and it was used to remarkable effect in the film's final scenes. Here, Alton's camera dollies mysteriously with a young boy on skates bathed in fog as he bumps into an angry Fantail before careering into an addled Joe. It is a wholly unnerving prelude to the muddled, grotesque shoot-out.

Having finally disposed of Rick, who is fittingly engulfed in flames before plunging hellishly out the window, a fatally wounded Joe dies cradled in Ann's arms. He can now tell Ann, "I got my breath of fresh air", while ironically enshrouded by fog and acrid smoke. The last words are left to the handcuffed Pat's despairing voice-over: "There's my Joe in her arms, a kind of happiness on his face. In my heart I know that this is right for Joe, this is what he wanted." Small comfort for the film's "genuinely working-class woman", who has to stomach the rawest deal of all.

Le Samouraï

dir Jean-Pierre Melville 1967, Fr/It, 95m
cast Alain Delon, Nathalie Delon, François Périer, Cathy Rosier, Jacques Leroy *cin* Henri Decaë *m* François de Roubaix

"There is no greater solitude than the samurai." Look carefully behind Melville's bogus quotation superimposed over the film's drab apartment room opener, and a lone figure, with a caged, chirruping bullfinch for company, is just visible. This is hitman Jef Costello (**Alain Delon**), preparing for his next kill, the manager of Martey's nightclub. In an anachronistic ritual, Delon pulls up his trenchcoat collar and runs two fingers along his snap-brim fedora – a detail copied from his Stetson-touting director.

Martey barely has time to question the laconic, white-gloved killer before being outgunned with a speed and dexterity rarely seen outside of a Sergio Leone Western:

Who are you?
It doesn't matter.
What do you want?
To kill you.

Solitary assassin Jef Costello (Alain Delon) prepares to deal with an unwelcome visitor in *Le Samouraï*.

Rounded up with a mass of criminal suspects – a sequence influenced by the line-up in Melville's favourite noir *The Asphalt Jungle* (1950) – Costello is freed by the inexplicable perjury of enigmatic nightclub pianist Valérie (**Cathy Rosier**) and the grudging testimonial of the sugar daddy of his lover Jane Lagrange. However, Costello will have to contend with both a tenacious superintendent convinced of his guilt (**François Périer**, superbly cast against type) and his gangster paymaster, suspicious of a hit with loose ends.

Although *Le Samouraï* is now regarded as Melville's masterpiece – a distillation of his recurrent themes of loneliness, betrayal and obsessive honour – the film's production and reception were troubled. Beset by delays, not least because Melville's studio burned down mid-production, the film would be a massive hit with the French public and popular press but treated contemptuously by the serious critical establishment. *Cahiers du cinéma*'s Serge Daney suggested that Melville's skills would be better employed making commercials about "a style in raincoats".

Querulous, fiercely independent and a man completely committed to cinema, Melville, in Périer's words, "knew exactly what he wanted and shot few takes". He also had a maddeningly acute sense of detail, even "down to the width of the brim of a hat". Assisting him in his mission "to make a colour film in black and white" was cinematographer **Henri Decaë**, who worked solely in a spectrum of deliberately cold colours (even the bank notes Costello receives for his contract would be black-and-white photocopies). By attempting to reinterpret the black-and-white cinematography of *This Gun For Hire* (see p.26), an iconic 1942 noir in which killer Alan Ladd is a key inspiration/source for Costello's look, Melville would raise that key conundrum in noir – can it exist in colour? (see p.31)

Double-crossed and wounded by a gunman (**Jacques Leroy**) at the Gare d'Orléans – in a frenetic montage of tracking shots, studied close-ups and disorienting long shots – Costello's behaviour becomes increasingly wilful and irrational. He brazenly returns to Martey's to seek out Valérie, for whom he has developed a fatal fascination, while attempting to discover the identity of the gangster behind his attempted murder. No need, as he is soon ruthlessly prizing the identity of the gangster boss Olivier Rey (**Jean-Pierre Posier**) from the returning gunman. He also finds out that he has instructions to fulfil one last contract-kill – on the now-compromised

Valérie, who happens to be Olivier's mistress. However, not before he pays a vengeful trip to Olivier...

Costello returns to Martey's one final time, his bloodied trenchcoat and fedora exchanged for an immaculate dark overcoat. Double-crossed by the gangsters, let down by a dismissive Valérie and with Jane pressured by the police to withdraw her alibi, the only thing left for Melville's isolated killer is to carry out his contract. However, with his world falling apart around him perhaps the Samourai's hari-kiri offers the one honourable alternative. Which will it be?

Scarlet Street

dir Fritz Lang, 1945, US, 103m, b/w

cast Edward G. Robinson, Joan Bennett, Dan Duryea, Rosalind Ivan *cin* Milton Krasner *m* Hans J. Salter

All that Chris Cross (**Edward G. Robinson**) has to show for his dull 25-year career as a cashier is a gold watch from his boss and an overbearing sense of loneliness. His home life is little more than a barrage of abuse and domestic demands from his harridan wife Adele (**Rosalind Ivan**), and all he wants is to be left alone to work on his Sunday paintings in his cramped bathroom studio. As he wanders through the nocturnal, labyrinthine Greenwich Village streets, Chris witnesses the sight of streetwalker Kitty (**Joan Bennett**) being beaten up by her boyfriend Johnny (**Dan Duryea**) and turns unlikely umbrella-swinging vigilante. Bedazzled by Kitty, clad in a sexy transparent raincoat, Chris persuades her to have a late-night drink with him. Eager to impress, he fails to correct her mistaken belief that he is a rich and successful artist.

As Chris returns to his cluttered Brooklyn apartment to add a few more daubs to his latest naive work, Johnny is plotting how Kitty can persuade Chris to part with his non-existent thousands. By now completely besotted with Kitty, Chris soon sets her up in a swanky studio apartment and is funding her and (unbeknown to him) Johnny's tawdry lifestyle by any means necessary. Thus begins his noirish descent into embezzlement, murder and guilt-ridden madness.

Scarlet Street and the state censors

Scarlet Street was granted a "B" rating ("objectionable in part") by the **Legion of Decency**, but was banned outright by the state censors in New York, Milwaukee and Atlanta. In Atlanta they cited the following reasons: "the sordid life it portrayed, the treatment of illicit love, [and] the failure of the characters to receive orthodox punishment from the police." The threat of losing such substantial markets sent **Walter Wanger** scuttling to various state dignitaries with editor **Arthur Hilton** and scissors in tow. After varying delays (the longest being ten months in Atlanta), the film was granted a certificate, along with a welcome dose of notoriety – which no doubt contributed to it being Universal's second most successful film of the mid-1940s after the noirish *Dark Mirror*. Its tussle with the censor meant that various *Scarlet Street* edits existed, and it was possible to view the murder with one, four or seven ice pick stabs, depending on the stipulations of each state censor.

Scarlet Street was adapted from Georges de La Fourchardière's novel, which had already been made into Jean Renoir's 1931 realist classic, *La chienne* (see p.14). Adapted by Dudley Nichols, it was the first picture produced by Diana Productions, the independent company run by Bennett's husband, Walter Wanger. Lang was granted complete authority over the production, exerting a fastidious control over props and actors. This gave rise to rumours after he spent an inordinate amount of time "rearranging the folds in Joan Bennett's negligée so she would cast a certain shadow he wanted". His relationship with Robinson was more professional, but in his autobiography, *All My Yesterdays*, the actor was dismissive of the film and failed to do justice to his own extraordinarily moving performance.

When Chris is forced to store his paintings with Kitty, Johnny tries another money-raising scheme and the result is that a leading New York gallery owner takes up the works. With his paintings now the toast of the art world, albeit under Kitty's name, and having extricated himself from his marriage (in a rather cumbersome plot twist), Chris calls on Kitty in order to propose, only to catch her with Johnny. When his efforts to win her over only prompt her taunts – "I've wanted to laugh in your face ever since I first met you. You're old and ugly and I'm sick of you, sick, sick, sick" – he grabs a handy ice pick and repeatedly stabs her in a sexual frenzy.

Chris's revenge is complete as he denies authorship of the paintings (and therefore any connection with Kitty), thereby sealing Johnny's murder rap and execution in Sing Sing. Shuffling back to his squalid rooms, intermittently lit by a flashing neon light, he is haunted by the voices of Johnny and Kitty while the camera pans and roams round the room in step with his deranged mind. Suicide evades him when neighbours drag him down from his attempt to hang himself, his body racked by sobs. The final image of his spectral figure shuffling past his portrait of Kitty in a Fifth Avenue gallery is one of the most desolate in film noir. As the camera cranes up over the street, the crowds dissolve to reveal him hunched and isolated, haunted by Kitty's lilting words: "Jeepers, I love you Johnny."

Se7en

dir David Fincher, 1995, US, 99m
cast Morgan Freeman, Brad Pitt, Gwyneth Paltrow, Kevin Spacey *cin* Darius Khondji *m* Howard Shore

Se7en opens insidiously: no studio fanfare, no titles, just a cacophony of threatening city sounds over an inky-black screen fading up to reveal Lt William Somerset (**Morgan Freeman**) preparing for his last week in Homicide. Quitting after 34 years of methodical and thankless service, he has become alienated by a rain-drenched city he no longer understands and a police department in terminal decline. On top of this, he has to spend the next seven days breaking in his cocksure, impulsive successor Dt David Mills (**Brad Pitt**), recently arrived from up state with his angelic wife Tracy (**Gwyneth Paltrow**).

Suddenly Kyle Cooper's iconic title montage plunges the film into the dark heart and mind of the third main protagonist, serial killer John Doe (**Kevin Spacey**) safety-blading off the pads of his fingertips before his hands are shown feverishly pouring out screeds of close-written diatribes on the deadly sins. This monstrous barrage – distorted, stretched and vying with scratched negatives, flash frames and searing blood-red negatives – seems like the unhinged scribblings of a madman.

Fresh from a Monday morning autopsy of Doe's first victim – a grossly obese man (**Bob Mack**) force-fed till bursting – Somerset pleads with his glaring superior (**R. Lee Ermey**): "This can't be my last duty, it's just going to go on and on and on." By Friday his instincts have been proved right; avaricious attorney Eli Gould (**Gene Borkan**) is discovered by Mills bled to death after having been forced to extract a pound of his own flesh, and a slothful drug-dealing pederast (**Michael Reid MacKay**) is found reduced to a cadaverous heap after a year-long starvation programme.

So with another four killings expected and nothing apart from Doe's preachy, misleading crime-scene messages to go by, the hapless detectives are stuck – as was screenwriter Andrew Kevin Walker. Cue one of the most clunky second act "hooks" of recent years as

Officer Mills (Brad Pitt) careers after serial killer John Doe in *Se7en*'s six-and-a-half-minute chase sequence.

the detectives track down the serial killer to his tenement apartment via his dubious FBI-tagged public library withdrawals. Not that it seems to matter once a wrong-footed Doe opens fire on them and a six-minute chase sequence ensues.

Although Doe eventually gives them the slip, the detectives gain access to the serial killer's apartment, their flashlights catching ghastly glimpses of his macabre home furnishings, including display cabinets devoted to each of his victims, a darkroom crammed full of photographs of his "life's work" and his countless journals. The weekend brings with it two further killings – a prostitute's shocking client-based encounter, followed by a model offered the choice between living defaced or committing suicide. Then in one of the most barnstorming entrances since Orson Welles's appearance in *The Third Man* (1949), a bloodied Doe turns himself in.

Se7en is a profoundly uneasy and unsettling film to watch and one in which it is virtually impossible to find one's bearings. Although filmed in Los Angeles, its unnamed city feels like a run-down, colourless, rain-drenched New York or Philadelphia. Bereft of establishing shots, its characters are dominated by cramped, cluttered locations often filmed in tight close-ups or medium shots from low levels. Looking more like a film out of the 1970s, its look was inspired by "the stylized work" of *Klute* (1971) and "the rawness and grittiness" of *The French Connection* (1971). This constant see-sawing of styles – for instance between the gothic look of the crime scene installations and the documentary feel of the squad car interiors – further disorientates.

Shooting the film was an exacting process. Fincher and many of the crew developed hacking coughs due to constant exposure to a vaporized mineral oil used to create a mist effect. Pitt severed a tendon in his wrist while running through traffic and his arm was in a cast for most of the filming. Freeman suffered an ankle injury during the many takes demanded by Fincher for the final denouement, in which the detectives agree to Doe's request to accompany him to an out-of-city scrubland in order to uncover his last two victims.

Fincher described the twists and turns of *Se7en* leading up to its nihilistic, crushing ending as follows: "First you thought it was gonna be a cop movie, then you thought it was going to be a thriller, and then at the end it's really a horror movie – it's the fucking *Exorcist*, you don't have any control over this, you're just along for the ride." Some bloody ride.

Tirez sur le pianiste (Shoot The Pianist)

dir François Truffaut, 1960, France, 84m, b/w

cast Charles Aznavour, Marie Dubois, Daniel Boulanger, Nicole Berger, Albert Rémy *cin* Raoul Coutard *m* Georges Delerue

In what appears to be a classic noir opening, a thickset man hurtles down a pitch-black city street chased by a menacing car, before slamming headlong into a lamppost. Helped to his feet by an avuncular stranger, the two men indulge in a lengthy conversation about marriage and fatherhood. It is a brilliant introduction to Truffaut's genre-hopping hybrid, in which comedy, romance, drama, melodrama, the psychological film and the thriller all struggle to break free from the film's pervasive noir atmosphere.

The man, Chico Saroyan (**Albert Rémy**), is pursued by two bumbling gangsters, Ernest (**Daniel Boulanger**) and Momo (**Claude Mansard**), who he and his wayward sibling Richard have crossed. By leading the gangsters to a rundown bar, he embroils its implacable piano player Charlie Koller (**Charles Aznavour**) – in fact Chico's estranged brother Edouard – in his criminal shenanigans. Charlie helps Chico escape, but later admits to the bar's lecherous owner Plyne (**Serge Davri**) just how scared he is, his face crumpling into a frightful grimace as he does so.

Over the next 36 hours Charlie – a once celebrated concert pianist with a tragic past – sees his anonymous life collapse around him. Fingered by the avaricious Plyne, Charlie and waitress Léna (**Marie Dubois**) are picked up by the gangsters the following morning. Not the most menacing of kidnappers, Ernest and Momo bicker about each other's driving before conversing uproariously about women's sexual appetites with their bemused passengers.

After an easy escape, Charlie discovers that Léna knows all about his past career and, rather worryingly, has a poster of the "old" Edouard Saroyan over the bed on which they will later make love. This prompts a lengthy flashback outlining Charlie's start as a struggling pianist, his rise to fame and the appalling consequences of his wife's efforts to secure him an influential music agent. Having faced up to his past, Charlie returns to the bar with Léna to quit their jobs. However, after knifing Plyne in self-defence, and with his adopted younger brother Fido (**Richard Kanayan**) now abducted by the gangsters, Charlie and Léna decide to head for the Saroyan family home.

Tirez sur le pianiste is Truffaut's darkest and most innovative film in a career peppered with neo-noir gems: its crushing commercial failure would profoundly shape the director's subsequent career. Adapted from David Goodis's pulp novel *Down There*, the director changes the book's location from Philadelphia and New Jersey to the outskirts of Paris and the Grénoble region. Using the basic plot as a springboard, Truffaut recreates the book's atmosphere of doomed desperation, combining it with his own slant on Charlie. In Aznavour's nuanced interpretation, the pianist becomes a much more timid character, racked by self-doubt and paranoia; a far cry from Goodis's embittered veteran and sado-masochistic brawler.

The film was shot entirely on location using a minimal crew but always with an extra camera operated by its cinematographer Raoul Coutard. Particular attention was paid to accentuating Charlie's isolation and awkwardness, for instance in the scene where he visits his agent Lars Schmeel (**Claude Heymann**). Here a slightly raised camera cranes backwards, shrinking his hunched figure down a seemingly endless corridor before he hesitates outside Schmeel's door. Attempting to ring the doorbell, three increasingly large close-ups of his trembling finger approach the buzzer before the door is opened.

By the time the main players reach the Saroyan home for the film's climax, Truffaut has already crisscrossed a gamut of film genres, from comedy, as the incompetent gangsters cross France telling increasingly outlandish stories to Fido, to romance, as Charlie and Léna journey through urban landscape to winter wonderland. However, it is in the final showdown that the film reaches its heady apogee in a melée of Western, slapstick and melodrama.

In the film's coda, Charlie returns to his old job, positioning himself protectively behind the upright piano. A small, trapped figure, his stare fixed in a frown of immobility, he represents the quintessential noir loner, a survivor trapped by his past, and now with even more reason to dread the future.

T-Men

dir Anthony Mann, 1947, US, 96m, b/w

cast Dennis O'Keefe, Alfred Ryder, Wallace Ford, Charles McGraw, John Wengraf *cin* John Alton *m* Paul Sawtell

Try to stop your eyes glazing over as a real–life US Treasury honcho addresses the camera in *T-Men*'s stilted opener because you might miss cinematographer **John Alton**'s masterclass in noir style. Here, in thirteen succinct shots, a secret service agent waits in the shadows as his informer is gunned down in a flurry of surreal compositions and a riot of night-time chiaroscuro. This is part of an investigation into a Los Angeles counterfeiting operation which is going nowhere. Time to bring in Treasury agents Dennis O'Brien (**Dennis O'Keefe**) and Tony Genaro (**Alfred Ryder**).

One of the particularly unsettling elements in this disconcerting semi–documentary is just how easily O'Brien and Genaro, set to infiltrate the counterfeiting ring, inhabit their criminal aliases as snugly as their sharply tailored suits. The transformation is complete when O'Brien dons his immaculate wide-striped suit saying, "It's a nice suit, hope the tax payers can afford it. I know I couldn't on my salary", before running his fingers along his snap-brim Fedora. At times he is virtually indistinguishable from his hoodlum counterpart Moxie (**Charles McGraw**), and beats up elusive counterfeiter Schemer (**Wallace Ford**) like a seasoned criminal pro. Genaro, meanwhile, has a weaselly, sweaty presence not unlike many of noir's more unsavoury criminal types.

What makes O'Brien's character still more ambiguous is how little is known about his personal life. He appears to take a perverse pleasure in receiving a group pummelling after infiltrating a gambling joint with counterfeit money, and his final gunfight is one of the strangest in noir. He repeatedly shoots at Moxie with no apparent fear for his own safety, almost inviting the punishing fire power. By the time his bandaged, bedridden figure smiles from the covers of *Look* magazine in the film's semi-realist coda, it is a world away from his angst-ridden face as he lies bleeding on the San Anselmo deck.

Another part of *T-Men*'s unsettling power stems from an uneasy balance between its semi-realist techniques and its intensely

Treasury agent O'Brien (Dennis O'Keefe) on the trail of diminutive counterfeiter Wallace Ford in *T-Men*.

dramatic and expressionist sequences, which tend to linger in the memory long after the stentorian voice-over or Treasury department footage have faded away. Mann could have been thinking along these lines when he admitted to being "fairly satisfied with certain sequences: the murder of Wallace Ford in the steam bath, for example, or the beating of Dennis O'Keefe."

In order to achieve this fusion of documentary and expressionist effects, Mann teamed with John Alton in noir's most fruitful partnership between director and cinematographer. As Alton wrote, "I found a director in Tony Mann who thought like I did … He not only accepted what I did, he demanded it." Not only was Alton adept at filming in the new postwar documentary style, but also his mystery lighting was unparalleled. He would make particular reference to *T-Men* two years later in his ground-breaking book, *Painting With Light*, referencing the low-angled grotesque lighting of Schemer "which distorted the countenance, threw shadows seldom seen in everyday life across the face" and his bizarre compositions "when, for example, there is the suggestion of fear or menace behind".

One of the outstanding examples of Alton's craft is the wide-angle shot in which a paranoid Schemer threatens his suave superior Shiv Triano (**John Wengraf**) on the phone, while the frame cuts him off just below the eyes and Genaro loiters in the background in deep focus. Not for long, as Genaro's cover gets blown disastrously and O'Brien sinks deeper and deeper into the workings of Triano's counterfeiting operation. And as drama and suspense vie with and finally replace *T-Men*'s documentary style, there won't be a chance for anyone's eyes to glaze over, least of all the cornered O'Brien.

Touch Of Evil

dir Orson Welles, 1958, US, 108m, b/w
cast Orson Welles, Charlton Heston, Janet Leigh, Akim Tamiroff, Marlene Dietrich *cin* Russell Metty *m* Henry Mancini

Just two hours into filming on the first day, Welles announced: "OK, that's a print! Wrap! We're two days ahead of schedule!" To the relief of concerned Universal International executives, Welles and his cinematographer **Russell Metty** had achieved the near impossible: filming *Touch Of Evil*'s complex twelve-page interrogation scene of suspected car bomber Manelo Sanchez (**Victor Millan**) in one continuous crab-dolly-defying shot.

A week later, Welles would further test his crew's ingenuity while directing the film's ground-breaking three-minute opener. Here, a camera rises from a saboteur bomb-rigging the convertible of local millionaire Rudy Linnekar. Then, floating over the cruising car in the bustling Mexican/US border town of Las Robles, it homes in on newlyweds Miguel "Mike" Vargas (a tanned, moustachioed **Charlton Heston**) and his American wife Susan (**Janet Leigh**, with a recently broken arm hidden under a cardigan) as they stroll maddeningly close to the mobile time bomb.

When the couple's evening border break is interrupted by Linnekar's explosive demise on the US side, Vargas (a Mexican government official) is compelled to postpone his honeymoon and acts as unwelcome observer to the US investigation, headed by Capt Hank Quinlan (**Orson Welles**, encased in 60lb of padding and ageing make-up). Separated from Susan – who unwisely takes refuge in a deserted mob-run border motel – Vargas becomes unwilling bystander to the unorthodox, instinctual police procedure of the racist, repugnant Quinlan.

Discovering that Quinlan (acting on one of his legendary hunches) has planted incriminating dynamite in Sanchez's apartment, Vargas makes an official complaint to uncomprehending Police Chief Gould (Harry Shannon) and disbelieving District Attorney Adair (**Ray Collins**). Meanwhile a paranoid Quinlan, off the wagon and back on the Bourbon, teams up with local mobster "Uncle" Joe Grandi (played by the toupee-touting, eyeliner-heavy **Akim Tamiroff**), who has his own personal reasons for avenging Vargas. After Susan is horrifically assaulted and "overdoses" in a seedy hotel next to Grandi's garrotted corpse, Vargas's reputation is in the balance and his accusation nullified. That is, until Quinlan's devoted assistant Lt Pete Menzies (**Joseph Calleia**) finds his boss's walking stick at the crime scene and starts to have serious doubts.

Welles radically reworked Paul Monash's adaptation of *Badge Of Evil* by Whit Masterson over an intense period before going straight into the film's six-week schedule. He changed the Anglo-Saxon Assistant District Attorney into Mexican national Mike Vargas, adrift in the racial undercurrents of Las Robles, and fleshed out Quinlan into a monumental, quasi-Shakespearean figure, one who remains noir's most uncompromisingly corrupt police officer. Scarred by his failure to bring his wife's strangler to justice, he now works, according to Vargas, like "a dog catcher putting

Evil restored

Eight months after *Touch Of Evil* wrapped, Orson Welles sent a staggering 58-page memo to Universal's studio boss Edward Muhler. In this document, the director responded eloquently to Universal's drastic re-edit of *Touch Of Evil*, the post-production process from which he was, by now, virtually excluded. Problems had begun six months before, when studio executives – bewildered by Welles's audacious rough cut – started replacing editors and even employed a jobbing director to film expository bridging sequences.

The director's impassioned feedback – a virtual masterclass in film technique – passed largely unheeded by the studio and for almost twenty years *Touch Of Evil* was only available in an emasculated 96-minute version. Despite this, its international reputation continued to snowball and, in the early 1970s, the memo came to light during **Peter Bogdanovich**'s interview sessions with Welles.

Then in 1975 UCLA academic Bob Epstein unearthed a 108-minute print from Universal's archives. Initially hailed as the lost director's cut, it was actually a preview version containing some of Welles's deleted scenes and extra material filmed by replacement director Harry Keller. This longer version rapidly replaced the 96-minute print, whereas its home video release combined elements of both.

Skip forward to 1992 and Bogdanovich's landmark interviews titled *This Is Orson Welles* is finally published by Harper Collins. The book's editor and Welles authority

Jonathan Rosenbaum – frustrated by the publisher's decision to omit the edited memo – submits it instead to *Film Quarterly* magazine. This revelatory article in turn prompts producer Rick Schmidlin to team up with veteran film editor **Walter Murch** and Rosenbaum to restore *Touch Of Evil* in line with Welles's original suggestions. That is, within the limits of the footage available.

By 1998 Murch's sensitive restoration was complete and the producer/editor team finally watched their new version with some trepidation. Schmidlin's reaction, as outlined in Laurent Bouzerau's excellent documentary *Reconstructing Evil* (1998), was as follows: "What we found was a more coherent, more commercial movie that made sense of every plot point." What made their achievement doubly extraordinary was that they had had no studio rough cut from which to qualify Welles's notes, suggestions and tweaks.

Comparing the reconstruction against the old version is a revelation. Gone are the clumsy titles besmirching the film's breathtaking opener, while Henry Mancini's strident music is replaced by atmospheric snatches of real sound and music from transistors and cafes; the transitions between Vargas and Susan's opposing stories now come at just the right dramatic moments and Susan's rape scene turns into an atmospheric sequence of eerie suggestion rather than barnstorming horror. And so the structural and specific changes continue adding yet greater layers of depth and resonance to the film.

criminals behind bars". Despite this, he is described by Adair as "one of the most respected police officers in the country" and has earned intense loyalty from Menzies after stopping a crippling bullet meant for him.

Unable to film in Mexico's Tijuana, Welles chose Venice, California as his principal location. He fell in love with the town's gone-to-seed faux Italianate arcades, crumbling interiors and oil derrick-cluttered canals, and gradually jettisoned Universal's specially prepared studio sets. The milieu is showcased to great effect in the film's hallucinatory ending where Menzies, driven to betraying his partner, ekes out a recorded confession from Quinlan while Vargas (with temperamental transmitter) tracks the couple over an angular terrain of derricks, walkways and industrial wasteland.

In the closing scenes, Welles elevated *Touch Of Evil* from a technically delirious noir policier to minor tragedy. Quinlan is transformed into an almost sympathetic figure as Menzies' betrayal gradually dawns on him. His only recourse is to continue working outside the law as he avenges his partner and attempts to frame Vargas. His vainglorious attempts would usher in a new type of police officer for neo-noir, described by his old flame Tanya (**Marlene Dietrich**) in her response to the closing words of Assistant District Attorney Al Schwartz (**Mort Mills**):

> Schwartz: Hank was a great detective alright…
> Tanya: …and a lousy cop. He was some kind of a man … What does it matter what you say about people?

The Woman In The Window

dir Fritz Lang, 1944, US, 99m, b/w
cast Edward G. Robinson, Joan Bennett, Dan Duryea, Raymond Massey, Edmond Breon *cin* Milton Krasner *m* Arthur Lange

As Milton Krasner's camera cranes down towards Professor Richard Wanley (**Edward G. Robinson**) lecturing on the "Psychological Aspects of Homicide", cast your eye to the blackboard behind him with its Mental Life definition, and prepare yourself for a surfeit of doppelgängers, id, ego and superego in one of noir's great Freudian fests.

Walking to his apartment after drinks at his stodgy New York club with friends Dr Barkstane (**Edmond Breon**) and District Attorney Frank Lalor (**Raymond Massey**), Wanley is captivated by a beautiful woman's portrait in a gallery window. As if in answer to his repressed subconscious desire, he is interrupted by the dreamy presence of the portrait's real-life sitter, Alice Reed (**Joan Bennett**), in figure-hugging sheer chiffon. And before he knows it, he is ensconced in her dazzling, mirrored apartment, sipping champagne. With the arrival of Alice's enraged lover, Mazard (**Arthur Loft**), Wanley has to grapple with his worst subconscious fears as he defends himself from Mazard's murderous attack only to end up with a scissor-skewered corpse to dispose of. To add to his troubles, he has to contend with a day-by-day update of the Mazard case from Lalor and also has to keep his cool with the blackmailing Heidt (**Dan Duryea**), who knows all about Alice's squalid affair with Mazard. With the forces of law relentlessly bearing down on the couple, and their scheme to poison Heidt a write-off, an exhausted, disillusioned Wanley commits suicide – or is the whole thing just a dream?

In a 1975 interview with noir specialists **Alain Silver** and **Robert Porfirio**, Lang justified the film's controversial dream ending, saying: "This movie was not about evil … it was about psychology, the subconscious desires, and what better expression of those than in a dream, where the libido is released and emotions are exaggerated." Other factors also mitigated against a more explicit suicide ending; it would never have got past the Production Code, and Lang also "felt that an audience wouldn't think a movie worthwhile in which a man kills two people and himself just because he had made a mistake by going home with a girl".

Lang's instincts were right on the nail; the film was a commercial success, although neither the film's producer/screenwriter Nunnally Johnson nor the critics were as impressed, prompting a Motion Picture Herald journalist to comment: "The shopworn and superfluous ending has all the impact of a stale peppermint upon a man who has just ordered a steak dinner." Nearly 25 years later, Lang claimed that he had unconsciously borrowed a technique (used to sinister effect in *Das Cabinet des Dr Caligari*, 1920) of having dream figures reappear as real-life characters. This is the moment when Wanley is caught off-guard by seeing Mazard as club cloakroom attendant and Heidt as its doorman.

The Woman In The Window's Freudian subtexts even extend to its props – everywhere you look in Alice's apartment there are symbolic paintings, ornaments and, above all, mirrors implying

Edward G. Robinson's repressed professor about to succumb to the "siren call" of Alice Reed (Joan Bennett).

alter egos and doubles. As for Alice, she is anything but a straight-forward *femme fatale*. Once she has changed her diaphanous dress for a more housewifely skirt and shirt she becomes Wanley's confidante and trustworthy accomplice throughout his calm efforts to evade the law. The last word, however, should go to monocled meddler Lang, who was an intense and humourless presence on the set, involved in all departments even "to the point of doing the make-up". He continually cued the actors "like puppets" with a peremptory flick of his fingers that kept his editors busy. His technical excellence came to the fore in the sequence in which the camera tracks towards a close-up of Wanley's pinched, overdosed, face as he slumps in his apartment chair. Slowly tracking back, the camera reveals the professor being woken from his post-dinner slumber. A rapid change of scenery and lightning change of jacket ensured that no cut was necessary. Technically, it is a breathtaking effect, but how much darker it would have been had he not woken up at all.

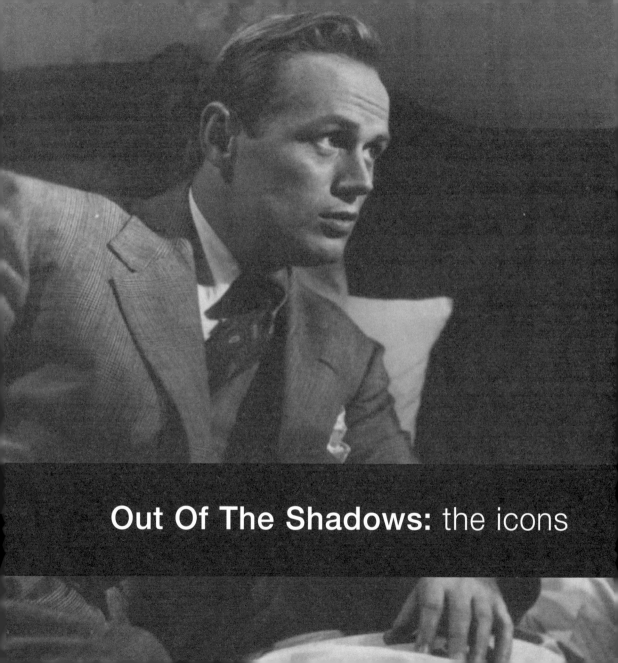

Out Of The Shadows: the icons

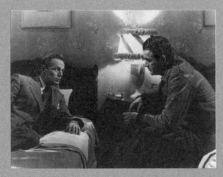

Richard Widmark (left) as gang leader Alec Stiles in *The Street With No Name*.

Out Of The Shadows:
the icons

The nature of the Hollywood studio system meant that directors, actors and all other members of the creative team weren't supposed to specialize in a single genre. The reality was that certain artists became strongly associated with a particular type of film and stamped their personalities on it. The following pages detail those key players who most helped define film noir – from actors like Robert Mitchum and Barbara Stanwyck to directors and cinematographers such as Fritz Lang and John Alton.

Robert Aldrich

Director, 1918–83

One of the great mavericks of the cinema, Robert Aldrich worked his way up through the ranks of Hollywood, learning his craft as assistant to such directors as **Jean Renoir, Charlie Chaplin, Lewis Milestone, Robert Rossen** and **Abraham Polonsky**. A respected enough figure in the US, his stock in Europe was much higher, largely as a result of the veneration of his noir masterpiece *Kiss Me Deadly* (1955, see Canon) by French cineastes.

The popular appeal of Aldrich's extremely tough action films has been largely to a male audience and his is a totally masculine universe (apart from an atypical foray into the world of female grotesques in *What Ever Happened To Baby Jane?* and *The Killing Of Sister George*). His vision is marked by its extreme cynicism: the choices people make are rarely connected to morality, motives are usually selfish and the difference between heroes and villains is hard to discern. While his films encompass a dizzying variety of genres – including some ground-breaking Westerns – it's in the crime and thriller field that Aldrich produced his most personal work.

The delirious *Kiss Me Deadly* may be his greatest film noir but it is by no means the only one. His second film, *World For Ransom* (1954), is a slightly disappointing big-screen extension of Dan Duryea's TV series *China Smith*, and dealt (in perfunctory fashion) with the kidnapping of a nuclear scientist in the Far East. His first fully achieved films followed in the same year, the Westerns *Apache* and *Vera Cruz*, the latter a virtual blueprint for Sergio Leone's Italian Westerns. *Kiss Me Deadly* exploded the following year, and Aldrich's credentials as a director of extreme cinema were consolidated. *The Big Knife*, also 1955, is a noirish melodrama about the venality of Hollywood with **Jack Palance** as an embittered matinée idol and Rod Steiger as a monstrous studio boss. *Autumn Leaves* (1956) is a bizarre, noir-

Robert Aldrich (left) on the set of *Kiss Me Deadly* rehearses the final apocalyptic scene.

ish **Joan Crawford** weepie, famous for one act of startling violence – **Cliff Robertson** hitting the luckless Crawford with a typewriter.

Aldrich's independence meant that he tended to work for himself or for the smaller studios. When Columbia hired him for *The Garment Jungle* (1957), a pro-union film noir about the garment industry, he was replaced over halfway through shooting for refusing to soften the script. His greatest commercial successes were the over-the-top psychodrama *What Ever Happened To Baby Jane?* (1962) and his nihilistic action movie *The Dirty Dozen* (1967). His final noir outing, *Hustle* (1975), co-produced by and starring Burt Reynolds, is one of the better noirs of the 1970s.

The Big Knife
dir Robert Aldrich, 1955, US, 111m, b/w

Made in the same year as *Sunset Boulevard*, this is a less subtle satire on the perils of Hollywood stardom. Jack Palance plays Charlie Castle, an alcoholic movie star, frustrated with his career, who wants to quit. Rod Steiger is the megalomaniac studio boss who will do anything to stop him. Aldrich allows his actors full rein with the histrionic script (based on a Clifford Odets play), while Ernest Laszlo's delirious camera-work adds another layer of anguish to the heady mix.

Hustle
dir Robert Aldrich, 1975, US, 118m

A slightly ungainly script but one with the requisite noir mood of disenchantment and despair. Phil Gaines (Burt Reynolds) is an LA cop investigating the murder of a young woman, while her grief-stricken and violent father breathes down his neck. The evidence seems to lead to corrupt attorney Leo Sellers (Eddie Albert), who also has a connection with Gaines's girlfriend, the prostitute Nicole (Catherine Deneuve). Inevitably, Gaines's attempt to fix his own small part of a corrupt world ends tragically.

John Alton
Cinematographer, 1901–96

No other cinematographer made more noirs than John Alton – a total of nineteen in nine years. His extraordinary filmography is proof positive that a bold visual style is a prerequisite of any serious noir. Most of these films, which include four classic collaborations with director **Anthony Mann** – *T-Men* (1947), *Raw Deal* (1948), *He Walked By Night* (1948), *Border Incident* (1949) – were filmed in just a few weeks on the no-budget B-movie treadmills of Eagle Lion and Republic.

A cosmopolitan intellectual, whose career included running the camera department at France's Joinville studios and overseeing the construction of two South American film studios, Alton cut an incongruous figure in the union-controlled macho atmosphere of the B-movie backlot. Photographs reveal a slight, dapper figure with the pose of a ballet choreographer – not the usual look of a Poverty Row, roughneck director of photography.

Opinionated, precocious, brilliantly innovative but envied and disliked by colleagues, Alton would spend much of his career trying to reform union-fixed studio lighting techniques. It resulted in making an A-movie career-wrecking enemy of John Arnold, the powerful head of MGM's camera department, at least until the 1950s. However, during his twenty-year Hollywood career (1940–60) Alton became a director's favourite with lasting partnerships with **Bernard Vorhaus** (*The Spiritualist*, 1948, and *Bury Me Dead*, 1947), **Allan Dwan** (*Slightly Scarlet*, 1955), Anthony Mann, **John Sturges** (*Mystery Street*, 1950, and *The People Against O'Hara*, 1951) and **Vincente Minnelli** – all of whom valued his skill in providing an A-picture look on a B-movie budget.

Despite his ignominious early retirement from the film industry, after being replaced by his old rival Burnett Guffey on *The Birdman Of Alcatraz* (1962), Alton lived long enough to live out the epigraph to his classic lighting primer *Painting With Light*: "Life is short, but long enough to get what's coming to you." What came were plaudits, retrospectives and the recognition that he was, in Paul Schrader's words, "perhaps the greatest master of noir, an expressionist cinematographer who could relight Times Square at noon if necessary".

 Hollow Triumph
dir Steve Sekely & Paul Henreid, 1948, US, 82m, b/w

With the mob closing in after a bungled casino heist, ex-con John Muller (Paul Henreid) takes on the identity of a psychiatrist to whom he bears a striking resemblance, with the unknowing aid of the shrink's assistant Evelyn Nash (Joan Bennett). An extraordinarily bleak film, Alton's touches of genius include camera tracks round a table of Muller and his cronies; the tension-filled casino hold-up, and the archetypically noir image of Muller silently awaiting his fate in his squalid hotel room, intermittently lit by a flashing neon sign.

Painting With Light

While directors of photography in 1940s Hollywood might get the occasional namecheck in a trade weekly or the odd quotation in an *American Cinematographer* article, what they did not do was write ground-breaking books on cinematography. Not, that is, until John Alton approached Macmillan to publish a collection of his *International Photographer* magazine articles.

First published in 1949, *Painting With Light* blew the lid off the hitherto secretive world of Hollywood cinematography. Part lighting manual (with pithy descriptions of equipment from Cookies to Dinky-Inkies) and part an unofficial technical manifesto of film noir, the book was infused by Alton's no-nonsense, low-lighting philosophy. For the illustrations he borrowed the facilities of Poverty Row studio Eagle Lion to duplicate lighting setups, and used gritty images taken from the studio's low-budget noir B-movies *T-Men* (1947), *Hollow Triumph* (1948), *The Spiritualist* (1948) and *Raw Deal* (1948). Despite being both a critical and commercial success – it ran to three reprints in the 1950s – it would be eight years before *American Cinematographer* magazine gave *Painting With Light* even a cursory review.

Among its 14 chapters are several that contain fascinating and revelatory insights into noir techniques: "Mystery Lighting" has sections devoted to criminal lighting and prison scenes; "Special Illumination" discusses lighting for fog effects and mirror illumination; while "The Hollywood Close-Up" details the aspects of angles, size and composition. However, this is just a small fragment of a book which consistently debunks traditional Hollywood lighting methods and controversially mixes professional and amateur film-making techniques. Alton is just as likely to advise on extricating a car stuck in the mud as he is to tell you how to make an amateur ocean cruise film.

Painting With Light was unavailable for three decades, ensuring cult status for both the book and author among cinematographers and noir aficionados alike. Thanks to Todd McCarthy, who lured the reclusive Alton to attend a 1993 retrospective of his work and spent many hours interviewing him, a new edition of *Painting With Light* appeared in 1995 with an insightful introduction by McCarthy and an updated filmography. It remains one of the great introductions to the art of cinematography.

Humphrey Bogart

Actor, 1899–1957

In 1963 the New York Theatre in Manhattan programmed the first retrospective of Bogart movies. A double bill of *To Have And Have Not* and *The Big Sleep* not only broke records at the theatre, but demonstrated that a younger college crowd had adopted Bogart as the new epitome of masculine cool – despite the fact that he wore suits and fedoras in an era of floral shirts, and that many of his movies were made before his audience was born. Why was Bogart, of all the great Hollywood stars, the one who spoke most eloquently to this new generation – and continues to do so to audiences today? It's a complex cocktail of elements: the blue-collar intransigence of the characters he played is subtly undercut by the actor's own middle-class origins, and his cool, uninflected delivery (exacerbated by his scarred, immobile upper lip) seemed a world away from the more ingratiating style most of his contemporaries had adopted. His battered looks and unexceptional physique marked him out as a more modern performer than the more conventionally handsome male stars of the day. Most of all, though, it was his acting that ensured the actor's screen immortality, even as his heavy smoking brought about his early death from cancer.

It was Bogart's emblematic appearance as a gangster in the 1936 film *The Petrified Forest* that signalled the arrival of an unusual screen presence; today, the film looks stagey and unconvincing, but Bogart's authenticity is unquestionable. Directors and audiences had not yet spotted the actor's leading-man capabilities, and his unsympathetic performance in Raoul Walsh's *The Roaring Twenties* in 1939 rendered his one-dimensional heavy far less interesting than that of his charismatic co-star, James Cagney. But a seismic change was just around the corner, with two films that defined the new Bogart: his tragic gangster Roy Earle in Raoul Walsh's *High Sierra* in 1941 and (in the same year) his definitive incarnation of Dashiell Hammett's Sam Spade in *The Maltese Falcon*, with John Huston's writing and directing perfectly honing the insolent charm and quietly self-assured toughness of his character. Having created one of the great American literary private eyes on film, Bogart went on to portray the other, Chandler's Philip Marlowe, in Howard Hawks's *The Big Sleep* (1946). Bogart's chemistry with Lauren Bacall (both on and off-screen) consolidated one of the screen's great romantic duos. After this, the actor rarely made a misstep, even demonstrating a talent for such disturbingly psychotic characters as the protagonist of Nicholas Ray's *In A Lonely Place* (1950, see Canon).

 Dark Passage
dir Delmer Daves, 1947, US, 106m, b/w

Bogart plays a man – wrongly convicted of murdering his wife – who has just escaped from prison. Taken in by Irene (Lauren Bacall), he changes his identity through plastic surgery (we finally see him when the bandages come off), and tracks down the real killers with her help. Not the greatest of the Bogart-Bacall vehicles, but still pretty atmospheric despite some unlikely plot twists and the fact that almost the entire first half is filmed from Bogart's subjective point of view.

Raymond Chandler

Writer, 1888–1959

Film noir had more than its fair share of brilliant writers, but none made more of an impact, both as an author of classic crime novels and as a scriptwriter, than Raymond Chandler. By creating the wisecracking loner Philip Marlowe, a private detective who maintains a core of integrity and honesty in the face of crime and corruption, he established a noir archetype that has maintained its hold to this day. Marlowe appears in Chandler's first novel, *The Big Sleep*, written in 1939, a work that immediately reveals his stylistic hallmarks – a partial debt to the hard-boiled style of **Dashiell Hammett**, and a brisk first-person narration peppered with outlandish, and often very funny, similes.

Chandler's involvement with Hollywood was a love-hate relationship, and he once wrote: "If my books had been any worse I should not have been invited to Hollywood and if they had been any better I should not have come." Having witnessed from a distance half-baked adaptations of *Farewell, My Lovely* and *The High Window*, he was signed up by Paramount to work on the script of **James M. Cain**'s novel *Double Indemnity* in 1943. The result was a masterpiece but a deeply miserable experience, with Chandler finding **Billy Wilder**, his co-writer and the director of the film, brash and overbearing.

The next year saw the first appearance on screen of Philip Marlowe in *Murder My Sweet* (see Canon), an adaptation of *Farewell My Lovely* starring **Dick Powell** as the private eye. It was followed by *The Big Sleep* in 1946 (see Canon), with the writers William Faulkner and Leigh Brackett perfectly capturing the tone of the book while never quite getting on top of the convoluted plot. Chandler was hired to work on the next adaptation of one of his books, *The Lady In The Lake*, but hated going over old ground with the result that MGM hired another writer.

In the meantime, Chandler had worked on three scripts, the best of which was the Alan Ladd vehicle *The Blue Dahlia* (1945, see Canon) – his only original screenplay. Chandler received an

Oscar nomination for his work, but the script was written at some personal cost as he felt obliged to consume large amounts of booze in order to complete it.

Despite Chandler's regular and vitriolic diatribes about Hollywood, his stock was still high enough for Universal to hire him in 1947 at $4000 a week with a promise not to interfere in his work. But the completed screenplay, *Playback*, was rejected and the frustrated writer decided to turn his back on the industry for ever. He did one final screenplay, for **Alfred Hitchcock**, in 1950, personally persuaded by the director to adapt Patricia Highsmith's first novel *Strangers On A Train*. It was another embittering experience as Hitchcock largely rejected Chandler's version and employed Czenzi Ormonde to rewrite it. From then on Chandler's life was a downward spiral of drink-fuelled depression, although he did manage to write what some consider his best Marlowe novel, *The Long Goodbye*, in 1953.

Since his death, filmmakers have continued to plunder his work with results that range from the sublimity of Robert Altman's revisionist *The Long Goodbye* (1973, see Canon), through the respectful *Farewell My Lovely* (1975) of Dick Richards to Michael Winner's utterly risible remake of *The Big Sleep* (1978).

The Lady In The Lake
dir Robert Montgomery, 1947, US, 105m, b/w

This is most notable for being filmed entirely from the point of view of protagonist Philip Marlowe (Robert Montgomery) as a way of replicating Chandler's first-person narrator. Hired by the editor of a crime magazine to trace the whereabouts of the proprietor's missing wife, Marlowe is hampered in his attempts by the police's brutal obstruction and their attempts to frame him. An interesting experiment, doggedly followed through, that is as irritating as it is intriguing.

The Brasher Doubloon (aka The High Window)
dir John Brahm, 1947, US, 72m, b/w

Ignore the fact that this is meant to be a Philip Marlowe story and it works quite well as the kind of darkly foreboding melodrama that John Brahm specialized in. The creepy widow Mrs Murdock (Florence Bates) hires a rather nondescript Marlowe (George Montgomery) to try to recover a prized rare coin, the Brasher Doubloon, which has been stolen by her son (Conrad Janis). Some excellent performances include a classy turn from the veteran German actor Fritz Kortner as the sinister Vannier.

Joan Crawford

Actor, 1906–1977

To appreciate Joan Crawford's achievements as one of Hollywood's most indestructible stars, it's necessary to strip away the accretions – most of which were firmly placed there by the actress herself. There was, of course, the "Mrs Coca-Cola" image, in which, as wife-then-widow of a soft drinks tycoon, she made herself quite as powerful a business player as the doughty protagonist in *Mildred Pierce* (1945, see Canon). Then there was the contentious route to Hollywood stardom, with rumours of porno films and the casting couch, not to mention the child cruelty tag perpetuated by her daughter Christina in her memoir *Mommie Dearest*. It's a formidable off-screen image which to a large extent overlaps with the characters she played on screen.

Crawford's career began in the 1920s, and she proved herself adept at a variety of genres, from musicals to comedy. She was a protégée of the much-feared **Louis B. Mayer**, who single-mindedly fashioned her into a major MGM star. Work with **Howard Hawks** in the 1930s (such as *Today We Live*, 1933) demonstrated that she was refining her craft, which was learnt rather than

instinctual. After a string of failures had made her "box-office poison", she bounced back with *Mannequin* (Frank Borzage, 1938) and the bizarre **George Cukor** movie *A Woman's Face* (1941) – her facial mutilation in this film looks forward to the horror films she would make later in her career with Robert Aldrich and William Castle. Her first really important role based on a book by a major crime writer came in the Michael Curtiz adaptation of James M. Cain's *Mildred Pierce*, in which Crawford grasped the dramatic ingredients with both hands, and demonstrated that what she lacked in nuance as an actress she more than made up for in sheer charismatic star power.

Later engagements with the crime genre included *Possessed* (1947), the noirish *Flamingo Road* (1949), with Sydney Greenstreet matching Crawford's basilisk intensity, and the noir melodrama *The Damned Don't Cry* (1950) in which she gets through men like a dose of salts. David Miller's tough and violent take on the "woman's picture", *Sudden Fear* (1952), won Oscar nominations for both Crawford and her co-star **Jack Palance**. Four years later another noirish woman's picture, *Autumn Leaves* (1956), had her as a lonely spinster pitted against a much younger Cliff Robertson. It was directed by **Robert Aldrich** who was to work with her again in the famous face-off with arch-rival **Bette Davis** in *What Ever Happened To Baby Jane?* (1962). More axe-wielding mayhem was to follow for William Castle in *Strait Jacket* (1964), but by now Crawford, like many of her generation, was trading in middle-aged grotesques. The earlier work, however, still shines brightly.

Possessed
dir Curtis Bernhardt, 1947, US, 108m, b/w

Highly atmospheric direction by German émigré Bernhardt sets Crawford up for one of her greatest performances as

Louise Howell, a woman whose desperate love for wastrel David Sutton (Van Heflin) leads to her mental disintegration. Having been rejected by David, Louise marries the man whose sick wife she has been nursing, but when David returns things start to go downhill fast. The whole sorry tale is told as a flashback after Louise is picked up off the streets of LA dazed and confused.

Sudden Fear
dir David Miller, 1952, US, 110m, b/w

Wealthy playwright Myra Hudson (Joan Crawford) is auditioning actors for her latest play. She rejects Lester Baines (Jack Palance) as not sufficiently romantic, but when they accidentally meet up later he successfully woos her and they marry. With his sexy ex-girlfriend Irene Neves (Gloria Grahame), Lester then contrives to murder his wife in order to inherit her money – but their plot has been recorded, prompting Myra to make a pre-emptive strike. An extraordinarily overwrought script (even by noir standards) is redeemed by red-hot performances from the three stars.

Hans Dreier
Art director, 1885–1966

Born in Bremen, Hans Dreier entered the German film industry in 1919, and in the late 1920s followed many of his compatriots to Hollywood. His career as a production designer was one of the most prolific and long-lasting in America, with nearly 500 films to his credit, along with 23 Academy Award nominations. Dreier, who had worked as an architect in South Africa before entering the film industry, swiftly rose through the ranks to become the head of Paramount's art department, and his sumptuous, highly individual sets were much in demand from such exacting directors as von Sternberg, Lubitsch and King Vidor.

Dreier's early films in the crime genre, such as *The Dragnet* (1937), featured relatively functional set designs, but by the time of *The Glass Key* in 1941, he had developed a style in which the marriage of design and the psychological trajectory of a film was complete. The most perfect example of this is *The Big Clock* in 1948, in which the Art Deco magazine headquarters – the setting for the psychological duel between tortured hero **Ray Milland** and villainous magnate **Charles Laughton** – becomes the visual correlative of both men's states of mind. A similar piece of legerdemain was effected by Dreier in *Sorry, Wrong Number* (1948), with **Barbara Stanwyck's** fussy, over-decorated apartment presented as something more menacing than the cosy domain that her character wrongly believes it is.

Dreier won an Academy Award for best black-and-white art direction on **Billy Wilder's** masterly *Sunset Boulevard* (1950) – once again, a drama in which décor is utilized to present an image of the damaged mind of a central character. The faded grandeur of the silent movie star was perfectly matched by the gothic extravagance of her vast Beverly Hills mansion. But Dreier's principal achievement was arguably as head of the Paramount art department, where he was able to perform a similar function to music department supremo **Alfred Newman**: in other words to benignly impose his own artistic personality on the many talented creators who worked under him, without cramping their individual styles. Like Newman, Dreier was regarded as a great teacher, and those who worked under his tutelage were grateful for the opportunity. But it is his own work (including such von Sternberg masterpieces as *Underworld*, 1927) that is his greatest legacy to Hollywood cinema, a legacy finally recognized in several gallery exhibitions of his work.

The gothic extravagance of a Beverly Hills mansion created by Dreier for *Sunset Boulevard*.

Samuel Fuller

Director, 1911–97

Of all B-movie directors, Sam Fuller was the nearest thing to a pulp novelist or a tabloid journalist. He could never be accused of sophistication but it's precisely this primitive quality that makes him (along with the equally direct Cornel Wilde) unique among Hollywood directors. If you are able to take the rawness of his sensibility, then Fuller's films are some of the most eye-opening in American cinema, especially in the way they confront controversial issues – like racial intolerance – head on.

After years as a screenplay writer on other people's films, his directorial debut was *I Shot Jesse James* (1948), a film told almost entirely in close-ups. Fuller worked in a variety of genres – the Western, the war movie and a mesmerizing exposé of journalistic ethics in *Park Row* (1952) – before producing his noir masterpiece, *Pickup On South Street* (1954, see Canon). However quaint the film's red-baiting, patriotic criminals seem today, Fuller's un-nuanced directness remains as powerful as ever, and is the perfect curtain-raiser for the director's subsequent essays in the crime genre.

Set in Tokyo, *House Of Bamboo* (1955) tells of how a criminal gang of former GIs is infiltrated by the army in order to expose it. It's notable for Fuller's masterful handling of CinemaScope and for the implicit homoeroticism between **Robert Ryan**'s gang leader and **Robert Stack**'s undercover man. Fuller's next noir, *The Crimson Kimono* (1959), dealt with interracial relationships with an unusual degree of sensitivity, while his take on the crime movie became both more assured and even bleaker in *Underworld USA* (1961, see p.37).

While the over-the-top duo of *Shock Corridor* (1963) and *The Naked Kiss* (1964) assured his place in the pantheon of French cineastes, their obviousness obliterates any possibility of the psychological penetration that (for instance) **Nicholas Ray** achieved with noir. This hardly mattered for such admirers as **Jean-Luc Godard**, who used the cigar-chomping American director on screen in *Pierrot le Fou*, growling that "film is a battleground". This was the perfect encapsulation of Fuller's cinematic world-view, an attitude that continued even as his career faltered.

Shock Corridor
dir Samuel Fuller, 1963, US, 101m, b/w & col

From the free-for-all performances to Stanley Cortez's fabulously demented camera-work, this is one of Fuller's crudest but at the same time most wildly energetic movies. The initial premise is mad enough: by having himself committed to an insane asylum, journalist Peter Breck (Johnny Barrett) hopes to solve the murder of an inmate and thereby win the Pulitzer Prize. Needless to say, it doesn't quite work out that way, as he encounters some truly bizarre characters and begins to lose his grip on reality.

The Naked Kiss
dir Samuel Fuller, 1964, US, 90m, b/w

A weird mixture of soap opera, film noir, psychological drama and kinky shocker, this shoestring masterpiece fiercely attacks the apparent security of the suburban family. Prostitute Kelly (Constance Towers) shows up in a small town and has an affair with the sheriff, who subsequently tries to run her out of town. Instead, she leaves her illicit past behind, opting to work with handicapped kids and finding love with the sheriff's best pal, only to make a dreadful discovery…

Gloria Grahame

Actor, 1925–81

The most quirky and unconventional of all film noir actresses, Gloria Grahame was rarely the *femme fatale* and more often the good-bad girl – sassy, wanting a good time and largely oblivious of the evil that surrounded her. She plays this role to perfection in *The Big Heat* (1953, see Canon), as Debby Marsh, the girlfriend of sadistic hoodlum **Lee Marvin**, who shockingly disfigures her with a jug of scalding coffee. It's the scene audiences remember, but Grahame's final confrontation with the cold-blooded widow of a corrupt police official is no less striking.

Having studied acting with her mother (the stage actress Jean Grahame), Gloria Grahame signed for MGM in 1944 after being spotted on Broadway by **Louis B. Mayer**. She was loaned out to Columbia to play the small-town tart in *It's A Wonderful Life* (1946) and the next year had her contract taken over by RKO. Her first noir role was in *Crossfire* (1947) and the conviction with which she played Ginny Tremaine, a smart-talking nightclub hostess with a heart, gained her an Oscar nomination.

The most significant personal and professional encounter of Grahame's life took place in 1948 when she married the director **Nicholas Ray**, who cast her in *A Woman's Secret* the same year. Apart from *Crossfire*, there was little to indicate just how much screen presence she possessed until Ray directed her in *In A Lonely Place* (1950, see Canon) shortly after their divorce. As the woman involved with a damagingly unstable writer, played by **Humphrey Bogart**, she not only held her own against one of Bogart's most riveting performances, but created a fully rounded and conflicted character in her own right.

The 1950s were undoubtedly her best years, in which she was able to display the whole range of her acting ability. There were two more noir roles in 1952, *Macao* and *Sudden Fear*, the same year that she won an Oscar for her performance as **Dick Powell**'s flirty wife in the noirish Hollywood satire *The Bad And The Beautiful*. She did more good work for Lang in *Human Desire* (1954), was a wonderful Ado Annie in *Oklahoma!* (1955), and had a final noir outing in *Odds Against Tomorrow*

Good-bad girl Gloria Grahame in *The Big Heat*.

(1959). From then on her film career nosedived, although she continued to have an active stage career. She died while acting in repertory theatre in the north of England – a long way from her birthplace in Los Angeles – her last days recorded by her sometime lover Peter Turner in a moving memoir, *Film Stars Don't Die In Liverpool*.

Human Desire
dir Fritz Lang, 1954, US, 90m, b/w

Not as consistently good as Renoir's version, Fritz Lang's adaptation of Emile Zola's *La bête humaine* provides Gloria Grahame with one of her finest roles as Vicki Buckley, the amoral and sexually manipulative wife of the brutish, and insanely jealous, railway worker Carl (Broderick Crawford). Glenn Ford plays the Korean War veteran and regular guy who is swept away by his desire for Vicki and is nearly persuaded to bump off her husband. Hobbled by the Production Code, the film looks good but never fully plumbs the depths.

Edith Head

Costume designer, 1897–1981

When **Carl Reiner** decided to make his comedic homage to film noir, *Dead Men Don't Wear Plaid* (see p.237), Edith Head was his first choice of costume designer. Then aged 84, she was the absolute doyenne of her profession, having spent nearly 60 years in Hollywood – 44 of them at Paramount – and notched up eight Academy Awards.

Unlike most of the other great Hollywood designers, however, she had neither a fashion nor a theatre background; instead she learnt her trade from the inside, bluffing her way into a job as a sketch artist at Paramount in the late 1920s. For most of her apprentice years, she assisted the flamboyant but erratic **Travis Banton**, and when he left in 1938 (due to a drink problem), Head succeeded him. It was not a unanimous choice:

several colleagues thought that she was too safe and lacked imagination, but in many ways her caution as a designer was also her strength.

Because movies were sometimes released a couple of years after they were made, Head was very careful that her costumes were not over-dependent on the fashion of the moment (she hated padded shoulders). Hence the classic, time-less look of many of her designs. She was also a good operator – consulting widely with colleagues and establishing good working relation-ships with the actresses she dressed, in particular **Barbara Stanwyck** and **Ingrid Bergman**. In her film noir work her leading ladies are always as elegant as they are seductive, however trashy the character they may be playing.

For Barbara Stanwyck in *Double Indemnity* (1944, see Canon), Head combined just the right degree of slinky allure and *nouveau riche* vulgarity, not least in her first stair-descending entrance: what the insurance salesman (and the viewer) first sees are the tantalizingly erotic anklet, the pom-pom-topped, high-heeled shoe and then the clingy white silk dress. Dressing Stanwyck again in *Sorry, Wrong Number* (1948), this time as a bed-ridden invalid, Head stresses the character's vul-nerability by a delicately feminine lace bedjacket. Her aim was always to match the costume not just to the role, but also to the mood of the moment. Her attention to detail was legendary and she was always seen in a pair of tinted spectacles, which she wore (so she claimed) in order to get the tonal relations right in black-and-white films.

Notorious
dir Alfred Hitchcock, 1946, US, 102m, b/w

In this noirish romantic thriller Ingrid Bergman plays Alicia Huberman, the daughter of a dead Nazi, who agrees to infiltrate a group of Nazi exiles in Rio de Janeiro. Cary Grant is her FBI contact but when the two fall for each other their burgeoning love affair is undermined by a mutual lack of trust. The first of several films for Hitchcock, Head created the perfect look for Bergman: from the midriff-exposing, zebra-striped blouse of the early scenes to the black velvet evening dress with its plunging back and neckline that she wears in the crucial party scene.

Alfred Hitchcock

Director, 1899–1980

At the site of the London studio where the British-born "Master of Suspense" made his first essays in the thriller genre, a gigantic bronze likeness of his head sits, Buddha-like and impassive. But although one of the few authentic geniuses of cinema is now appropriately celebrated in his own country, Hitchcock's greatest influence began in 1940, when he moved to Hollywood and made his adaptation of Daphne du Maurier's *Rebecca* for producer **David O. Selznick**. That Hitchcockian blend of jet-black humour and what was to become known as his "transference of guilt" theme had already appeared in such British films as *The Man Who Knew Too Much* (1935) and *The Lady Vanishes* (1938). But these by-products of his cockney wit and Jesuit upbringing were to be developed with far greater rigour in such American films as *Suspicion* (1942), *Shadow Of A Doubt* (1943) and *Strangers On A Train* (1951). While Hitchcock always had an appreciative audience, the real juggernaut of critical acclaim was set in motion by such French cineastes as **Claude Chabrol** and **François Truffaut**. Hitherto, British and American critics had taken the director at his own estimate – as a consummate craftsman and light entertainer – but with the attention of the *Cahiers du cinéma* critics came a radical reappraisal of his worth, one that has held sway to this day.

Hitchcock came to be seen as a serious and powerful commentator on the darker aspects of the human condition, a filmmaker who (however much he himself might have disdained such analyses) rivalled more obviously "serious" directors in terms of moral complexity. Films such as his adaptation of **Patricia Highsmith**'s *Strangers On A Train* had been constrained by the censorship straitjacket of the day (the "swapped murders" theme of the book had to be altered so that only the villain committed a crime), but still the moral queasiness at the heart of Hitchcock's universe was a world away from straightforward entertainment products. It remains debatable whether his thrillers – being so clearly forged from his own preoccupations – are ever straightforwardly noir, or rather his own unique manipulation of noirish themes.

The masterpieces of the 1940s were followed by the director's greatest work: *Rear Window* (1954), a more complex version of the **Cornell Woolrich** source from which it was adapted; *Vertigo* (1958), with its uncompromising picture of the hero's obsession and fetishism; and the high point of his achievements, *Psycho* (1960). Whole generations of filmmakers have carved out careers utilizing the tropes and themes of "The Master", and even at the beginning of the twenty-first century, there is every sign that his influence refuses to wane.

Shadow Of A Doubt
dir Alfred Hitchcock, 1943, US, 103m, b/w

Joseph Cotton plays nice Uncle Charlie, hero-worshipped by his young niece, also called Charlie (Teresa Wright), when he comes to stay with her and her family in the quiet town of Santa Rosa. But gradually it emerges that he may not be as nice as he seems, in fact he may be very nasty indeed. Hitchcock's manipulation of the audience, and the intense, symbiotic relationship between the two Charlies, is handled with the greatest skill and a sly wit.

Strangers On A Train
dir Alfred Hitchcock, 1951, US, 101m, b/w

This compelling study of guilt by association begins with the chance encounter on a train between tennis champion Guy Haines (Farley Granger) and Bruno Anthony (Robert Walker). A casual conversation leads to Bruno proposing an exchange of murders – Bruno to kill Guy's wife, Guy to kill Bruno's father. Guy treats it as a joke, but when his wife is murdered and Bruno demands payback, things start to get difficult. Guy's attempts to avoid Bruno's hold on him culminate in an explosive finale at a fairground.

Jean Louis

Costume designer, 1907–97

Having learnt the couturier's art at the prestigious House of Agnes-Drecoll in his home city of Paris, by 1942 Jean Louis Berthault was working in New York for the firm of Hattie Carnegie. One of his private clients was Jean Cohn, wife of Columbia Studios boss Harry Cohn, and in 1944 Jean Louis joined the studio as an assistant to the legendary **Travis Banton** (who had trained up **Edith Head**, see p.190) but was very soon running the department himself.

Among the many female stars whose image he helped to create, the most significant was **Rita Hayworth**. With Jean Louis designing for her, Hayworth's style became sexier and more sophisticated, famously in *Gilda* (see Canon) where, apart from the famous low-cut black dress in which she performs a provocative song and dance routine (see p.95), her wardrobe consisted of one superbly glamorous outfit after another. From the flouncy off-the-shoulder white chiffon dress she wears for her first appearance to the sober pinstripe suit at the end, all the gowns emphasize her elegant curvaceousness.

For *The Lady From Shanghai* (see Canon), directed by her ex-husband **Orson Welles**,

Hayworth played Elsa Bannister, a more ruthless character than in *Gilda*. Her ambiguity is reflected in her clothes; one minute overtly sexy, the next demure. In one stunning outfit (worn in a semi-chase sequence through Acapulco backstreets) she combines the two with a low-cut white dress topped by a cape with a collar that would be positively nun-like were it not for the fact that it is see-through.

Other great noirs for which Jean Louis designed the gowns include *The Big Heat* and *In A Lonely Place*, both with **Gloria Grahame**, and *The Reckless Moment* with **Joan Bennett**. Neither of these two women plays a classic *femme fatale*, so the emphasis is on smart-sexy rather than beguiling-sexy. Bennett's character, as an over-controlling housewife and mother, is brilliantly conveyed through her elegant but slightly prim outfits.

Dead Reckoning
dir John Cromwell, 1947, US, 100m, b/w

This is atmospheric enough but with an over-complex plot that sometimes makes it seem like a noir parody. Humphrey Bogart plays Rip Murdock, who gets entangled with the beautiful Mrs Chandler (Lizabeth Scott) as he investigates the disappearance of his soldier-buddy. Scott's gowns reveal Jean Louis at his most fetishistic, with lots of accessories – big belts, gloves and an especially flouncy polka-dot bow.

Burt Lancaster

Actor, 1913–94

After a brief career as a circus acrobat and a Broadway actor, Burt Lancaster hit the big time with his very first film. **Robert Siodmak's** *The Killers* (1946, see Canon) showcased Lancaster's flawed and tragic male beauty as the doomed Swede, sleepwalking to his death after an encounter with *femme fatale* **Ava Gardner**. It was as if the actor already knew that straightforward, one-dimensional heroic figures were not for him. The prison drama *Brute Force* (1947) demonstrated the actor's sweaty power – in marked contrast to his more carefully groomed peers. The following year saw Lancaster in a trio of noirs, the best of which was Siodmak's *Criss Cross* (1948, see Canon) in which he played another doomed reluctant crook, this time bewitched by Yvonne De Carlo.

Lancaster's first attempt at more overt menace in *Sorry, Wrong Number* in the same year, for Anatole Litvak, seemed strained, as did more self-consciously "actorly" performances in such films as Daniel Mann's *Come Back, Little Sheba* (1953). But his performance as the all-powerful Broadway columnist J.J. Hunsecker in Alexander Mackendrick's *Sweet Smell Of Success* (1957) was his finest to date. Coolly wrecking the lives of those around him (and suggesting an incestuous desire for his young sister), Lancaster definitively demonstrated that there was much more to him than the acrobatic athleticism of such films as *The Crimson Pirate* (1952) or *Trapeze* (1956).

By all accounts, Lancaster could be extremely difficult and prickly, but he was able to synthesize this aspect of his personality with the charismatic good looks and muscular physique that had been his calling cards. An encounter with **Robert Aldrich** engendered some of his best work as the rebel Indian in *Apache* (1954) and several subsequent films for the director. As his looks faded in middle age, he seemed even more considerable an actor, exuding gravitas and authority, notably as the Sicilian aristocrat in Visconti's *The Leopard* (1963). There were many duds in his later years but his beautifully observed performance in Louis Malle's *Atlantic City* (1980) was one of several distinguished codas to a remarkable career.

 Atlantic City
dir Louis Malle, 1980, Can/Fr, 105m

Lou Pascal (Burt Lancaster) is an elderly, self-deluding criminal living in Atlantic City, where he runs a small-time numbers racket and takes care of Grace, a gangster's widow. Lou gets involved with his pretty neighbour Sally (Susan Sarandon) when she gets mixed up in a drugs deal following the arrival of her pregnant sister and ex-husband. When it transpires that the drugs were stolen from the mob, things start to get serious. A noir premise, given a humane twist by Malle's always sensitive emphasis on character development rather than action.

Fritz Lang

Director, 1890–1976

Of the German expats who brought their dark visions to Hollywood (see p.11), Fritz Lang is arguably the greatest, directing around a dozen films that are at the heart of any definition of film noir. His reputation worldwide was established by the visual extravagance of his Teutonic epic *Die Nibelungen* (1924) and his sci-fi masterpiece *Metropolis* (1926), but it was his ground-breaking crime movies, *Dr Mabuse der Spieler* (1924) and *M* (1932, see p.11), that provide the link with the films of his highly successful Hollywood career.

According to Lang (and it is a story that has been challenged), his panicky flight from Germany was precipitated by an offer from Dr Goebbels to play a major role in the film industry of the Third Reich. A brief period in France was followed by twenty years in the US, where he started as he meant to go on with the masterly *Fury* (1936). With its terrifying vision of an innocent man at the mercy of a lynch mob, *Fury* had a nightmarish force far more potent than most native directors were expressing at the time. It was followed by *You Only Live Once* (1938), the story of a ex-criminal trying to go straight who is jailed for a robbery and a killing of which he is innocent. Both films focus on the plight of a wronged individual, and on how fear and alienation become self-perpetuating.

Though Lang trained as a painter and his German films are associated with expressionism, the visual style of his US films is very much tied to their subject matter – from the baroque stylization of the nightmare films *Ministry Of Fear* (1944, see p.26) and *Secret Beyond The Door* (1950) to the relatively restrained *Clash By Night* (1952) and *The Blue Gardenia* (1953) – the latter two shot by the subtlest of noir cinematographers **Nicholas Musuraca** (see p.198). More than any visual signature, it's his great skill as a storyteller that shines through Lang's films: plots unfold with an inexorable clarity and logic through the careful accumulation of telling human detail. Despite his on-set reputation as a martinet, his films mostly tell of ordinary people caught up in extraordinary events. This is particularly true of the two masterpieces with Edward G. Robinson, *The Woman In The Window* (1944, see Canon) and *Scarlet Street* (1946, see Canon), and the finest of his 1950s noirs, *The Big Heat* (1953, see Canon).

His final two US movies were intriguing, flawed crime stories, betrayed to some extent by their low budgets. *While The City Sleeps* (1956, see p.34) is a quirky newspaper drama, dripping with Lang's cold-eyed perception of humanity, while *Beyond A Reasonable Doubt* (1956) has Dana Andrews confessing to a murder he didn't commit in a plot as unlikely as it is ruthlessly compelling.

and then narrowly escapes a lynching as a frenzied mob burn down the jail. Believing Joe to be dead, the DA charges several of the townspeople with murder and, in a brilliant touch, Lang intercuts newsreel footage of the crowd as individual "alibis" are read out. The embittered Joe eventually steps forward but a powerful point about suspicion and hysteria has been made.

Ordinary folk: Andes and Monroe in *Clash By Night*.

 Fury
dir Fritz Lang, 1936, US, 94m, b/w

Lang got off to a blinding start with his first American movie, despite massive studio interference. Spencer Tracy plays Joe, who is arrested as a suspected kidnapper

 Clash By Night
dir Fritz Lang, 1952, US, 104m, b/w

This noirish melodrama – a kind of anti-romance – brings together two powerful noir regulars, Barbara Stanwyck and Robert Ryan. She plays the urbane Mae Doyle who, having returned to the seaside town of her birth, meets up with fisherman Jerry D'Amato (Paul Douglas), an acquaintance from her youth, and his cynical friend Earle Pfeiffer (Ryan). The emotional havoc the three wreak on each other is contrasted with the love of Mae's brother Joe (Keith Andes) for his girlfriend Peggy (Marilyn Monroe).

Beyond A Reasonable Doubt
dir Fritz Lang, 1956, US, 80m, b/w

Dana Andrews plays Tom Garrett, a novelist who with Austin Spencer (Sidney Blackmer), a newspaper publisher (and the father of his fiancée), comes up with a scheme to show the evils of capital punishment. Tom will take the rap for a murder he didn't commit, but before being executed he will reveal the subterfuge. All goes to plan, except that Austin Spencer – the only one who can prove his innocence – gets killed. Lang's unforgiving vision ratchets up this minor piece several notches and adds an intriguing sting to its tail.

Anthony Mann
Director, 1906–67

Few Hollywood directors have had such a ready facility for switching between genres as Anthony Mann. In his series of Westerns with **James Stewart**, made in the 1950s, he introduced a markedly more psychological, even noirish, approach to the genre. Similarly, when the economics of the film business demanded blockbuster historical epics from him, he responded with the same degree of intelligence and ambition. But it's the director's 1940s crime movies that many admirers cite as his most complex and interesting work, and the reputation of such films has grown considerably in recent years.

In 1947, *Desperate* and *Railroaded* marked Mann out as among the most authoritative filmmakers at work in the tough action movie genre, but only hinted at the exuberant achievements of *T-Men* (see Canon) in the same year and *Raw*

Deal in 1948 (see Canon). The latter two films were given an added noir depth by the work of cinematographer John Alton (see p.181), who became a frequent collaborator with Mann. Interestingly, the two men were able to transfer the same noir sensibility to a period thriller of 1949, *Reign of Terror*. Although set during the French Revolution, Mann treated the narrative with the same terse authority as his noir pieces, losing all trace of the historical so often associated with costume dramas.

In the same year, Mann made two films which were as distinctive as his best work: *Border Incident* and *Side Street*. *Border Incident* maintains the format that Mann had used so consummately in *T-Men*. While the style of the movie suggests the documentary form (cool presentation of facts, realistic depiction of current social issues), Mann brilliantly sidesteps such expectations with underpinnings of sudden violence and betrayal. With *Side Street*, as so often with Mann, the end-of-the-tether psychology of the hero is of most interest to the director: not for Mann the uncomplicated hero who is clearly on the side of right. But this is not a totally pessimistic vision – Mann's heroes may be crushed by the exigencies of fate, but we're always presented with the possibility of the redemption of the human spirit. His protagonists may be criminals or policemen undercover, but their world is always one of existential danger: whether or not a Mann hero survives, he has invariably played out his life and desperate choices with personal authenticity.

Desperate
dir Anthony Mann, 1947, US, 73m, b/w

Trucker Steve Randall (Steve Brodie) is tricked into taking part in a warehouse heist which he then tries to prevent. Forced by gang leader Walt Radak (Raymond Burr) to take the rap for a policeman's death – actually committed by Walt's brother – Steve and his young wife flee, with the cops and Walt both in pursuit. The moral complexity of Mann's later work is sketchily drawn here, but the film still packs a punch not least because of Burr's deeply sinister turn as a sadistic hood.

Border Incident
dir Anthony Mann, 1949, US, 96m, b/w

A film about the attempts of two undercover immigration officers (from both sides of the border) to infiltrate a gang – led by a psychotic rancher named Parkson (Howard da Silva) – who are smuggling poor Mexicans into California as cheap labour. In this dangerous landscape, moodily shot by John Alton, human life is cheap and, when they've outlived their usefulness, the expendable Mexicans are dispatched in a particularly brutal fashion.

Side Street
dir Anthony Mann, 1950, US, 83m, b/w

Farley Granger plays Joe Norson, an ordinary guy who makes a wrong move. Having stolen money that turns out to belong to some murderous blackmailers and to be a far larger sum than he thought, Joe decides to return it. But it's not that easy so he stashes it with barman Gus (John Gallaudet) who runs off with it and gets himself murdered. Set in a stunningly shot New York City, this is classic noir territory with events running rapidly beyond the control of the hapless protagonist.

Robert Mitchum

Actor, 1917–97

The appreciation of Robert Mitchum as one of Hollywood's finest was slow in coming, partly due to the attitude of the man himself. Critics were inclined to take Mitchum at his own estimate, and he delighted in conveying the laid-back image of a man who didn't take acting too seriously and who "phoned in" most of his performances. Certainly, Mitchum's early work in films such as *The Human Comedy* (1943) and Tay Garnett's *Bataan* (1943) suggested an actor who, while visually imposing

with his solid physique and heavy-lidded good looks, was little more than competent.

William Castle's *When Strangers Marry* (1944) was the first tentative demonstration that Mitchum could be a more subtle and intelligent performer. But it was *Out Of The Past* (1947, see Canon) that established him as one of the most considerable actors of his generation, as well as making him an emblematic film noir figure. The actor's remarkable combination of vulnerability and menace was uniquely his own and, in the role of ex-private eye Jeff Bailey, Mitchum appeared as much a man of thought as a man of action, despite the tough guy accoutrements. The trajectory of his career after this was firmly upwards, with solid work in films for **Don Siegel** (*The Big Steal*, 1949) and **John Farrow** (*Where Danger Lives*, 1950). But it was Nicholas Ray who, in *The Lusty Men* (1952), coaxed from Mitchum what is arguably his most multi-faceted performance. As injured rodeo rider Jeff McCloud, Mitchum convincingly conveys an unhappy man attempting to deal with the poor hand that life has dealt him.

But Mitchum also took on a great deal of grimly uninspiring work, and his lack of involvement in many films was patent. However, **Charles Laughton**'s *The Night Of The Hunter* (1955) had at its centre one of the actor's most terrifying creations, the psychotic preacher who is the embodiment of evil. In fact, Mitchum did evil particularly well, and his later incarnation of the murderous criminal menacing Gregory Peck and his family in **J. Lee Thompson**'s *Cape Fear* (1961) was an object lesson in screen menace, much more sinister than Robert De Niro's approach to the character in Martin Scorsese's remake.

Mitchum's finest films date from the 1940s and 50s but in the 1970s he was once again exploited for his authentic noir credentials – effectively in *The Friends Of Eddie Coyle* (1973), *The Yakuza* (1975) and *Farewell My Lovely* (1975), humiliatingly in the execrable remake of *The Big Sleep* (1978).

Where Danger Lives
dir John Farrow, 1950, US, 82m, b/w

Doctor Jeff Cameron (Robert Mitchum) is at the start of a promising career, that is until he saves Margo (Faith Domergue) from suicide and then falls in love with her. Unfortunately, the psychotic Margo manages to persuade Jeff that her husband (Claude Rains) is actually her father – a misunderstanding from which Jeff emerges concussed and believing that he is responsible for the husband's

death. The two lovers then flee for Mexico. This unlikely tale is made plausible by Mitchum's riveting delineation of Jeff's decline into bewilderment and near hopelessness.

Farewell My Lovely
dir Dick Richards, 1975, US, 95m

The second adaptation of Chandler's novel – after *Murder, My Sweet* (1944) – stays closer to the original story of Philip Marlowe's search for nightclub performer Velma, the missing girlfriend of petty criminal Moose Malloy (Jack O'Halloran). Shot by John A. Alonzo (of *Chinatown* fame), its wonderfully burnished period look raises it above most retro-noirs. But

Vulnerable man of action and noir icon Robert Mitchum in *Out Of The Past* with Rhonda Fleming.

what really seals its quality is Robert Mitchum's authoritative and world-weary Marlowe. He may be a decade too old but he manages to make the character more three-dimensional and convincingly human than any other actor.

Nicholas Musuraca

Cinematographer, 1892–1975

Italian-American cinematographer Nicholas Musuraca is a shadowy but exalted figure in film noir, and despite the longevity and diversity of his career his biographical details are sketchy. His reputation depends on a batch of black-and-white movies he photographed while under contract at RKO which feature some of the most dreamlike and atmospheric sequences in the noir canon. In contrast to **John Alton** (see p.181), Musuraca always aimed "for simplicity and logic instead of technical window dressing". But however straightforward his methods, the results – such as the flamboyant nightmare sequences suffered by the helpless protagonists in *Stranger On The Third Floor* (1940) and *Spiral Staircase* (1945) – are not easy to define.

In *Stranger*, Mike (John McGuire) doubts his reliability as a star witness in a murder case, prompting a daydream in which he takes the place of the wrongly accused killer (Elisha Cook Jr). His descent to the electric chair takes him through a vast corridor, cell and courtroom peopled by his laughing defence lawyer, a disbelieving fiancée and baying jurors – all filmed from dizzying angles, enshrouded by jagged or crosshatched shadows and peppered with low-key lighting.

As a cinematographer who thrived on diversity, Musuraca would not have enjoyed being pigeonholed – as he often is – as the master of chiaroscuro lighting: his contribution to noir style is far more complex than this. Throughout

his work, threatening or noirish sequences are not always dominated by low-key or shadowy lighting. Rather they are sometimes set in high-key, almost overexposed rural settings – for instance the bucolic scene in *Out Of The Past* (1947, see Canon) where the deaf-mute boy sends Paul Valentine's assassin to a precipitous death with the flick of a fishing rod.

Musuraca's constant experimentation and versatility continued up to his last noir outings with **Fritz Lang**. Both *Clash By Night* (1952) and *The Blue Gardenia* (1953) were tightly budgeted and scheduled, with the result that director and cinematographer relied heavily on a new scuttling camera cart (a prototype crab-dolly), which enabled the crew to navigate long, complex sequences in each of the film's main locations.

A key scene in *Roadblock* (1951) proves, conclusively, that Musuraca was much more than just a master of chiaroscuro. Just before honest Joe Peters (Charles McGraw) makes his irreversible decision to turn felon, he lights up a cigarette in front of a safe-deposit store. It has all the makings of an archetypal noir image until his jagged silhouette is cast over the store window's Venetian blinds. It is a harrowing reflection of his fractured, corrupt mindset and a world away from noir's traditional slatted shadowing.

Roadblock
dir Harold Daniels, 1951, US, 73m, b/w

Insurance detective Charles McGraw manages on $350 a month, until he falls for Joan Dixon's voluptuous "chiseller" Diane. Teaming up with her sugar daddy (Lowell Gilmore), he decides to keep her in the furs to which she aspires. It is a doomed decision as the heist he engineers and then investigates leaves a trail of evidence leading back to him. Fleeing to Mexico with roadblocks at every turn, Joe and Diane end up cornered in the Los Angeles riverbed – preceded by a helter-skelter seven-minute car chase orchestrated by Musuraca.

Otto Preminger

Director, 1905–86

The image of Preminger as a bullying martinet who frequently reduced his actors to tears has tended to get in the way of his achievements as a director. In a career spanning some fifty years, he made a number of outstanding noirs for Twentieth Century-Fox in the 1940s and 50s before branching out as an independent producer/director. His independent work is notable for the way it regularly took on controversial issues – drug addiction in *The Man With The Golden Arm* (1955), homosexuality in *Advise And Consent* (1962) – and dealt with them in a direct and honest way, often defying the censors in doing so. He was also almost unique as a director who went out of his way to provide film projects in which black performers played major roles.

Born into a distinguished Austrian-Jewish family (his father had been the attorney-general of the Austro-Hungarian Empire), Preminger studied law at the University of Vienna before deciding to become an actor. He rapidly rose through the ranks of the legendary **Max Reinhardt** company and, after directing one film in Austria (*Die grosse Liebe*, 1931), moved to the US in 1935. Signed up by Fox, Preminger became something of a protégé of producer **Darryl Zanuck** before blowing his big chance with his lame direction of *Kidnapped* (1938). Despite this setback he managed to wrest back control of his next film, *Laura* (1944, see Canon), and the result was a masterpiece, a unique "drawing-room" noir which subtly dissects the deceits and frailties of its glamorous but brittle characters.

Much of the languorous, dreamlike feel of *Laura* was achieved through the claustrophobic camera-work of **Joseph LaShelle**, with whom

Preminger was to work on three more noirs. The first of these was *Fallen Angel* (1945), another tale of *amour fou* which, like *Laura*, starred Dana Andrews, this time playing a drifter and small-time con man who falls for *femme fatale* Linda Darnell, over whom the camera lingers with an almost fetishistic intensity. This was followed two years later by *Whirlpool* (1949), which reunited Preminger with the star of *Laura*, **Gene Tierney**. Once again he skilfully presents a situation – an apparently happy marriage – which turns out to cover dark secrets, mistrust and unhappiness.

Sitting pretty: Preminger at work.

With the start of a new decade, Preminger was impatient to shake free of studio control, but continued to produce solid work within the system, such as *Where The Sidewalk Ends* (1950) – the tale of a maverick cop (Dana Andrews) whose uncontrolled violence places him under suspicion of murder. The next year came his last noir for Fox, the melodramatic *The 13th Letter* (1951), a thriller about a series of poison–pen letters, shot in Canada, that failed to improve upon the French film, *Le Corbeau* (1943), on which it was based. His final true noir was *Angel Face* (1952), made for **Howard Hughes** and showcasing a memorable psychopathic *femme fatale* from **Jean Simmons**, desperate to get her claws into a gullible **Robert Mitchum**.

There were to be two more highly accomplished crime movies: *Anatomy Of A Murder* in 1959, a leisurely but hypnotic courtroom drama notable for its censor-baiting sexual frankness, and *Bunny Lake Is Missing* (1965), the director's last decent movie before some late career disasters.

Fallen Angel
dir Otto Preminger, 1945, US, 98m, b/w

Dropped off in a strange town, an unscrupulous drifter (Dana Andrews) makes his way to the warmth of Pop's Diner, where he falls under the spell of small-town *femme fatale* Stella (Linda Darnell). She won't marry him because he has no money, so he hatches a plot to marry the respectable church organist (Alice Faye) for her money and then divorce her. But then Stella gets murdered and he becomes a major suspect. A flimsy plot but, as always with Preminger, the lust and despair are palpable.

Angel Face
dir Otto Preminger, 1952, US, 91m, b/w

Preminger's finest noir after *Laura* has an enigmatic Jean Simmons as the gorgeous but mad Diane Tremayne, who becomes infatuated with ambulance man Frank

Jessup (Robert Mitchum) when he's called out to treat the mysterious gas poisoning of Diane's stepmother. Frank's selfishness and naiveté mean that he's putty in her hands, and he's soon caught up in a murder plot that goes badly wrong. Preminger's cool, objective direction makes the psychological machinations all the more disturbing.

David Raksin
Composer, 1912–2004

If **Rita Hayworth**'s black satin outfit in *Gilda* is the iconic noir dress, then the haunting theme from *Laura* (1944) is the iconic noir melody. Composed by David Raksin in a weekend, and in the knowledge that his wife was about to leave him (see p.127), it is completely identified not just with the title character but with how she is perceived by those around her. While linking a musical theme to a particular character was not unusual, writing a mono-thematic film score was an act of great daring for a composer on his first major film.

Raksin, a talented Broadway arranger, had arrived in Hollywood in 1935 where his first job was to put into effect the musical ideas of Charlie Chaplin – who couldn't read music – for his "silent" film *Modern Times*. Encouraged by top movie composer **Alfred Newman**, Raksin settled in Los Angeles and started taking private lessons with **Arnold Schoenberg**. By 1942 he was working for Twentieth Century-Fox but only got the nod for *Laura* when both Alfred Newman and Bernard Herrmann turned the job down.

Raksin made two more noirs for Preminger. *Fallen Angel* (1945) has a typical noir opening with a night-time bus journey given an added urgency by Raksin's pulsing music, while *Whirlpool* (1949) boasts a remarkably subtle score which moves between the musical conventions of horror and romance, cleverly conveying the disturbed protagonist's internal state and mood swings.

For Polonsky's *Force Of Evil* (1948) Raksin provided his most heterogeneous score – from the pounding ascending and descending scales that presage the movie's big redemptive tune to the almost Korngoldian schmaltz of the love scenes between corrupt lawyer Joe (John Garfield) and his brother's secretary Doris (Beatrice Pearson). Even here the scoring is much sparer than that of the old-school Hollywood composers, and this modern approach comes into its own in the scene where Joe is seen running through a completely deserted Wall Street to the angular strains of a lone bassoon.

After *Laura*, Raksin's most celebrated scores are for Preminger's bodice-ripper *Forever Amber* (1947) and **Vincente Minnelli**'s cynical dissection of Hollywood *The Bad And The Beautiful* (1952). But he had one final noir outing in 1955 with **Joseph Lewis**'s *The Big Combo*, for which he composed the most jazz-inflected of all his scores, beginning with a jaunty big-band melody over the opening credits. The sultry but plaintive sax melody that emerges from this is used to represent Lt Diamond's barely acknowledged desire for the gangster's girlfriend and it reappears as the two are ambiguously united at the film's close.

Whirlpool
dir Otto Preminger, 1949, US, 98m, b/w

Gene Tierney plays Ann Sutton, a rich socialite with a dark secret – kleptomania! Married to a neglectful psychoanalyst (Richard Conte), she falls prey to David Korvo (Jose Ferrer), a hypnotherapist with an evil plan. The musical high point occurs when Ann's hypnotic trance is triggered by the striking of a clock: Raksin takes the notes of the chimes and builds them into an increasingly insistent and sustained passage of music as Ann drives to the house of her rival.

Nicholas Ray
Director, 1911–79

Nicholas Ray is the great justification for the *auteur* theory – a Hollywood professional who was given little attention for many years until critics – notably the French – spotted just how individual and challenging his work was within the constraints of the studio system. The theme of the rebellious outsider struggling to make their way in a hostile society was meticulously threaded throughout his work. But while he was always concerned with tough social criticism – notably in *They Live By Night* (1949) and *On Dangerous Ground* (1951, see Canon) – his strongly held views were never aired at the expense of a powerfully involving narrative.

He began life as an architect, briefly studying with **Frank Lloyd Wright**, before moving to New York in 1934. There, his involvement in left-wing theatre brought him in contact with director **Elia Kazan**. When Kazan came to direct his first full-length feature film, *A Tree Grows In Brooklyn*, in 1945 he allowed Ray to observe the process from beginning to end. Two years later Ray made his own cinematic debut with the moving couple-on-the-run picture *They Live By Night*, although it wasn't released until 1949. The treatment of youth here differs radically from earlier Hollywood films, and Ray's intelligent sympathy with these marginalized characters prefigures his better-known *Rebel Without A Cause* (1955).

They Live By Night was followed by four more noirs, two of which – *In A Lonely Place* (1950, see Canon) and *On Dangerous Ground* (1951, see Canon) – rank among his finest work, while the other two – *Knock On Any Door* (1949) and *Party Girl* (1958) – are flawed but intriguing. Another examination of juvenile delinquency, *Knock On Any Door* is arguably just a little too schematic in the way it unravels the causes that lead a young hoodlum to murder. It teamed Ray up with **Humphrey Bogart** for the first time, a partnership which bore greater fruit in the masterly *In A Lonely Place* (1950), a film that deals with another perennial Ray fascina-

tion – the psychological impulses that lie behind actions of extreme violence. Uncontrolled male anger also underlies *On Dangerous Ground*, in which a dangerously embittered New York cop is sent to the country to assist in a local murder case, and is forced to question his very identity when he falls in love with the fugitive's sister. Finally, the last of Ray's noirs is the oddball *Party*

A couple on the run: Ray's sympathetic portrait of youth, *They Live By Night*.

Girl, a luridly colourful homage to the gangster movies of the 1930s. Dismissed as an aberration until relatively recently, it is now seen as a film that transcends the limitations of its material.

Party Girl
dir Nicholas Ray, 1958, US, 99m

Robert Taylor is a bent lawyer (whose limp is an index of his psychological state) who falls in love with Vicki Gaye (Cyd Charisse), a nightclub dancer. Lee J. Cobb escapes the director's control as a psychotic gangster Rico. A plot that is clichéd when it isn't implausible is transformed by Ray into a baroque extravaganza of dark emotions and brutal violence. Few directors have used colour cinematography quite as dramatically to suggest the psychological turmoil of his characters.

Edward G. Robinson

Actor, 1893–1973

Short and squat but with a powerful and compelling presence, Edward G. Robinson was one of the finest character actors in the history of Hollywood. Born Emmanuel Goldenberg in Romania, he began his acting career on the New York stage and made his film debut in 1923. His career-changing moment came with **Mervyn Le Roy**'s seminal *Little Caesar* in 1930, instantly assuring the actor a place in the pantheon of great screen mobsters. Inevitably he was offered similar parts, like Tod Browning's *Outside The Law* in the same year, but Robinson was too canny an actor to allow himself to be typecast, and he began to make an equally strong mark in such films as *Five Star Final* (1931), as a ruthless newspaper editor, and **Howard Hawks**'s *Tiger Shark* (1930), in which he played a fisherman. Once he had established the breadth of his range, Robinson felt comfortable about moving into the crime genre once again, with striking

roles in *The Last Gangster* (1938) and *Bullets Or Ballots* (1936), in which he played a detective.

In the 1940s Robinson appeared in a sequence of noirs that illustrate just how versatile and profound an actor he could be. First up was his wry insurance investigator in **Billy Wilder's** *Double Indemnity* (1944, see Canon), a marvellously quirky portrait of a man devoted to his work but with a compassionate affection for his murderous colleague. Even more impressive were his two astonishing performances for **Fritz Lang** in *The Woman In The Window* (1944, see Canon) and *Scarlet Street* (1945, see Canon). In both these films, Robinson poignantly delineates a doomed everyman figure, lured into crime and murder by a beguiling *femme fatale* who seems to promise the fulfilment of his frustrated dreams. The actor's restrained but intense performances perfectly meshed with Lang's American-period expressionism. Robinson returned to his gangster schtick in *Key Largo* (1948), where he was effectively pitted against regular colleague Humphrey Bogart in an old-fashioned, and slightly wordy, acting duel.

House Of Strangers
dir Joseph L. Mankiewicz, 1949, US, 101m, b/w

The story of an Italian-American banking family ruled over by the patriarchal Gino Monetti (Edward G. Robinson) with despotic force. Of his four sons, Gino reserves the greatest affection for lawyer Max (Richard Conte) who relates the film's narrative after his release from prison, where he has served seven years for bribing a juror. His father now dead, Max plans to get even with his disloyal, self-seeking brothers who now run the bank. This corrosive study of a family tearing itself apart from the inside gets full-throttle treatment from Conte and Robinson.

Edward G. Robinson as doomed everyman Professor Richard Wanley (*The Woman In The Window*).

Miklós Rózsa

Composer, 1907–95

Miklós Rózsa was one of Hollywood's most revered and innovative composers and one with an impeccable classical pedigree. He was born in Budapest into a musical family, learning piano with his mother and later studying in Leipzig.

As a result of writing music for a London ballet company in 1935, Rózsa was hired by his compatriot **Sir Alexander Korda**, who was head of London Film Productions. When World War II forced Korda to move his production of *The Thief Of Bagdad* to Hollywood, Rózsa went with him and never returned. Initially working for several studios, he was contracted to MGM from 1949.

As a composer for film noir Rózsa broke new ground, beginning with *Double Indemnity* (1944), one of his very finest scores. The mood is immediately established over the credits: as the silhouette of a man on crutches walks towards the viewer, a portentous four-note motif strikes up. This theme will recur throughout the film and seems to signal the inevitability of Walter Neff's fall into corruption. It occurs again, for instance, when Walter and Phyllis dump the body of her husband on the railway. For Walter's soliloquies – his confession into the dictaphone – a scurrying background motif is used suggesting the anxiety that Walter's relatively resigned voice-over doesn't reveal. As with the film, there is very little tenderness in the music, indicating the superficiality of the lovers' relationship – merely a hint of a love theme as the two kiss following the murder, and a plaintive cello solo when they shoot each other. Paramount's music director initially vetoed Rózsa's music, but Wilder and the studio boss both approved it.

No

With *Double Indemnity* Rózsa set the seal for a number of great noir scores: his achievement lay in creating atmosphere and mood through angular melodies and often astringent harmonies rather than relying on lushly orchestrated "big tunes". But the extent to which a composer was circumscribed by what a director wanted can be clearly seen if you compare the music for two Rózsa-scored noirs. Directed by **Lewis Milestone**, the melodrama *The Strange Love Of Martha Ivers* (1946) is one of his crudest scores, with every emotional moment underlined by overblown "symphonic" music. Four years later, *The Asphalt Jungle* (1950) revealed a much more subtle and dramatically effective approach. The film uses just five minutes of music, divided between the opening and closing sequences – edgy, angular and spare music as **Sterling Hayden** dodges a

city police car in the early morning light; then at the end anxious contrapuntal writing as Hayden and his girl drive into the country, culminating in a briefly lyrical passage as he collapses in a field and is nuzzled by horses.

Other dark dramas enhanced by Rózsa's contribution include *Spellbound* (1945) for Hitchcock and *The Lost Weekend* (1945) for **Billy Wilder**, both of which employed the eerie, wavering tones of the theremin – in the first to indicate Gregory Peck's mental attacks, in the latter for the nightmarish DTs that afflict the alcoholic Ray Milland. Rózsa also worked to great effect for Robert Siodmak, a musically sensitive director, especially in *The Killers* (1946) and *Criss Cross* (1948). Rózsa was always looking to expand the vocabulary of film music, especially when attempting to unnerve, even going so far – in Lang's *Secret Beyond The Door* (1948) – as to write and record a piece of music backwards and then play the recording backwards so that it was then the right way around but eerily distorted. Other outstanding noirs included *Brute Force* (1947) and *The Naked City* (1948), both of which were directed by **Jules Dassin**.

Robert Ryan

Actor, 1909–73

Robert Ryan's film roles, particularly in noir, suggest a classic case of Hollywood typecasting. In film after film the tall, handsome Ryan got to play violent men, bordering on the psychotic and sometimes well beyond. The truth is that he was outstandingly good in such roles, possessing a quality of latent menace even when in repose, with a deep-lined face and piercing eyes that suggested a neurotic anguish that was just waiting to explode into violence. By all accounts the man himself was nothing like the roles he played.

After graduating from Dartmouth College in 1932, where he was the college's unbeaten boxing champion, Ryan drifted into acting, studying with Max Reinhardt in California. His breakthrough in the movies came in 1947 – after several years in Hollywood and a wartime stint in the Marines – when he played the anti-semitic GI in **Edward Dmytryk's** *Crossfire*. Bigots became something of a Ryan speciality: he was the small-town tyrant who murders a Japanese farmer in the noirish modern Western *Bad Day At Black Rock* (1955) and the racist ex-con who reluctantly teams up with Harry Belafonte in *Odds Against Tomorrow* (1959).

Ryan always brought depth to his characterizations, even when the script didn't suggest it. One that did, and which provided him with one of his finest roles, was Nicholas Ray's *On Dangerous Ground* (1951, see Canon), in which he played an out-of-control New York cop who gets sent on an upstate assignment to assist the investigation of a child murder and is forced to confront his own demons. It was followed the next year by **Fritz Lang's** taut emotional melodrama *Clash By Night* (1952), in which he played the nihilistic odd man out in a destructive triangular relationship opposite **Barbara Stanwyck** and **Paul Douglas**.

Villains in Westerns were another part of the Ryan repertoire, the best of which was in **Anthony Mann's** noirish *The Naked Spur* (1952). The prey of a neurotic bounty hunter (James Stewart), Ryan – when captured – cleverly manipulates his captors, turning them against themselves. This capacity for conveying a complexity behind the villainy is also in evidence in *House Of Bamboo* (1955), a **Sam Fuller** movie set in Tokyo. Ryan plays Dawson, a former GI now running a criminal gang that targets US ammunition trains: he's a vicious psychopath but he also has a tenderness that even hints at homoerotic feelings for one of his gang.

Top-of-the-bill roles largely ended in the 1960s, but Ryan continued to give always reliable and often outstanding performances, including a final crime thriller outing, the underrated *The Outfit* (1973), shortly before he died of cancer.

The Set-Up
dir Robert Wise, 1949, US, 72m, b/w

The greatest of all boxing movies (including *Raging Bull*, which it influenced) has Ryan convincingly portraying Stoker, a washed-up fighter competing against a younger opponent and not expected to win. His trainer (George Tobias) is so convinced that Stoker will lose that he doesn't even bother to tell him that he has fixed up a deal for him to throw the fight. The sleazy, nocturnal ringside atmosphere is brilliantly conveyed by Wise and, for a change, Ryan plays a man of dignity and integrity.

House Of Bamboo
dir Sam Fuller, 1955, US, 102m

A remake of *Street With No Name*, this – one of Fuller's finest films – was shot in Cinemascope in Japan, with a wealth of colourful local details that reflect the director's enthusiasm for the country. A rather wooden Robert Stack plays a military policeman who infiltrates a gang run by ex-GI Dawson (Robert Ryan). Macho codes of honour, racial tension, loyalty and betrayal – all the key Fuller themes are here; and there are thrilling set pieces including the initial train heist and the final shoot-out in an amusement park.

Robert Siodmak

Director, 1900–73

Of all the great Austro-German directors who influenced film noir, Robert Siodmak is the least celebrated and the least well-known. This is largely because he was more of a jobbing director than the rather more independent-minded

Fritz Lang, Billy Wilder or Otto Preminger, and thus has a less unified body of work. Siodmak tackled whatever came his way – for instance, the dramatically executed horrors of *Son Of Dracula* (1943), to a script by his brother Curt, or the high-camp Technicolor idiocies of *Cobra Woman* (1944). But from 1944's *Phantom Lady* onwards, producers quickly realized that his skill lay with the dark thriller, and his career (right up to his last film in 1969) was studded with some of the most impressive examples in American cinema.

Before his first Hollywood sojourn, Siodmak had made his mark in his native Germany beginning with *Menschen am Sonntag* (*People On Sunday*, 1929), a pioneering documentary-style film co-directed by **Edgar G. Ulmer** and with brother Curt and **Billy Wilder** as scriptwriters. Four years later, with the Nazis in power, he headed to France where he made a handful of films before arriving in the US in 1939. *Phantom Lady* was his breakthough, a film that demonstrated the director's highly sensitive use of actors (Franchot Tone and Ella Raines) and was burnished with the delirious visual style that was the hallmark of German directors.

Siodmak's ability to handle actors with skill was consolidated in *The Suspect* (1944), in which he coaxed from a recalcitrant **Charles Laughton** one of his finest performances as the essentially mild man who murders his nagging wife when she threatens to expose his affair with a younger woman. The insecurity of home and the unreliability of the family unit are recurring themes in Siodmak's films, notably in *Christmas Holiday* (1944) – with **Deanna Durbin** married to a **Gene Kelly** who is not all that he seems – and the spooky *The Spiral Staircase* (1946) in which a vulnerable deaf-mute (Dorothy McGuire) is threatened in the very home where she should feel most secure.

If *Phantom Lady* was the breakthrough, then it was Siodmak's adaptation of Hemingway's *The Killers* (1946, see Canon) that established him as the pre-eminent German director of the nihilistic thriller. It also highlighted emerging Siodmak trademarks, such as the use of multiple flashbacks to create a web of narrative ambiguity (the film starts with the tense assassination of its fatalistic protagonist). *The Killers* is often claimed as its director's greatest work but, arguably, *Criss Cross* (1949, see Canon) is even better. Both films starred **Burt Lancaster** as a naive young man, completely in thrall to a seductive young woman who leaves him in the lurch. In *Criss Cross*, however, the lovers – who have been married – have a rather more real relationship, with Yvonne De Carlo's fears and misgivings making her seem less wholly bad than Ava Gardner in *The Killers*.

While Siodmak branched out into other genres, including the hugely enjoyable Technicolor swashbuckler *The Crimson Pirate* (1952), he never matched the consistency or vision of the half-dozen or so noirs he made in the 1940s.

Phantom Lady
dir Robert Siodmak, 1944, US, 87m, b/w

When the wife of Scott Henderson (Alan Curtis) is strangled, his alibi – that he was out on the town with a young lady in a hat whose name he does not know – looks pretty implausible. He faces execution unless the "phantom lady" can be traced, and only his loyal secretary, Kansas Richman (Ella Raines), believes in him. One jump ahead of Inspector Burgess (Thomas Gomez), Kansas aims to track the mystery woman down. Directed with real flair by Siodmak, the film is famous for its "orgasmic" montage in a sleazy nightclub, a scene that somehow got past the censor.

The File On Thelma Jordon
dir Robert Siodmak, 1949, US, 100m, b/w

Often compared to *Double Indemnity*, this has Barbara Stanwyck playing a young woman, Thelma Jordon, who embarks on an illicit love affair with the unhappily married

Assistant DA Cleve Marshall (Wendell Corey). But when Thelma's rich aunt is shot, Marshall gets in deeper than he should. Although Thelma is acquitted, the whole sorry tale starts to unravel as the levels of her duplicity become apparent. Over-elaborate and slow to get going, this is nevertheless a compelling study of emotional dependency and self-delusion with Barbara Stanwyck in sparkling form.

Barbara Stanwyck

Actress, 1907–90

Born Ruby Stevens, Barbara Stanwyck had the kind of underprivileged upbringing that was written into many of her characters, but very quickly demonstrated a versatility lacking in most of her peers. More than **Bette Davis** or **Joan Crawford**, her early work foregrounded the erotic, and in Stanwyck's case, that was steamy stuff indeed. In Frank Capra's *The Bitter Tea Of General Yen* (1932) she radiated an upfront sexuality, while *Baby Face* (1933) could only have been filmed in the pre-Hays Code 1930s, as a manipulative Stanwyck manoeuvres her way to the top of a company by sleeping with a series of her bosses.

By the 1940s, the dead hand of censorship was ensuring that most adaptations of celebrated crime novels were being effectively neutered, but **Billy Wilder** managed to retain much of the scabrous tone of James M. Cain's *Double Indemnity* (1944, see Canon), and in Stanwyck, he had one of the screen's great incarnations of a *femme fatale* – languidly seductive and always in control of Fred MacMurray's morally weak insurance agent. Two years went by before she turned to crime films once more, taking on the title role in *The Strange Love Of Martha Ivers* (1946), a lurid family melodrama in which Stanwyck played a single-minded businesswoman pushing her passive, weak-willed husband (Kirk Douglas) into political office, while covering up a guilty secret.

More solid work in the crime genre followed, this time in the potential victim role: first in *The Two Mrs Carrolls* (1947), where she's menaced by husband **Humphrey Bogart**, then in *Sorry, Wrong Number* (1948) in which marriage to Burt Lancaster turns out to have been no less a mistake. She was back in the driving seat in *The File On Thelma Jordon* (1949), a *Double Indemnity*-style plot which had her murdering her aunt and getting her lover, an Assistant DA (Wendell Corey), to get her off the hook. Soon after, the two were paired up as lovers again in Anthony Mann's noirish Western *The Furies* (1950), but there's no doubt that Stanwyck's great love in the film is for her patriarchal rancher father (Walter Huston), whose second marriage she tries to prevent.

Best of all Stanwyck's later noir outings was **Fritz Lang**'s *Clash By Night* (1952), in which all the facets of the actress's screen persona (toughness, vulnerability, sensuousness) were brought together in a marvellously nuanced performance which is well matched by the equally tough yet vulnerable Robert Ryan. Her final two noirs were relatively conventional but she still gave committed performances in each, as victim in the first and aggressor in the second. *Witness To Murder* (1954) is literally that – a woman sees her neighbour murder his mistress but he manages to convince the authorities that she is insane and should be put away. In *Crime Of Passion* (1957) Stanwyck is a successful columnist on a San Francisco paper who abandons her job to marry a cop. She then takes it upon herself to further his career, by any means at her disposal.

From the 1960s, the cinematic glory days were largely over for Stanwyck and she worked mainly in TV, moving into comfortable Grand Dame territory epitomized by her implacable matriarch in the long-running series *The Big Valley*.

The Strange Love Of Martha Ivers
dir Lewis Milestone, 1946, US, 116m, b/w

After attempting to run away with her friend Sam, Martha Ivers is provoked into attacking her tyrannical aunt (Judith Anderson) who is accidentally killed. The event is witnessed by Walter, the son of Martha's tutor, and when an innocent man gets framed for the death Martha inherits a fortune. Years later Sam (Van Heflin) returns and looks up his childhood – and now married – friends Martha (Barbara Stanwyck) and Walter (Kirk Douglas), but they suspect his motives. A compellingly rich and moralistic melodrama in spite of Milestone's plodding direction.

The Two Mrs Carrolls
dir Peter Godfrey, 1947, US, 99m, b/w

Another creaky melodrama but it does pair up the king and queen of noir for the first and only time, so it can't be all bad. Humphrey Bogart plays Gerry Carroll, an artist who falls for the wealthy Sally (Barbara Stanwyck) while on holiday. But he already has a wife who he is painting as "The Angel of Death" before proceeding to bump her off. He then marries Sally but, after a few revealing chats with Gerry's daughter Bea (Ann Carter), she decides that maybe he has similar plans for her.

Not one but two Mrs Carrolls: Barbara Stanwyck ponders her portrait.

Fatal women

The most memorable staple character in film noir was the *femme fatale*, an archetype developed from the vamp of early cinema via the more modern, liberated "flapper" of the 1920s. Sexy in a highly glamorous way, she was habitually duplicitous (and often deadly), with a desire to control her own destiny. Men were used and abused as a means to an end.

Some have seen the *femme fatale* as reflecting male anxiety about the increased liberation and independence of women during the interwar period, and the *femme fatale* character was often contrasted with another archetype, that of the homebuilder – the loyal, reliable wife and mother.

The *femme fatale* role was a great opportunity for a beautiful actress to make her mark and many did so, either in just one or two performances or by becoming so identified with the type that it was almost all they were ever asked to play. Here are ten of the very best, drawn from both the classic and the neo-noir eras:

1 **Barbara Stanwyck** as Phyllis Dietrichson in *Double Indemnity* (1944).

2 **Rita Hayworth** as Elsa Bannister in *The Lady From Shanghai* (1947).

3 **Jane Greer** as Kathie Moffatt in *Out Of The Past* (1947).

4 **Yvonne DeCarlo** as Anna Dundee in *Criss Cross* (1949).

5 **Joan Bennett** as Kitty March in *Scarlet Street* (1945).

6 **Ava Gardner** as Kitty Collins in *The Killers* (1946).

7 **Kathleen Turner** as Matty Walker in *Body Heat* (1981).

8 **Linda Fiorentino** as Bridget Gregory/Wendy Kroy in *The Last Seduction* (1994).

9 **Gene Tierney** as Laura Hunt in *Laura* (1944).

10 **Mary Astor** as Brigid O'Shaughnessy in *The Maltese Falcon* (1941).

Orson Welles

Actor and director, 1915–85

After his amazing success as actor-manager of the avant-garde Mercury Theatre Company – and an early radio brush with the crime genre, in which he played crime-busting vigilante "The Shadow" – Orson Welles was invited to Hollywood where he made the greatest debut feature film in the history of the medium, *Citizen Kane* (1941, see p.20). Ostensibly a fictional biopic (loosely based on newspaper magnate William Randolph Hearst), the format of *Kane* was partially borrowed from the crime genre: the investigator who uncovers dark facts about a powerful deceased figure is a standard device of the detective story. He was to use the same technique, rather less successfully, in the similarly themed *Mr Arkadin* (1955). But Welles's troubles – and his precipitate fall from grace – had begun almost before *Kane* was in the cinemas, where it did unexceptional business. His second film, *The Magnificent Ambersons* (1942), was famously mauled by RKO who began to see him as a problem director.

Still hanging on to his wunderkind image, Welles's next project (actually shot back-to-back with *Ambersons* and using some of the same cast) was an adaptation of **Eric Ambler**'s spy thriller *Journey Into Fear* (1942). Directed by Norman Foster, but with a huge input from Welles, including one of his hammiest turns as Colonel Haki the Turkish police chief, the film has some great moments (usually involving the silent assassin Benat, played by Welles's manager Jack Moss) but is ultimately pretty slight. *The Stranger* (1946) had Welles acting and directing once again, but determined to salvage his reputation and bring the project in on time and to budget. Its Nazi-hunting plot, set in small-town Connecticut, was more coherent than *Journey Into Fear* and conveyed a palpable sense of threat. Unfortunately, this is undercut by a banally over-romanticized score and a range of different acting styles – from the restrained but effective **Edward G. Robinson** to Welles's own barnstorming caricature of the murderous Hun on the loose.

It was left to the delirious *The Lady From Shanghai* (1948, see Canon), made to fulfil a contractual obligation, to reveal just how Welles's battery of expressionist stylings could be effectively put at the service of the crime thriller. Intriguingly, it starred Welles's recently ex-wife **Rita Hayworth** as the murderous double-crossing *femme fatale*, with Welles himself as the love-lorn Irish adventurer who gets mixed up with her and her reptilian husband (Everett Sloane). Sadly, it was still too experimental for the Columbia bosses who had the film re-edited, cutting much of its (now famous) hall of mirrors climax.

Welles's participation as an actor in the classic Carol Reed/Graham Greene film *The Third Man* (1949) was crucial to the film's success, with his charismatic delineation of the black marketeer Harry Lime creating one of the cinema's most ambiguous villains. *Mr Arkadin* (1955) showed a distinct faltering, the director shamelessly indulging several slumming actors (such as Michael Redgrave) in over-drawn cameos. It's an extravagantly filmed and often intriguing investigation into the power and corruption of a rich man, played by Welles in a terrible false beard, without the focus or energy of *Citizen Kane*.

Welles subsequently produced his noir masterpiece, *Touch Of Evil* (1958, see Canon), a doubly remarkable achievement for being produced on time and for containing a truly mesmerizing performance from the director as the grotesque, overweight and utterly corrupt cop Quinlan. It's a technical *tour de force* set on the US side of the border with Mexico and co-starring Charlton Heston and Janet Leigh. Almost inevitably, the studio butchered it, shooting new and unnecessary footage, and released it as a B-movie in support of a lurid Hedy Lamarr vehicle, *The Female Animal*. *Touch Of Evil* was only released in something like Welles's intended form in 1998, after a painstaking restoration job (see p.172).

Journey Into Fear
dir Norman Foster, 1942, US, 69m, b/w

This is standard spy thriller fare, but Welles's stamp is firmly in place (though the film is credited to Norman Foster). Joseph Cotton, who wrote the script, plays a naval engineer in Istanbul trying to evade assassination by Nazi agents. With its cast of sleazy and exotic characters (largely recruited from Welles's Mercury Company), its claustrophobic atmosphere and rain-soaked climax, this has a sufficiently noir feel to compensate for its rambling plot. A bonus (of sorts) is Welles's amusing performance as the malign Turkish secret police chief, Colonel Haki.

The Stranger
dir Orson Welles, 1946, US, 95m, b/w

Welles's inspiration as a director is notably burning low on this workaday effort, but he does manage to obtain a magnificent performance from Edward G. Robinson as an FBI man keeping a watchful eye on Nazi war criminal Franz Kindler (Welles). Kindler (aka Professor Rankin) plans to marry the gauche Mary (Loretta Young), who is unaware of her betrothed's past. The details of small-town American life are conveyed quite as unnervingly as in Hitchcock's *Shadow Of A Doubt* and there's a very Hitchcockian ending.

Richard Widmark

Actor, 1914–

Few film debuts are as memorable or as disturbing as Richard Widmark's Tommy Udo in Henry Hathaway's *Kiss Of Death* (1947, see Canon). The psychotic giggle, the nervously darting eyes, the sense that the character was one of the most lethally unpredictable criminals ever presented on screen, and – most of all – the murder of a woman by pushing her wheelchair downstairs.

It's a performance that made most criminals previously seen on screen seem demure by comparison. But how to follow it? Widmark, who had a background in theatre and radio, found himself in a series of similar gangster roles, none quite as memorable as his debut. There was, however, plenty of good work: in **William Keighley's** *The Street With No Name* (1948) and **William Wellman's** *Yellow Sky* (1948).

Widmark's next outstanding film involved the actor playing a fish out of water in an adapta-

All-purpose authority: Widmark as gang leader Alec Stiles in *The Street With No Name*.

tion of cult British crime writer **Gerald Kersh**'s celebrated novel *Night And The City* (1950, see Canon). Widmark played the increasingly terrified petty criminal, menaced on all sides in a threatening London, and few actors could have conveyed the tension and paranoia with such flesh-creeping vividness. But he was no less adept at handling heroic protagonists, notably in **Elia Kazan**'s *Panic In The Streets* (1950) as a doctor trying to track down the criminal carriers of a plague. Another excellent director, **Joseph L. Mankiewicz**, brought out the best in the actor in *No Way Out* (1950), which showcased one of Widmark's pointed studies in bigotry.

Two years later, Widmark worked for the great primitive maverick of American cinema, **Samuel Fuller**, in *Pickup On South Street* (1952, see Canon), in which his pickpocket, dangerously out of his depth, is one of the actor's most powerful performances. He played another gangster in the Henry Hathaway segment of the portmanteau film *O. Henry's Full House* (1952), and was a discreet support for **Marilyn Monroe** in *Don't Bother To Knock* (1952).

But as middle age beckoned, Widmark showed that he could easily supply a series of all-purpose authority figures (corrupt or otherwise) in a lengthy string of movies. While his success as a jobbing actor was assured, he also ventured into production with three Cold War thrillers beginning with *Time Limit* in 1957. His association with crime cinema had a prestigious late-1960s revival in **Don Siegel**'s *Madigan* (1968), in which his tough, anti-authoritarian cop was a dry run for Siegel's later *Dirty Harry*.

The Street With No Name
dir William Keighley, 1948, US, 91m, b/w

One of those docu-noirs that emerged in the late 1940s, complete with plenty of location work, real FBI men in bit parts and portentous narration. It's raised above the ordinary by Widmark's sharp performance as fight promoter and gang leader Alec Stiles, a raging hypochondriac who seems to take a bit of a fancy to new gang member Gene Cordell (Mark Stevens). In fact Cordell is an undercover agent reporting the gang's movements back to the FBI, and when Stiles finds out…

Panic In The Streets
dir Elia Kazan, 1950, US, 93m, b/w

This time Widmark gets to play the good guy, Dr Clinton Reed, a public health official who is the only person truly aware of the enormity of what might engulf New Orleans. A murder victim is found to have pneumonic plague, so the murderers – almost certainly carriers – must by tracked down. Police chief Tom Warren (Paul Douglas) is the man responsible for finding the infected criminals (Jack Palance and Zero Mostel), but is he up to the job? Often veering between genres, the film climaxes with a brilliantly sustained chase sequence through the grimy labyrinth of the docks.

Billy Wilder
Director, 1906–2002

By the end of his career, when his films had lost the razor-sharp edge that distinguished both his comedies and crime movies, Billy Wilder was notably bitter about the young "beards" who had taken over Hollywood (the then-new generation of Steven Spielberg, Brian De Palma and George Lucas). But this disillusionment was not just an old man's resentment: Wilder's acerbic, outsider's view of American society had also informed his classic movies, along with a very German respect for the word.

Born in Sucha in southern Poland, then part of the Austro-Hungarian Empire, Wilder moved to Berlin as a young man, working as a dancer and a journalist before starting in films as a scriptwriter. With Curt Siodmak he co-scripted

Menschen am Sonntag (*People On Sunday*, 1929), a slice of Berlin life directed by **Robert Siodmak** and **Edgar Ulmer**, and he worked again with Robert Siodmak on the blackly comedic crime movie *Der Mann, der seinen Mörder sucht* (*Looking For His Murderer*, 1931). When the Nazis came to power in 1933, Wilder (who was Jewish) left for France where he directed his first film, *Mauvaise graine* (*Bad Seed*, 1934). In the same year, he arrived in America. Astonishingly, for someone whose reputation hangs on his brilliance as a wordsmith, his English was pretty basic when he arrived. But he was soon writing scripts, mostly in tandem with Charles Brackett with whom he worked for twelve years, a collaboration which produced some brilliantly constructed films, including *The Lost Weekend* (1945) and *Sunset Boulevard* (1950) – both also directed by Wilder.

His first great film, and one of the greatest of all film noirs, was *Double Indemnity* (1944, see Canon), written with **Raymond Chandler**, whose mark can be discerned in the wisecracking, sexually charged dialogue between insurance salesman Walter Neff and Phyllis Dietrichson. But the cynicism of the vision, and at the same time the humanity, is entirely Wilder's own. His brief venture into noir territory – just four films if you count *The Lost Weekend* – is remarkable for being rooted in a recognizably real world, so that while the visual stylistics are strong (three of the films are stunningly lit and photographed by John F. Seitz), they never obtrude on or overwhelm the characters.

After *Double Indemnity* Wilder's career alternated such sardonic visions of human greed with almost equally dark comedies, of which *Some Like It Hot* (1959) was the apogee. Although not a crime film, *The Lost Weekend* (1945) was informed with a deeply noir sensibility, as alcoholic writer **Ray Milland** watches his life fall

apart. Similarly, in *Sunset Boulevard* (1950) Wilder turns his unflinching gaze on the film industry itself, with **Gloria Swanson** playing a once great star dreaming of her comeback, who hires a failed scriptwriter to feed her self-delusion as he loses his self-respect. A year later came Wilder's most savage film, *Ace In The Hole* (1951), in which **Kirk Douglas** gave a lacerating performance as a cynical newspaper reporter manipulating facts and situations, as well as endangering lives, in order to get "the big story".

Witness For The Prosecution (1958) was an altogether gentler riff on the crime genre for Wilder, with a mechanical but satisfying plot enlivened by husband-and-wife team **Charles Laughton** and **Elsa Lanchester** playing a barrister and his fussy nurse. By now in harness with a new writing partner, former maths genius I.A.L. Diamond, Wilder concentrated on comedies, producing some of the greatest ever, usually featuring his leading men of choice – **Jack Lemmon** and **Walter Matthau**.

The Lost Weekend
dir Billy Wilder, 1945, US, 99m, b/w

Wilder enjoyed tackling taboo subjects head on, in this case alcoholism. Ray Milland plays Don Birnam, a once successful writer who – despite a sympathetic brother and fiancée (Jane Wyman) – will not face up to his drink problem. With them out of town, he goes on a bender, finishing up with the DTs in a terrifying hallucination sequence. Not strictly a noir, the film utilizes the milieu of grimy New York streets and a local bar complete with worried barman and cute good-time girl Doris Dowling. The trite ending (forced on the makers) is the only false note.

Casting Shadows:
noir locations

Christopher Lambert running for the train in *Subway*.

Casting Shadows:
noir locations

Most early noirs were staged in the confines of the studio. However, with the rise of location filming in the late 1940s, an increasing number of noirs showcased authentic, dramatic locations, in particular capitalizing upon the diverse, atmospheric urban locales of Los Angeles, San Francisco and New York. But noir was not just a US creation, and international locales were also utilized in the classic era. In the ongoing neo-noir age, filmmakers continue to look back to LA's classic noir persona in films such as *L.A. Confidential*, but also look forward to a future-noir vision of the metropolis, as in *Blade Runner*. The following pages describe noirs, both classic and modern, that have memorably and inventively made use of real locations.

Los Angeles

No city has gripped the dark imagination so much as the homeland of Hollywood, in so many ways the cradle of noir (see Origins). A string of key films have been set in the city, including *Double Indemnity* (1944) and *Kiss Me Deadly* (1955). This dark love affair has never abated, prompting filmmakers to home in on specific areas of the city such as the Chinatown district (*Chinatown*, 1974),

and even specific roads (*Sunset Boulevard*, 1950, *Mulholland Dr.*, 2001). With LA centre stage in the past, present and future, the city is noir's very own capital city in every respect.

White Heat
1949 (see p.27)

This film provides a textbook example of the striking propensity of noirs to locate their narrative climax at an industrial location. *White*

Heat's highly memorable finale – in which James Cagney, surrounded by flames, shouts skyward with mad glee: "Made it, Ma! Top of the World!" – was filmed at the **Torrance Refinery**. You can no longer see it as it was then, as it was completely rebuilt in 1965. Today, it's the **Exxon Mobil Refinery**, located at 3700 West 190th Street, Torrence, in southern Los Angeles.

Double Indemnity
1944 (see Canon)

The "death house" of this seminal film noir, where Fred MacMurray and Barbara Stanwyck meet and plot murder, and where their twisted love affair finally reaches its disastrous climax, still stands high in the Hollywood Hills. It can be found amidst a maze of small lanes at **6301 Quebec Street** – off Beachwood, not Los Feliz as the film states – north of Franklin Avenue, in Los Angeles. Although the home looked rather secluded in the original film, these days it's in a densely packed area of (pricy) houses.

Sunset Boulevard
1950 (see p.33)

Unfortunately, the gorgeous mansion in which Gloria Swanson's fading movie star resides in Billy Wilder's seminal satirical noir was demolished in

White Heat: Cagney on top of the world (in an LA refinery).

1957 to be replaced by the headquarters of the Getty Foundation. However, you can still view the apartment of William Holden's broke screenwriter, in all its Mediterranean-style splendour, at **Alto Nido Apartments**, 1851 North Ivar Street. Also in the film, Swanson visits Cecil B. DeMille on set at the world-famous **Paramount Studios**, located at **5555 Melrose Avenue**, although, because the studio has expanded considerably in recent decades, the entrance is no longer the Paramount archway, as seen in the film. If you want to see it, you'll need to sign up for one of the walking tours around the studio – available three times a day at fifteen bucks a wander.

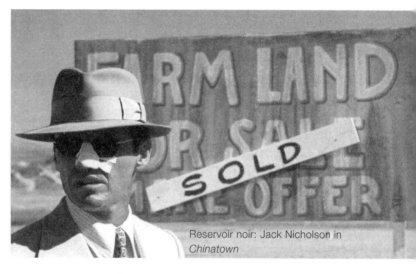

Reservoir noir: Jack Nicholson in *Chinatown*

(1949) and *Angel's Flight* (1965). The area has been extensively redeveloped in recent years and is now home to the Walt Disney Concert Hall and a thriving upscale community.

Kiss Me Deadly
1955 (see Canon)

Robert Aldrich's masterful 1955 rendition of the Mike Hammer detective story was primarily filmed in the **Malibu** area, but also made use of the **Bunker Hill** region of LA. Until the end of World War I, Bunker Hill was a wealthy district with a very low crime rate. During the 1920s and 30s, however, the area went into decline and was soon plagued by criminals and vandals. The Victorian houses fell into disrepair and the crime rate soared, making the area a slum. Thanks to this well-timed lapse into urban decay, Bunker Hill became the perfect visual metaphor of all things noir and was a popular setting for filmmakers. As well as *Kiss Me Deadly*, it was also used as a location for such noirs as *Criss Cross*

Chinatown
1974 (see Canon)

One of the all-time great neo-noirs, *Chinatown* is packed with LA locations. The lake at the centre of the film's story about corruption within the city's water programme is **Lake Hollywood**, a reservoir built in 1925 by Water Commissioner William Mulholland. (Interestingly, that man's own tragic life may be the reason why David Lynch chose to use the LA street named after him for his 2001 movie *Mulholland Dr.*) The memorable scene in which Jack Nicholson's gumshoe Jake Gittes gets his nose sliced by a thug's knife was shot at **Point Fermin Park** in San Pedro. Gittes's first meeting with John Huston's man-behind-the-plan, Noah Cross, occurs on

Catalina Island, which is just off the coast of LA, while the mansion of Gittes's doomed love interest Evelyn Mulwray (Faye Dunaway) was located on **South Oakland Avenue** in Pasadena. And if you find yourself in need of refreshment after all that sightseeing, try **The Prince**, 3198 West 7th Street in Koreatown – the location for the scene between Mulwray and Gittes, called the Brown Derby Restaurant in the film.

Blade Runner
1982 (see Canon)

Now considered a peerless example of future noir, Ridley Scott's extraordinarily vivid dystopian vision of a permanently rain-swept and polluted LA of 2016 was mostly shot on the Warner Bros backlot, but it also made magnificent use of LA locations. Some, such as the cylindrical towers of the **Bonaventure Hotel**, located on 404 South Figueroa Street, are incorporated in the stunning FX-enhanced views of the future city.

The film's most memorable set is the overwhelmingly waterlogged apartment of the toy maker Sebastian, where the film's climactic showdown between Harrison Ford and his quarry Rutger Hauer takes place, culminating in Hauer's "Tears in the rain…" speech. This is the **Bradbury Building**, located on 304 South Broadway. Unremarkable on the outside, its real beauty is the inner skylight-covered courtyard, along with a magnificent wrought-iron stairwell and cage elevators, surrounded by marble. After years of neglect – it was run-down when *Blade Runner* was filmed – it has now been lovingly restored.

A further architectural beauty was used for Deckard's apartment: the Frank Lloyd Wright-designed **Ennis-Brown House** on 2607 Glendower Avenue, built in 1924 and featuring beautiful geometrically tiled walls, inside and out.

L.A. Confidential
1997 (see Canon)

Curtis Hanson's utterly masterful 1950s-set neo-noir was shot almost entirely on location throughout LA – only "The Victory Motel" was a constructed set, albeit among the oilfields of **Baldwin Hills**. The office of Danny DeVito's sleaze-rag journo was located beneath the revolving, neon-lit spire of **Crossroads of The World** (6671 Sunset Boulevard), which in fact is a shopping mall designed in the 1930s to look like an ocean liner. DeVito's staged "movie premiere pot-bust" was shot at a bungalow at **1714 Gramercy Place**, while the movie's cops operate out of LA **City Hall**, which is downtown

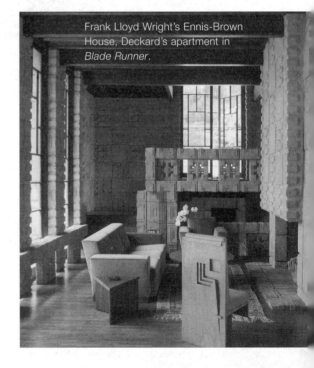

Frank Lloyd Wright's Ennis-Brown House, Deckard's apartment in *Blade Runner*.

at 200 North Spring Street. The Nite-Owl café, which hosts the massacre that drives the film, is the **J&J Sandwich Shop** – downtown LA on 119 East 6th Street. Just opposite is the **Pacific Electric Building**, where hothead cop Russell Crowe dangles the corrupt DA from a window.

One of the film's best-looking locations is the exceedingly classy pad of pimp Piers Patchett – **Lovell House** is in fact widely regarded as an architectural masterpiece. Located on 4616 Dundee Drive, Los Feliz, it was designed in 1929 by famed architect Richard Neutra. Finally, the Hollywood bar where ambitious cop Bud White inadvertently hassles the real Lana Turner is the **Formosa Café**, situated at 7156 Santa Monica Blvd, which in real life was a fabled hangout for such legends as Bogart, Clark Gable and Marilyn Monroe.

New York

New York has always been at the cutting edge. *Kiss Of Death* (1947), starring a psychotic Richard Widmark, and Jules Dassin's *The Naked City* (1948) were both at the forefront of a move in noir towards filming mostly or entirely on location. History repeated itself in the 1970s when a somewhat run-down Big Apple appeared in *Taxi Driver* (1976), the film credited with spearheading neo-noir, shortly after *The French Connection* (1971) had shown us more of Manhattan than Marseille.

The Naked City
1948 (see Canon)

Jules Dassin's docu-noir informed audiences that "There are eight million stories in the Naked City; this has been one of them." What made Dassin's particular tale so engrossing – and influential – was the extensive location shooting on New York's streets, something that was done rarely at the time and produced footage that was markedly different from studio-bound fare. The police station is the **10th Precinct**, located in the Chelsea district at 230 West 20th Street. The murder that the cops investigate occurs on New York's **Upper West Side** at 52 West 83rd Street. Segments of the film were also shot at the hub of New York's financial district, **Wall Street**, and the climactic confrontation was filmed at the **Williamsburg Bridge**, where the villain dies falling into the East River.

The French Connection
1971 (see p.42)

A seminal cop thriller that, like *Dirty Harry*, perfectly captured the cynicism of the times, William Friedkin's film about an unorthodox cop's near-obsessive hunt for a French drug dealer was, save for the Marseille-set introduction, produced in New York to compelling effect.

The sleazy bar where Gene Hackman's Popeye Doyle habitually gets sloshed is on **South Street** by Manhattan Bridge on the Lower East Side. Hackman and Roy Schneider's early morning stakeout is **Ratner's Restaurant** on 138 Delancey Street, again on the Lower East Side. Schneider first comes across their target, "Frog One" (Fernando Rey), at the entrance of the **Roosevelt Hotel**, East 45th Street on Madison Avenue, while the hotel that Frog One stays at is **The Westbury**, on 15th East 69th Street. Elsewhere in the movie, the slippery Frenchman evades Hackman by ducking into the **Ronaldo Maia Flower Shop** and, later, by using the get-on-get-off subway trick underneath **Grand Central Station**.

The film's famous chase sequence, shot over five weeks and rather illegally at full speed in the midst of unsuspecting bystanders and real traffic, begins at **Bay 50th Street Station**. The bulk of the chase follows the 26-block-long **Bensonhurst Elevated Railway**, moving from 50th Street along Stillwell Avenue to 86th Street and from there on to New Utrecht Avenue, culminating at 62nd Street Station, where Popeye Doyle puts a bullet in Frog Two's back.

Taxi Driver
1976 (see p.42)

This is not just one of the best movies to come out of the so-called Second Golden Age of Hollywood, but also the film that is widely perceived to have started noir's transformation into "neo-noir". As for the Big Apple locations featured: the cab office that Robert DeNiro's progressively unhinged Travis Bickle works from is located on **57th Street at 11th Avenue**. Unfortunately, the Belmore Cafeteria, where Travis hung out with his fellow cabbies, no longer exists. The porno theatres, which Travis cruises during daylight hours, were along **48th Street and 8th Avenue**. Travis is picked up by underage prostitute Iris (played by Jodie Foster) outside the **St Regis Sheraton Hotel** at 2 East 55th Street. The thoroughly sleazy hotel at which Travis takes Iris – and which is also the location of the startling climactic blood bath – is located at 226 13th Street.

Hackman as Popeye Doyle under the Bensonhurst Elevated Railway.

San Francisco

The city's famous hills, the Golden Gate Bridge and nearby Alcatraz Island are only a few of the local landmarks that directors have taken to their hearts and then put on screen. John Boorman's *Point Blank* (1967) was the first film to be given access to the famous penitentiary (now a popular tourist attraction) but from Delmer Daves's *Dark Passage* (1947) to *Dirty Harry* (1971) dubious characters have been at large on the streets of San Francisco. And then of course there is the ultimate Bay Area film, *Vertigo* (1958).

Dark Passage
1947 (see p.183)

In Delmer Daves's 1947 noir, a convict escapes from prison, hooks up with Lauren Bacall and, thanks to the miracle of plastic surgery, is transformed into Humphrey Bogart. The prison that Bogart escapes from is the notorious **San Quentin**, located in Marin County, just across the bay from San Francisco. An especially beautiful aspect of the film is the unbelievably stylish Art Deco apartment that Bacall's character resides in. It's located at **1360 Montgomery Street** and, remarkably, the building has hardly changed. It is at the top of Filbert Steps, which is a seemingly endless public stairway that Bogart, immediately post-surgery, struggles to climb at the film's start.

Vertigo
1958 (see p.31)

Although technically not a film noir, Alfred Hitchcock's *Vertigo* (1958) is as good as, being a psychological thriller of the first order, in which ex-detective Scottie (James Stewart) becomes entangled in a nightmare of acrophobia and sexual obsession. *Vertigo* is famous for its extensive location footage of San Francisco, and many would claim the city itself as an important character in the story.

Fort Point on Marine Drive, at the southern point of the Golden Gate Bridge, is the marine wall where Kim Novak memorably takes a plunge and is rescued by Scottie. He takes her to his apartment, located on **900 Lombard Street**, a few blocks downhill from the famous "crookedest street in the world". Although the door has been repainted, the entrance to Scottie's apartment is easily recognizable, save for a few small changes to the patio. The doorbell and the mailbox, which Novak uses to deliver a note to Scottie, are exactly the same as they were in the movie. At **351 Buena Vista East** is the sanatorium where Scottie recovers after suffering a nervous breakdown. Formerly St Joseph's Hospital, now Park View condominiums, the building looks much the same from the outside.

The film's exceedingly tense climax takes place at **San Juan Batista**, located ninety miles south of San Francisco. The all-important tower was in fact a matte painting, since the original tower had been torn down thanks to extensive decay from dry rot. The original was in fact much smaller and less dramatic than the matte version.

Dirty Harry
1971 (see p.42)

Shot entirely on location, Don Siegel's thriller about Clint Eastwood's anti-authority, near-fascist cop hunting for a serial killer still retains enormous potency. The film's opening sees Scorpio performing an assassination from the rooftop of the **Bank of America World HQ** (555 California Street), instantly killing the girl frolicking in the rooftop pool of **The Holiday Inn** at Chinatown on 750 Kearney Street. Unfortunately, if you want to see the place where Harry delivers his immortal question, "Do you feel lucky…?", to the gunned-down thug, you're out of luck – it was the only studio-bound scene. The Police Department that Harry operates from, however, is the **Pacific Gas and Electric Building**, located in the financial district on 245 Market Street.

The brilliant sequence in which Scorpio runs Harry over town, via orders issued over public phones, culminates at the impressive concrete cross at the top of **Mount Davidson**, the highest point in the city. Eventually, Harry tracks Scorpio down to **Kezar Stadium** in Golden Gate Park, where Harry practically tortures his quarry after shooting him in the leg. In the film's climax, Scorpio hijacks a school bus filled with young children, travels over the **Golden Gate Bridge**, on to **Sir Francis Drake Boulevard** and from there on to **Highway 101**. The final showdown – conforming to noir tradition by taking place in an industrial location – is at the **Larkspur rock quarries**, now completely redeveloped.

Paris

Nightlife and noir go together, hence in French noir Paris's nightclubs and street life appear centre-stage. It took an American, Jules Dassin, to set the ball rolling, brilliantly utilizing the city's centre in his classic heist movie *Rififi*. Director Jean-Pierre Melville created a smoke-filled, trench-coat-laden image of the underworld in *Bob le flambeur* (1955) and *Le Samouraï* (1967). This epitome of criminal cool was updated but still located mostly in the shadows in Luc Besson's *Subway* (1985).

Rififi
1955 (see p.259)

The target for the heist is English jewellery store Mappin and Webb, then situated on the **Rue de la Paix** very close to the **Place Vendôme**. The thieves initially case the joint from a café across the street which, as Dassin has revealed, was simply a table placed on the pavement with a window stuck in front of it. When Tony (Jean Servais) tracks down the kidnapped son of his friend Jo, he does it by shadowing a man from the Métro stop at **Port Royal** all the way to the end of the line at **Saint-Rémy-Les-Chevreuse**.

Le Samouraï
1967 (see Canon)

Hugely influenced by American noirs, director Jean-Pierre Melville turned the most romantic of European cities into a suitably noirish environment with *Le Samouraï* (1967). Hitman Jeff Costello (played with impeccable cool by Alain Delon) is a perfectionist who always plans his murders carefully and never gets caught. However, after killing a nightclub owner, he's seen by witnesses. While the entire film makes excellent use of Parisian locations, the best example is the film's chase sequence, as Delon desperately tries to dodge the law.

While on the **Champs-Elysées**, Delon first escapes by ducking into the entrance of **1 Rue Lord Byron**, emerging at **116 Bid**, near The Lido, then into the **George V Métro Station**. He then takes the Vincennes line to **Porte d'Ivry**, where he's shot and wounded upon meeting his contact. There follows a chase on the Métro system where the police hunt him from the **Télégraphe Métro** to **Place des Fêtes**. He gets off at **Jourdain**, finally giving them the slip at **Châtelet-Les Halles**, where he leaps off the travelator.

Christopher Lambert avoiding
the rush hour in *Subway*.

Subway
1985 (see p.260)

Luc Besson's enormously stylish neo-noir *Subway* provided Paris with a neon sheen, making vivid use of the Parisian underground system, where the bulk of the film was shot. Christopher Lambert plays safe blower Fred, who takes refuge in the Paris Métro after being chased by the henchmen of a shady businessman from whom he has just stolen some documents. While hiding out, Fred encounters a subterranean society of eccentric characters and petty criminals. The station where Christopher Lambert escapes the hitmen is **Dupleix**, located on Boulevard Grenelle, south of Pont de Bir-Hakeim. Lambert listens to the sax player at the eastern Paris station **Gallieni**, while Jean-Hughes Anglade's roller-skater is followed onto the train at **Concorde**, before being handcuffed to a carriage pole at **La Motte Picquet-Grenelle**. Most of the film's action takes place at the world's largest underground station, **Châtelet-Les Halles**.

London

Arthur Woods was the first native director to take real advantage of London's Dickensian-style gloom with the hard-hitting crime film *They Drive By Night* (1939), but it was Jules Dassin who gave the city an authentic noir edge when he crossed the Atlantic to make *Night And The City* in 1950. Since then the capital has proved a perfect showcase for seediness and criminal sleaze, from *Performance* (1968) to John Mackenzie's *The Long Good Friday* (1980).

Night And The City
1950 (see Canon)

In 1950, director Jules Dassin achieved the considerable feat of transposing film noir – then a determinedly American style – to the more genteel climes of London with the film *Night And The City*. The results were hugely successful and mightily atmospheric. Richard Widmark is exceptional as the venal hustling promoter Harry Fabian who has lofty ambitions of hitting the big time and a willingness to achieve it by any means. Dassin shot London wholly free of grace and charm and it shows in every frame: cold, dank, dark, shrouded in mist and with danger lurking in every corner.

The film begins with Fabian fleeing his creditors down the impressively wide steps in front of an imposingly lit **St Paul's Cathedral**. The (fictitious) Silver Fox nightclub, meanwhile, is located in Covent Garden's **New Row**, just off St Martin's Lane, opposite **The Salisbury pub**. Fabian meets the shady nightclub owner (played by Francis Sullivan) at tourist hot spot **Trafalgar Square**, while the terrace in front of **County Hall**, located on **Westminster Bridge Road**, is where Fabian pretends to obtain a drinks licence. At the film's climax, Widmark finally gets his comeuppance beneath **Hammersmith Bridge**.

The Long Good Friday
1980 (see p.255)

Thirty-two years later, London was similarly employed to marvellously grimy effect in the British neo-noir classic *The Long Good Friday*. Bob Hoskins provided an incendiary performance as the ferociously patriotic Thatcher-era gangster Harold Shand, whose hard-won empire comes under threat from rivals. While the London of *The Long Good Friday* is not one shrouded in shadows, it nonetheless possesses a thoroughly noirish maze-like and permanently dangerous quality, and is home to no shortage of duplicitous and dangerous denizens.

Harold gives the mafia bosses an expletive-heavy piece of his mind outside the **Savoy hotel**, where they dump him just before he is abducted by the IRA. Its restaurant on Wigmore Street is where Harold's right-hand man gets spat on during a meal with the shady London councillor. **The Villa Elephant Italian restaurant** provided the interior for Harold's casino, and the film's elaborately mirrored restaurant was in the **Rainbow Room** on **Kensington High Street**. Harold and Helen Mirren's moll character entertain the shady Americans on their boat, which is moored at **St Katharine's Dock** in the East End.

Another pub named **The Salisbury** (this one located on Grand Parade, Green Lanes) doubled as the Irish pub Fagan's. **St Patrick's Church**, Green Bank, is where Harold's mother narrowly avoids getting killed, thereby triggering Harold's drive for revenge. **Ladywell Leisure Centre**, in Lewisham, contains the swimming pool where

Harold Shand (Bob Hoskins) contemplates his prospects, with Tower Bridge in the distance.

Harold's right-hand man is killed by a member of the IRA (played by an exceedingly young Pierce Brosnan). **Villa Road in Brixton** is the site of another of the film's gruesome murders, as it contains the home of "Errol the Grass" who gets cut up by "Razors".

Vienna

Vienna may not be the setting for many noirs but this former imperial capital and cradle of psychoanalysis has plenty of historical shadows of its own which can add a certain gravitas to proceedings. Nick Roeg's erotic thriller *Bad Timing* (1980) is very aptly set in Freud's home city (mostly in art galleries) but no film can compete with the impact made by Carol Reed's postwar classic *The Third Man* (1949). Cue a minor industry of *Third Man* walking tours around the city and even beneath its streets.

The Third Man
1949 (see p.254)

Cinematically, Vienna never had a more vivid or dramatic showcase than when it appeared as the central location of Carol Reed's mesmerizing noir *The Third Man* (1949), starring Orson

Orson Welles avoids the military police in Vienna's sewer system.

Welles as the racketeer Harry Lime, who casts a large shadow over the rubble-strewn city. Joseph Cotton's naive Western writer Holly Martens, arriving in Vienna to accept a job offer from his pal Harry Lime, first appears at Vienna's West Railway Station (**Westbahnhof**), subsequently going to Lime's apartment block, the palatial exterior of which was **Palais Pallavicini**. This is where Martens learns that Lime has "died". Lime finally makes a memorable entrance in the beautifully ornate doorway of **8 Schreyvogelgasse**, and the vast cobble-stoned square where Lime disappears is to be found at **Am Hof** – although there is no kiosk hiding a secret entrance to the sewers; that was just a prop.

One of the film's most memorable scenes is the meeting between Lime and Martens at the giant Ferris wheel, where Lime gives his "cuckoo clock speech". It was filmed at the **Riesenrad** Ferris wheel, which still stands today, located at the vast **Prater** park, which lies between the Danube river and the Danube canal. (The Ferris wheel makes a more romantic appearance in the Timothy Dalton Bond film *The Living Daylights*, 1987.)

Later, a trap is set to capture Lime at **Hoher Markt**, which is a seventeenth-century square that possesses a striking "nuptial" fountain. The trap fails, of course, sending Lime fleeing into the city's labyrinthine sewer system for the movie's climax. If you so desire, you can take a tour of the sections of the sewer system that Reed used to film Lime's demise.

Is there such a thing as rural noir?

In the classic era, film noirs were so anchored in the forbidding urban environment of the city that excursions to rural locations were rare. There were exceptions, however: 1945's *Leave Her To Heaven* bases its murderous love story in the romantic, colourful environs of New Mexico. Generally speaking, the appearance of a rural locale in a film noir signified a release or refuge from the claustrophobic urban setting, such as in the climax of *The Asphalt Jungle* (1950) or the wintry scenes of *On Dangerous Ground* (1952).

However, it is far easier to identify a sub-genre of "rural noir" within the (now considerable) confines of neo-noir/postmodern noir. An excellent starting point would be Lawrence Kasdan's *Body Heat* (1981), set in the searing heat of a Florida summer. Likewise, the Coen brothers' seminal neo-noir *Blood Simple* (1984), Dennis Hopper's *The Hot Spot* (1990) and John Sayles's *Lone Star* (1996) make exquisite use of Texas. John Dahl set *Red Rock West* (1993) in the isolated plains of Wyoming, while David Lynch's *Wild At Heart* (1990) took in the sweat-drenched environs of New Orleans. And not forgetting the Coen brothers' *Fargo* (1996), set in the frozen wastes of North Dakota.

It's a sub-genre that is not teeming with films, but what releases there are constitute excellent examples of noir. More recently, in 2005, cinema audiences were treated to an exceedingly potent example of rural noir with the release of David Cronenberg's *A History Of Violence*, in which the peace of a small town in Indiana is shattered when diner-owner Viggo Mortensen's past catches up with him, suddenly infesting this bastion of Americana with big-city gangsters bent on revenge.

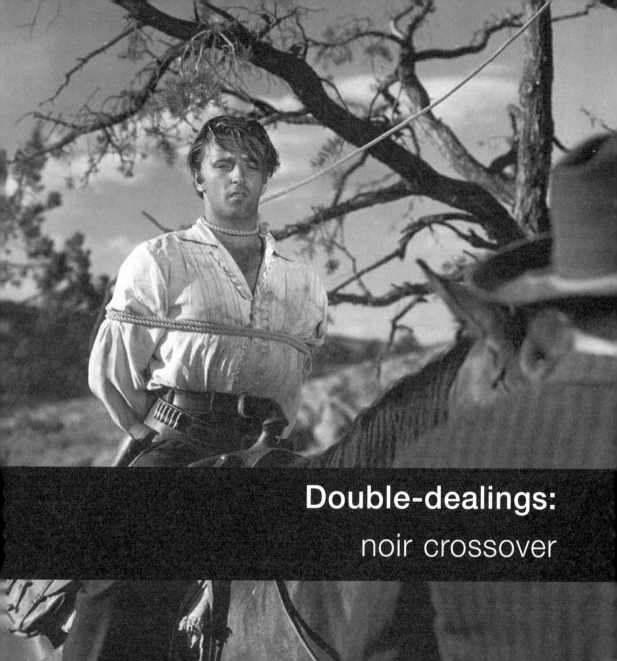

Double-dealings:

noir crossover

Robert Mitchum as Jeb Rand in the finest of all
noir Westerns, Raoul Walsh's *Pursued* (1947).

Double-dealings:
noir crossover

Given film noir's prevailing atmosphere of darkness and despair, it would be easy to assume that its influence on established Hollywood genres would be minimal. This is not the case. In both the classic era, and more recently with neo-noir, there have been several examples of successful cross-pollination and even the emergence of whole new hybrid sub-genres.

A large part of noir's continuing impact on other genres can be put down to the immense influence that classic movies have had on the directors who emerged in the postwar era. This began with French *nouvelle vague* auteurs, such as Truffaut and Godard, in the 1950s and 60s and continued with the so-called "movie-brats" of the 1970s (Scorsese, Coppola, DePalma, et al) who embraced noir's stylistic and thematic sensibilities as a means of plying their own brands of harder-edged, crime films.

More pertinently, a great many of the younger directors and writers – the **Coen brothers**, **Christopher Nolan** – working across today's film industry eagerly cite noir's enormous influence on their work. Consequently, noir has

proven itself a highly enduring and widespread presence, with a variety of cinematic genres and sub-genres routinely bearing noir characteristics.

This chapter will examine the most notable areas of crossover that film noir has produced, focusing on the best and most successful examples.

Animation

That the traditionally brash, knockabout, fun-filled and colour-drenched medium of animation has found itself infiltrated by noirish elements is testament to just how wide-ranging noir's influence has been. Not that it took long in this case: as far back as the 1940s, animated shorts – particularly Warner Bros' legendary *Looney Tunes* series – featured some masterful parodies of noir themes and motifs. A prominent example was the 1946 cartoon *Bacall To Arms*, which, as the title implies, featured a *femme fatale* based on the then new star, Lauren Bacall.

Not that there are that many examples of cartoons directly mixing with noir; the only one to achieve absolute classic status is *Who Framed Roger Rabbit* (1988), which took several noir motifs (the private investigator searching for redemption, the *femme fatale*, etc) and paired them with Looney Tunes-esque zaniness to vastly enjoyable effect. More recently, the 1990s animated incarnation of *Batman* (see box opposite) abounded with noir characteristics, a not insignificant part of the series' success. Equally, Pixar's brilliant *The Incredibles* (2004) has a well-developed and knowing noirish feel.

Who Framed Roger Rabbit
dir Robert Zemeckis, 1988, US, 103m

What's the first thing that comes to mind when recalling this knockabout comedy? The title character's supremely slinky heartbreaker of a wife, Jessica (voiced with magnificent huskiness by Kathleen Turner), an improbably voluptuous *femme fatale* who effortlessly reduces Bob Hoskins's private eye to mush. Very much a cinematic milestone thanks to its still supremely impressive interaction of the animated and live-action elements, Zemeckis's "toon-noir" has aged wonderfully and remains one of his career's high points.

especially visually, resulting in some remarkable work over the last two decades. Most notably, **Katsuhiro Otomo**'s seminal *Akira* (1988) and **Mamoru Oshii**'s *Patlabor 1* (1995) rank among the very best feature-length examples. On the small screen **Chiake Konaka**'s *The Big O* (1998–2001) centered around a private eye-like "freelance negotiator" who operates in a doomed metropolis; *Nightwalker* (1998) had a Japanese detective solving cases while dealing with his double life as a vampire; and – best of all – *Noir* (2001) revolved around the uneasy alliance between two female assassins for whom the description *femme fatale* is only too apt. A more classical-looking hybrid of noir and anime exists in Shinichiro Watanabe's excellent "Detective Story", which was one of the principal contributions to the animated spin-off to *The Matrix* film franchise, *The Animatrix* (2003), replete with vividly rendered 1940s settings.

Noir
Kôichi Mashimo and Matt Greenfield, 2001, Jap

Known as *Nowâru* in Japan, this excellent series focuses on a female assassin, Mireille, who receives a message from a young girl named Kirika who has lost her memory, but who similarly displays incredible talents as a killing machine. As the pair strive to discover Kirika's past, they set themselves up as a hit team named Noir, travelling worldwide while evading a secret society bent on stopping their discoveries. With the focus on characters and plot as opposed to guns and explosions, this is a surprisingly affecting and often beautiful series.

Anime

While not as widespread an influence as cyberpunk, an entire sub-genre of anime has nonetheless been infused with tech-noir elements,

Comedy

With paranoia, danger, violence and death all key elements of the noir universe, it might seem that there is not much room left for laughter - other

Dark Knight rising

Originally appearing in comic books as early as 1939, Batman is without doubt the *noirest* of the super-heroes. Not only do his crime-fighting adventures take place in the classically noir environment of Gotham City, but he is also surrounded by a textbook cast of gangster crime lords, blundering police chiefs and, of course, *femmes fatales*. Also significant are Batman's beginnings – one of the few superheroes to possess no "super powers", Batman found his calling after witnessing the murder of his parents. Thus, in true noir style, Bruce Wayne's alter ego searches not for *truth* or *justice*, but good old-fashioned vengeance as a means of quenching his own inner turmoil. There have been many small-screen and big-screen incarnations of the character also known as "The Dark Knight", many of which should be swiftly forgotten. Here are the choicest three, which each in their own way, stay true to the original, dark, noirish DC Comics vision.

Batman
dir Tim Burton, 1989, US, 126m

A huge cultural phenomenon as well as a massive blockbuster, Burton's visually stunning film played a key role in eradicating memories of Adam West's campy 1960s Dark Knight and restoring some darkness to the character. At the film's core was a notable sense of Stygian psychosis, implying that both Batman (Michael Keaton) and his nemesis, The Joker (Jack Nicholson), are psychotically deranged, fighting for the city's soul. The film has a very noirish Art Deco look, with sharply dressed gangsters, corrupt cops and glamorous molls.

Batman: The Animated Series
1992–95, US, 3 seasons

Routinely lauded as a masterpiece of modern animation and held up by fans as the purest screen incarnation of the Dark Knight, this magnificent show is an undiluted joy. Visually, the series drew heavily from noir, with a postmodern style dubbed "Dark Deco", in which Gotham City has an ostensibly 1940s look – from clothes to transport – but also features computers and supervillains alongside zoot-suited hoodlums.

Batman Begins
dir Christopher Nolan, 2005, US/UK, 141m

Nearly a decade after the franchise-stalling *Batman & Robin* (1997), the Dark Knight received masterful reinvigoration from Nolan, who not only injected a sense of realism, but also imbued the film with a surprisingly forthright quota of dark psychology. The noir tone was furthered by a flashback-filled narrative and the grimly cavernous Gotham setting, ruled by gangsters and psychopaths instead of the more garish and theatrical villains that had populated some of the earlier Bat-fare.

Christian Bale as the Dark Knight in *Batman Begins*.

than the hysterical. Surprisingly, humour occurs quite regularly in classic-era noirs, and actually becomes something of a cliché in the form of the sardonic, wisecracking private investigator, epitomized by **Raymond Chandler**'s Philip Marlowe. Chandler also worked as a scriptwriter, and his work with **Billy Wilder** on *Double Indemnity*

Out of his depth and into a new genre: Bob Hope does comedy noir with Dorothy Lamour.

(1944, see Canon) has some of the sharpest, wittiest dialogue of any film of the period.

It is also surprising just how quickly the noir style and its attendant clichés started to be parodied. *Lady On A Train* (1945) had the bubbly **Deanna Durbin** as an avid crime fiction reader who fails to convince anyone that she witnessed a murder as she pulled into Grand Central Station. *My Favorite Brunette* (1947, opposite) was a **Bob Hope** vehicle in which he plays a baby-photographer who masquerades as a private eye when the detective in the adjacent office goes away on a case.

1951 saw one of the great accidental comedy-noirs with **John Farrow**'s *His Kind Of Woman*. It begins in conventional noir territory, with **Raymond Burr** as a gangster planning to take over the identity of gambler **Robert Mitchum**. Then, halfway through, Vincent Price turns up (with Jane Russell in tow) as a Shakespeare-quoting actor of heroic proportions, and the whole thing explodes into surreal parody. **John Huston**'s bizarre *Beat The Devil* (1953), with its over-elaborate script by Truman Capote, strives a little too hard for a similar effect – although there are great moments of self-parody from Humphrey Bogart.

There's a large degree of parody, and even pastiche, in a lot of neo-noir, for instance in *Body Heat* (1981, see canon), which shamelessly mimics the flirty dialogue in *Double Indemnity*. An even more blatant and affectionate homage appeared the following year in *Dead Men Don't Wear Plaid* (1982), starring Steve Martin. There is also much humour in the **Coen brothers**' sly variants on noir, in particular *The Big Lebowski* (1998), a delightfully comedic spin on a Chandleresque mystery, and *The Man Who Wasn't There* (2001, see p.51), starring Billy Bob Thornton and shot in black and white. In recent years, the finest comedy-noir hybrid was undoubtedly the ludicrously underrated *Kiss Kiss Bang Bang* (2005, see Canon), which melded the crime thriller and black comedy to great comic effect.

Lady On A Train

dir Charles David, 1945, US, 94m, b/w

With moody camera-work from Woody Bredell, a rather breathless score from Miklós Rósza and Dan Duryea as a (possible) bad guy, what further noir ingredients do you need? Well probably not the charming Deanna Durbin breaking into song and changing her outfit and hairstyle at regular intervals. Nevertheless, this gentle send-up of noir, and crime fiction in general, is enjoyable enough.

My Favorite Brunette

dir Elliott Nugent, 1947, US, 87m

Baby-photographer Ronnie Jackson (Bob Hope) is taking phone calls for the private eye (a trench-coated Alan Ladd) in the neighbouring office when gorgeous, wide-eyed Dorothy Lamour walks in. Explaining to Ronnie how her uncle has been captured by spies, he decides to step into the breach. Faced with the bad guys, including a gormless Lon Chaney Jr and a mean Peter Lorre, it's not long before Ronnie is completely out of his depth.

Dead Men Don't Wear Plaid

dir Carl Reiner, 1982, US, 89m, b/w

Expertly utilizing the gimmick of intercutting scenes from classic noirs with modern 1940s-spoofing material featuring Steve Martin's private eye uncovering a sinister plot, this loving homage to the genre is a masterful piece of absurdist comedy. Something of a forgotten film, it's notable for being the last outing for noir legends costume designer Edith Head and composer Miklós Rósza (with him rescoring his own work).

The Big Lebowski

dir Joel Cohen, 1998, US, 127m

This is a kind of comedic *Cutter's Way* (see p.45) with Chandleresque overtones, as LA slacker Jeffrey "The Dude" Lebowski (Jeff Bridges) is mistaken for a millionaire with the same name who owes the mob some money. His troubles escalate as he agrees to act as a conduit between his

namesake and the bad guys who have kidnapped his wife. A wonderfully rambling and fantastical plot, complete with a Busby Berkeley-style dream sequence, makes this one of the most endearing Coen movies.

Documentary

The late 1940s saw a significant shift in the style of film noir, from highly stylized studio-based work (in films like *The Maltese Falcon*) to a greater reliance on location work. The influence came from documentary filmmakers, most notably **Louis de Rochemont** (see p.22), the producer of the pioneering *March Of Time* series. Films were no less melodramatic, but there was a greater emphasis on events that had actually happened, and a blurring of the difference between fiction and fact by mixing the actual participants with professional actors. De Rochemont's director of choice in these early docu-noirs was Henry Hathaway who made the *The House On 92nd Street* (1945), *Kiss Of Death* (1947, see Canon) and *Call Northside 777* (1948).

With the decline of noir at the end of the 1950s and with documentary filmmakers favouring a more *cinéma-vérité*, fly-on-the-wall approach in the 1960s, the relationship between noir and documentary faltered. The notable exception to this rule is **Errol Morris's** *The Thin Blue Line* (1988), a film that investigates the case of a man, Randall Adams, awaiting execution for a murder of which he claims to be innocent. Though this type of subject matter has been frequently handled by documentarists, Morris's approach is highly original in the way he clothes the story in an eerie, dream-like and decidedly noirish beauty.

Call Northside 777
dir Henry Hathaway, 1948, US, 111m, b/w

Remarkable for its location shooting in and around Chicago, this tells the story of Frank Wiecek (Richard Conte) – found guilty of killing a policeman and sentenced to life. Enter James Stewart as reporter P.J. McNeal, to reinvestigate the long-closed case, and gradually come to believe in the man's innocence. A tough and unsentimental film, both in the way it depicts the reality of life for the urban poor and the way it shows the reluctance of the authorities to admit to a miscarriage of justice.

The Thin Blue Line
dir Errol Morris, 1988, US, 101m

Forty years on and another case of wrongful imprisonment following the death of a policeman. But Morris's approach couldn't be more different from Hathaway's. With its highly stylized dramatic reconstructions, its bizarre characters and hypnotic Philip Glass score, this is much more of a meditation on the elusive nature of truth. The result is the same, however, as gradually the viewer becomes aware of the innocence of Randall Adams. As a result of this film he was eventually released.

Gangster movies

Just as the gangster movie genre of the 1930s exerted a considerable formative influence on film noir (see p.6), so noir – in the decades since the classic era ended – has had a similarly potent influence on the gangster movie. In some cases, it is difficult to decide where the one ends and the other begins, with the 1940s producing such gangster-noir hybrids as *High Sierra* (1941) and *White Heat* (1949). Clearly, in the classic era, noir introduced a degree of moral and narrative complexity into the crime movie which it hadn't possessed before. But in the post-classic era, things are not quite so clear-cut.

Certainly, most modern gangster movies have benefited from the exposed moral conflicts evident in noir, the most celebrated examples being **Francis Ford Coppola**'s *The Godfather Parts I to III* (1972/1974/1990). **Brian De Palma**'s remake of *Scarface* (1983) made explicit comment on the deleterious effects of capitalism, reminiscent of **Abraham Polonsky**'s *Force Of Evil* (1948), while *Carlito's Way* (1990) focused on the killer's doomed-to-fail efforts at redemption to stunning effect. Martin Scorsese, of course, is responsible for the brilliant *Goodfellas* (1990), which made memorable use of the noir staples of voice-over narration and flashbacks, as well as the temptation of crime. He would revisit similar territory with 1995's *Casino*. The Coen brothers, with typical flair, have reinvigorated the gangster genre while employing classic noir motifs with *Miller's Crossing* (1990).

The Godfather Parts I to III
dir Francis Ford Coppola, 1972/1974/1990, US, 175m/200m/162m

At its core, Coppola's much-lauded Mafia saga is about power: its inheritance, the internal and external struggles to maintain it and the massive loss it engenders. As such, Coppola's trilogy is entrenched in a very noir environment, brilliantly encapsulated by Al Pacino's performance as the increasingly soulless Michael Corleone. Gordon Willis's cinematography expertly enhances this fact, with darkness creeping into every frame.

Miller's Crossing
dir Joel Coen, 1990, US, 115m

Another masterpiece from the Coens, this one amply recalling the 1930s gangster movies from which film noir sprang – albeit with a contemporary level of violence. Gabriel Byrne plays an advisor to a Prohibition-era crime boss who tries to keep the peace between warring mobs, but gets caught by divided loyalties. The Coens' seemingly effortless ability to take genre clichés and give them a fresh spin remains thoroughly impressive.

Black gangster

The rise of neo-noir in the mid- to late 1970s immediately followed the short-lived reign of "Blaxploitation" cinema – low-budget action movies aimed at black audiences – which borrowed elements of film noir with its visions of dimly lit urban ghettos infested with cut-throats, pimps and hustlers, memorably exemplified in films such as *Superfly* (1972), *Coffy* (1973), *Foxy Brown* (1974) and *Sheba Baby* (1973), the last three starring **Pam Grier** as an altogether different brand of *femme fatale*.

Noir's influence on Black cinema would resonate more explicitly – though far less colourfully and with far greater seriousness – in the black gangster movies that proliferated in the early 1990s, most notably John Singleton's powerful *Boyz N The Hood* (1991),

New Jack City (1991), *Juice* (1992), *Dead Presidents* (1995) and *Menace II Society* (1993), all of which superbly chronicled the black urban experience.

New Jack City
dir Mario Van Peebles, 1991, US, 97m

Though borrowing heavily from rise-and-fall gangster films such as *Scarface*, Van Peebles (son of Blaxploitation legend Marvin) concocts a brutally effective story of black urban lives embroiled in the world of drugs and the lure of gangster power. Wesley Snipes is terrific as the drug dealer who thrives selling cocaine to his poor fellow blacks and Van Peebles grants the film a captivating authenticity of life amongst such rampant crime.

Nino Brown (Wesley Snipes) considers his next move in *New Jack City*.

Road To Perdition
dir Sam Mendes, 2002, US, 117m

Tom Hanks is the Prohibition-era assassin who embarks on a mission of vengeance with his son when his wife and child are murdered by his mob overlords. Beautifully elegiac, Mendes's film is anchored on a man struggling with the light and dark aspects of his existence, unable to escape the truth of what he is.

Gothic melodrama

The influence of horror movies on film noir has been explored in an earlier chapter (see p.11). Both had roots in nineteenth-century stage melodrama – a theatre of sensational events and heightened emotionalism – which in turn was influenced by the gothic novel of the late eighteenth and early nineteenth centuries. In the twentieth century a gothic and melodramatic strand continued in both literature and film, often focusing on the image of a single, vulnerable woman insidiously preyed upon either physically or psychologically. Such material need not be, but often was, set in the historical past, and often blurred the boundary between noir and horror. So *Dr Jekyll And Mr Hyde* (1941) and *The Picture Of Dorian Gray* (1945) are regarded as horror, whereas *Rebecca* (1940) and *Spiral Staircase* (1946) are (more or less) noir.

Shadows from the past: Anthony Mann's *Reign Of Terror.*

The vogue for such material was at its height during the 1940s and included a surprisingly large number of films. Many of these were based on works by British authors, including **Daphne du Maurier** whose *Rebecca*, filmed by Hitchcock in 1940 (see p.26), is the outstanding example of modern gothic; and **Patrick Hamilton** whose play *Gaslight* and novel *Hangover Square* both got the Hollywood treatment in 1944. Both of Hamilton's works were set in a shadowy fog-filled Victorian London, whereas *Reign Of Terror* (1949), filmed by top noir director Anthony Mann, made a more daring time leap into eighteenth-century Paris at the height of the French Revolution. Other outstanding noir melodramas with a gothic edge include *Spiral Staircase* (based on a thriller by Ethel Lina White) and a late example, *The Night Of The Hunter* (1955, see p.34).

The Spiral Staircase
dir Robert Siodmak, 1946, US, 83m, b/w

With the brilliant noir team of Siodmak and cameraman Nicholas Musuraca in top form, this is one of the finest of all period thrillers. Set in a provincial American town at the start of the twentieth century, a serial killer is on the loose targeting young women who have a physical disability. Dorothy McGuire plays Helen, a young mute working as a nurse for the elderly Mrs Warren (Ethel Barrymore) in the perfect "old, dark house". As the killer closes in, the tension becomes almost unbearable.

Sorry Wrong Number
dir Anatole Litvak, 1948, US, 89m, b/w

An untypical role for the powerful Barbara Stanwyck, here playing a bedridden invalid, Leona Stevenson, who is also the daughter of a millionaire. Trying to phone her husband (Burt Lancaster), she gets a crossed line and overhears two men planning a murder. Gradually she comes to realize that she is the intended victim. Based on a radio play and largely set in one room, the palpable sense of claustrophobia is enhanced by Hans Dreier's detailed designs and some nice expressionist touches from director Litvak.

Reign Of Terror
dir Anthony Mann, 1949, US, 89m, b/w

Possessing a gritty, crime-movie feel that wholly belies the eighteenth-century costume drama setting (unsurprising as Mann shot this in the wake of his noir classics *T-Men* and *Raw Deal*) and filmed with great economy, this taut, claustrophobic tale of suspense concerns the attempts by an operative of the newly formed Republic to obtain the black book of contacts belonging to a would-be dictator. This is excellent proof of how adaptable noir elements could be.

Musicals

The noir-musical – now that, surely, is an oxymoron. How could a style so determinedly dark as film noir be applied to the one genre whose teeming, ever-present optimism it specifically sought to counterbalance? The truth is that there are several musicals that have dark elements (*Carousel*, *West Side Story*), but is there a fully fledged noir musical? The most cited noir moment in a musical is the eleven-minute jazz ballet sequence, "The Girl Hunt", that occurs in the **Vincente Minnelli**-directed *The Band Wagon* (1953). Brilliantly choreographed by Michael Kidd as a parody of Mickey Spillane-style pulp novels, this has Cyd Charisse as a leggy *femme fatale* (complete with Louise Brooks hairstyle) leading Fred Astaire's private dick astray.

Other films that are sometimes suggested include the Betty Hutton vehicle *Red, Hot And Blue* (1949). Directed by seasoned noir specialist **John Farrow**, this is a flimsy musical comedy with songs by Frank Loesser (who also appears as a gangster). But the only serious candidate to fit the bill convincingly is *Carmen Jones*. The brainchild of librettist Oscar Hammerstein II, it first appeared as a Broadway show in 1943 and was filmed by classic noir director **Otto Preminger** in 1954. Closely based on Bizet's opera *Carmen* (1873), the musical updates the action to the US in World War II and gives it an all-black cast. Plot and characters are decidedly noirish, with Carmen the archetypal *femme fatale* and the hero a good but gullible man who goes off the rails because of her. Filmed in widescreen Technicolor, there is little in visual terms that identifies it with the noirs of the period.

 Carmen Jones
dir Otto Preminger, 1954, US, 105 mins

Lured off the straight and narrow by good-time girl Carmen Jones (the fabulous Dorothy Dandridge), Joe (Harry Belafonte) abandons a potential career as a pilot and his loyal girlfriend, for a half-life in Chicago dodging the military police. Carmen soon tires of this and goes off with boxing champ Husky Miller (Joe Adams). Despite great performances by the leads and some clever lyrics, the film is marred by Hammerstein's irritating attempts at black idioms (all "dis", "dat" and "deys") and the fact that the singing voices (Belafonte's in particular) are inappropriately dubbed by others.

Science fiction

Despite being firmly rooted in the fantastic, the science fiction of the 1950s, like noir, eagerly drew upon the pervading mood of fear, paranoia and distrust that had engulfed America in the wake of World War II. In particular, there was a preoccupation with the Cold War, an anxiety which had been significantly enflamed by the Communist witch-hunts led by Senator McCarthy. .

Two fine examples of this displaced anxiety can be found in **Don Siegel**'s *Invasion Of The Body Snatchers* (1956) and Gene Fowler Jr's *I Married A Monster From Outer Space* (1958). Despite their silly titles, both – especially the for-

mer – are very powerful films that amply capture the hysteria of the time and transform it into an oppressive, doom-laden noirish atmosphere. However, the outstanding noir of this period to touch on both scientific and Cold War themes remains **Robert Aldrich**'s *Kiss Me Deadly* (1955, see Canon).

In the decades since, hybrids of sci-fi and noir – dubbed variously as "future noir", "cyber noir" but predominantly "tech noir" – can lay claim to being among the most creative, visually arresting and enjoyable manifestations of noir's ongoing legacy. Following sci-fi's widespread re-emergence in the late 1970s, courtesy of the playful *Star Wars* (1977), the optimistic *Close Encounters Of The Third Kind* (1977) and the earnest *Star Trek: The Motion Picture* (1979), noir traits started to appear in sci-fi, notably in **Ridley Scott**'s starkly pessimistic *Alien* (1979), which, while technically a space-bound horror movie, was rooted in a prevailing atmosphere of entrapment, fear, hopelessness and death.

Tech noir's crowning moment, however, came in 1982 with Scott's now-celebrated *Blade Runner* (see Canon), which to this day remains the model for a successful merging of noir and sci-fi. The iconic nature of this movie's blatant noir stylings pretty much drew a line in the sand that few have dared to cross. The result was that noir-inflected sci-fi became the exception rather than the rule, and usually as part of a vision of dystopia. Both *The Terminator* (1984) and *Robocop* (1987) offered such a view, while *Nineteen Eighty-Four* (1984) saw Orwell's classic tale of totalitarianism imbued with an overwhelming, noirish sense of desperation and fear. *Brazil* (1985), in turn, was a retro-futuristic dystopia anchored in black comedy.

Since the 1990s, tech-noir stylings have had a routine – and profitable – presence at the cinema, with films such as *The Matrix Trilogy* (1999–2002)

The noir look will never be out of fashion: William Hurt sometime in the future, *Dark City* (1998).

and *Minority Report* (2002) bolstering their vividly dark visions with blockbuster-sized earnings.

This period also witnessed an array of lightly noir-dusted movies, feeding off a pervading millennial angst. **Kathryn Bigelow**'s *Strange Days* (1995), set on the eve of the new millennium, featured a hustler (Ralph Fiennes) who sold sexy and violent digital content fed directly into the cortex of the brain. The cyber-age thriller *Virtuosity* (1995) had Russell Crowe as a computer-generated, virtual reality killer pitted against LA cop Denzel Washington. Another movie that ticked many of the right noirish boxes was Andrew Niccol's directorial debut, *Gattaca* (1997), with its futuristic tale of genetic engineering. You can also add to this list such movies as *Equilibrium* (2002) and the much-lauded *Children Of Men* (2006), though best of all was Alex Proyas's labyrinthine, visually inspiring *Dark City* (1998), a combination of science fiction and crime melodrama set in a futuristic, postmodern, urban locale with a story about a malevolent alien race.

A final movie worth highlighting is **Wong Kar Wai**'s *2046* (2004), which, though largely set in 1960s Hong Kong, is draped in the lighting and mood of classic 1940s noir, thanks to the efforts of cinematographer Christopher Doyle.

Invasion Of The Body Snatchers
dir Don Siegel, 1956, US, 80m, b/w

Based on the pulp novel by Jack Finney, Siegel concocted both a chilling tale of unseen alien invasion and a potent indictment of Cold War hysteria (although he claimed the latter was never intended) and it remains a defining moment in science-fiction cinema, remade no less than three times since its release.

Strange Days
dir Kathryn Bigelow, 1995, US, 145m

Set in the closing days of 1999, Ralph Fiennes is the disgraced ex-cop who deals illegal "clips"– recordings of memories downloaded direct from the brain – and who, along with mate Angela Bassett, becomes embroiled in a murder conspiracy that threatens to unleash a racial apocalypse. While the story might be pure shopworn pulp, Bigelow's film is primarily distinguished by an extremely stylish visual inventiveness.

Dark City
dir Alex Proyas, 1998, US, 115m

Something of a film noir fever dream, this hugely atmospheric mixture of sci-fi and crime melodrama is blessed with astounding visual elements, most notably the heinously sinister and permanently dark city that literally changes before the eyes of confused amnesiac and murder suspect Rufus Sewell, who happens to be the only witness to the mysterious goings-on because the city's inhabitants fall into a dead sleep come midnight. Delightfully creepy.

2046
dir Wong Kar Wai, 2004, Fr/Ger/HK/China, 116m

A kind of sequel to Wong Kar Wai's earlier romance *In The Mood For Love,* the confusing but beguiling story revolves around a womanizing writer (Tony Leung) and a series of encounters with women, all coloured by his lost love

(Maggie Cheung). The action constantly shifts, flashback-style, between the writer's complicated life and scenes from the sci-fi novel, *2046*, that he is penning about an android that develops emotions.

Serial killer films

Thanks to films such as *Henry: Portrait Of A Serial Killer* and *Manhunter*, both released in 1986, the serial killer movie gained a sheen of sophistication and depth. With the enormous success of *Silence Of The Lambs* (1991), this particular sub-genre became even more firmly established. Many of these films – such as *Copycat* (1995), *Se7en* (1995, see Canon), *Hannibal* (2001), *Roberto Succo* (2001), *Tattoo* (2002) – employed noir stylings to create a mood of oppressiveness.

Visually and tonally, noir's influence is obvious, with such films habitually trading on a bleak, fear-laden mood drenched in darkness. However,

Video game noir

In the last decade, the gap between cinema and video games has closed considerably, with games now habitually possessing cinematic features, not just visually but also in the employment of sustained story lines replete with nuanced dialogue and detailed characters to go along with the customary mayhem. As you'd expect, film noir has been heavily drawn upon by game designers in their efforts to achieve this, and many games can now be found to feature noir traits.

In particular, the more overt appropriations have given rise to the term "game noir" and games such as *Under A Killing Moon* (1994), *Grim Fandango* (2001), *Condemned: Criminal Origins* (2005) and *The Godfather* (2006) to name but a few, feature no shortage of both loving homages to, and inspired uses of,

the noir style. To date, however, the best – and most successful – example of game noir exists in the stunning *Max Payne* series of games.

Max Payne 1 & 2
2001/2003, Take 2 Interactive

From an action perspective, *Max Payne* is deeply indebted to the movies of John Woo, but in just about every other aspect – story, characters, dialogue, atmosphere – this incredibly popular third-person shooter is an out-and-out homage to classic film noir – and a magnificently executed one, too, which follows the internal and external troubles suffered by a cop in a supremely dark and sinister vision of New York.

noir's greatest influence lies in these films' treatment of the serial killer. As shown in many noirs of the classic era, the killer can be a dark prism through which society is viewed and, in the case of Hannibal Lecter, even made unexpectedly charismatic!

The Silence Of The Lambs
dir Jonathan Demme, 1991, US, 118m

Thanks to Demme's taut direction, a performance from Anthony Hopkins as Hannibal Lecter that is both highly theatrical and utterly chilling, and Jodie Foster as the FBI agent brave enough to tackle him, this film remains the most entertaining of the serial killer movies. In Lecter, pure evil never appeared so charming and the complexities of his relationship with Agent Starling provide the film with a compelling moral centre.

The Western

The Western provides an interesting example of the way that the noir sensibility could infiltrate an established genre. At first sight the whole concept seems antithetical to the noir approach. Most obviously, the Western's locations are usually wide open spaces rather than modern cities, and it tends to deal with moral certainties – it's always easy to distinguish the good guys from the bad. But following World War II, the genre developed a greater degree of moral complexity. The iconic figure of both the cowboy and the lawman often resembled the classic noir protagonist – isolated and threatened, on a less than heroic quest and following a personal moral code rather than the law. He is often obsessive, driven by revenge and capable of extreme violence.

Significantly a number of directors who excelled at noir also made some excellent Westerns. Chief among these was **Anthony Mann** who in a total of ten Westerns introduced a much harsher degree of violence and characters who carry a lot of psychological baggage. The folksy **James Stewart** was Mann's favourite lead, who – in films like *Winchester 73* (1950) and *The Naked Spur* (1952) – tapped into an anger and intensity that he had rarely shown before. Even darker than these two movies was *Man Of The West* (1958), in which **Gary Cooper** played a reformed criminal faced with some harsh decisions.

The first great example of a noir-inflected Western was *The Ox-Bow Incident* (1943), a deeply pessimistic tale of the lynching of three innocent men. No less powerful was **Raoul Walsh**'s *Pursued* (1947), in which **Robert Mitchum** plays a man weighed down by the demons of his past. Mitchum crops up again in *Blood On The Moon* (1948), this time playing a cowboy who drifts into a dispute between ranchers and homesteaders, switching his help to the latter when he discovers that he's been working for a crook. In *The Gunfighter*, released in noir's peak year of 1950, **Gregory Peck**'s eager-to-retire gunslinger has to face up to the dangerous reality of his reputation in a taut, suspenseful tale about a tragic and lonely man.

The early 1950s even saw the Western take on the issues raised by McCarthyism, most famously in the controversial *High Noon* (1952), in which Gary Cooper plays a marshal who risks his life for what he believes. Written by the soon-to-be-blacklisted **Carl Foreman**, ironically the film was also admired by some conservatives as showing a man motivated by duty. **Alan Dwan**'s *Silver Lode* (1954) took a more overtly anti-McCarthy stance with **Dan Duryea** playing a villain (named McCarty) who successfully turns the townspeople against respectable rancher Dan Ballard (John Payne) in order to settle a grudge.

Pursued
dir Raoul Walsh, 1947, US, 101m, b/w

Shot by James Wong Howe with a pitch-black intensity that immediately put it at odds with the Western's conventional sunniness, this is one of the first truly psychological Westerns. Centring on a family feud worthy of a Greek tragedy, the tale unfolds through a series of flashbacks. As a man who has spent his entire life being pursued by unseen assailants and his own terrible memories, Robert Mitchum brilliantly conveys a sense of all-consuming paranoia.

Jeb Rand's demons finally catch up with him. Robert Mitchum in *Pursued*.

High Noon
dir Fred Zinnemann, 1952, US, 85m, b/w

A *tour de force* of unbearable, slow-burning tension, this masterfully produced tale – now regarded to be the first "adult" Western – finds Gary Cooper on stoic form as the beleaguered retiring marshal. To this day, the alternating imagery of ticking clocks, tolling bells and the gradually increasing anxiety on Cooper's face as his date with destiny inexorably approaches still exerts a powerful punch.

The Gunfighter
dir Henry King, 1950, US, 101m, b/w

Jimmy Ringo (a moustachioed Gregory Peck) is trapped by his past. He may wish to end his gunfighting career, but his legendary reputation means that everyone treats him like a celebrity. *The Gunfighter* is set mainly in the claustrophobic atmosphere of a saloon, where Ringo awaits his estranged wife and the son he has never seen, hoping for a new life. Tension builds as word gets round that he's in town. Everyone wants a piece of him, including a young punk who wants to know just how fast he really is.

Man Of The West
dir Anthony Mann, 1958, US, 100m

One of the darkest of all Westerns has Gary Cooper as reformed criminal Link Jones, who inadvertently stumbles on his old confederates as they try to rob the train he's travelling on. When the train leaves him behind, Link holes up at a farmhouse with fellow passenger and saloon girl Billie Ellis (Julie London). The unfolding drama becomes increasingly fraught with violence, deceit and sexual tension, as Link confronts the gang and its brutish, amoral leader Dock Tobin – who just happens to be his uncle.

Unforgiven
dir Clint Eastwood, 1992, US, 131m

This rare neo-noir Western pays its respects to *Man Of The West*. William Munny (Eastwood), a gunman turned farmer, resumes a life of violence because he needs the money. Recruited as a bounty hunter after a group of prostitutes offer a reward for the two men who disfigured one of them, Munny arrives at Big Whiskey, a town presided over by a corrupt and sadistic sheriff, Little Bill (Gene Hackman). There is no hint of redemption as a train of violence is unleashed in this decidedly unromantic vision of the old West.

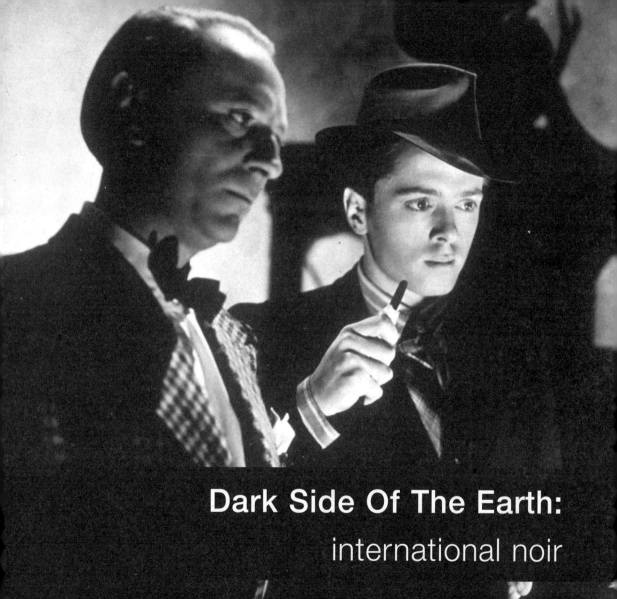

Dark Side Of The Earth:

international noir

Richard Attenborough (centre) at his most disturbing, aided by William Hartnell (left) in *Brighton Rock*.

Dark Side Of The Earth:

international noir

Just as European cinema made a significant contribution to the formation of the noir style, so, in turn, did US crime movies have a wide-ranging influence on the film cultures of other countries. This chapter examines the noirs and neo-noirs that are the result of this symbiotic relationship, with special emphasis on the rich profusion of films that emerged in Britain and France.

Britain

In the period just prior to World War II, a general darkening of mood and style, as well as a greater degree of violence and moral ambiguity, began to be apparent in British cinema – just as they were in the films of France, Germany and the US. Of course, crime movies had always been popular in Britain, as illustrated by the career of **Alfred Hitchcock** whose first significant film,

The Lodger (1926), explored one of his (and noir's) recurrent themes, that of a man – in this case a highly suspicious one – accused of a crime he did not commit. But the origins of British crime films came from a tradition of sensationalist Victorian melodrama and, despite strong links with German studios, the use of expressionistic camera-work to suggest inner psychological states was largely absent from the repertoire of most British filmmakers.

The most prolific and successful British crime writer of the century's first thirty years was **Edgar Wallace**, whose work was eagerly seized upon by the film industry. Despite being the first British writer to focus on police procedure, his work falls into the category of lurid melodrama, and it wasn't until the 1930s that a younger generation of writers emerged who wrote in a more realistic vein, in some cases directly influenced by the hard-boiled crime fiction of US writers like Hammett and Chandler. These included **James Hadley Chase**, **Gerald Kersh**, **Peter Cheyney** and **James Curtis**, while **Eric Ambler** brought the spy thriller up to date. A fascination for the underbelly of British society can also be found in the work of both **Patrick Hamilton** and **Graham Greene**.

But at the risk of over-straining the colour metaphor, it would be true to say that Graham Greene was the real *eminence grise* of British film noir. Between 1935 and 1940 he was an influential film critic for *The Spectator* and *Night And Day*, regularly attacking what he saw as the banality and sentimentality of most Hollywood films while praising Fritz Lang's *Fury* (1936) and the French film *Pépé le Moko* (1937), and singling out **Carol Reed** as an English director to watch. *The Green Cockatoo* (1937), taken from a Greene story, starred John Mills (in James Cagney mode) helping naive country girl Rene Ray escape gambling racketeers who have framed her for the murder of Mills's brother (Robert Newton). It's sometimes credited as the first British noir, but a rather better candidate (and a much better film) is *They Drive By Night* (1939), based on a James Curtis novel and directed by **Arthur Woods**. This has the authentic down-at-heel atmosphere, with a sordid murder and a wrongly accused ex-con pounding the wet London streets, aided in his quest for justice by a dance-hall hostess with a heart of gold.

During World War II the British film industry did its bit for the war effort, with morale-boosting films that were either heroic or jauntily optimistic. A dark noirish edge crept into a few films, however. *Gaslight* (1940), based on the play by Patrick Hamilton, was a gothic noir set in a suitably dark and dismal Victorian London where suave but sinister **Anton Walbrook** tries to drive his wife mad in order to stop her finding out his guilty secret. More near-madness surfaced in *The Night Has Eyes* (1942), in which **James Mason** (who specialized in morally ambivalent characters) played a shell-shocked composer living in an isolated house on the Yorkshire Moors, into which stumble a pair of young women searching for a missing friend. At the end of the war came **Robert Hamer**'s *Pink String And Sealing Wax* (1945), a Victorian thriller set in a seedy Brighton where *femme fatale* pub landlady Googie Withers sweet-talks a naive Gordon Jackson into helping her murder her husband.

The high water mark of British noir occurred in the years just after the war, a period when the country was attempting to recover and cope with shortages of nearly all basic commodities. Rationing continued until 1954, so even when spivs and black marketeers do not figure as major characters in films (which they often did), there is usually a background feel of struggle and deprivation. The year 1947 alone produced a handful of strong titles, including *The Upturned Glass*, *October Man* and *It Always Rains On A Sunday*. Three other films stand out from that year. *They Made Me A Fugitive*, with Trevor Howard as an ex-RAF pilot who falls in with a (for the time) pretty nasty bunch of criminals, has an authentically brutal noir tone which is very close to its US equivalents. *Odd Man Out*, directed by Carol Reed, stars James Mason as a wounded Irish Republican gunman on the run through the labyrinthine streets of Belfast after a heist goes wrong. Its shadowy cinematography by Robert Krasker was something of a dry run for *The Third Man* two years later. Most famous of all was *Brighton Rock*, an adaptation of Graham Greene's novel of the same name about a young psychotic hoodlum and his nemesis – the jolly barmaid turned sleuth, Ida.

The following year Greene and Carol Reed were teamed up by producer Alexander Korda, and the result was two of the finest British films not just of the decade but of all time. The first of these, *The Fallen Idol* (1948), has the noir premise of an unhappily married and adulterous man who is accused of murdering his bullying wife. The central relationship of the film, however, is between the man (Ralph Richardson as an embassy butler) and the young boy – the ambassador's son (Bobby Henrey) – in his care. Reed and Greene's next collaboration was a more thorough-going noir. *The Third Man* (1949) takes place in war-damaged Vienna, where the lack of basic facilities means that its citizens are at the mercy of black marketeers like Harry Lime, who peddles contaminated penicillin to devastating effect. But it is also a film about betrayal and the limitations of friendship.

Meanwhile in the US, friendship and loyalty within the filmmaking community was at breaking point as the House Committee on Un-American Activities (HUAC) attempted to root out all hint of left-wing thinking from Hollywood (see p.24). One result was that several blacklisted figures came to England, including director **Edward Dmytryk** (of *Murder, My Sweet* fame), who in 1949 made *Obsession*, the morbid tale of a jealous husband (Robert Newton) who imprisons his wife's lover (Phil Brown) in a basement with the intention of murdering him and then dissolving his body in an acid bath.

Richard Attenborough (centre) in one of his greatest roles as psychopath Pinkie Brown.

Ironically, when Dmytryk reappeared before HUAC a few years later, one of the people he named as a Communist fellow-traveller was **Jules Dassin** who had already made his one contribution to British noir, with the outstanding *Night And The City* (1950, see Canon). Based on a novel by Gerald Kersh, it was shot in London and has two Hollywood stars (**Richard Widmark** and **Gene Tierney**) holding their own amidst a plethora of English character actors.

In terms of production, most British noirs were B-features (see p.23) – emanating from small independent companies such as Alliance, Anglo-Amalgamated, Butchers, Danzigers, Independent Artists and Hammer Films, interspersed with the occasional prestige feature. There was also some Hollywood involvement: *They Drive By Night* was made as a "quota quickie" for Warner Brothers at their studios in Teddington, *The Third Man* was a co-production between Korda's London Film

Production and David O. Selznick, and *Night And The City* was made for Twentieth Century-Fox in London. Critical reaction to British noir was varied, but the grimmer, more downbeat mood of crime films was certainly noted. Arthur Vesselo, writing in *Sight And Sound* about *They Made Me A Fugitive*, mentioned the film's "unpleasant undertone" and "sordidness, corruption and violence almost unrelieved". *Sunday Times* critic Dilys Powell, on the other hand, was highly enthusiastic about *Odd Man Out*, commenting on the "erratic shadows spinning along lamp-lit walls, children playing in the shining dark night streets" and comparing it advantageously with the best American thrillers.

The production of British noir continued throughout the 1950s but the overall standard declined and, as in America, there were many occasions when films lapsed into cliché and self-parody. Among the directors who made more than a fleeting impression were Hammer studio stalwarts **Ken Hughes** and **Terence Fisher** and two American blacklistees now resident in England, **Cy Endfield** and **Joseph Losey**. Hammer's crime films were clearly made with an eye across the Atlantic and frequently had one or even two American stars. Fisher's *Stolen Face* (1952) starred **Lizabeth Scott** and **Paul Henreid**, the latter as a plastic surgeon who replicates the face of a woman who has jilted him on a former prisoner whom he then marries. The best of Ken Hughes's several noirs is probably *The House Across The Lake* (aka *Blackout*, 1954), a British *The Postman Always Rings Twice* set in the Lake District and again starring two Americans – Alex Nicol as a struggling writer and Hillary Brooke as the *femme fatale* who persuades him to bump off her husband (Sid James).

Rather classier fare was served up by Joseph Losey, who had already made three excellent noirs with a social edge in the US, including a remake of Fritz Lang's *M* in 1951. In Britain he directed the excellent *Time Without Pity* (1957), a gripping tale of a neglectful father (Michael Redgrave) who has 24 hours to save his son (Alec McCowen) from being executed for a murder he didn't commit. It was followed in 1959 by *Blind Date*, with Stanley Baker (a key collaborator with both Losey and Endfield) as a policeman investigating the apparent murder of an elegant French woman (Micheline Presle) by her young, art student lover (Hardy Kruger). Both films bring an outsider's perspective to British class and sexual mores, themes that would be developed by Losey in later, more sophisticated films. Meanwhile his fellow exile Cy Endfield contributed *Hell Drivers* (1957), a melodramatic slice of social realism starring Stanley Baker and Patrick McGoohan as rival truck drivers, part of a team of macho tough guys (including Sean Connery) paid by the delivery, so pushed to outdrive each other at top speeds down country lanes.

Two strong crime films – both starring **Stanley Baker** – brought the decade to an end and kick-started the 1960s. In Val Guest's *Hell Is A City* (1959) Baker played a hard-driven police officer, in pursuit of a ruthless criminal through the dark and dirty streets of Manchester. Shot with a documentary immediacy, the film was especially memorable for its unusually tough and uncompromising realism. In Joseph Losey's *The Criminal* (1960) Baker is now on the wrong side of the law, banged up in prison and caught between the rock of sadistic warder Patrick Magee and (after his release) the hard place of Sam Wanamaker's criminal "Mr Big", desperate to get his hands on the hidden takings from a racetrack heist.

The fact that most British noirs were B-features ultimately determined their demise, since after 1964 cinemas ceased to have double-bills.

Following this change, film noir in Britain surfaced only sporadically, with a couple of examples late in the decade marking the arrival of a more contemporary approach. *The Strange Affair* (1968) and *Performance* (1970) are early examples of British neo-noir; both are in colour and both reflect a more radical and questioning attitude – a strong reflection of the times in which they were made. **David Greene**'s *The Strange Affair* takes an almost sympathetic view of police corruption, as a new and keen police constable (**Michael York**) is gradually sucked into the harsh reality of police work, until he's persuaded to plant some evidence in order to nail a known criminal and lands himself in prison. The more experimental *Performance* was filmed in 1968 before being shelved for two years while worried Warner bosses wondered what to do with it. The brainchild of **Donald Cammell**, a counter-cultural figure who mixed with both the London art set and the underworld, *Performance* is both a critique and an expression of the permissiveness and narcissism of the 1960s, with the incongruous pairing of rock star Mick Jagger and gangster James Fox gradually fusing in a kaleidoscopic half-world of fantasy and reality.

Directed by **Mike Hodges**, *Get Carter* (1971) was the other key neo-noir of the period. A relentlessly disturbing film, it focuses on the single-minded mission of ice-cold hitman Jack Carter (**Michael Caine**) as he travels up to Newcastle to investigate and avenge the death of his brother. Carter is a bleak man in a bleak landscape, something that is reinforced by the dispassionate, long-lens cinematography of Wolfgang Suschitzky. Both *Performance* and *Get Carter* traded off the new image of the British gangster established by the Kray brothers' high-profile celebrity status, but without overtly endorsing it in the way that several later British gangster movies would.

Get Carter – though it would later become an influential cult film – proved something of a false dawn. The withdrawal of foreign investment, especially from the US, and a reduction in state subsidies plunged the British film industry into crisis. With the exception of **John Mackenzie**'s *The Long Good Friday* (1979), which was essentially a gangster film, noir did not get much of a look in until the next decade.

The 1980s was the era of Thatcherism which, with its tight controls on public expenditure and its emphasis on the individual rather than society, was highly divisive – a fact that many filmmakers responded to. *Mona Lisa* (1986), *Hidden City* (1987) and *Stormy Monday* (1987) were three outstanding neo-noirs which looked at the moral and spiritual decay at the heart of British cities, as the gap between the haves and the have-nots widened. *Mona Lisa* focused on the sex trade; *Hidden City* posited the idea of London as a labyrinth of historical secrets and lies hidden just beneath its surface; while *Stormy Monday* took a very cynical view of the special relationship between Britain and the US, with a story of a rapacious American businessman/crook (Tommy Lee Jones) moving in on the re-development of Newcastle.

Since then, British neo-noir high points have been few and far between. The most notable achievement was *Croupier* (1999) – Mike Hodges' return to features after a ten-year absence. Aspiring writer Jack (**Clive Owen**) finds material for his novel when he resumes his old job as a casino croupier – a role that begins to take him over. Paul Mayersberg's sophisticated script both references classic noir, with its voice-over narration and existential protagonist, and functions as the sting in the tail of the Thatcher era, as Jack becomes divided between being a detached observer and wanting "to fuck the world over".

They Drive By Night
dir Arthur B. Woods, 1939, UK, 93m, b/w

A "lost" masterpiece of British prewar noir? Possibly. It certainly conjures up a powerful atmosphere of grimy London streets, populated by spivs, tarts and perverts. Recently released from jail, Shorty (Emlyn Williams) visits his girlfriend and discovers that she's just been strangled. Aware that he will be the prime suspect, he goes on the run, hitching rides with lorry drivers and aiming to hunt down the real killer. He's helped by Molly (Anna Konstam) and a sinister criminal psychologist named Hoover, played by Ernest Thesiger at his campest, creepiest best.

They Made Me A Fugitive
dir Alberto Cavalcanti, 1947, UK, 78m, b/w

The Brazilian Cavalcanti brought a documentarist's cool eye to this tough tale of Clem, an ex-RAF officer (Trevor Howard) at a loss after the war. Caught up with a gang of black marketeers, working out of a funeral parlour and led by the sharply dressed Narcy (Griffith Jones), Clem gets framed for killing a policeman and sent to Dartmoor. After escaping, he heads back for London – via a woman who wants him to kill her husband – hell-bent on revenge. With brilliant art direction and some striking camera-work from Otto Heller, this relative obscurity is the real thing.

Brighton Rock
dir John Boulting, 1947, UK, 92m, b/w

A baby-faced Richard Attenborough is genuinely disturbing as psychotic gang leader Pinkie Brown, settling scores and running protection in a grotesque Brighton of seedy streets, down-at-heel boarding houses and scruffy pubs. Greene co-wrote the screenplay from his own novel, and managed to retain the guilt-saturated, Catholic undertow of the original. Pinkie is the embodiment of evil, but the naive and besotted waitress Rose thinks she can redeem him. The personable Ida (Hermione Baddeley) thinks otherwise.

The Third Man
dir Carol Reed, 1949, UK, 104m, b/w

Essentially a political thriller, the story focuses on the search by author Holly Martins (Joseph Cotton) for his old friend Harry Lime (Orson Welles) in a Vienna still devastated by war. What he eventually has to face is the fact that his friend is involved in black-marketeering of a particularly unpleasant nature. The fusion of Greene's sharp script, Welles's insouciant charm, Robert Krasker's inventive camera-work and the famous zither theme tune adds up to the finest of all British noirs, with the final chase through the sewers just one of many marvellous moments.

Time Without Pity
dir Joseph Losey, 1957, UK, 85m, b/w

With the killer revealed as the rich and powerful industrialist Robert Stanford (Leo McKern) at the film's beginning, the tension lies in whether failed writer and drunk David Graham (Michael Redgrave), will manage to get his estranged son (Alec McCowan) off a murder rap with only a day left before his execution. Despite the story unfurling at a frenetic pace and Losey trying to cram too many issues in (it's clearly anti-capital punishment), this is a superbly performed dissection of British social and sexual hypocrisy with a distinctly noirish edge.

Hell Is A City
dir Val Guest, 1960, UK, 98m, b/w

This neglected British crime thriller is something of a docu-noir in the vein of Dassin's *The Naked City*, with much of it filmed on location in a grey and grimy Manchester. Hard-as-nails Inspector Martineau (Stanley Baker) is determined to track down an escaped prisoner, Don Starling (John Crawford), now back in Manchester and wanted for murder. Meanwhile, at home Martineau's disgruntled wife (Maxine Audley) is giving him a hard time. Simultaneously downbeat and riveting, the whole thing is propelled along by a great jazz score from Stanley Black.

Performance
dir Donald Cammell and Nicolas Roeg, 1970, UK, 105m

Chas (James Fox) is a young, sadistic East End gangster looking for a place to hide when a job gets out of hand, so he holes up in the house of decadent, charismatic rock star, Turner (Mick Jagger) and his two women (Anita Pallenberg and Michele Breton). The men's two worlds seem miles apart, but after much drug-induced, psychological game playing a weird elision of their personalities seems to take place. Along with *Blow Up*, this is the film that best conveys the darker side of the "Swinging London" scene, helped by Cammell's elliptical script and non-linear editing.

Get Carter

dir Mike Hodges, 1971, UK, 93m

This startlingly raw debut from Hodges features Michael Caine's darkest performance as a thoroughly brutal London hitman, Jack Carter, who travels to Newcastle to investigate his brother's mysterious death. While there, he gets caught up in the local gangland scene and makes a terrible discovery about his niece Doreen (Petra Markham). Carter then proceeds to exact a relentless and bloody revenge. With its harsh industrial backdrop, the film's realism and deeply pessimistic tone perfectly captured the widespread social discontent of the period.

The Long Good Friday

dir John MacKenzie, 1979, UK, 114m

Bob Hoskins gives an electrifying performance as Harold Shand, a sadistic gangland boss and warped patriot who wants a slice of the redevelopment of London's Docklands and invites American Mafia boss Eddie Constantine to lend a hand. A mystery adversary has other ideas, and Shand's visions of respectability is soon undermined as a whole lot of bombs start going off. The film is often seen as presaging Thatcherism in its emphasis on naked self-interest masquerading as enterprise and entrepreneurship.

Mona Lisa

dir Neil Jordan, 1986, UK, 104m

A genre-crossing noir of doomed romance and wasted lives. Bob Hoskins plays George, an ineffectual ex-con who is hired by his sleazy former boss Dinny Mortwell (Michael Caine) as a driver for high-class hooker Simone (Cathy Tyson). Gradually driver and call-girl start a friendship and George agrees to help her find Cathy (Kate Hardie), a young woman who is also on the game. All three eventually escape to Brighton but are unable to evade Mortwell and a violent denouement.

Stormy Monday

dir Mike Figgis, 1988, UK, 93m

Mike Figgis's debut movie – he also wrote the bluesy jazz score – is a moody thriller set (like *Get Carter*) in Newcastle. Brendan (Sean Bean) is a young Irish drifter, working for jazz club owner Finney (Sting). But when he falls for waitress Kate (Melanie Griffiths), it turns out that she is in the pay of rapacious American business man Cosmo (Tommy Lee Jones), who is trying to force Finney to sell his club. Their troubled romance and divided loyalties add a compelling element to this character-led neo-noir.

Croupier

dir Mike Hodges, 1997, UK, 91m

Ignored in the UK upon release, but popular in the US, Hodges' erratic career got back on track with this incisive neo-noir about a struggling writer (Clive Owen) with a strong penchant for gambling who takes a job as a croupier in a seedy casino. Increasingly addicted to the late-night lifestyle, he becomes involved with a punter, Jani (Alex Kingston), and, through her, a planned heist. The script rather labours the existentialism angle but Hodges generates a claustrophobic atmosphere aided by some down-at-heel settings and a cooly laconic turn from Owen.

France

The French invented the idea of film noir, but saw it as an exclusively American phenomenon. Prewar critics had sometimes used the term, usually pejoratively, when discussing some of the darkly fatalistic French movies of the 1930s (see p.13), but when **Nino Frank** applied it to a handful of American crime thrillers, in his 1946 essay "Un nouveau genre policier: l'aventure criminelle", he made no link with earlier French films. Similarly, in their pioneering survey *Panorama du film noir américain* (1955), the authors Etienne Chaumeton and Raymond Borde were positively dismissive about French crime movies.

Nowadays the connection between the "poetic realist" films of prewar France and American film noir is widely acknowledged (and outlined in the Origins section on p.13). What separated French critics from their memories of 1930s films was, of course, World War II. In the war years France, as an occupied country, had its film industry kept on a very tight leash by the Vichy government, which meant a diet of largely positive and upbeat films, with gloom and moral ambiguity kept firmly at bay. Now and again, however, something darker would slip through the net, as was the case with Clouzot's *Le Corbeau* (*The Raven*, 1943), a murky tale of back-biting and murder in a small provincial town.

Le Corbeau's misanthropic vision offended practically everybody – the Germans for its dark anti-authoritarian tone, and patriots for being "anti-French". After the war Clouzot was given a lifetime ban from working in film, a sentence later reduced to two years. He followed *Le Corbeau* with a handful of bleakly noirish films beginning with *Quai des orfèvres* (1947) about a down-at-heel musician (Bertrand Blier) and his wife, the ambitious chanteuse Jenny Lamour (Suzy Delair), who are implicated in a murder. Concentrating on milieu and character rather than plot, the film has an authentically seedy feel despite its unfeasibly happy ending.

Quai des orfèvres was based on a novel by Belgian crime writer **Stanislas-André Steeman** who, along with his compatriot **Georges Simenon**, introduced a greater realism into the *policier* (as both the crime novel and crime movie was called), with both writers favouring sardonic, slightly crumpled detectives as protagonists. Crime fiction in France was given a further boost when the publisher Gallimard launched its *série noire*, of mostly translated American hard-boiled detective novels, in 1945. Two homegrown Gallimard titles, published in the early 1950s, were *Touchez pas au grisbi* by **Albert Simonin** and *Du rififi chez les hommes* by **Auguste Le Breton**. Both were rapidly turned into outstanding films. *Grisbi*, directed by **Jacques Becker** in 1953, is a stylish, character-based gangster movie starring an impassive **Jean Gabin** as the mastermind of a successful heist (that is never seen), whose retirement is scuppered when his weak-willed partner boasts about the theft to his two-timing girlfriend (**Jeanne Moreau**).

In *Du rififi chez les hommes* (1955) you definitely see the heist, which forms the nail-biting central moment of the film. Directed by American **Jules Dassin**, working in Europe because of the Hollywood blacklist against Communist sympathizers, *Rififi* was hailed as "the best film noir I have ever seen" by François Truffaut and it formed an important stylistic link between French and American cinema. The following year saw another highly significant contribution to French noir with the release of *Bob le flambeur* (*Bob The Gambler*), based, like *Rififi*, on a novel by Le Breton. This was the first of a spate of great *policiers* by **Jean-Pierre Melville**, the most consistent of French noir directors who created a unique universe, one that is a highly controlled synthesis of American archetypes – he adored American films – and his own particular poetic vision. It's an almost exclusively male world, in which the protagonist – usually trench-coated and fedora-wearing – is as concerned with image as he is with identity.

Louis Malle's debut film, *Ascenseur pour l'échafaud* (*Lift To The Scaffold*, 1957), had the same cinematographer, **Henri Decaë**, as *Bob le flambeur* and a similarly vibrant approach to location shooting. It also had a political edge by virtue of the fact that the murderer is an ex-serviceman who has served in Indochina and Algeria, while his victim is a businessman who has profited from the colonial wars. Along with *Bob le flambeur*, Malle's film is seen as paving the way for the *nouvelle vague*, the new wave of young filmmakers (most of whom began as critics) who venerated certain Hollywood noir directors – in particular B-movie figures like Sam Fuller – for the directness of their vision and the vitality of their shooting style.

A bout de souffle (*Breathless*, 1959) was the seminal *nouvelle vague* film. Directed by **Jean-Luc Godard** and co-written with **François Truffaut**, the film revolutionized not just the *policier* but movies in general. The most startling innovation was the jump-cut, whereby a section of film would be cut from the middle of a shot so that the action on screen would suddenly jump forward, or a shot would abruptly cut to a close-up. The result was a restless, nervous energy that added a spontaneous, improvised quality to the narrative. The film is also highly self-conscious about American culture – popular and otherwise. The anti-hero (**Jean-Paul Belmondo**) is an existential hoodlum who reads William Faulkner and is obsessed with the screen style of Humphrey Bogart.

Godard's trailblazing masterpiece was followed a year later by Truffaut's *Tirez sur le pianiste* (*Shoot The Pianist*, see Canon), another overt homage to American noir loosely based on Dave Goodis's pulp novel *Down There*. It's more romantic than *A bout de souffle*, with **Charles Aznavour** as a melancholy barroom pianist trying to escape his past. The other *nouvelle vague* director to fixate on the Hollywood thriller was **Claude Chabrol**, although his reference point was Alfred Hitchcock rather than Hollywood's B-movie auteurs. Beginning with *Le beau Serge* (1959), Chabrol revealed a fascination with ordinary human relations and the strains they endure from both social and individual notions of morality and guilt. His increasingly well-crafted thrillers arguably reached a peak in the late 1960s with *Que la bête meure* (*The Beast Must Die*, 1969) and *Le Boucher* (*The Butcher*, 1970).

The cinematic flirtation of first Melville and then the *nouvelle vague* directors with all things

American marked the beginnings of neo-noir in France and, arguably, elsewhere. Three English-language films – *Point Blank* (1967), *Bonnie And Clyde* (1967) and *Performance* (1970) – all owed a stylistic debt to the innovations of Godard in particular. From this point on there was a self-referential quality to noir, an overt acknowledgement of looking over your shoulder to a specific tradition and at the same time renewing it. Godard continued to use noir conventions as a springboard for his increasingly experimental films, notably with *Bande à part* (*The Outsiders*, 1964), *Alphaville* and *Pierrot le fou* (both 1965), while Truffaut's *La mariée était en noir* (*The Bride Wore Black*, 1967), based on the novel by Cornell Woolrich, was an only partly successful homage to both Hitchcock and Jean Renoir, starring Jeanne Moreau as a vengeful widow.

Interestingly, it was Melville (a kind of honorary uncle of the *nouvelle vague* but more commercially minded) who produced the most convincing noir *policiers* of the 1960s, with a trio of brilliant films – *Le doulos* (*The Finger Man*, 1962), *Le deuxième souffle* (*Second Breath*, 1966) and *Le Samouraï* (1967, see Canon). The first two are in black and white and based on *série noire* novels, but all three take place in a bleak and abstracted milieu – a self-contained noir world where personal codes of friendship, trust and loyalty are regularly tested. Melville continued to be a major figure up to his death in 1973, with *Le cercle rouge* (*The Red Circle*, 1970) and *Un flic* (*A Cop*, 1972) – both starring the icily cool Alain Delon.

Following the events of May 1968, when demonstrations by radical students developed into a national strike leading to the downfall of the government, certain filmmakers utilized the thriller to make political points or tell political stories. The French-educated Greek **Costa Gavras** led the way with the highly influential

Z in 1968. Based on the actual assassination of a member of the Greek parliament, the film investigates the death of a similar figure and gradually uncovers a whole world of government corruption and collusion with extremists. The following year Jean-Pierre Melville made *L'armée des ombres* (*Army In The Shadows*), about the Resistance to the German occupation of France during World War II, still a painful subject shrouded in silence and half-truths. He did so by employing the same style and methods of his noir *policiers* to highly powerful effect.

Another extremely sensitive subject in French politics concerned the tactics employed by the French as the colonial rulers of both Morocco and Algeria, countries that won their inde-pendence in 1956 and 1962 respectively. **Yves Boisset**'s film *L'attentat* (*The Assassination*, 1972) was a fictionalized account of the mysterious death of Moroccan revolutionary and dissident Mehdi Ben Barka in Paris in 1965, a subject that was revisited in 2005 by Serge Le Péron in *J'ai vu tuer Ben Barka* (*I Saw Ben Barka Get Killed*).

By the 1970s there was a whole new generation of filmmakers engaging with *policiers* (or *polars* as they were now more popularly known), although few of their films made a strong impression outside of France. Among the best were **Bertrand Tavernier**'s Simenon adaptation *L'horloger de Saint-Paul* (*The Watchmaker Of St Paul*, 1973), an old-fashioned character study of a man (Philip Noiret) forced to confront his own

Ex-con Figon (Charles Berling) dominates the screen in *J'ai vu tuer Ben Barka*.

attitudes to justice when he discovers that his son has committed a murder. The other outstanding figure to emerge was **Alain Corneau** who in the mid-1970s made a string of gutsy crime movies, culminating in the outstanding *Série noire* (1979), a bleak but moving tale of social misfits in the blighted no-man's-land of the Paris suburbs.

The new decade was ushered in by *Diva* (1981), the film that kick-started the so-called "cinéma du look" in which the emphasis was on a flashy, surface style – borrowed from advertising, fashion and comic books – avoiding any political or social dimension. **Luc Besson** was the director who most successfully applied a layer of postmodern chic to film noir with his exciting but two-dimensional thrillers *Subway* (1985), *La femme Nikita* (1990) and *Léon* (1994).

Polars that did not succumb to the fashion for fantasy continued to be made, among them **Bob Swaim**'s hard-hitting, American-style *La balance* (1982), about how a whore and her pimp/boyfriend are worked over by the police, **Maurice Pialat**'s restrained but powerful *Police* (1985), and **Patrice Leconte**'s *Monsieur Hire* (1989) – the tale of a lonely voyeur and the suspicion he engenders. More recent standouts include Tavernier's *L.627* (1992), a searing indictment of the drugs trade and the police's inability to deal with it, and two remarkable films from **Jacques Audiard**: *Sur mes lèvres* (*Read My Lips*, 2001) and *De battre mon coeur s'est arrêté* (*The Beat That My Heart Skipped*, 2005).

Le Corbeau (The Raven)
dir Henri-Georges Clouzot, 1943, Fr, 93m, b/w

A deeply gloomy and oppressive film in both looks and subject matter. A town is turned inside out as a spate of poison-pen letters – signed "The Raven" – breeds an atmosphere of escalating malice and paranoia. One of the targets is urbane local doctor Rémy Germain (Pierre Fresnay) who is conducting affairs with Laura (Micheline

Francey), the wife of a colleague, and the crippled Denise (Ginette Leclerc). He is also accused of conducting abortions. A brilliant allegory of the fear and mistrust engendered by occupation, it was remade in Hollywood as *The 13th Letter* (1951).

Du rififi chez les hommes (Rififi)
dir Jules Dassin, 1955, Fr, 117m, b/w

A battered-looking Jean Servais plays Tony Le Stéphanois, fresh out of prison and planning a raid on a swanky Parisian jewellery store with two friends and a specialist safe-breaker, César (played by director Dassin). The elaborate heist is a detailed 28-minute sequence, played in almost complete silence, as the thieves tunnel through the floor of the flat above the shop. It all starts to unravel when César spills the beans to a rival gangster who kidnaps the young son of one of the thieves. The bleak denouement is matched by the wintery Parisian landscape in which it takes place.

Bob le flambeur (Bob The Gambler)
dir Jean-Pierre Melville, 1956, Fr, 95m, b/w

Bob le flambeur concerns an amiable, silver-haired gambler and former robber (Roger Duchesne), who inhabits the *demi-monde* with an easy-going style. When he runs out of cash, Bob plans a final heist at the Deauville Casino before retiring, enlisting the help of his young protégé Paolo (Daniel Cauchy). Needless to say, things don't go according to plan. With its plentiful location work, the film is a hymn to a disappearing Paris with a great opening shot of a tram descending from Montmartre where Bob lives to Pigalle where he operates.

Ascenseur pour l'échafaud (Lift To The Scaffold)
dir Louis Malle, 1957, Fr, 89m, b/w

Julien Tavernier (Maurice Ronet) plans to murder his girlfriend's husband who also happens to be his boss. But after completing the killing, Tavernier gets stuck in a lift while at the same time two teenagers steal his car before shooting a German tourist. In the meantime, the girlfriend (Jeanne Moreau) wanders the streets wondering what has happened to him and thinking the worst. All three plot lines are juggled with amazing assurance and the whole film is bound together by a breathtaking Miles Davis score.

A bout de souffle (Breathless)
dir Jean-Luc Godard, 1959, Fr, 90m, b/w

In this relatively simple story Jean-Paul Belmondo plays a petty hoodlum who steals a car in Marseilles, then inexplicably shoots the policeman who stops him for speeding on his way to Paris. In Paris, he spends much of his time trying to make out with an American girl – the iconic Jean Seberg in striped T-shirt and cropped blonde hair – who he encounters (in a famous scene) selling the *Herald Tribune* on the Champs-Elysées. Nearly fifty years on, the film still has a startling in-your-face energy, due to both the editing and Raoul Coutard's noirish camera-work.

Le doulos (The Finger Man)
dir Jean-Pierre Melville, 1962, Fr/It, 108m, b/w

Recently released from jail, Maurice Faugel (Serge Reggiani) kills his friend Gilbert (Rene Lefevre) in an act of revenge and then steals some jewels. Later, when he attempts a robbery, the police are waiting for him but he escapes wounded. Is his old friend Silien (a suitably ambivalent Jean-Paul Belmondo) the "doulos" (finger man or nark) who tipped off the police? And if so why? Melville deftly handles a convoluted script and adds a revealing twist three-quarters of the way through.

Le deuxième souffle (Second Breath)
dir Jean-Pierre Melville, 1966, Fr, 150m, b/w

Big bad Gu Minda (a formidable Lino Ventura) has escaped from prison and decides to do "one more job" before retiring. He first sorts out a couple of hoods bothering his sister but this alerts the police in the shape of Commissaire Blot (Paul Meurisse), and a classic game of cat and mouse ensues. There's a fair amount of talk and some heavy violence plus one stupendous piece of action – the hold-up of an armoured truck loaded with platinum on a lonely mountain road.

Le boucher (The Butcher)
dir Claude Chabrol, 1970, Fr/It, 94m

The setting is a charming French village, the protagonists Helene, a withdrawn school teacher (Stephane Audran), and Popaul (Jean Yanne), an ex-soldier and now the local butcher. Each is drawn to the other, but the relationship is compromised by their own damaged psyches and the series of brutal murders that occur in the neighbourhood.

Like the best of Hitchcock, the film is subtly unnerving in the way it presents a surface social normality while hinting at the pain and trauma seething underneath.

Série noire
dir Alain Corneau, 1979, Fr/It, 94m

Taking a Jim Thompson novel, *A Hell Of A Woman* (scripted by Georges Perec), Corneau creates a harrowing spin on the perennial noir theme of a pair of losers trying to make new lives for themselves by crime. Patrick Dewaere is terrifyingly convincing as the unstable Franck Poupart, a door-to-door salesman who, with his teenage lover (Marie Trintignant), rapidly descends into a vortex of deceit, murder and despair. This is among the bleakest visions of urban alienation and imploding social structures in all of French noir.

Police
dir Maurice Pialat, 1985, Fr, 113m

What seems like a powerful police procedural about drug dealing – remarkable for its exploration of Paris's Muslim community – suddenly changes gear as Gerard Depardieu's earthy cop Mangin finds himself falling for the beautiful but duplicitious Noria (Sophie Marceau) who has stolen a large stash of money from her drug-dealing confederates. By foregrounding the messiness of human emotions and vulnerability, Pialat establishes a uniquely sombre but dangerous mood and, almost incidentally, creates a quietly tragic love story.

Subway
dir Luc Besson, 1985, Fr, 102m

Lighthearted, noirish notes from the underground as Fred (Christophor Lambert), raffish wannabe musician turned safe-breaker, flees into the Métro having stolen some valuable papers after gate-crashing the party of beautiful but bored Helena (Isabelle Adjani). Down in the depths, among the various social misfits, he must evade the clutches of both the police and Helena's husband. *Subway* still retains a stylish charm, not least because the "look" was overseen by legendary veteran designer Alexandre Trauner.

La femme Nikita
dir Luc Besson, 1990, Fr, 93m

In this hugely stylish thriller, Besson provided an intriguing new take on the assassin: Nikita is a teenage junkie who, following a bungled robbery in which she kills a cop, is tried and given a stark choice by the French secret service – work as an assassin or be executed for her crimes. Proving surprisingly talented, she is eventually allowed to have a life again (plus boyfriend), but her "job" creates inevitable conflict. The premise may be hideously far-fetched, but it's hard not to succumb to such high-octane entertainment.

De battre mon coeur s'est arrêté (The Beat That My Heart Skipped)
dir Jacques Audiard, 2005, Fr, 108m

This remake of James Toback's *Fingers* boasts a full-throttle performance from Roman Duris as Thomas Seyr which almost outdoes De Niro in its bottled-up intensity. Working as a brutal enforcer for a dodgy property dealer (a criminal life modelled on his father), Thomas is also a talented pianist (like his absent mother) who resumes playing and hires a Chinese teacher (Linh Dan Pham) to bring him up to scratch. Veering between these two contrasting worlds, while avenging the death of his charismatic, amoral slob of a father, this is a compelling study of the thin line between genius and psychosis.

J'ai vu tuer Ben Barka (I Saw Ben Barka Get Killed)
dir Serge Le Péron, 2005, Fr, 102m

The events leading up to the real-life kidnap and death of left-wing Moroccan dissident Ben Barka (Simon Abkarian) in 1965 is hardly standard neo-noir. That is, until ex-con turned impresario Georges Figon (Charles Berling) is introduced in a lifeless heap and his voice-over starts charting his dubious involvement in the case. His downfall unravels via a trio of complex overlapping flashbacks which he wholly dominates. Imagine the intensity of Lino Ventura combined with the fervour of Richard Widmark and you get a flavour of Berling's magnetic performance.

Germany

German Expressionist movies exerted a profound stylistic influence on American film noir of the classic era, with many of the key personnel of the German film industry leaving the country (as did their Austrian colleagues) after the Nazis came to power in 1933 (see p.9). Of all the German directors who left, **Fritz Lang** was the one who already had a strong track record with crime movies: in the silent era with his two-parter about a criminal mastermind, *Dr Mabuse der Spieler* (*Dr Mabuse The Gambler*, 1922); and with his first sound picture *M* (1931), in which **Peter Lorre** provided a star-making (if controversial) turn as a child-killer on the prowl in 1930s Berlin (see p.11). This particular film's shadow-drenched cinematography was highly influential on the films that would eventually comprise film noir, and its star would become one of the great villains of American noir.

The collapse and division of Germany after World War II had one very interesting consequence for film: the emergence of the *Trümmerfilme* genre, whose name derived from the ruins (or rubble) of the German postwar urban landscape. The films featured several signature noir characteristics, including low-key lighting and exaggerated shadows, complex flashbacks, and moral dilemmas revealing themselves as character traits. *Zwischen Gestern und Morgen* (*Between Yesterday And Today*, 1948) was one of the most successful of these films, but probably the best known was the wonderfully morbidly titled *Die Mörder sind unter uns* (*The Murderers Are Amongst Us*, 1946), made by the East German film company DEFA. The big difference between these films and Hollywood noir was a real clarity over moral issues. Nazi characters were evil: no shades of grey here.

With the end of the war some of noir's heavy hitters returned to Germany from Hollywood. **Robert Siodmak** (see p.206) made the serial killer thriller *Nachts, wenn der Teufel kam* (*The Devil Strikes At Night*, 1957) and in 1960 **Fritz**

Lang released *Die tausend Augen des Dr Mabuse* (*The Thousand Eyes Of Dr Mabuse*), which harked back to Lang's *Dr Mabuse* films of the expressionist 1920s. Both reflected on the Nazi past, Siodmak through his setting, Lang through allegory. But the most startling contribution came from Peter Lorre in *Der Verlorene* (*The Lost One*, 1951). Directing himself as Dr Rothe, a quiet doctor with a Nazi past, he elicited more than a few echoes of his role in *M*. But German audiences weren't impressed and Lorre returned to Hollywood, his directing career over.

The majority of films released in Germany in the 1960s were genre works, and among the most popular of these were a series of films based on the crime novels of **Edgar Wallace**. As early as the silent movie era, German film producers had discovered that Wallace's novels were easily adapted to the screen. Though there have been countless Wallace movie adaptations, the cycle of 32 films produced by the Rialto film company between 1959 and 1972 are the best known. The first, *Der Frosch mit der Maske* (*Face Of The Frog*, 1959), was so successful that it sparked off a fad of crime films, known in Germany as "Krimis". The Wallace adaptations contained a number of distinct stylistic traits, most notably in the films of **Harald Reinl** (five movies) and **Alfred Vohrer** (fourteen movies). Reinl preferred long dolly shots, pans and exterior shots, while Vohrer's films are known for their slight overacting and their distinct zoom and editing styles. Although shot mostly in Germany, the films recreated Wallace's British locations – mostly London and

Peter Lorre: before and beyond noir

Originally born in Hungary as Laszlo Loewenstein in 1904, Lorre studied acting in Vienna, making his mark as the child serial killer in Lang's *M*. The horror film *Mad Love* (1935; see p.13) added the mad scientist to his portfolio of deranged characters. And he played two key roles for Hitchcock, as a quirky nihilist in *The Man Who Knew Too Much* (1933) and the volatile, flamboyant "Hairless Mexican" in *The Secret Agent* (1936).

From 1933, Lorre lived as an exile, first in Paris, then in Britain and the US. Even before the Nazis used extracts from *M* to vilify him in the anti-Semitic propaganda film *Juden ohne Maske* (*Jews Without A Mask*, 1940) he struggled to shrug off the creepy murderous persona that had brought him to attention in Lang's film. One of his more measured roles (in a career strewn with melodramatic and exaggerated turns) was in the key noir *The Maltese Falcon* (1941) as the wheedling Joel Cairo, one of a trio of villains that included Sydney Greenstreet and Elisha Cook Jr. *Casablanca* (1942) was another respite from

a career with more than its fair share of psychopaths and sadists. In that film, he once again acted as a foil for Humphrey Bogart and Sydney Greenstreet, as the ordinarily murderous Ugarte. Lorre was also capable of some playful self-parody, as in the noirish comedy *Arsenic And Old Lace* (1944) and Bob Hope's noir send-up *My Favorite Brunette* (1947).

With such a talent for portraying the deranged and hunted, it was surprising that Lorre didn't feature in more classic noirs. But his child-like yet sinister moon-round face was the opposite of the ordinary matinee-idol looks and even his villains could seem a little too unsettling for your everyday tale of the streets. By the time he directed *Der Verlorene* (1951) his career was beginning to slide. Though unpopular at the time with both audiences and critics, its reputation nowadays suggests Lorre might have had a future as a noir director. Instead he returned disappointed to Hollywood, where he featured in a few horror spoofs with the likes of Boris Karloff and Vincent Price.

its surrounding area – with the characters moving through old castles, mansions or country houses as well as seedy nightclubs, asylums, dark basements and Scotland Yard. But despite the noirish locales, the films often went for upbeat endings in which the detectives were paired off with threatened females, and though they remain popular, the films are now appreciated mostly for their kitsch value rather than noir cool.

The 1970s saw German cinema attain a level of international critical regard that had not been seen since the days of the Weimar Republic. Two key directors of this period, dubbed "New German Cinema", were **Rainer Werner Fassbinder** and

Wim Wenders. Two of Fassbinder's earliest low-budget films, *Liebe ist kälter als der Tod* (*Love Is Colder Than Death*, 1969) and *Der Amerikanische Soldat* (*The American Soldier*, 1970), were gangster films with an auterist edge. They replay the classic film noir theme of a jealous woman who comes between two male friends, resulting in violence, death and deception. However, *Veronika Voss* represents Fassbinder's biggest and finest tribute to Hollywood noir, with his intimate knowledge of classic-era Hollywood evident even in the film's most striking departures from that template. Wim Wenders' *The American Friend* (1977) drew even more closely on American sources. An

Veronika Voss, Fassbinder's gorgeous theatrical homage to classic noir

adaptation of one of Patricia Highsmith's Ripley novels, it marries the American crime film with European art-house cool. Some have claimed that this hybridity reflects Wenders' famous remark about the Americans colonizing the German "subconscious". The noir connection was even more apparent in a later Hollywood-sponsored Wenders film, *Hammett* (1982), a kind of biopic-noir of hard-boiled author Dashiell Hammett, with Brechtian trimmings reflecting on the nature of narrative. But the über-noir pastiche style of these films didn't open any further doors in Tinseltown and Wenders returned to Germany. His most effective use of black-and-white photography probably remains the Berlin angel scenes of *Der Himmel über Berlin* (*Wings Of Desire*, 1987).

After reunification in 1989 German cinema has increasingly focused on popular genres including crime. **Rainer Kaufmann**'s Tarantino-styled *Long Hello And Short Goodbye* (1998) was succeeded by *Meschugge* (1999), which, though set in New York, reflected again on Germany's Nazi past, and *Paths In The Night* (*Wege in die Nacht*, 1999), perhaps the most noirish of the wave of films reflecting on the experiences of citizens of the former East Germany. More noirs of all kinds are sure to follow.

Die Mörder sind unter uns (The Murderers Are Amongst US)
dir Wolfgang Staudte, 1946, Ger, 85m, b/w

A traumatized surgeon can't get over his part in a war incident in which his platoon killed a number of innocent civilians. He suffers nightmares, depression and a tendency to hit the bottle. Re-encountering the officer responsible – now a thriving capitalist – he resolves on revenge. This is a bleak and somewhat melodramatic glimpse back at the horrors war leaves behind.

Der Verlorene (The Lost One)
dir Peter Lorre, 1951, Ger, 98m, b/w

Vaclav Viche's gloomy cinematography and a grim plot that pitches two guilty Nazis against each other combine impressively in a very downbeat kind of way. After a long career playing psychopaths, Nazis and insane scientists, this is Lorre's acting *tour de force* (in which he manages to unite all three of these roles), a piece of perfect self-typecasting with the imagery to match.

Der Amerikanische Freund (The American Friend)
dir Wim Wenders, 1977, Ger, 93m

Probably the least known of the film adaptations of Patricia Highsmith's Tom Ripley books – this one takes on *Ripley's Game* – it's actually one of the better ones, with Dennis Hopper playing the charming psychopath with an air of tragedy. Even so, Wenders is somewhat weighed down by an incessant need to remake classic noir motifs, rather than update them. Look for cameos by acclaimed classic noir directors Nicholas Ray and Samuel Fuller.

Die Sehnsucht der Veronika Voss (Veronika Voss)
dir Rainer Werner Fassbinder, 1982, Ger, 104m

Veronika Voss is a UFA actress who supposedly had an affair with Goebbels. Now in decline, she is kept afloat by her doctor and morphine. When she attempts a comeback, she can no longer act even the simplest scene, but this intrigues a journalist, who suspects her doctor could be to blame. Loosely based on the career of actress Sybille Schmitz and influenced by Billy Wilder's *Sunset Boulevard* (1950), this is a gorgeous-looking film full of noirish touches.

Italy

An Italian equivalent of film noir first surfaced at the height of World War II, when **Luchino Visconti**, a Marxist and former assistant of Jean Renoir, directed his first film, *Ossessione* (1943). The second filmed version of James M. Cain's steamy, hard-boiled crime novel *The Postman Always Rings Twice* (the first was *Le deuxième tournant* in 1939), *Ossessione* is often cited as the first example of neorealism, an Italian film movement that lasted until 1952 and focused on the hardships endured by ordinary working-class people in a war-damaged Italy. Although condemned by the fascist authorities as condoning adultery, Visconti's version of Cain's story reached audiences several years before Hollywood dared film it (see p.26) and was not itself shown in the US until much later, owing to alleged copyright infringement.

An offshoot of neorealism was *neorealismo nero* (black neorealism), which is considered to be related to noir. Films such as *The Bandit* (1946) dealt with the dislocation created by the return of Italian soldiers after the war, and newly thriving criminal hotspots such as the ports. As Visconti had done in *Ossessione*, *neorealismo nero* blended elements of the Hollywood crime film with native melodramatic traditions. **Michelangelo Antonioni**'s *Cronaca di un Amore* (*Chronicle Of A Love Affair*, 1950), in which a detective investigates the past of a businessman's wife, touched on everyday ennui and alienation, themes which the director was to take into art-house territory in his later films.

Despite these efforts, film noir wasn't widespread in Italian cinema until the 1960s and even then it was via a very distinct regional style – albeit one quite similar to noir – called *giallo* (pronounced JAH-loh). Encompassing both literature and film, *giallo* mingled horror, crime and eroticism. The name originally emerged as a term to describe a series of mystery and crime pulp novels published by the Mondadori publishing house from 1929 onwards. Released as cheap, yellow-covered paperbacks, the majority of titles were whodunits, much like their American

counterparts. Many of the earliest "gialli", however, were English-language novels translated into Italian (a similar situation to the *série noire* books in France). Established foreign mystery and crime writers such as Agatha Christie, Edgar Wallace and Georges Simenon were also labelled "gialli" on first publication in Italian. This led to the word "giallo" becoming a synonym of the mystery, crime and detective story genre.

The film genre that emerged from these novels in the 1960s began with close adaptations of the books, but soon developed on a separate path to become a unique genre in its own right. *Giallo* films were characterized by extended – and very bloody – murder sequences featuring stylish camera-work and unusual musical arrangements. The whodunit element was retained, but it was combined with modern slasher horror, and filtered through Italy's venerable traditions of opera and *grand guignol* drama. The films also generally included generous amounts of nudity and sex, and typically introduced strong psychological themes of madness, alienation and paranoia.

The film that created *giallo* as a cinema genre is *The Girl Who Knew Too Much* (1963), directed by **Mario Bava**, who would become a key figure in the *giallo* movement. In Bava's 1964 film *Blood And Black Lace*, the emblematic talisman of the *giallo* was introduced: the masked murderer with a shiny weapon in his black-leather-gloved hand. *Giallo* had its heyday in the 1970s, when dozens were released. The most notable directors working in the genre were **Dario Argento**, Mario Bava, **Lucio Fulci**, **Aldo Lado**, **Sergio Martino**, **Umberto Lenzi** and **Pupi Avati**. High-contrast lighting and shadows (alongside excessive blood-red and yellow colour) were all part of the gothic trimmings in *giallo* films, but Argento took things further towards noir, often using a criminal investigation to catalyse the action. He became the leading cult name amongst *giallo* directors for international audiences. *Giallo* continued to develop as a genre in the 1970s, moving into political territory as it hinted at conspiracies and murky links between Italian politicians and criminal elements. Bertolucci's *Il Conformista* (*The Conformist*, 1970), which looked back to the fascist past, gained international plaudits. Other films with social themes (or *giallo politico*) did not.

More recently one of the closest rapprochements with noir Hollywood style was an adaptation of a Patricia Highsmith novel. *Gioco di Ripley* (2002) was released overseas as *Ripley's Game*, with John Malkovich supplying a typically queasy turn as the ageing Ripley for director **Liliana Cavani**. Like the novel, the film traded on Italy's architectural and artistic splendours and proved once again that although Italian cinema doesn't quite have a recognizable noir tradition in the same way as Britain or France, it can be depended upon to blend noir elements with its own native traditions, be they neorealism, horror or art-house chic.

Ossessione
dir Luchino Visconti, 1942, It, 139m, b/w

Visconti's first feature – now considered the first major example of neorealism – was the sexiest of the four adaptations of James M. Cain's novel *The Postman Always Rings Twice*. Strikingly different from the prevailing Italian cinema of the time, the film was shot in the Italian countryside in a determinedly naturalistic style. It remains a hugely powerful and highly passionate examination of the boundaries between lust and morality.

The Conformist (Il Conformista)
dir Bernardo Bertolucci, 1970, It, 108m

Bertolucci's finest film examines the connection between sexual repression and fascist politics. A weak-willed Italian (Jean-Louis Trintignant) becomes a fascist henchman who is sent abroad to organize the assassination of his old teacher, now a political dissident. Torn between two women and his political beliefs, he self-destructs. Bertolucci's adaptation of Alberto Moravia's original novel is impressive but is exceeded by cinematographer Vittorio Storaro's visuals, which beautifully capture the decadence of 1930s Italy.

The Bird With The Crystal Plumage (L'Uccello dalle piume di cristallo)
dir Dario Argento, 1969, It, 98m

In Italy, American writer Sam Dalmas (Tony Musant) sees the attempted murder of the owner of an art gallery, a couple of days before his return to the US. Staying with his girlfriend Julia (Suzy Kendall), Dalmas tries to help the police in their investigation, while the serial killer stalks them both. Argento crafts a compelling murder-mystery with a thick atmosphere of suspense.

Japan

It is not surprising that Japan should have one of the finest film noir traditions outside of Hollywood. Not only did Japanese cinema have its own expressionism in the 1920s (as well as taking note of the Germany variety) but crime movies such as the French *policiers* were also widely admired in Japan, imitated and sometimes surpassed. Add to this some of the world's densest urban landscapes, home-grown postwar alienation and a wide range of masterful practitioners of the art of cinematography, and you have most of the ingredients needed for noir to flourish.

Early traces of film noir in Japanese cinema came from its greatest talent: **Akira Kurosawa**. His *Drunken Angel* (1948), with its striking imagery and sharp-suited gangster anti-hero played by **Toshiro Mifune**, proved captivating. Though the humanistic emphasis of Kurosawa's filmmaking ensured that the overall impact of the film was not cynical and world-weary like much of noir, so many brilliant stylistic touches echo or anticipate the genre that it was obvious that Kurosawa was a master of the dark art and the crime film in the making. His next project was the police procedural *Stray Dog* (1949), a flawless application of US noir tone and style to a Japanese setting, in which a rookie cop frantically tries to track down his lost gun in Tokyo. In his 1960 film *The Bad Sleep Well* a young man plots to expose corruption within the large corporation which caused his father's death. For all its dark visuals the film wasn't an out-and-out noir. But Kurosawa returned decisively to the genre with *High And Low* (1963), whose depiction of a drug-fuelled urban hell packed a heavier punch than much of Hollywood's stylish urban decay. In both these films there was a potent social message highlighting both the differences and the similarities between rich and poor, the police and their prey.

Kurosawa moved on to other genres, but this did not mark the end of Japan's noir cinema. Homegrown *yakuza* films – a staple for decades – led the way. In these films, noir style could be prevalent or it could, just as in Hollywood films, be simply drowned out in a blaze of bullets. It was, however, an excess of style that cost prolific cult director **Seijun Suzuki** his job when his studio boss viewed *Branded To Kill* (1967). Shot entirely in black and white, and drenched in wonderful high-contrast photography and memorable images courtesy of cinematographer **Kazue Nagatsuka**, it was in stark contrast to Suzuki's film of the previous year, *Tokyo Drifter*, which was a garishly colourful and slightly more conventional gangster film. The studio chief was distraught at having funded a film in which plot had been sacrificed to directorial flamboyance.

Nervous Toshiro Mifune is the cop on the lookout for his gun in *Stray Dog*.

Suzuki had previously staked out his maverick credentials with a sequence of prostitute films including *Gate Of Flesh* (1964) but this time there was to be no reprieve. He was not to make another film for cinema for a decade. When he finally returned to noir, aged 78, with a sequel of *Branded To Kill* called *Pistol Opera* (2001) he abandoned the über-noir style in favour of the garish palette of *Tokyo Drifter*.

With Suzuki languishing out of favour with the studios, the 1970s were not a high point for mainstream noir thrillers in Japan. **Nomura Yoshitaro**'s *The Castle Of Sand* (1974), a slow-burn detective drama with a classical music score and rural settings, lacked the directness and cynicism of earlier films. **Kinji Fukasaku**'s updating of the *yakuza* tradition in such films as *Battles Without Honour Or Humanity* (1973) upped the body- and bullet-count but could not deliver the cool and style of Suzuki's films. By the 1980s and 90s other types of film were centre-stage in Japanese cinema. In *anime*, noir sometimes contributed a certain bleakness of tone and darkness of styling to a dsytopic future. Elements of tech noir (see p.242) were common but not often pervasive in any single *anime*. *Wicked City* (1987) featured a *femme fatale* in the form of a spider, and the hitmen of *The Professional: Golgo 13* (1983) sported classic noir-era trenchcoats, but even the landmark films *Akira* (1998) and *Ghost In The Shell* (1995) showcased only a reliably dingy metropolis amidst the noir-lite action and futuristic musings for *Blade Runner* fans.

The return to form of the *yakuza* film, courtesy of Takeshi Kitano, sparked renewed hope for Japanese crime movies. Kitano's films mixed goofball humour – he was a comedian by training – with introspective and elegiac episodes, most noticeably in *Sonatine* (1993) and *Hana-Bi* (1997). But it is debatable whether any of his films, or the hundreds of other contemporary gangster films from East Asia, really qualify as noir. They include scenes that are dark and noir-styled but so, to varying degrees, do the *anime* mentioned above, and even a number of soft-erotic or "pink" films, such as **Shinya Tsukamoto**'s monochrome *A Snake Of June* (2002), in which the shadows of impersonal city life and rain-drenched settings are testimony to fine camera-work wasted amidst casually exploitative scripting. Japan may just be too post-postmodern for noir. Indeed, it may be that the clearest links to noir (as in many films nowadays, including Hollywood's) are to be found in noir parodies or pastiches. The best example of this is perhaps *The Most Terrible Time In My Life* (1993), which looked back to Suzuki as well as to classic Hollywood in a knowingly amused way a year before Tarantino's *Pulp Fiction*. As the shadow of the twenty-first century lengthens we can expect Japanese film to remain at the forefront of noir.

Drunken Angel (Yoidore tenshi)
dir Akira Kurosawa, 1948, Jap, 98m, b/w

An alcoholic doctor played by Takashi Shimura tries to help an ailing callow gangster (the iconic Toshiro Mifune) in a seaside town shortly after World War II. Images of diseased water (the source of the tuberculosis from which the criminal suffers) and a wistful score give a noirish sheen to what is essentially a character two-hander. More *Bicycle Thieves* than *Double Indemnity*, it makes for fascinating comparisons with Hollywood noir of the time.

Stray Dog (Nora inu)
dir Akira Kurosawa, 1949, Jap, 122m, b/w

A tortured young Tokyo cop (Toshiro Mifune again) searches desperately for his gun, which was stolen and later used as a murder weapon by persons unknown. Kurosawa adopts noir style, using low-key lighting as his morally ambiguous hero disappears into an urban underworld on an obsessive quest. He also adds innovations, such as optical wipes and documentary-like street scenes captured with hand-held camera, most notably at the film's climax at a sports stadium, much copied by thrillers since.

High And Low (Tengoku to Jigoku)
dir Akira Kurosawa, 1963, Jap, 143m, b/w

Rich businessman Gondo (Mifune) is forced to pay ransom to an unknown and unseen kidnapper as police camp out in his luxury hilltop apartment. Kurosawa crafts a cool and tense first half reminiscent of a Michael Mann thriller. But the second part of the film shifts the focus abruptly as the police descend into squalid drug-infested dens with more than a hint of *Blade Runner* about them. This is an astoundingly modern-feeling film, in which Mifune once again exudes authority, humility and gravitas.

Branded To Kill (Koroshi no rakuin)
dir Seijun Suzuki, 1966, Jap, 91m, b/w

"Number 3" killer (Jo Shishido) gets in over his head and faces a show down with the "Number 1". As a morbid obsession with a *femme fatale* and other bizarre goings on result in "Number 3" losing it, the director opens up a dazzling array of cinematic tricks more "out there" than Godard or the John Boorman of *Point Blank* (1967). This is quite simply baffling, bizarre, sexy and thrilling.

Latin America

Film noir has always been attracted to the lands south of the border, with *Border Incident* (1949) and *Touch Of Evil* (1958) notable examples of southern exotic, but its connection with South America could be said to date back to the moment when legendary noir cinematographer **John Alton** (see p.181) accepted an invitation from an Argentinian millionaire to design a film studio in San Ysidro, just outside Buenos Aires. He stayed for seven years. Sadly none of the surviving films directed or shot by Alton were proto-noirs, though the likes of *Los tres berretines* (*The Three Buddies*, 1932) displayed the visual flair of Alton's "painting with light" (see p.182). One three-handed interrogation scene was illuminated by a single overhead light bulb. With Alton back in Hollywood after World War II, domestic variants on urban melodrama became popular in Argentina, Brazil and especially Mexico.

Family melodramas vied for attention with the Mexican brothel or *cabaratera* film in which a "fallen woman" typically becomes a prostitute or nightclub worker and music and dance (often provided by sexy Cuban singer-actress **Ninón Sevilla**) are mixed in a heady cocktail with noir and melodrama. The most highly acclaimed of these films was Alberto Gout's *Aventurera* (*The Adventuress*, 1949). Mexican neo-realistic filmmaking emphasizing the grittier side of urban life was represented in the films of **Ismael Rodríguez Ruelas** and **Alejandro Galino**, who made cinematic hay out of urban poverty with the latter directing two films in 1948 about the travails of an urban bus driver, *¡Esquina … bajan!* (*Stop At The Corner!*) and *Hay lugar para… dos* (*There's Room For …Two*). Only a short time later, avant-garde Spanish director **Luis Buñuel** painted a dark and violent picture of Mexico City youth in

Los olvidados (*The Young And The Damned*, 1950) and, two years later, filmed the gripping tale of an "enforcer" who sees the error of his ways in the noirish *El Bruto*. Other Mexican directors churned out urban gangster melodramas, the best of which (*El Suavecito*, 1950, directed by **Fernando Méndez**), according to critic Eduardo de la Vega Alfaro, stands comparison with Robert Wise's *The Set-Up* (1949). Just as Hollywood noir was excelling itself, something of a golden period occurred in Mexican cinema. Amongst the notables working at this time were **Emilio "El Indio" Fernández** (Mexico's John Ford) and his cinematographer **Gabriel Figueroa**. Figueroa's camera-work under Fernández's direction, though it often strayed into other genres, demonstrated a prowess with the camera to set alongside Hollywood's finest in such films as *Salón Mexico* (1949) and *Víctimas del Pecado* (1951).

From 1955 onwards, however, there was a sharp decline in the industry. Thereafter, Mexico

Bad company for Ninón Sevilla (left) in *Aventurera*.

has struggled to make much of an impact on noir. Fernández later made it as a character actor in Hollywood, in such roles as the insane General Mapache in Peckinpah's *The Wild Bunch* (1969), but he never recaptured the triumphs of his directorial heyday.

Neo-noir, however, particularly in all the variant forms that have emerged since the 1990s (see p.233), has yielded some riches in Latin America. Mexican director **Arturo Ripstein**'s *Deep Crimson* (1996) attracted attention not just for its submerged incest theme, which he had treated more openly in the spicy *cabaratera* remake *La mujer del puerto* (*Woman Of The Port*, 1991), but also for its cool detachment. And John Alton was not the only Western filmmaker to make a mark in Mexico. Liverpudlian **Alex Cox**, best known for his Sex Pistols biopic *Sid And Nancy* (1986), directed the compromised cop thriller *Highway Patrolman* (1992), with Mexican co-funding. Brazilian cinema, with its long tradition of *favela* (slum) movies, went one better and really broke into the international big time with the energetic *City Of God* (2003). Brazilian noir, however, extends before and after 2003, taking in the Lisbon setting of the black-and-white *Foreign Land* (1995) and the fleshpots of Salvador da Bahia in *Lower City* (2005). But the most intriguing neo-noir of the twentieth century

must be the Argentinian rural noir *El Aura* (*The Aura*, 2005), which proceeds far less frenetically than any of the Brazilian films, rather like the David Lynch of *Twin Peaks*. Sadly director Fabián Bielinsky died shortly after its completion. Unlike in most recent neo-noir crime films, any debt to Tarantino is in the structured plotting rather than in glib pop-cultural references or knowing genre pastiche. The cinematography is also excellent. John Alton would have approved.

 Aventurera (The Adventuress)
dir Alberto Gout, 1950, Mex, 101m, b/w

Elena Tejero (Ninón Sevilla) is forced to become a nightclub dancer and hostess after her drink is spiked. She fights back. Fans of classic noir will appreciate the clothes and décor, the foggy street scenes and backlit lighting served up with an occasional dash of real menace in a very polished-looking production. And then there are the song and dance numbers...

The striking monochrome imagery of Salles's *Foreign Land*.

Deep Crimson (Profundo carmesí)
dir Arturo Ripstein, 1996, Mex, 115m

Set in 1940s northern Mexico, this macabre and perverse film re-tells the story of "The Lonely Hearts Killers", a famous pair of murderers who made victims of lonely and wealthy widows in the US. The story was originally told in *The Honeymoon Killers* (1970), but here it's filtered through black comedy and a thoroughly heartless tone by Ripstein, one of Mexico's best-known directors who started out as an assistant to Luis Buñuel.

Highway Patrolman (El patrullero)
dir Alex Cox, 1992, Mex, 93m

An episodic look at a young man's life in Mexico's national highway patrol. Pedro Rojas journeys from cadet training and a rookie assignment in a northern border area, to a quick courtship, the taking of bribes and a slow exposure to drug smuggling and the compromise of his ideals. Cox turns what could have been a very formulaic piece into an intense chronicle of a man in deep conflict.

Foreign Land (Terra estrangeira)
dir Walter Salles and Daniela Thomas, 1995, Braz, 100m, b/w

Combining elements of road movie, thriller and American indie film, *Foreign Land*'s memorable black-and-white imagery demonstrated why director Salles (*The Motorcycle Diaries, Central Station*) would become a name to conjure with. Lisbon is Sin City Central as drug dealers, Angolan immigrants, gangsters and an inflammatory *femme fatale* lead a naive young man on a bewildering and dangerous trail before he fights back. This is an unknown gem, in which a suspense-drenched scene in a Fado café is worth the admission price alone.

City Of God (Cidade de Deus)
dir Fernando Meirelles, 2002, Braz, 130m

Taking place over the course of a few decades, *City Of God* tells the story of two parallel lives in a *favela*. A stylish, unstinting look at life in Brazilian slums that received universal acclaim, this is both shocking and captivating. Far better than the gangster film tag with which it is so often labelled, the noir element is resonant mostly in the voice-over narration and the sheer intelligence of the proceedings.

Lower City (Cidade Baixa)
dir Sérgio Machado, 2005, Braz, 93m

Not the next *City Of God,* nor even perhaps much of a noir, this Brazilian *Jules et Jim* – two friends come to blows over a sexy hooker – meanders around the fleshpots and street life of Salvador. All three leads are very convincing. A vibrant Latin fatalism pervades the sleazy proceedings as once again crime fails to pay and messing with guns proves to be a bad idea.

El Aura (The Aura)
dir Fabián Bielinsky, 2005, Arg, 126m

Downbeat epileptic taxidermist Esteban finds an opportunity to get involved in an unlikely robbery. Throughout his journey from half-hearted hunting holiday to botched heist it is never clear whether Esteban is a patsy, an everyman noir victim or a real villain in the making. The easy pace – rather like a television two-parter – gives the film a take it or leave it feel but this unusual slow-burn thriller has an understated excellence well worth checking out.

Scandinavia and Nordic Countries

Though Scandinavia can match the gloom of any cinematic tradition – think Ingmar Bergman – the two key figures in terms of modern internationally recognized noir are the divisive Danish director **Lars von Trier** and deadpan Finnish helmer **Aki Kaurismäki**. Prodigy von Trier started his career with two astonishing low-budget monochrome noirs, *The Element Of Crime* (1984, see Canon) and *Europa* (1991). Both films attracted wide international attention but their humourless intensity made it difficult for audiences to embrace the illusions and box-office success did not follow critical acclaim. Von Trier later abandoned such meticulously manufactured films in favour of movies more aligned with the

Scandinavian traditions of melodrama (*Breaking The Waves*, 1996) and the back-to-basics style of filmmaking espoused by the Dogme group (of which von Trier was a member). Hollywood homage of the noir kind was henceforth out.

Aki Kaurismäki has never been one to be taken too seriously, with many of his films on the borderline between social realism, comedy and noir. He often draws on noir style and conceits, from the London-set *I Hired A Contract Killer* (1990) to his Finnish trilogy, including *The Man Without A Past* (2002). In his films a mood of exhausted ennui provides the bass notes to exquisite cinematography and sometimes rousing music. Noir aficionados are probably best advised to begin with *I Hired...* But, once obtained, a taste for Kaurismäki's films is not easily lost. His latest film, *Lights In The Dark* (2006), which sees a lonely night-watchman entangled with a *femme fatale* and a dodgy crook, suggests that the dark droll filmmaker will continue in the same vein.

The most exciting thing for years in the region was Norwegian **Erik Skjoldbjærg**'s *Insomnia* (1997). Set in the midnight sun, the film is a noir of the purest kind with Hollywood (in 2002) quick to see the remake potential (see p.53). Sadly Skjoldbjærg hasn't quite managed to follow this up, with the drugs and depression

A world of shadows

Nearly every country's filmmakers have been drawn down noir's dark alleys from time to time. Here are just a few outstanding films from around the world

My Friend Ivan Lapshin (Moy Drug Ivan Lapshin)
dir Alexei Gherman, 1986, USSR, 99m

The Stalinist terror of the 1930s provides the backdrop to a low-key rendering of ordinary Soviet life, local criminal gangs and a police chief struggling to cope with the stresses of his work, his home life and his hopeless courting of a beautiful actress. The historical setting supplies the vital ingredient of foreboding, stylishly framed in vivid black-and-white vignettes. A striking and highly original historical noir.

Kiss Or Kill
dir Bill Bennett, 1997, Aus, 96m

Nikki and Al take flight into the Australian outback after a botched robbery, pursued by the police and a threatening footballer named Zipper Doyle. Sounds like *True Romance* in Australia? Well, you'd be right, and while this makes it just one amongst the avalanche of post-Tarantino films released in the 1990s, it has its moments, prompted mostly by the vivid array of offbeat characters the pair meet on their travels.

Fallen Angels (Duolou Tianshi)
dir Wong Kar Wai, 2000, HK, 96m

No one does urban solipsism quite so artfully as East Asia's art-house darling Wong Kar Wai. In this film a lovelorn hitman and a mute ex-con who occupies himself by reopening shops closed for the night are just two amongst a group of loners cast adrift in the night. In a dryly humorous depiction of missed opportunities and uneasy solitude, Hong Kong's neon lights and dingy diners are splendidly captured via the director's trademark wide-angle and slow-motion shots.

Live Flesh (Carne trémula)
dir Pedro Almodóvar, 1997, Sp, 101m

Almodóvar has long claimed a keen admiration for film noir and in this film it shows. Based on a Ruth Rendell novel, the film opens with pizza-delivery man Victor arguing with junkie Elena. Reacting to the noise, two cops, David and Sancho, arrive at the scene and a biopic *Prozac Nation* (2002) being the sum total of his Hollywood career and the *Insomnia* remake being entrusted to **Christopher Nolan**.

Europa (Zentropa)
dir Lars von Trier, 1991, Den, 113m, b/w and col.

Von Trier's low-budget experimental masterclass in claustrophobic noirish style and cinematography is a very European kind of über-noir. The plot concerns an *ingénu* American in postwar Germany captivated by a *femme fatale* but menaced by the Nazi forces of the mysterious Werewolves organization. Much of the "action" takes place in railway carriages speeding overnight across Germany, creating a tunnel-like feel: hypnotic, dark and repetitive. If only it felt just a little more sincere.

I Hired A Contract Killer
dir Aki Kaurismäki, 1990, Fin, 79m

Henri Boulanger is made redundant from his London job. Shocked, he attempts suicide, but can't go through with it, so he hires a hitman to murder him. But almost immediately he falls in love with Margaret, a flower-seller. When he goes back to the bar to cancel the contract, it has been demolished – and there's no way he can get in touch with the killer. Despite being effectively melancholic in mood, the film suffers from badly miscast characters, especially loud-mouthed Liverpudlian Margi Clarke, who fails utterly to convince as a viable love interest.

---

gun accidentally goes off. Four years later David is a wheelchair basketball star and married to Elena and Victor is released from prison and out for revenge. A superb ensemble piece.

Suzhou River (Suzhou He)
dir Lou Ye, 2000, Ch, 83m

Shanghai's river is centre-stage in a teasing story of crime, obsession, nightclub mermaids and motorcycle couriers. An offscreen world-weary narrator (who "films" the action), petty crime and alienating urban landscapes all ensure the film sails smoothly into deep noir waters. Austere and beguiling, this is 21st-century noir for real.

Lantana
dir Ray Lawrence, 2001, Aus, 121m

This multi-award-winning neo-noir is well worth seeking out. Set in suburban Sydney, the film revolves around the entwined relationships of a group of people connected to the disappearance and death of a local female psychiatrist. Anthony LaPaglia is brilliant as the rumpled cop who investigates, while dealing with his hugely screwed up personal life.

Blind Shaft (Mang Jing)
dir Yang Li, 2003, Ch, 92m

Two Chinese coal miners develop a successful scam: murder one of their fellow miners, make the death look like an accident, and claim money from those in charge to keep the event hushed up. Their latest target is a naive teenager from a small village. But then things start to get complicated. Highly acclaimed abroad but banned back in China, Yang Li makes excellent use of authentic mining locations and seedy urban backwaters, as well as the universal theme of man's eternal greed for money.

Where The Truth Lies
dir Atom Egoyan, 2005, Can, 107m

Set in a glossy 1970s celebrity bubble, the film stars Colin Firth and Kevin Bacon as two US comedians in the vein of Dean Martin and Jerry Lewis, who are traumatized by the death of a female high-school fan in their hotel suite. Trademark Egoyan sleaze titillated American audiences unused to such queer goings on in an otherwise fairly mainstream thriller. Sadly this is not the classic the director and cast (Firth apart) might have been capable of pulling off.

Insomnia
dir Erik Skjoldbjærg, 1997, Nor, 95m

A detective, Jonas (Stellan Skarsgård), investigates a murder in a small town but then becomes involved in a second killing – of his colleague Erik (Sverre Anker Ousdal). Better than the star-studded 2001 remake with Al Pacino and Robin Williams – which itself was very good – this is a superb neo-noir that compellingly turns a classic noir convention on its head: instead of an environment filled with darkness, you have one of ever-present daylight that conveys guilt and confusion just as effectively. Simple, yet brilliant.

Insomnia: no clear view for detectives Jonas and Erik (left).

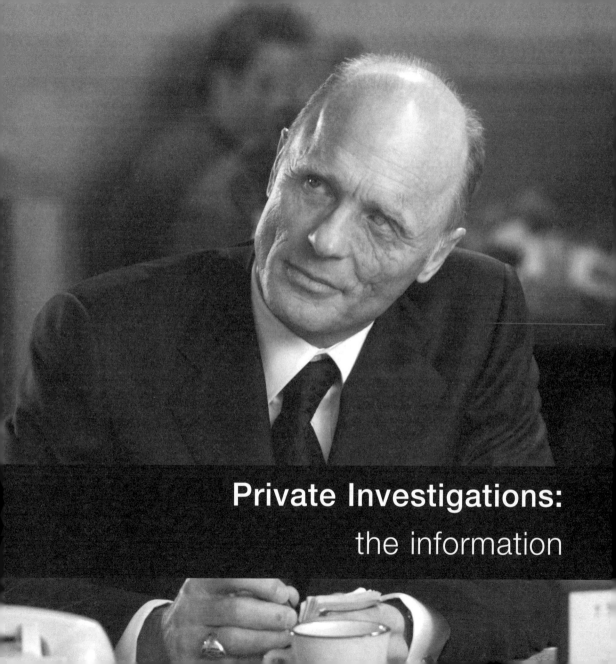

Private Investigations:
the information

Ed Harris plays the disfigured Fogarty in the
2005 movie version of *A History Of Violence*.

Private Investigations:
the information

It was inevitable that a movement as visually stylish and dramatically rich as film noir would attract the attention of other mediums eager to appropriate some of its magic. Noir's darkness swiftly and effectively infiltrated other areas of popular culture. In this chapter – which is by no means exhaustive – we cover the major variations on noir's dark theme and provide an array of resources to help you weave your way through the shadows.

Small-screen shadows

The popularity of TV in the 1950s had a real impact on film, not least in making potential cinema audiences less eager to leave the comfort of their homes. As a consequence, Hollywood had to completely rethink its approach. That meant, in part, offering widescreen spectaculars with vast casts, in glorious Technicolor and full of an optimism that covered over some profound problems rumbling just beneath the surface of American society.

However, while it's generally assumed that film noir, in its original form, had more or less ended by 1959, it had actually migrated to television, along with many of its key personnel – actors, directors, producers and writers. Its influence was immediate: TV shows about crime were exceptionally popular in the 1950s, most notably *Dragnet* (1950), in which cleaner-than-clean cop Joe Friday upheld the letter of the law. It has been estimated that between 1949 and 1975 over one hundred detective shows, mostly hard-boiled in tone, were produced for television.

During the 1960s, when noir was virtually absent from cinema screens, it still exerted a powerful influence on programme makers who wanted to infuse their shows with its dramatic motifs. For example…

The Fugitive
1963–67

When producer **Roy Huggins** pitched this series in 1960, one executive lambasted the idea as "the most repulsive concept ever for television" while another praised it as the best idea he'd ever heard. Whichever camp you find yourself in, you can't deny the creation of the longest chase sequence in television history. The plight of Dr Richard Kimble (**David Janssen**) – on the run for a crime he didn't commit, and perennially searching for "the one-armed man" who was the actual perpetrator – gripped American TV audiences for 120 episodes. Kimble finally cleared his name in a climactic ending reportedly seen by three-quarters of the US population.

At its core, *The Fugitive* twinned the classic noir theme of a man trapped in circumstances beyond his control with the Western motif of the rootless loner wandering the American landscape.

With Kimble's travels taking him to small-town America, the show has some distinct elements of rural noir, and, with its tight shooting style, traces of docu-noir (see p.237), though here the protagonist is actually a victim of police procedure, much like Henry Fonda's Balestrero in the 1956 Hitchcock feature *The Wrong Man* (1956).

The Twilight Zone
1959–64

While this incredibly popular and influential anthology series was rooted in the realms of science fiction and fantasy, noir exerted a powerful influence on the series, especially in the opening two seasons. *The Twilight Zone* regularly dropped characters into desperate situations and forced them to struggle with noirish circumstances beyond the realm of their regular lives; this regularly culminated in a signature twist ending. Creator and host **Rod Serling** possessed a vast experience of writing hard-hitting drama and it's in *The Twilight Zone* that you get many wonderful opportunities to see his combustible mixture of noir and the fantastic.

Perhaps the most potent example of this synthesis can be seen in the first season episode "The Four Of Us Are Dying", in which a man, Arch Hammer, possesses a chameleon-like power to assume the identities of other people. He transforms into the recently deceased boyfriend of a singer in order to romance her, then proceeds to extort cash from a gangster so the pair can run away together, only to change identities again to escape retribution. But Hammer ultimately chooses the wrong person to impersonate, finally enduring a suitably grim comeuppance. Lacking Serling's typical sentiment, it was a gripping piece of TV.

Johnny Staccato
1959

Appearing at the very end of noir's classic period and running for just one season of 27 episodes, **John Cassavetes** (prior to his better-known guise as one of the leading lights of US Indie cinema) is terrific as a jazz musician moonlighting as a private dick. With many of the episodes conducted against the backdrop of Waldo's jazz club in New York City's Greenwich Village, the show had a distinctly "hip" feel that offset the violent nature of the stories. In fact, one of the series' best elements was its jazz score, with a main theme composed by the legendary **Elmer Bernstein**. Still, the show routinely fell foul of the censors, eventually ensuring its cancellation.

Moonlighting
1985–89

The launch pad for **Bruce Willis**'s career, as well as being rightfully regarded as the gold standard for sexual tension on TV, *Moonlighting* managed to take the traditionally rumpled, world-weary outcast private eye and imbue him with a quite unbelievable level of sexiness. Willis's David Addison was a cocky, swaggering charmer all the way, and his rapport with **Cybill Shepherd**'s model turned detective agency owner Maddie Hayes was, simmering lust aside, routinely distinguished with sharp, witty dialogue.

Throughout the series the influence of noir was proudly worn on the show's sleeve, most notably with a number of black-and-white fantasy sequences (especially a great one that lasted an entire episode and featured **Orson Welles** in his final screen appearance) in which the sight of Willis in a white tuxedo instantly recalls a young Humphrey Bogart. Common wisdom has

it that this show went irretrievably downhill the moment Maddie and David consummated their sexual tension. Nevertheless, twenty years on, the show remains wilfully entertaining.

The Singing Detective
1986

Noir plays a vital role in this **Dennis Potter** serial, now considered a masterpiece of twentieth-century television drama. **Michael Gambon**'s misanthropic novelist Philip Marlow, bedridden and immobile thanks to a particularly nasty skin disease, mentally rewrites his early Chandleresque thriller *The Singing Detective*, incorporating his childhood memories and installing himself as a private eye/nightclub crooner investigating a labyrinthine murder plot in a noir-rich fantasy realm.

Potter masterfully utilizes the private eye figure to imbue Marlow's "existence" with measures of independence, forthright masculinity and victory through determination – classic PI attributes that have been cruelly stripped from his languid form in his hospitalized reality. Similarly, the genre's signature dark sexuality and misogynistic violence fuels his inner voyage of self-discovery. Potter's postmodern use of noir motifs provided a powerful assessment of how youthful cruelties can wreak havoc decades later.

Miami Vice
1984–89

One of the most influential and ground-breaking shows of the 1980s, the crime-busting adventures of Miami undercover 'tecs Crockett and Tubbs may have dated somewhat, thanks mainly to the show's decidedly period fashions (suit jackets with rolled-up sleeves, shoes worn without socks) and a rather garish visual palette dominated by pastel colours, but the show's uncharacteristic grittiness – episodes rarely climaxed with a happy ending – and determinedly cinematic feel (thanks to producer Michael Mann) created an eminently watchable and gripping cop drama.

Just as noir features drew on the accentuating power of music, so too did *Miami Vice*: in this case formulating a perfect marriage between the stylish imagery and a soundtrack of chart-topping tunes, most memorably Phil Collins's "In The Air Tonight", starting a trend that is utilized instinctively by shows today.

Fallen Angels
1993–95

What links Tom Cruise and film noir? It's this utterly wonderful but little-seen anthology series, an episode of which the Cruiser directed (his only directing effort to date). Originally shown on US channel Showtime, the show's tales were set in a sombre Los Angeles between the end of World War II and the election of JFK. In retrospect, everything about *Fallen Angels* is almost absurdly top-drawer: the production values were flawless, the stories were solely drawn from noir fiction greats (Hammett, Chandler, Spillane, Ellroy), the directors were high profile and eclectic (Steven Soderbergh, Peter Bogdanovich, Alfonso Cuarón, John Dahl and Tom Hanks) and the various casts read like a who's who of Hollywood.

Over two years, the show managed just twenty episodes, but each one was gorgeously faithful to the classic era of noir. The show was aired in Britain, re-titled *Perfect Crimes*, and, in typical fashion, filled a graveyard slot where no one saw it. Worse, the show is yet to appear on DVD.

Until then, there are two compilation videos that are well worth tracking down. You won't regret it – it's an outright cult gem.

The X-Files
1993-2002

While noir obviously didn't influence *The X-Files*'s signature themes of alien abduction and general paranormal activities, its sway was greatly evident elsewhere. The most obvious link being this zeitgeist-defining series' routine showcasing of lurking, shadow-drenched environments (indeed, one of its most memorable visual motifs was high-powered flashlight beams penetrating a thick darkness).

The poster on the wall of Fox Mulder's dingy broom-cupboard office.

The lead character of Fox "Spooky" Mulder was undoubtedly a contemporary spin on the private eye – a social and professional outcast, yet doggedly determined and fanatically dedicated to a personal code. Over the course of the series, Mulder would tangle with some highly alluring yet decidedly duplicitous *femmes fatales* in his search for "The Truth", and while his unshakeably sceptical partner, Scully, was similarly alluring, she was more often than not charged with the classic noir role of the damsel in distress.

Comic book noir

Just as television has made eager use of film noir's visual and dramatic strengths, so too has the significantly less-appreciated medium of comics. However, the 1931 debut of square-jawed detective Dick Tracy in the *Chicago Tribune* suggests that comics already had a popular relationship with the crime genre nearly a decade before noir's perceived beginnings. Chester Gould's strip found resonance in a public fascinated by gangsters and G-men, leading to the swift appearance of competing characters distributed by rival publishers.

Most notably, **William Randolph Hearst**, who controlled King Features Syndicate, told his president to start a crime comic strip immediately: "And I want **Dash Hammett** to write it," Hearst demanded. The magnate generally got what he wanted, and in early 1934 Hammett began work on *Secret Agent X-9*. He was paid $500 a week (an astronomical sum for the time), and delivered dialogue and continuity for approximately two years before growing bored and walking away to occasionally consult on *Red Barry*, which critic Anthony Boucher later declared was "vigorously in the Hammett tradition".

Crime comics displayed tremendous popularity throughout the 1940s and 50s, despite constant scrutiny from the over-zealous eye of the censors, which led to the infamous Senate hearings about violence in comics in the 1950s. As a result, while these comics would have utilized noir motifs and characters, there was never the opportunity to truly explore the genre's moral darkness and violence. It wasn't until the 1980s that a concerted push towards darker and grittier material occurred, allowing comics the room and support to truly explore the noir form.

Comic book noir is a small, but very potent sub-genre in the comics medium, often containing some of the best examples of narrative and visual innovation. Also, with censorship no longer the potent and undeniable force it was back in the 1940s and 50s, comics are now able to delve into considerably darker territory in terms of violence and sexuality than the original noir films were ever able to touch.

The Spirit
DC Comics

Dubbed "the *Citizen Kane* of comics", **Will Eisner**'s pioneering and legendary strip about a cop turned masked crime-fighter appeared in 1940, the same year as the first film noir. While noir couldn't have played a part in the genesis of

Eisner's signature work, he was clearly drawing from the same influence, as his style showed the motifs of German expressionist cinema. In the years following World War II, noir's influence on *The Spirit* was noticeably more evident, not least by the fact that Eisner increasingly darkened his backgrounds, making his layouts look cinematic while heightening the feeling of danger in the unknown. Even more pointed was the introduction of an array of *femmes fatales* to vex the hero, each one a duplicitous heartbreaker with a wiggle like a Siren's call, especially **P'Gell**, a Jane Russell lookalike with a habit of losing husbands violently. It was in these postwar years that *The Spirit* truly reached the greatness for which it, and its creator, have become known.

Sin City
Dark Horse Comics/Titan Books

Frank Miller had routinely – and memorably – infused mainstream comic characters like Batman and Daredevil with his love of gritty crime fiction, but it wasn't until the debut of his *Sin City* series that he had the opportunity for a pure, uncompromising and often ferocious expression of the genre. The first four books – filled with such suitably dark fare as a psychopath avenging a beloved hooker's death, an aged cop on a crusade to protect a child from a deranged pederast, the murder of a cop that leads to a turf war between the mob and a community of Amazon-like prostitutes and, most noir-like, the destructive allure of a supremely insidious *femme fatale* – are uniformly brilliant, filled with anti-heros whose well-intentioned actions land them on the wrong side of the law. Each man a bone-crusher, they're driven by warped senses of devotion, honour and justice and are routinely prone to hideous acts of violence.

Miller also delivers stunning artwork – highly stylized black and white with an occasional inclusion of a single colour – that makes Basin City a fearsome and disgusting yet oddly captivating place. While the excellent 2005 film version (see p.52) may have exposed *Sin City*'s murder and whores (and murderous whores) to a new audience, it's unfortunate that the most recent book entry, *Hell And Back*, was self-indulgent nonsense that verged on outright parody and was not a patch on those early, undoubtedly classic tales.

100 Bullets
Vertigo/Titan Books

A mysterious man gives you a briefcase. Inside is a handgun, one hundred untraceable rounds and a file that contains concrete proof that someone has wronged you most grievously. Revenge is yours – and you *will* get away it. The question is: will you take it? From such a delicious moral

A typical member of the "Basin City" community, armed to the teeth and presented in Miller's characteristic noirish black-and-white style.

conundrum emerges one of the very best crime comics available and without doubt a towering example of neo-noir.

Brian Azzarello's writing displays masterful handling of the most gut-wrenching of situations and his ear for authentic street dialogue is absolutely impeccable, providing the series with a strong streak of gritty realism. While the series' overarching storyline is a tantalizing mix of the conflict between warring criminal families, a secret society of enforcers and a massive conspiracy to cover up the true origins of America, *100 Bullets* is most effective when focusing on the individual moral plights of the characters. Deeply compelling stuff.

5 Is The Perfect Number
Drawn and Quarterly/Jonathan Cape

Peppino is a retired mob hitman, quietly living out the twilight of his life in rural Italy. When his beloved son, also a hitman, is killed during what should have been a routine job, Peppino, desperate for vengeance, puts aside his fishing rod and picks up the pistols that dominated his old life. He embarks on a quest for revenge, searching for his son's murderers and the new pistol he gave his son on the last night of his life.

Both written and drawn by renowned Italian cartoonist **Igor Tuveri** (otherwise known as Igort), this is a tale both hugely atmospheric and very gritty, rendered in a beautifully spare fashion rife with romantic melancholy, infusing the much-explored Mafia gangster genre with a true sense of beauty. With captivating duotone artwork that incorporates elements of Japanese cinema and manga, Igort captures with supreme elegance and power the echoing tragedy of a father outliving his son.

Blacksad
Dargaud/iBooks

Don't be put off by the fact that all the characters in this murder mystery are anthropomorphized animals: this ain't no Disney feel-good. On the contrary, this is good old-fashioned, stone-cold noir through and through, in which feline private eye Blacksad investigates the death of an old flame, treading an increasingly dangerous path that leads to the highest echelons of the big city.

Writer and artist duo **Juan Diaz Canales** and **Juanjo Guarnido** perfectly relate creatures to their stereotypical characteristics (an assassin is a snake, assorted lowlifes are lizards and rats, a couple of heavies are a grizzly bear and a rhino, a lawyer is a fox), but the effect is anything but cliché. You quickly forget that the characters are animals as you're drawn into a hunt for justice evoking the themes and techniques of some of the most memorable noir efforts of the 1940s.

Batman: Year One
DC Comics/Titan Books

Having made a monumental impact on Batman with the seminal *The Dark Knight Returns*, Frank Miller's superb elaboration on Batman's origin is even more overtly noir in tone and presentation. Almost entirely stripped of the character's trademark fantastic gadgetry and garish villains, the crux of Miller's story is the crisis of identity. Both Bruce Wayne and Commissioner James Gordon struggle to walk the true path among the overwhelming, morality-sapping grimness of Gotham City. Wayne is searching for the implacable guise that will enable him to conduct an all-consuming war on crime, while Gordon is trying to be an honest cop in a corruption-riddled police force that doesn't appreciate his type.

A major inspiration for 2005's *Batman Begins* film (see p.235), Miller's Chandleresque narrations for Wayne/Batman and Gordon are considerably bolstered by the hugely impressive artwork of **David Mazzucchelli**, which eschews traditional exaggerated comic-book layouts for a realist approach in which deep, dark shadows infiltrate every panel. The result ranks as one of the single best Batman stories ever published.

Stray Bullets
El Capitan Books

While not nearly as high-profile a crime comic as *Sin City* or *100 Bullets*, **David Lapham**'s *Stray Bullets* is without question on the same level, perhaps even better. Indeed, to label this excellent series, running since 1995, as straight crime fiction would be doing it something of a disservice. Lapham's exquisitely crafted stories are not centred around hard-boiled archetypes, but something rather more interesting and very noir-like: characters who are severely impacted by events far beyond their control. The series chronicles the reactions to these events and the effect they have on their lives. Lapham utilizes cinematic techniques, such as flash-backs and flash-forwards, to get further into these characters' psyches while providing a tantalizing glimpse of a larger picture. Deeply unpredictable, occasionally unbearably dark, and sometimes very funny, *Stray Bullets* delves into personal shadows with compelling brilliance.

A History Of Violence
Paradox Press/DC Comics

A long-underrated comics gem, this breathlessly tense and hugely shocking tale of an apparently upstanding and peaceful small-town family man whose hideously violent past comes back to haunt him has deservedly received a significant amount of exposure thanks to the 2005 film adaptation by **David Cronenberg** (staring Viggo Mortensen and Ed Harris). Cronenberg, ironically, wasn't even aware that he was adapting a graphic novel until well into the film's production.

In either medium, *A History Of Violence* is an exquisite example of rural noir. The film made significant alterations to the story, while the book benefits from **John Wagner**'s altogether more layered tale – it's considerably more violent and bloody than Cronenberg's film too, which is really saying something. And **Vince Locke**'s sketchy but hugely dynamic artwork generates a truly memorable tale of past crimes and present consequences.

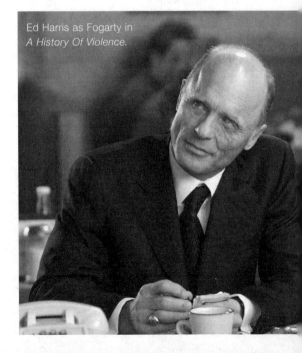

Ed Harris as Fogarty in *A History Of Violence.*

Raymond Chandler's Marlowe: The Graphic Novel
iBooks

An interesting and enjoyable collection of three previously unpublished stories featuring Raymond Chandler's legendary and flawed private eye: *The Goldfish*, *The Pencil* and *Trouble Is My Business*. Writers Tom De Haven, Jerome Charyn and James Rose provide elegant and faithful translations of Chandler's work while, visually, two of the three stories settle for a classical black-and-white approach. Illustrator David Lloyd's work on *The Pencil* is notably cinematic, while **Lee Moyer** and **Alfredo Alcala** define *Trouble Is My Business* with a style reminiscent of 1930s standout J.C. Leyendecker. The only hue comes from Rian Hughes's restrained colours on *The Pencil*, offering a duotone style that accentuates shadows and provides a sepia look. Chandler aficionados would approve.

The Bogie Man
Paradox Press / DC Comics

On the rain-soaked streets of modern-day Glasgow, a rather familiar, trench-coated figure who goes by the name of Bogie is searching for the legendary Black Bird while trying to avoid the Fat Man and his gang of hardened killers. But there are problems with this "familiar" scene, and serious ones at that. "Bogie" is, in fact, escaped mental patient Francis Clunie, the Black Bird is actually a generously sized frozen turkey and his so-called adversaries are law-abiding citizens who have become unwittingly drawn into Clunie's fantasy. Not that it matters, because Bogie always cracks the case…

Something of a cult classic, **John Wagner** and **Alan Grant**'s brilliant send-up of all things hard-boiled offers a vast array of prime comedy moments.

Books

Film noir has generated a massive amount of books, ranging from highly academic studies to uncritical enthusings. Titles easily number in the hundreds and, as this book proves, they keep on coming.

The Big Book Of Noir
Ed. Lee Server, Martin H. Greenberg, Ed Gorman, 1998 (Carroll & Graf)

A huge – and hugely valuable – reference guide that utilizes an impressive cast of contributors to cover all areas of noir. The mixed format includes such varied material as interviews with **Fritz Lang**, discussions of the scores of classic and obscure films, and a look at key crime writers and comic book noir.

Dark City: The Lost World Of Film Noir
Eddie Muller, 1998 (St Martin's)

With infectious enthusiasm, noir specialist Muller provides an entertaining summary of film noir, utilizing a mix of critical, biographical and historical material. Beautifully illustrated with a wealth of stills, one of the high points is a full-colour poster gallery.

Film Noir: An Encyclopaedic Reference To The American Style
Ed. Alain Silver & Elizabeth Ward, 1992 (Overlook)

An essential purchase, this massive volume pores over nearly 300 film noirs produced between the 1920s and the 1970s, concentrating on the classic period. Endlessly fascinating and hugely authoritative.

Femme Noir: Bad Girls Of Film
Karen Burroughs Hannsberry, 1988 (McFarland)

The stars behind famous *femmes fatales* receive biographical treatments by film historian Hannsberry in this tribute to the genre's most alluring element. A-list celebs and almost-forgotten players are treated with equal respect.

Film Noir
Alain Silver & James Ursini, 2004 (Taschen)

Focusing on the core 1940–59 era of film noir, this book offers a brisk overview, covering the genre's main themes, motifs, characters and types of film. As is Taschen's hallmark, the book is stuffed with gorgeously reproduced film stills.

Bad Boys: The Actors Of Film Noir
Karen Burroughs Hansberry, 2003 (McFarland)

The private and public lives of over ninety actors who starred in the noirs of the 1940s and 50s are presented, with an appendix that focuses on the actors who were least known but frequently seen in minor roles. Most of the volume treats these "bad boys" in depth, in A to Z entries ranging from five to twelve pages in length.

Voices In The Dark: The Narrative Patterns of Film Noir
J.P. Telotte, 1989 (University of Illinois Press)

Packaged in a beautiful noirish jacket, Telotte's in-depth discussion of classic film noir draws on the work of Michel Foucault to examine four dominant noir narrative strategies.

Hard-Boiled: Great Lines From Classic Noir Films
Peggy Thompson & Saeko Usukawa, 1995 (Chronicle Books)

Collects 300 inordinately snappy lines from around 150 classic noirs alongside a fantastic selection of pictures.

Film Noir Reader
Eds. James Ursini & Alain Silver, 2004 (Limelight)

An abundant anthology that reprints all the key early writings on film noir alongside many newer essays, including a few pieces commissioned specifically for the project. There are three further volumes – all just as indispensable as the first: Vol.

2 is a further collection of 22 essays including Paul Schrader's essential and pioneering "Notes on Film Noir";Vol. 3 contains 18 interviews with filmmakers of the classic film noir period while Vol. 4 covers the key films and themes of noir.

Women In Film Noir
Ed. E. Ann Kaplan, 1998 (BFI Publishing)

Very influential and much referenced, this is a second edition of a seminal collection that explores the murky and complicated gender politics of classic and 1970s neo-noir from a feminist perspective.

The Art Of Noir: The Posters And Graphics From The Classical Era Of Film Noir
Eddie Muller, 2002 (Overlook)

With a clear love for and expertise in his subject, Muller tracks the evolution of the form through 275 posters (338 full-colour illustrations in all), many of them full-page plates, which look nothing short of spectacular in the book's oversize format. Supremely captivating eye candy.

Virgin Film: Film Noir
James Clarke, 2005 (Virgin)

While the format of the Virgin Film series has always been disappointingly spreadsheet-like, the excellent coverage and analysis has routinely made up for it. Here, a decent overview of the genre is offered, along with broad analysis of twenty features, both classical and neo-noir.

Film Noir Guide: 745 Films Of The Classic Era 1940–59
Michael F. Keaney, 2003 (McFarland)

A good ready-reference covering a large amount of the film noir produced during the classic era. Entries resemble the IMDB format, with cast and crew lists, a star ratings system, a synopsis and some easily digested review comments.

Dark City Dames: The Wicked Women Of Film Noir
Eddie Muller, 2002 (Regan Books)

An enjoyable portrait of six of the greatest *femmes fatales* – Jane Greer, Marie Windsor, Ann Savage, Evelyn Keyes, Audrey Totter, and Coleen Gray – all of whom Muller interviews. Like his other books, Muller's sheer love of noir leaps from the page.

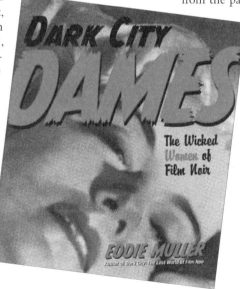

Death On The Cheap:
The Lost B Movies Of Film Noir
Arthur Lyons, 2000 (Da Capo Press)

The well-informed Lyons delves deep into the forgotten realms of noir, filling every page with hugely fascinating information on the films that helped keep cinemas filled in the 1940s and 50s.

European Film Noir
Ed. Andrew Spicer, 2007 (Manchester University Press)

A solid and enlightening round-up of noir and neo-noir in France, the UK, Germany, Spain and Italy; a shame there is no East Asian counterpart.

The Noir Style
James Ursini & Alain Silver, 1998 (Overlook)

Pre-eminent noir experts Ursini and Silver analyse the look of noir, tracing it back through the likes of Edward Hopper and police photographer Weegee.

More Than Night: Film Noir In Its Contexts
James Naremore, 1998 (University of California Press)

One of the most intelligent analyses of the subject written by an academic who knows how to write. Naremore treats film noir as a cultural phenomenon within the history of ideas, looking not just at the films but at the wide range of literature surrounding them.

Pocket Essentials: Film Noir
Paul Duncan, 2000 (Pocket Essentials)

Short and sharp, this is a great primer for those who want a general overview of noir.

Mean Streets And Raging Bulls: The Legacy Of Film Noir In Contemporary American Cinema
Richard Martin, 1997 (Scarecrow Press)

A short but very incisive assessment of film noir's enormous influence on modern film.

Websites

The Internet Movie Database
www.imdb.com

Without doubt, this is the best online film resource available and a great start for anyone wishing to find out more about individual examples of the noir genre. Many of the famous films will have an indispensable wealth of information.

The Danger and Despair Knitting Circle
www.noirfilm.com

The "Knitting Circle" trades, swaps, buys and sells film noir on video and 16mm film; it also regularly screens classic noirs in San Francisco. Its website has become a thoroughly impressive resource, featuring a fascinating blog, interviews with experts and articles on noir-related topics.

Green Cine – Film Noir

www.greencine.com/static/primers/noir.jsp

A snappy primer on the genre, written by the almost ubiquitous Eddie Muller.

Filmsite – Film Noir

www.filmsite.org/filmnoir.html

An excellent hub of information about the genre.

UC Berkeley Film Noir Essays

www.lib.berkeley.edu/MRC/Noirtext.html

This site draws together a short but useful list of links to full-text articles and essays on film noir available via various e-magazines. Topics range from the *femme fatale* in noir films to noir composer Miklós Rózsa.

Classic Noir Online

www.classicnoir.com

An online community devoted to noir, this expansive site includes articles, recommendations and detailed information on more than 600 films.

The Incredible World of Bowling Noir

http://members.aol.com/bobbuttman/bowlingnoir/bowlingnoir.htm

A daft diversion – but an amusing one.

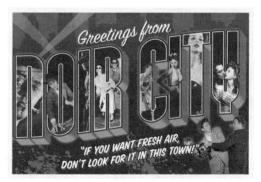

Festivals

Noir City

www.noircity.com/noircity.html

Run by the **Film Noir Foundation** and hosted by noted noir historian Eddie Muller, this San Francisco-based festival runs every January and represents a wide-ranging appreciation of noir in various arts. Guests at the 2005 edition included Sean Penn, James Ellroy and Stanley Rubin.

Palm Springs Film Noir Festival

www.palmspringsfilmnoir.com

Held over three days in early June, this festival screens a dozen noirs from the classic and modern eras, bolstered with a typically high calibre of guest appearances.

Merchandise

Murder One
www.murderone.co.uk

Billed as "Europe's foremost Crime and Mystery Bookshop", and it's not an empty boast: this is a veritable Mecca for the crime fiction enthusiast, offering a peerless array of books both new and second-hand. Located at London's traditional centre of bookshops, Charing Cross Road.

Forbidden Planet
www.forbiddenplanet.com

Britain's pre-eminent chain of sci-fi/fantasy shops, with a vast flagship store located on London's Shaftesbury Avenue. While not teeming with noir material, the latest reference books are usually available alongside a decent selection of DVD material and the odd piece of memorabilia.

The Cinema Store
www.websonic.co.uk/cinemastore/default.asp

Located on London's St Martin's Lane, this thoroughly excellent – if rather pricey – store provides a wealth of material devoted to noir. It is split into two adjoining shops: one offers books and videos, the other merchandise and Region 1 DVDs.

Play.com
www.play.com & www.playusa.com

A phenomenally popular "e-tailer", the Jersey-based (and therefore tax-exempt) Play has swiftly become the place to get a vast array of DVDs for exceptionally good prices. Play's sister site, PlayUSA, offers Region 1 fare – and far more classic noir features. Free UK delivery and orders are dispatched first class within 24 hours.

M Is For Mystery
www.mformystery.com

The San Francisco Bay Area's leading mystery bookstore offers a large selection of new crime and detective fiction, as well as bestsellers, used books, first editions and other collectibles.

Dr. Noir's Crime Posters
www.drnoir.com

A fantastic site with vintage noir prints for sale, ranging from the 1930s to the 1960s in sizes from lobby cards to six sheets.

Picture Credits

The Publishers have made every effort to identify correctly the rights holders and/ or production companies in respect of the images featured in this book. If despite these efforts any attribution is incorrect, the Publishers will correct this error once it has been brought to their attention on a subsequent reprint.

Cover credits

Fred MacMurray and Barbara Stanwyck in *Double Indemnity* (1944) Courtesy of Universal Studios Licensing LLLP

Illustrations

Corbis: 25 © Bettmann/CORBIS, 220 © Tim Street-Porter/Beateworks/Corbis; Kobal: 8 Paramount Pictures/Famous Players-Lasky Corporation, 1, 14 Sigma/Vauban Productions/Les Films Vog/Studio Canal, 141; Movie Store Collection: 10 Paramount/Nero-Film AG, 12 Metro-Goldwyn-Mayer Corp, 17, 29 Loew's/MGM, 22 MGM/Loew's Incorporated, 32 Parklane Pictures Inc/MGM, 37 Metro-Goldwyn-Mayer, 40 Bil/Phillips/Judeo Productions/Columbia Pictures Corporation, 50 Good Machine/Mike Zoss Productions/The KL Line/Working Title Films/USA Films, © Gramercy Films LLC, 52 Dimension Films/Troublemaker Studios, © Miramax Corp, 55, 58 Allied Artists Pictures Corporation/Security Pictures Inc./Theodora Productions, 62 Warner Bros. Pictures, Inc, 65 Run Run Shaw/Shaw Brothers/The Ladd Company, Warner Bros, © The Blade Runner Partnership, 70 Paramount Pictures Inc, 73 Warner Bros Corp, © The Ladd Company, 81 Cardinal Pictures, United Artists, © Cardinal Pictures Inc, 84 Producers Releasing Corporation, 94 Columbia Pictures Corporation, 100 Santana Pictures Corporation/Columbia Pictures, 105 Harris-Kubrick Productions/United Artists, 108 Warner Bros Pictures/Silver Pictures, 112 Twentieth Century-Fox Corporation, 117 Monarchy Enterprises B.V./Regency Enterprises/Warner Bros Pictures, 123 Incorporated Television Company, October Fims, 131 E-K-Corporation/Lions Gate Films, © United Artists, 134 Warner Bros Inc, 136 Warner Bros Pictures, 146 Warner Brothers Pictures, 149 RKO Radio Pictures, 154 20th Century Fox, 164 © 1995 New Line Productions, Inc, 175 International Pictures Inc/ RKO Radio Pictures, © Christie Corporation, 177, 212 Twentieth Century-Fox Corporation, 180 Parklane Pictures, Inc/ United Artists, 187 Paramount Pictures, 189 Columbia Pictures Corporation, 197 RKO Radio Pictures, 199 Moviestore Collection, 202 RKO Radio Pictures, 204 International Pictures Inc/RKO Radio Pictures, © Christie Corporation, 209 Warner Bros Pictures, 215, 225 Gaumont International/Les Films du Loup/TF1 Film Productions/TSF Film Productions/ Island Pictures, 218 Pinnacle Productions/Seven Seas Corporation/Becaon Productions Inc/J.D.Trop/States Rights Independent Exchanges, Warner Bros, 219 Paramount Pictures/Penthouse, © Long Road Productions, 222 D'Antoni

PICTURE CREDITS

Productions/Schine-Moore Productions, © Twentieth Century-Fox Corporation, 227 Black Lion Films Ltd/British Lion Film Corporation/Calendar Productions, © HandMade Films, 228 British Lion Film Corporation, © London Film Productions, Canal +, 231, 246 United States Pictures/Warners, 235 Warner Bros Pictures/Syncopy/DC Comics,© Patalex III Productions Limited, 236 Paramount Pictures/Hope Enterprises Inc, 239 Jacmac Films/Warner Bros Inc, 240 Walter Wanger Productions/Eagle-Lion Films, 243 New Line Cinema/Mystery Clock Cinema/Dark City Productions Pty Limited, 247, 251 Charter Films Ltd/Associated British Picture Corporation/Pathe Pictures International, 258 Maïa Films/Casablanca Film Production/Mallerich Audiovisuales S.L./Films Inc./Studio Mac Tari/Arte France Cinéma/Ciné Cinémas/TPS Star/Soread-2M/Televisió de Catalunya (TV3)/Centre National de la Cinématographie/Centre Cinématographique Marocain/Generalitat De Catalunya Institut Catala De Les Industries Culturals (ICCA)/Région Ile-de-France, Films Distribution/Rézo Films, 274 Nordic Screen Production AS/Norsk Film A/S/Norsk Filminstitutt, 275, 284 New Line Productions/Bender Spink/Media 1! Filmproduktion Munchen & Company, New Line Cinema; Other: 270 Cinematográfica Calderón S.A, Facests Multimedia Distribution, 280 Twentieth Century Fox Television/Ten Thirteen Productions, 283 © Dark Horse Comics, 286 University of Illinois Press, 287 Regan Books, 289 www.noircity.com; Ronald Grant Archive: 88 Per Holst Filmproduktion, Det Dankse Filminstitut, 120 Columbia Pictures Corporation/Mercury Productions Inc, 159 Compagnie Industrielle et Commerciale Cinématographique (CICC)/Fida Cinematografica/Filmel/TC Productions/S.N. Prodis, 169 Edward Small Productions/Eagle Lion Films, © Pathé Industries Inc, 194 RKO Radio Pictures/Wald/Krasna Productions, 263 Laura Film/Maran Film/Rialto Film/Tango Film/Trio Film/Filmverlag der Autoren, 267 Film Art Association/Shintoho Company Ltd/Toho Company/Toei Company, 269 Videofilmes Produçoes Artisticas Ltda.

Index

Page references to films discussed in the Canon chapter and people described in the Icons chapter are indicated in bold.